THE YOUNG ALEXANDER

THE YOUNG ALEXANDER

The Making of Alexander the Great

ALEX ROWSON

WILLIAM
COLLINS

William Collins
An imprint of HarperCollins*Publishers*
1 London Bridge Street
London SE1 9GF

WilliamCollinsBooks.com

HarperCollins*Publishers*
1st Floor, Watermarque Building, Ringsend Road
Dublin 4, Ireland

First published in Great Britain in 2022 by William Collins

1

A catalogue record for this book
is available from the British Library

ISBN 978-0-00-828439-8 (hardback)
ISBN 978-0-00-828440-4 (trade paperback)

Typeset in Adobe Garamond Pro by
Palimpsest Book Production Ltd, Falkirk, Stirlingshire

Printed and bound in the UK using 100% renewable electricity
at CPI Group (UK) Ltd

MIX
Paper from
responsible sources
FSC
www.fsc.org
FSC™ C007454

This book is produced from independently certified FSC™ paper
to ensure responsible forest management.

For more information visit: www.harpercollins.co.uk/green

To Clan Rowson

CONTENTS

LIST OF ILLUSTRATIONS

Integrated:

Andronikos' 'Alexander' from Tomb II, Vergina: DEA / G. DAGLI
    ORTI / Getty Images

Lion hunt mosaic, House of Dionysos, Pella: DEA / G. DAGLI
    ORTI / Getty Images

Samothrace: author

Illustration of the Pella curse tablet: E. Voutiras and I. Kiagias

Terracotta figurine of a boy in Macedonian dress, the British
    Museum: © The Trustees of the British Museum

View from the Aiani acropolis: author

Macedonian guards at Aghios Athanasios: Alto Vintage Images /
    Alamy Stock Photo

Demosthenes, Ny Carlsberg Glyptotek: ullstein bild Dtl. / Getty
    Images

Olynthos: Werner Otto / Alamy Stock Photo

Aristotle, Athens Archaeological Museum: agefotostock / Alamy
    Stock Photo

The Nymphaion at Mieza (Isvoria): Shutterstock

A possible Macedonian tower at Kabyle: author

Ateas coin: D. Draganov

The battlefield of Chaironeia: author

The Macedonian burial mound at Chaironeia: author

The Philippeion at Olympia: Sklifas Steven / Alamy Stock Photo

The sacred house and oak of Dodona: Wolfgang Kaehler / Alamy Stock Photo

The palace of Aigai: robertharding / Alamy Stock Photo

The theatre of Aigai: Sean Burke / Alamy Stock Photo

The Abduction of Persephone from Tomb I, Vergina: Wikimedia Commons

Tomb II, Vergina: Ntinos Lagos / Getty Images

Alexander meets Diogenes statue, Corinth: author

The Danube, Rousse region, Bulgaria: author

The Tsangon pass: author

Thiva (ancient Thebes): author

The Giannitsa Alexander, Pella Archaeological Museum: DEA / G. DAGLI ORTI / Getty Images

Alexander at the battle of the Granikos: PRISMA ARCHIVO / Alamy Stock Photo

Colour Plates:

Third-century AD gold medallion depicting Olympias: the Walters Art Museum, Boston

Third-century AD gold medallion depicting Philip II: CPA Media Pte Ltd / Alamy Stock Photo

Third-century AD gold medallion depicting Alexander the Great: the Walters Art Museum, Boston

Views of Macedonia after exiting the Tempe pass: author

Warrior's helmet with gold mask from Sindos: DEA / G. DAGLI ORTI / Getty Images

Aghios Antonios Peak, Mount Olympos. The location of a Hellenistic mountaintop sanctuary dedicated to Olympian Zeus: author

The Derveni Krater: DEA PICTURE LIBRARY / Getty Images

NOTE ON SPELLING

There are still no rules that are universally agreed upon when it comes to spelling Greek names in English. In this book, the transliterated Greek form is used, except for names that are already well known in their Latinised form, such as Alexander, Philip, Aristotle, Macedonia, Athens, etc. Latinised spellings are also used for ancient authors and their surviving works. In citations, from both ancient translations and modern works, the original spelling of the publication is retained.

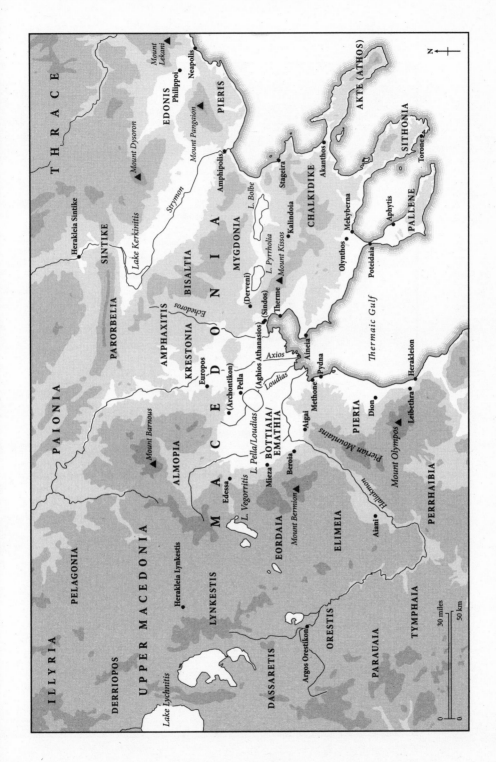

Macedonia in the time of Philip II and Alexander

ILLYRIA

PAIONIA

Bylazora

Strymon

Nestos

Epidamnos

Lake Lychnitis

MACEDONIA

Philippoi

Apollonia

ILLYRIA

Haliakmon

Mieza

Pella

Amphipolis

Stageira

CHALKIDIKE

Aigai

Methone

CHAONIA

Aoos

Pydna

Olythnos

EPEIROS

Dion

Poteidaia

MOLOSSIA

Passaron?

Dodona

THESPROTIA

Pelinna

Larissa

Vale of Tempe

MAGNESIA

Peneios

THESSALY

Pheral

Pagasai

Pharsalos

Crocus Field, 352 BC

Ambrakia

Pindos Mts

Halos

Ionian Sea

AKARNANIA

Acheloos

AITOLIA

PHOKIS

EUBOIA

Kephallenia

Amphissa

Mt. Parnassos

BOIOTIA

Chalkis

LOKRIS

Delphi

Chaironeia, 338 BC

Thebes

ACHAIA

ATTIKA

ELIS

CORINTHIA

Athens

Elis

Corinth

ARGOLIS

Olympia

Zakynthos

ARKADIA

Argos

Epidauros

LAKONIA

MESSENIA

Sparta

Mediterranean Sea

0   50 miles

0   30 km

Greece, the Balkans and Asia Minor (fourth century BC)

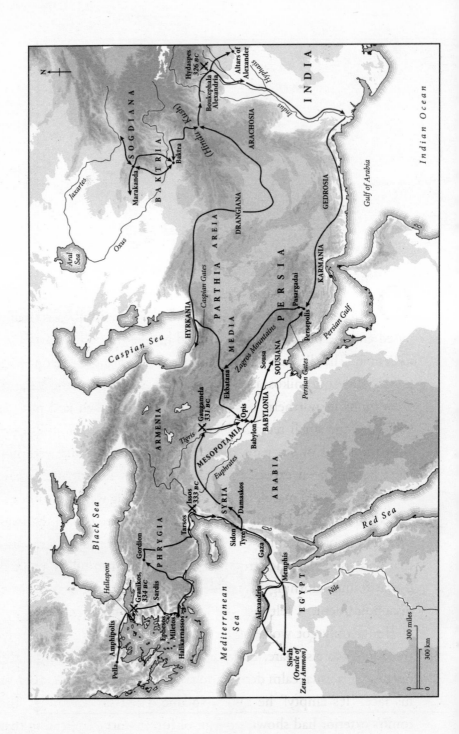

Alexander's Asian Campaign (334–323 BC)

PROLOGUE

On 8 November 1977, the Greek feast day of the Archangels Michael and Gabriel, the keystone of the tomb was finally raised and the burial chamber inhaled its first fresh air in over two millennia. The dig team gathered expectantly around the opening as Manolis Andronikos, the archaeologist in charge of the Vergina excavations in northern Greece, carefully bent down and put his head into the small rectangular hole, the dark interior still heavy with the smell of stagnant time. His first observations were not what he had been expecting. His torch beam illuminated a pair of coarsely worked marble doors; the surrounding walls were undecorated and even lacked the finishing coat of white stucco that was common in other tombs. Considering the massive earthen mound that had concealed the structure, along with an exquisite painted mural found adorning its façade, the plain interior was a bitter disappointment. 'I felt lost,' he later wrote in his memoir.[1]

Things only got worse as he noticed that the floor in front of the doors was also bare. He momentarily lifted his head from the opening, his usual calm demeanour vanished, anxiety etched across his face. 'It's empty!' he said.[2] No one dared say anything. The tomb's exterior had shown no sign of forced entry, indicating that it was another sad victim of ancient tomb robbers – how could it be empty? Unable to believe his own words, Andronikos plunged his head back inside for another look. This time he leant further into the space and aimed his torch directly downwards, and what he saw made him want to shout for joy. For the benefit of his colleagues he began to describe the scene, listing each wonderful item in turn in his slow, authoritative voice: 'Immediately down from the opening, very close to the wall, there is a small marble sarcophagus. On my right I see many bronze vessels, one bronze shield, a pair of greaves and other bronze and iron things. On the left there are silver vessels. On the floor I see residues of organic objects, I assume that they may be rotten wood. In the background I see the backside of an internal marble door. In the centre of the room, on my right, there is a rather strange cuirass. The walls have no decoration.'[3] When he finally stood up his face was serious, but, as one on-site archaeologist records, also 'lit by an impercep-tible ecstasy'.[4] The tomb was intact. Andronikos had finally come face to face with what he later called 'the living truth of the past'.[5]

The contents of the tomb, its location in ancient Aigai – the ancestral centre of ancient Macedonia or Macedon, and the burial place of its kings – combined with other historical and archaeo-logical research, allowed Andronikos to suggest that it belonged to none other than Philip II. This was a Tutankhamun moment; the study of Macedonia would never be quite the same again. But while Howard Carter had discovered the remains of a fairly insig-nificant boy king, Andronikos claimed to have found the final resting place of one of the most famous leaders in the Classical world. The man who had transformed the weak and fragile kingdom into the dominant power in the Aegean. It was one of the greatest archaeological finds of the twentieth century.

As the team set about meticulously recording the tomb and its artefacts, Andronikos' eyes settled on an assortment of miniature ivory body parts hiding among a spray of decomposing organic material. They belonged to figurines that had once adorned the façade of an elaborate wooden dining couch. Their tiny faces, around an inch high, were intricately carved, and the first one he picked up was that of a middle-aged man with prominent nose and trimmed beard. The portrait was similar to the depiction of Philip on a gold medallion from Tarsos. Andronikos believed that he held in his hands the image of the tomb's original occupant. The next face he found was quite different, youthful, with a clean-shaven chin, a gentle upwards tilt of the head and two sullen eyes staring into the distance. Andronikos identified it as Philip's son and successor, Alexander the Great. He could scarcely believe what he was seeing: 'I lost it . . . I am not a kid anymore to start screaming, but inside me I could hear trumpets.'[6]

Andronikos had opened up a portal to the past, to a seminal moment in world history. The funeral of Philip was one of Alexander's first acts as king, an event not related in any detail by the ancient sources. The discovery provided a visceral snapshot of real events, the moment that he stepped out from beneath his father's shadow. It was an encounter with antiquity that only archaeology can provide.

Alexander III of Macedon, also known as Alexander the Great (356–323 BC), would go on to profoundly change the world around him. In 334 BC, a few years after Philip's death, he launched his invasion of Persia. In a blaze of brutality and brilliance, he conquered Asia Minor, the Levant, Egypt, the Middle East, parts of Central Asia, and north-western India, bringing the vast lands of the Persian Empire under Macedonian control. His story often reads like fiction: son to a snake-loving mother and a battle-scarred father, tutored by Aristotle, this youth from the periphery of the Greek world took part in his first campaign aged sixteen, becoming king of Macedon at twenty, and king of Asia by twenty-five. Along with his famous horse Boukephalas, he led his men into battle like a Homeric hero, seeking to rival the deeds of all who had gone before, both men and immortals, even believing himself to be the son of a god. When he died in Babylon in 323 BC, eleven years after beginning his Asiatic campaign and a month short of his thirty-third birthday, he left behind him an achievement that would never be replicated, but the changes he wrought continued to reverberate throughout the ancient world. His many self-named city foundations (Alexandrias) facilitated trade and exchange between East and West. Homer began to be read by Persian schoolboys, the tragedies of Sophocles and Euripides were staged in new exotic locations, Delphi's words of wisdom were displayed in far-off Baktria (Afghanistan); the mixing of Greek and eastern cultures spawned a multitude of ideas and art forms. It was the dawn of a vibrant new age, commonly known as the Hellenistic (323–31 BC), set between the Classical era of the Greek city-states and the establishment of the Roman Empire, a time of great innovation and productivity that rivals any in human history.

Alexander's style of leadership, even the way he presented himself, became the model for those who sought to follow in his footsteps, including the Successors (or *Diadochi*), the king's former commanders, who carved up the newly won empire and established their own independent kingdoms. Later Roman generals and emperors were also inspired by his example. Pompey mimicked his appearance, wore his cloak, and accepted the cognomen Magnus or Great. A young Julius Caesar was apparently moved to tears on reading about Alexander's achievements: 'Do you not think', he said to his friends, 'it is matter for sorrow that while Alexander, at my age, was already king of so many people, I have as yet achieved no brilliant success?' Augustus for a time used the image of Alexander to stamp imperial documents, while the maniacal Caracalla actually believed he was the Macedonian king reincarnated. Alexander's tomb in Egyptian Alexandria became a place of pilgrimage for those who travelled the lonely path of power, until it disappeared sometime in the third or fourth century AD.[7]

But his ghost did not vanish with it. Alexander has had an extraordinarily active afterlife, moving seamlessly into legend, in part owing to the popularity of a fictionalised account of his life known as the *Alexander Romance*, which was in circulation by the third century AD. It remained ever popular and was greatly embellished over the following centuries, with numerous versions or recensions; it has been called the most influential work of historical fiction ever composed, the king endlessly reinvented for new audiences and times.[8] By the Middle Ages he was a protector of Christianity and chivalric knight, a fearless adventurer and sage, an inventor who plumbed the ocean's depths in a diving bell and took to the skies in a rudimentary flying machine, a Muslim and Prophet of God. His story even reached distant Britain. An invented letter between Alexander and Aristotle about the marvels of India is among the earliest surviving works written in Old English, while a fourteenth-century romance sought to link Alexander with Arthurian legend, and Chaucer could even write in his 'Monk's Tale' that Alexander was so well known that everybody had heard somewhat of his fortune.[9] Today our fascination continues, with Alexander being the subject of numerous books and films.

Yet his reputation, from the very beginning, has always been one of sharp contrasts. In the Persian tradition, for example, he is the 'Accursed One', a destroyer supreme, as well as a legitimate king and swashbuckling hero. It is a well-known adage among modern scholars that everybody has their own Alexander, depending on how you interpret the sources on his life. Each generation has peered through the frosted glass of history and come to their own conclusion, be it enlightened ruler, military genius, megalomaniac, drunkard or despot. He was undoubtedly a deeply complex man, a man of incredible drive and ambition, capable of great acts of compassion and crushing feats of inhumanity, who strived to reconcile his own heroic ideals with the realities of ruling the largest empire that had ever existed. His reign continues to confront us with difficult questions that now seem more relevant than ever – the relationship between East and West, the legacy of colonialism, the impact of authoritarian rule. Love him or loathe him, there has never been anyone quite like Alexander.

When Andronikos gazed upon the youthful features of that ivory face in the darkness of Philip's tomb, over two thousand years of history, myth and cultural import were held in the tiny eyes. But here he was not the great conqueror – those deeds were yet to come. He was merely a prince of Macedon, the man yet to be Great. It reminds us that he did not burst forth from his father's head fully formed and ready for battle like the goddess Athena, and that his unique personality was forged in the crucible of Macedonian culture, a result of a complex mixture of influences and experiences that endowed him with the potential for greatness long before he decided to head east. By the time he embarked on his Persian campaign, at the age of twenty-one, he had already loved, lost, killed and conquered. His fame may have been secured in Asia, but the man was made in Macedon.

This part of Alexander's story is rarely told, and for good reason. Written accounts about his upbringing are scarce and those that do survive are beset by romance, myth and legend. The poor state of the historical record from his native land has further hampered investigation; numerous Macedonian writers are known but none of their works have survived. Along with the Spartans, Carthaginians and Etruscans, they have often been called one of the silent peoples of antiquity.[10] Archaeology, however, is finally giving them a voice.

The exploration of Macedonia's buried past began slowly. The British Admiralty's 1920 handbook on the region could claim that, in the forty years prior to publication, it was less traversed by western

Europeans than any other part of Europe south of the Arctic regions.[11] Mainland Greece and the islands, with their impressive ruins and famous sites, had long drawn the attention of travellers, scholars and antiquarians, but the mysterious lands to the north were largely ignored. Things started to change in the nineteenth century, when a few energetic individuals ventured into Macedonia, braving bad weather, bandits and malaria. They pioneered a new approach to the region's past, one that was rooted in the examination of physical remains rather than relying solely on historical accounts; a revolver, Turkish fez, small medicine chest and plentiful supply of insect repellent were the essential items in any traveller's kit, while a moderate stock of good humour was also recommended.[12] They succeeded in locating many of the kingdom's lost settlements, recording inscriptions and collecting artefacts, and in doing so they laid the groundwork for the development of Macedonian studies, which is now a discipline in its own right.

With the collapse of Ottoman rule in Europe (1912–13), the majority of Macedonia's historical territory was incorporated into the Greek state.* New excavations followed, the unveiling of the past aided by a number of large-scale infrastructure projects that have since transformed the landscape – marshes have been drained, rivers canalised and dammed, forests reduced, motorways driven through mountainsides, new settlements created. But it is a land that still remembers Alexander, and it's now possible to explore the sites and cities that he once knew.† Work continues to this day and each year heralds new finds and fresh revelations. With each fragment

---

* Ancient Macedonia or Macedon was the land inhabited and/or ruled by the Macedonians. In this book Macedonia is used for the geographical area and Macedon the kingdom.

† These sites are located in today's Macedonia region of northern Greece, not to be confused with North Macedonia, a separate country to the north which in Philip and Alexander's time was Paionian territory.

of this shattered past, unearthed by shovel, pick and trowel, the world of ancient Macedonia is coming back into focus; a new history is being written in broken pottery and corroded iron, human remains and priceless treasures. The forgotten story of young Alexander is in the process of being unearthed, one dig at a time.

Andronikos' 'Alexander'
from Tomb II, Vergina

PART ONE

THE PRINCE
(356–336 BC)

I.

FIRE FROM HEAVEN

A little over a hundred years ago there was almost nothing to see of one of antiquity's greatest cities. Pella had been destroyed by an earthquake early in the first century BC, reduced to a cemetery of tiles. Only a few areas remained occupied until they too were abandoned, whereupon the great metropolis was lost and then forgotten. 'Few cities as important and as rich in memories have left fewer traces of their existence,' remarked one nineteenth-century visitor.[1] Besides a local spring known as the 'Baths of Alexander the Great', a few plundered tombs and an assortment of ancient finds, gathered from the fields by farmers along with their crop, there was scant trace of the glory that had once been Pella. Excavations began immediately after Macedonia's incorporation into the Greek state following the Balkan Wars (1912–13). Two field seasons (1914–15) revealed sections of late Hellenistic houses, the remains of a fountain and some small finds, but the First World War brought a premature close to the investigation; Pella slipped from memory once more.

The major breakthrough came in early 1957, when a local family began to dig a cellar for their village house in what is now Old Pella, the modern settlement that overlaps the ancient one.[2] They hit some Ionic column drums and called in archaeologist Photios

Petsas, who was already investigating the lost city. He quickly realised the significance of the find and managed to secure some money for a small exploratory excavation. The column drums were found to be still in situ, and more appeared to extend beyond the boundaries of the would-be basement. Over the following months, the archaeologists slowly revealed the building's plan as courtyards, walkways, antechambers and banqueting rooms began to emerge from the sun-baked earth. It was a massive Hellenistic house, one of the largest ever discovered, occupying an entire city block. Among the finds were a stunning set of river-pebble mosaics, some of them displaying geometric patterns. Others were of pictorial scenes from myth, including Dionysos riding a leopard – the mosaic that gives the house its modern name, the House of Dionysos. But one of them stood out as different; rendered in white pebbles and outlined in terracotta tracery were two men in heroic nudity, their bodies almost luminescent against the dark background, hair and lips picked out in hues of orange and red. With billowing cloaks and weapons raised, they confront a muscular mountain lion at the centre of the composition, ready for the kill. Petsas would later suggest that the scene represented Alexander and one of his Companions on a royal hunt; here was no mythical event but one rooted in real life.

It was an extraordinary discovery. The excavations had, in a matter of weeks, revealed one of Greece's greatest treasures. There could be no more fitting introduction to the archaeological richness that lay just beneath the soil. Roof tiles bearing the stamp 'Of Pella' put the identification of the city beyond doubt and excavations continued until 1963. They resumed in 1976, lasting up to the present day. The combined toil and endeavour of generations of archaeologists, conservators and stonemasons have now succeeded in resurrecting the ancient city. Their work has brought Pella back from the dead.[3]

Lion hunt mosaic, House of Dionysos, Pella.

The remains that can be seen today, including the House of Dionysos, mostly date to the Hellenistic period (323–31 BC), when the city was redeveloped and enlarged with riches acquired during Alexander's conquests. It was organised according to a Hippodamian plan – a design accredited to the ancient civic planner Hippodamos – with city blocks and public buildings set within a neat grid of avenues and roads. Water pipes spread out underfoot like the veins of a leaf, while the streets were crammed with shops, shrines, bathhouses, and private residences of varying size and grandeur; the bare Greek light reflects harshly off their friable white limestone remains. A massive agora or marketplace, the commercial heart of Pella, dominates the city; an expansive rectangle of open land enclosed by colonnades with rooms behind, where roads and people converged, it is the largest known forum complex from antiquity. At its zenith, Pella rivalled those other great beacons of Hellenistic civilisation, Pergamon, Alexandria and Antioch. It was the capital of Macedonia, but is better known today as the birthplace of Alexander the Great.

The Pella that Alexander knew, however, was much smaller and has proved harder to trace. It has only been uncovered in a few areas, where archaeologists have been able to delve below the later layers or investigate plots still under cultivation. Excavations have established that it was laid out on a grid plan from its foundation. A Classical cemetery was discovered under the eastern parts of the agora, and, along with a surviving section of the northern fortification wall, the core of the early city has been placed further to the south, on the fringes of what was once a large inland lake, which by the early twentieth century had become a sprawling swamp and was subsequently drained, the land being turned over to agriculture. A fortified islet known as Phakos, now a low bump in a farmer's field, was located just offshore; connected to the mainland via a wooden bridge, it functioned as a citadel, prison and royal treasury. An outlet of the river Loudias provided access to the Thermaic Gulf and the Aegean Sea. Pella was originally a port city.

On a normal day, some 2,300 years ago, the surrounding harbour would have been alive with activity. The sound of hammer and saw emanating from the ship sheds, piles of Macedonian timber stacked high along its length; fishermen setting out onto the lake with their flat-bottomed boats, casting nets for the daily catch, perhaps tossing a morsel or two to the pelicans that also called Pella home; flocks of glossy ibis occasionally rising from the surrounding reed-beds, painting the sky with their iridescent wings. In the city's many workshops, men set to work fashioning pottery or huddled around their forges, ready to mould, bend and temper their metal products. Women cloaked in colourful shawls could sometimes be seen venturing out from their houses, carrying offerings to the sanctuaries of the local healing god Darron, or Athena Alkidemos (Defender of the People). Boys played at knucklebones under shaded eaves, merchants hollered from their market stalls, men clustered together in the public spaces, ready to exchange gossip or talk politics, stray dogs picked at stinking middens.

Outside the cocoon of the city's walls, families could be found among the cemetery mounds and thickets of gravestones that bore the names and images of the dead, saying prayers to the departed and leaving graveside gifts to sustain their beloved's lives in the next world. Around them lay extensive vineyards and water-meadows, the ponding of rivers and protective marshes serving to shield Pella from potential invaders; one Roman general later commented that it had not been chosen as the capital without good reason.

During the winters, fog could quickly envelop the land, bringing days without dawn, dank and muffled mornings, life trapped in vapour; snowfall could often be heavy, a blanket of white stretched over terracotta roofs and open spaces, an icy wind that barrelled down the Axios valley chilling residents to the bone. Spring, and the welcome return of swallows, brought a resurgence of life, the opening of the sailing season attracting new people and wares to the city. With the hottest months came swarms of insects, thick as altar smoke, plaguing the horses of the royal stud and herds of cattle. The locals were then surely thankful for the nearby streams that stayed cool despite the rising temperatures, while those rich enough headed out to their country estates; the city turned drowsy towards the dog days of summer. Standing on the southern edge of the archaeological site, with fields of cotton and wheat extending into the distance, the views bisected by a modern motorway, it can be hard to reimagine the scenes, but hidden below the dusty plain lies the memory of this rich waterfront city, the place that Alexander once called home, where he was born and grew up and which, in 334 BC, he left never to return.[4]

Pella had emerged as the new centre of Macedon towards the end of the fifth century BC.[5] Aigai, identified with modern Vergina to the west, remained the ancestral and ceremonial capital, but because Pella was better situated to exercise control over the kingdom, it became a co-capital, an administrative and military hub; its name was likely derived from the ashen coats of the local herds, the image of a grazing cow being stamped onto the city's coinage and official clay seals.[6] It quickly grew into Macedonia's greatest city, and was further enlarged by Philip.[7]

The move from Aigai to Pella is usually attributed to a previous Macedonian king, Archelaos (413–399 BC), who did much to develop the infrastructure of the kingdom.[8] One of his royal projects was a new palace, decorated by Zeuxis, the most celebrated painter of the day, and such was its magnificence and fame that people apparently came to Macedonia to see the palace rather than the king.[9] Although it is not specifically stated by the sources, it is generally believed that Archelaos' palace was built at Pella, and that it was the principal royal residence for his descendants for much of the fourth century BC, including Philip and his family. It remains the most likely candidate for Alexander's birthplace and childhood home.

The Classical palace has so far eluded firm identification. It may have been close to the waterfront, where the Loudias flowed into Pella's lake. One Athenian visitor was accused of attempting to hold secret talks with Philip by taking a canoe along the river; others ridiculed the king's court as a dwelling in an outflow of slime.[10] Another possible location is further to the north, on the site of the later Hellenistic palace that crowns the heights of a low hill overlooking the city. For many years it remained closed off to the public, the shaggy grass growing up around metal canopies that sheltered the exposed remains, a playground for butterflies and other insect life, the understorey patrolled by tortoises, going nowhere slowly. Areas have recently been reno-vated and opened to the public, allowing the visitor to walk the corridors of power and to admire the regal views across the land, the sparkling waters of the Thermaic Gulf lying in the distance,

Mount Vermion and the Pierian range scoring a jagged line across the western sky which the eye can trace south towards the peaks of Olympos, home of the gods.

During the Hellenistic era, the palace was a labyrinthine complex, stretching across some seven hectares; buildings were terraced into the hill at various levels, linked together by corridors, halls, gateways, courtyards and stairs. Its grand façade towered above the rest of the city, a bank of bright white stucco, rich colours picking out the decorative architectural details. The roof was of strong Macedonian timber and held the great weight of large terracotta tiles that are now stacked in piles across the site, patinated with lichen and bleaching under the sun; when the clouds above began to boil and bruise, the weather breaking like a fever over the plain, the rain beat down upon them, the water gushing out of marble lions' heads positioned along its length. A monumental entrance afforded a carefully controlled passage into the palace, each of the interior buildings being based around a central courtyard, the spaces subdivided and given over to special-ised functions – meeting halls, feasting rooms, private residences, an exercise yard and service quarters. It has been suggested that the palace's core may reflect the original blueprint of Archelaos' building, but the dating remains uncertain.[11]

The beginnings of Alexander's life, his earliest years, are similarly difficult to retrace. Besides his birth, they are not alluded to in any of the surviving accounts. It is perhaps not surprising, then, that the most enduring portrait of the infant Alexander comes from a writer of fiction: Mary Renault. In 1969 her novel *Fire from Heaven* was published, in which she imaginatively recounts Alexander's journey from boy to man. Some fifty years after its publication, it still has the ability to transport the reader into the past, helping to place the young Alexander back into Pella's forgotten spaces. Renault begins her story in the private apartments of Archelaos' palace, when a silent intruder stirs a four-year-old Alexander from his sleep:

> The child was wakened by the knotting of the snake's coils about his waist. For a moment he was frightened; it had squeezed his breathing, and given him a bad dream. But as soon as he was awake, he knew what it was, and pushed his two hands inside the coil. It shifted; the strong band under his back bunched tightly, then grew thin. The head slid up his shoulder along his neck, and he felt close to his ear the flickering tongue.[12]

Renault's Alexander is a strange and extraordinary child, with pale white skin, blond hair that would not hold a curl, and a unique, adventurous spirit. He is different from other children, not afraid of snakes in the dark. This portrait was the result of Renault's lifelong fascination with Alexander. She had first come under his spell in the 1920s when she encountered a plaster-cast bust of him in Oxford's Ashmolean Museum. She later confessed to her friend Kasia Abbott that this face had come to haunt her, 'the amazing eyes, the way his hair springs from his brow, and what must already early in his twenties have been his weather-beaten beauty, his skin burnt almost black and his hair almost white with sun.'[13] A postcard of the original bust was one of her most prized possessions and took up permanent residence in her beachfront cottage near Cape Town.

Sadly, Renault never managed to visit Alexander's homeland. Two previous trips around Greece and the islands, undertaken in 1954 and 1962, had been enlightening but also exhausting. She was in her early sixties when she started work on *Fire from Heaven*. There was talk of a visit but it never materialised. Instead she began collecting archaeological reports and articles, anything that could help enrich the novel's setting. Her study, with views of the rolling Atlantic surf, became crammed with research material: 'There was literally a book behind a book and behind that there were books again,' reports one of her biographers.[14] At the same time, she pored over the ancient sources that detailed Alexander's life, of which there is a small collection of surviving accounts.[15] The earliest – provided by Diodorus Siculus – was produced in the first century BC, some three hundred years after Alexander's death; the rest appeared during the Roman Empire. But they all drew on earlier works and it has been the task of historians to peel back the layers of rhetoric and propaganda in order to get closer to contemporary views.

Two in particular deal with Alexander's youth. The fictionalised *Alexander Romance*, attributed to an anonymous author referred to as Pseudo-Callisthenes, provides a fantastic version, where Alexander is the son of the last Egyptian pharaoh and sorcerer: Nektanebo II. Fleeing a Persian invasion, Nektanebo leaves Egypt and takes up residence at Pella, where he manages to seduce Philip's queen, Olympias, by disguising himself as the god Ammon of Libya. Alexander is born to great claps of thunder and streaks of lightning, the world shaken. Alexander later kills Nektanebo, who with his dying words reveals that he is his true father. He is buried in Macedonia, enabling the author to reflect on the remarkable proof of divine providence, whereby an Egyptian is buried in a Greek grave while Alexander would be laid to rest in an Egyptian one. The prince goes on to tame a man-eating horse, and compete and win at the Olympics games, before becoming king. Despite these questionable historical details, the *Romance* does preserve unique information pertaining to Alexander's youth, such as a list of his various tutors, and is therefore of some value, but it is the other source that provides the basis for any real reconstruction.

Plutarch's *Life of Alexander* forms part of his series of *Parallel*

Lives – twinned biographies of famous Greek and Roman individuals – that were produced in the late first and early second century AD. Alexander's *Life* is coupled with that of Julius Caesar, and the author was able to draw upon a number of lost sources that dealt with his upbringing.[16] Plutarch was not so much concerned with Alexander's military achievements as with those stories that illuminated his character, reminding the reader in the introduction to the work that he is writing lives not history.[17] It was an approach that chimed with Renault's interests and she relied heavily upon his account, finding much of interest within it. She shared her excitement with a long-time correspondent in America, Jay Williams: 'They [historians] say again and again how he [Alexander] was enigmatic and complex and contradictory; yet the little that Plutarch has space to say about his youth, is enormously significant in itself, and very much more so if one takes the trouble to line it up against contemporary history . . . I may have got the answers all wrong, but I have never studied anything more interesting.'[18]

By the late 1960s, Renault had already written four other books of historical fiction.[19] She was a deft hand at rooting stories in the strange and alien ancient world. Her meticulous research made many believe that she had an almost psychic understanding of life in the distant past. *Fire from Heaven* remains important for many reasons. Not only is it an enthralling read but also, by reimagining Alexander's early life, Renault forces the reader to consider the realities of the time along with the influences that shaped his personality. Central to this understanding was Alexander's relationship with his parents, Philip and Olympias. Renault introduces them in dramatic fashion.

Alexander, believing the snake to be one of his mother's pets, sneaks out of the nursery, leaving behind his slumbering baby sister and nanny. He ventures down the dark palace corridors, past the on-duty guard and up the stairs to his mother's chamber. They lie together alone in the royal bed, snuggling up to each other, Alexander asking her who she loves best. He shows her the snake, but she does not recognise it; she says that it is Alexander's *daimon*, an intermediary between gods and men that can help guide an individual's fate. He calls it *Tyche* or Fortune.

This idyllic world is suddenly torn apart by the entrance of a drunken Philip. The door flies open. Without even looking at the bed, he starts to undress, making ready to take what is his by marriage. Alexander cowers under the blankets, his blue-grey eyes wide with fear. Through a peephole he observes his father naked and aroused, pockmarked with scars, one eye blinded by an arrow. Olympias protests at the intrusion and the two exchange insults: 'you Molossian bitch,' he says; 'you wineskin,' she counters. Philip lunges at her – like the mythical cyclops Polyphemos on his prey – but he reels in shock when he discovers Olympias' pet snake, Glaukos, sleeping at her side. 'How dare you,' he shouts, 'when I forbade it, bring your filthy vermin into my bed? Sorceress, barbarian witch . . .' His one good eye then comes to rest on the child. Father and son exchange steely looks. He notices Alexander's snake-*daimon*, still wrapped around his waist. 'What's that upon the boy? . . . are you teaching *him* now? Are you making *him* into a back-country, snake dancing, howling mystagogue?'

A heated argument erupts over their respective ancestry and experience, each one trying to trump the other's claims to Greekness. Philip moves to strike his wife but little Alexander stands up on the bed, coming to her defence. 'Go away! She hates you!' he cries, jabbing with his tiny fists at Philip's outstretched arm. 'Go away! She will marry me!' He ends up being thrown from the room by his father, like a rag doll tossed aside by squabbling children.

In just a few pages Renault encapsulates one of the strangest family dynamics in history, a dysfunctional father-mother-son relationship as tempestuous as a winter's sea. This is not all fiction; ancient sources attest to difficulties between the family members, albeit from a later time when Alexander had grown to adulthood. The lives of Philip and Olympias have long been overshadowed by their famous son, but there's no doubting that they were two extraordinary individuals, and that their influence on Alexander went way beyond mere genetics; they would both leave their own indelible impression on his character and life. Any story about the young Alexander must begin with his parents.

INTO THE MYSTIC

In antiquity, the island of Samothrace (or Samothraki) was famed for three things: onions, flat-horned goats and the mysteries of the Great Gods – a strange religious cult that was only accessible via a secretive initiation ceremony.[20] It was forbidden to divulge any information about the mysteries and, as such, very little is known about them. Even the identity of the Great Gods remains enigmatic. One Hellenistic scholar records that they were four in number, Axieros, Axiokersa, Axiokersos and Kasmilos, chthonic or underworld deities, whom he identifies with Demeter, Persephone, Hades and Hermes.[21] A central role in the cult was also reserved for a Great Mother figure, a goddess of fertility, who is depicted on local coins. Collectively they are called Kabeiroi on the mainland but inscriptions on Samothrace refer to them only as 'Gods' or 'Great Gods' (*Megaloi Theoi*), and anonymity may well have been part of their appeal. What is known is that they appear to have had the power to avert shipwreck, and promised to make initiates more pious, more righteous – just better in every way.[22] For the ancients their lure was strong, and despite the island's remote location, the mysteries possessed a lengthy list of famous initiates, including Jason and the Argonauts, the travelling hero Odysseus, the historian Herodotus, and, in the mid fourth century BC, the parents of Alexander the Great. According to Plutarch, it was here that they first met.

The event probably took place in 357 BC. Philip, son of Amyntas III, was then in his mid-twenties, and had come to power some three years previously. His brother, the former king Perdikkas III, had been killed in battle against the Illyrians, along with over four thousand of his men. He left behind a son, also named Amyntas, but he was too young to rule. Although the situation is debated by scholars, it seems likely that Philip first became guardian of Amyntas and that no new king was proclaimed.[23] With rivals and enemies appearing from every direction, Macedon was on the brink of collapse, but Philip managed to rescue the situation. Using a mix of speed, diplomacy and cunning, he brought valuable time to consolidate his position and build the army. As a boy, he had spent time as a hostage in both Illyria and Thebes – the dominant city-state in Greece at the time – and these experiences endowed him with a shrewd understanding of Greek and barbarian mentalities, as well as fostering new military ideas. Within a year he was ready to go on the attack. He defeated the Paionians to the north (in today's North Macedonia), securing their allegiance, and then marched his new model army west, towards the Illyrians. After a grudge battle against the veteran king Bardylis, Philip emerged victorious. The Illyrian threat was, for the time being, nullified; it was the biggest shift in the region's power dynamics for over a generation.[24] In the aftermath, he managed to unite the desperate independent cantons of Upper Macedonia under his rule, effectively doubling the size of his kingdom. In Thessaly, he re-established good relations with the city of Larissa, helping to resolve a dispute with their neighbours – the tyrants of Pherai – and then turned his attention to the east. The key port of Amphipolis, situated on the river Strymon close to the eastern borders of Macedon, had been an Athenian foundation but had declared its independence during the Peloponnesian War. The Athenians, who occupied various ports along Macedonia's seaboard, were desperate to reclaim it. Philip indicated that he would help them to do so, and a lengthy siege ensued, but once the city had fallen he decided to keep it for himself. In a short span of time Philip had proved his credentials and it is likely around this date, either late 357 or early 356 BC, that he was acclaimed king by the Macedonians. It was now his sons, if he could produce them, who would succeed, should the circumstances allow. There had been ancient prophecies that Macedon would achieve great things under one of the sons of Amyntas III, and these were finding their fulfilment under Philip.[25] It may well have been after the great victory at Amphipolis that he headed to the island of Samothrace, a day's sail away. Here he would meet a young princess from the kingdom of Molossia, in north-western Greece. She was called Polyxena and also Myrtale (Myrtle), but would later become known as Olympias.[26]

Robust ferries now make the voyage between the mainland town of Alexandroupolis and Samothrace, their steel bellies transporting tourists rather than pilgrims to the island. Across the inky-blue expanse of sea, Samothrace rears its mountainous head, slowly shrugging off its ethereal haze and taking on crisp definition. As the ferry tracks west, towards the main port, Mount Saos sharpens into a fierce point, its surface as grey and foreboding as Athena's eyes, the summit often haloed with cloud. It has an ominous aura. Lawrence Durrell, who wrote a travel book on the Greek islands, never managed to make it ashore but recorded his impressions from the sea: 'It's gloomy, it's barbaric; I didn't like it one bit; I felt the cannibals warming up the cooking pots.' He opted to stay on board his ship.[27]

At first, the island appears inhospitable, a desolate chunk of rock amid the Aegean's rippling waters, but then a shelf of surrounding land is revealed, extending out to north and west and providing space for yellowing pasturage and crop. Groves of olive, chestnut, plane and oak add welcome dashes of greenery, bunching around the base of the mountain and dissipating among the upper slopes where clusters of white houses cling like barnacles to the island's sides. Its geology is known to have a magnetic quality; those with iron-rich blood can quite literally feel the pull of Samothrace on their bodies.

The arrival of each ferry breathes fresh life into the port town of Kamariotissa. Supplies are unloaded and cafés begin to hum with activity; one set of visitors is exchanged for another; a host of cicadas greet all newcomers with their deafening drone. Many of the new imports are teenagers. They colonise the island's northern campsites in the summer, the holiday months passing in a carefree blur of firelit parties and twilight swims – a modern rite of passage

Samothrace

for young Greeks. With its deep forests, spectacular waterfalls and long stretches of pebbled beach, Samothrace feels quite unlike anywhere else in the vast tapestry of Greek islands.

The sanctuary of the Great Gods lies roughly six kilometres east from the port, buried in a cleft in the mountain's side. The nearby ancient town of Samothrace – now known as Palaiopolis (Old Town) – functioned as the gateway to the site, spreading across an open slope of Saos, the fifty-acre space providing ample room for houses, shops and public areas. This was where the pilgrims relaxed and prepared before the excitement of the mysteries which took place at night; the blanket of darkness helped to enhance the disorientating otherness of the rituals; the secrets of the immortals were not to be given away easily. The Macedonian and Molossian parties may have arrived for the annual festival, believed to have been held in the summer, but if not, initiation was available at any time, in part due to the difficulty in reaching the island.

Little survives of the ancient town except for its impressive encircling walls, in places standing well over six feet high. The remains of gates and towers are dotted along its length, the local goats often using them as convenient perches to spy on visitors. One section of the defences trudges uphill towards the summit of Fengari – Moon peak – where Homer relates that Poseidon once watched the unfolding of the Trojan War. Every now and then colossal bursts of wind are dispatched from its heights, twisting the trees into strange shapes and imbuing the island with a raw, untameable character. Storms can blow up quickly here; in the past, those caught at sea would call on the Great Gods for deliverance. With hands raised to the sky on the decks of their pitching ships, they promised votive gifts and sacrifices in order to survive the ordeal. The sanctuary was littered with such memorials, although one cynic slyly observed that 'There would have been far more, if those who were not saved had set up offerings.'[28]

With the Roman Empire's official adoption of Christianity in the fourth century AD, the cult of the Great Gods withered and eventually died. The sanctuary was abandoned and fell into decay. It re-enters the history books in 1444, when Cyriac of Ancona, an Italian merchant and prodigious traveller, came to the island. He was part of the Renaissance's humanist movement, and his life's mission was to search out noble memorials of antiquity, to record and, where possible, to help preserve them; when once asked why he undertook such a task he replied, 'to wake the dead.'[29] Cyriac was aware of the island's connection to Alexander's story and he set out to explore what was left of its ancient celebrity. In his diary, he recorded encounters with a distant age, including the city walls and the vast remains of a temple, which he ascribes to Neptune/Poseidon, along with 'fragments of immense columns, architraves, and statue bases and doorways decorated with garlanded boukrania [cattle skulls] and other very beautifully and artistically sculptured figures', one of which he mistook for Aristotle.[30] With the island's governor, he spent an October afternoon documenting some of his key discoveries, making sketches and transcribing inscriptions. In doing so he was pioneering a new discipline: archaeology. Other inquisitive minds have since followed in his footsteps. Greeks, Austrians, Germans, French, Czechs, and most recently Americans, have all contributed to disentangling the jumbled remains of the sanctuary.[31] Their work has made it possible to reconstruct elements of the initiation experience, to reimagine the circumstances that led to Philip's fabled meeting with Olympias.

The prospective initiates and veterans of the cult gathered at the town's western gate towards dusk. Together under an Alizarin-flecked sky they watched the sunset over the ravine that concealed the sanctuary, the pallid face of Lady Moon appearing overhead, climbing the peak that takes her name, bathing the land in a fragile, silvery glow. Finally, the signal was given. A line of torches

and flickering oil lamps moved in single file through the narrow
gateway, past a scattering of olive trees, and down towards a
mountain stream that marked the boundary between the sacred
and profane, the ice-cold water purifying all those who wished to
enter the realm of the Great Gods. Not all were allowed to cross
the threshold. There was first a sacred pronouncement that deter-
mined who was suitable to take part in the mysteries; the impure
were barred from proceedings.[32] As part of the screening process,
prospective candidates may have been asked to declare the worst
thing they had ever done.[33] Philip was a typical Macedonian royal,
with more than a few skeletons locked away in his strongbox. He
may have sidestepped the awkward question by replying in the
same manner as the Spartan Antalkidas: 'If any such deed has been
committed by me, the gods themselves will know it.'[34]

Once inside the sanctuary, the initiates descended onto the
eastern hill that overlooked the valley, the cult buildings remaining
hidden below. Following their trail, a mysterious saucer-like structure is the first to emerge from the gloom: the so-called Theatral
Circle. The moonlight shines bright on the paved steps, where the
initiates would have taken up their places, not sitting but standing.
It is estimated that the circle could cater for around three hundred
people, although smaller groups were more common.[35] The shared
experience of being initiated on the same night served to bind
them together – strangers from many distant lands became one
community. The circle is a likely location for the sacred instructions
for the mysteries that were to follow, where each initiate received
a special cup for libations, the wine to be poured on the sanctuary's
many rock altars and ritual pits, portals to the underworld that
punctured the sacred space. The ritual of enthronement (*thronosis*)
may also have occurred here, the participants being seated on a
special chair where they were surrounded by fearsome warrior
dancers who whirled around them with sword and spear, their war

cries, the clash of cymbals and beat of drums designed to terrorise and disorient.[36] One of the most famous Samothracian myths was the meeting and marriage of the Phoenician hero Kadmos to Harmonia, which took place on the island. 'And even now in Samothrace they go in quest of her [Harmonia] in their festivals,' says one ancient writer.[37] The initiates, re-enacting the myth, may have embarked on a sacred hide-and-seek in order to bring about the mythical union.

The Sacred Way leads from the Theatral Circle down into the sanctuary proper. The descent is hazardous, the sense of anticipation growing with each step. The sanctuary is cradled by the valley's steep sides and cleaved by a mountain torrent. It is an intimate location, even more so at night. The silhouettes of ancient buildings are everywhere; they represent a mosaic of different ages, their broken forms emerging like monsters in the dark. The archaeologists' painstaking work has helped to restore and date the majority. In the mid fourth century BC, there were only a handful of cult buildings. The most important was probably a rectangular hall or chamber that occupied the centre of the valley, underneath which the earliest ritual activity has been discovered – a layer of ash, pottery and burnt bone dated to the seventh century BC.[38] Its central location suggests that it was the final destination for the initiates.

Plutarch likens their journey to the flight of the soul at death: 'In the beginning there is straying and wandering, the weariness of running this way and that, and nervous journeys through darkness that reach no goal, and then immediately before the consummation every possible terror, shivering and trembling and sweating and amazement.' On entering the hall of initiation, they encountered an extraordinary light, where the reunion of Kadmos and Harmonia may have taken place. Plutarch continues, 'there are voices and dancing and the solemn majesty of sacred and holy visions.'[39] The revelation of the ancient mysteries typically included 'the things done, things shown, and things said', whereby the initiates gained a deeper understanding of the cult's secrets and saw the sacred objects.[40] The magnetic geology of the island may have had a role to play in the final rituals. The Roman writer Lucretius claimed to have observed 'Samothracian iron dance, and at the same time iron filings go mad in a bronze bowl, when this magnet stone was applied underneath: so eager seems the iron to escape from the stone'.[41] To superstitious eyes, the act could easily be interpreted as a manifestation of the Great Gods' power; a version of this simple trick perhaps constituted one of the 'things seen'. Whether the initiates understood the stories surrounding these rituals can only be guessed. The priests used many archaic words during the ceremony which probably sounded like gibberish to the majority of the participants.[42]

A purple sash and iron finger ring were handed out to each new member, talismans that represented their new status as initiates of the cult. Celebrations surely followed, the air of intoxicating sanctity giving way to more music and dance, stamping feet throwing up clouds of dust illuminated by torch-light, bodies moving in time to cymbal, drum and flute. Feasting later took place on the western hill. Fasts were broken and much wine consumed, song, laughter and sexual chemistry mixing in the mystic night. The footprint of the earliest banqueting rooms can be traced along the banks of the mountain stream, sheltered by plane trees and home to swooping bats. It is a fitting location to consider the story of Philip and Olympias' meeting, recorded by Plutarch: 'And we are told that Philip, after being initiated into the mysteries of Samothrace at the same time with Olympias, he himself being still a youth and she an orphan child, fell in love with her and betrothed himself to her at once with the consent of her brother, Arymbas [= Arybbas].'[43]

The story has had its fair share of doubters, an island romance appearing a little too good to be true. There are certainly some elements that are suspect: the stated ages given by Plutarch are problematic and his introductory phase, 'and we are told', allows no scrutiny of the original source on which he drew.[44] The love at first sight drama may be an embellishment, but there is reason to believe the truthfulness of the Samothracian setting. Philip, like Alexander, took an interest in famous sanctuaries when in their vicinity, while emulation of the former heroes, who had also been initiated into the cult, could have been another strong motivator. The Kabeiroi/Great Gods had many followers in Thrace and the northern Aegean and, for Philip, it may have been a chance to broadcast his piety in an area where he was increasingly active. Moreover, Macedonia was one of the principal sources and exporters of ship timber. It cannot have hurt to have a ruler who was devoted to gods that promised salvation at sea.

The meeting had likely been arranged in advance, although it is unknown who initiated it. The Molossians had travelled the greater distance, for their homeland lay in Epeiros, a mountainous region to the west of Macedonia. They too had suffered from Illyrian aggression in the recent past. An invasion by Bardylis had forced the evacuation of many of the residents to neighbouring Aitolia, and it was only by employing guerrilla tactics that they managed to rescue the kingdom.[45] Some of the cantons of Upper Macedonia had been aligned with the Molossians and Philip's policy of unification may have influenced their decision to seek out a new alliance. King Arybbas – Olympias' uncle – probably made the journey to Samothrace in the hope of a more stable future; conversely, for Philip, it offered a chance to secure his western frontier.

Olympias was probably in her mid to late teens, a good marriageable age in antiquity. She belonged to the ruling Aiakid family – descendants of Aiakos, father to Peleus and grandfather to

Achilles. Her mother may have been a Chaonian, another Epeirote people that traced their linage back to the kings of Troy.[46] Her DNA was distinctly Homeric. Neoptolemos, Olympias' father, had shared the kingship with Arybbas for a time, until his death in around 360 BC. Olympias and her siblings – Alexander and Troas – had then come under Arybbas' guardianship. He was married to Troas and now sought to use Olympias to help consolidate and expand his rule, but an enduring alliance would have hinged on her ability to produce children. Her feelings on the matter are not known. Marriage was often a traumatic experience for young maidens, wrenched from their family and left to make their own way in a strange household. But it also offered a chance to escape the shadow of Arybbas' kingship, and to represent Molossian interests in a new society that was growing in power and influence. Philip was young and handsome, and there may have been some mutual attraction. The engagement was made and the two were to marry back in Macedonia – a new Kadmos had his bride.

Following the end of the celebrations, the pilgrims began to file out of the sanctuary, leaving their ritual vessels at the Theatral Circle and heading back to their own lands. Philip took with him not only a new prospective wife but an enduring connection to Samothrace. Archaeologists have discovered that, in the middle of the fourth century BC (c.340), a grand structure with two deep chambers and a porch lined with Ionic columns was built in the centre of the sanctuary, incorporating part of the older cult building. This has been dubbed the Hall of Choral Dancers in honour of frieze depicting a line of dancing maidens that once girdled the upper exterior. The building was the first entirely marble structure in the sanctuary and has all the hallmarks of Macedonian-sponsored architecture. Philip is the obvious patron, while Alexander apparently later criticised his father for re-visiting

Samothrace when he should have been busy with other things.[47] His investment caused a chain reaction of redevelopment on the island, later Hellenistic kings and Romans following his lead. The valley sprouted many more marble creations and votive gifts, including the famous Nike or Victory of Samothrace. The statue was most likely a gift from a forgotten victor, perhaps one that had benefited first-hand from the Great Gods' power to aid those at sea. The now headless winged goddess resides in the Louvre, draped in diaphanous robes and standing on the prow of a warship, it had once overlooked the sanctuary's theatre. The masterpiece has become the icon of Samothrace and it is difficult to pass any shop on the island without encountering one of its miniature progeny, jostling for the tourist's attention on overladen shelves. The sanctuary became one of the most celebrated in antiquity, the mysteries second only to those in Eleusis near Athens. For Philip, it provided a stage on which he could display his burgeoning power; it was the beginning of a dialogue between a new and ambitious Macedonian leader and the outside world.

Philip and Olympias were married in one of the royal centres of Macedon, perhaps at the end-of-year festivals to Zeus that took place that autumn in 357 BC, a popular time for weddings. Set up in her new home at Pella, Olympias quickly became pregnant. As her belly began to swell, Philip remained active; the Samothrace pilgrimage and later celebrations had been but a short interruption in his continuing policy of expansion. He went on to claim the port city of Pydna on the Thermaic Gulf, taking it from the Athenians, and then formed an alliance with the powerful Chalkidike League, located on the three-pronged Chalkidike penin- sula, close to Macedon's south-eastern borders, and headed by the city of Olynthos.[48] As part of the agreement, he helped them capture Poteidaia, another Athenian-occupied stronghold that helped control the western stretches of Chalkidike. In the summer of 356 BC, on the very day he took the city, three messages arrived at his camp simultaneously. The first reported that his general Parmenion had defeated the Illyrians in another battle to the north, the second that his racehorse had won at the Olympic games; the third announced the birth of a baby boy, Alexander. The seers proclaimed that a son whose birth coincided with three victories (the Poteidaian, Illyrian and Olympic) would be invincible. Philip was undoubtedly having a good year and prayed for some minor setback in order to offset his lucky streak.[49] For the inhabitants of Asia, however, the omens were not so favourable. On the same day, a terrible fire was said to have consumed the temple of Artemis in Ephesos – one of the seven wonders of the ancient world. Hegesias of Magnesia claimed that such an accident was to be expected as the goddess was away in Macedonia overseeing the birth of the future conqueror. The local Magi believed it was an indication of the devastation to come.

GROWING PAINS

Alexander was born on the sixth day of the Macedonian month Loos, around 20 July, 356 BC.[50] It was believed that the three Fates (*Moirai*) visited the child soon afterwards, their task to assign mortals both good and ill, their destiny on earth. Ethnologists and antiquarians who visited Macedonia in the early twentieth century recorded the continuing rituals that may echo those of ancient times.[51] At midnight on the third day following the birth, the goddesses descended from Olympos to spin the child's future. Preparations were made to encourage a favourable visit: dogs were tied up, furniture moved aside, offerings were laid out on a table in the nursery, a single light was left burning to allow them to find the cradle. On arrival, they fussed over the child, debating with each other about their night's work. Klotho – the spinner – took out her wool and began spinning the thread. Lachesis – the apportioner – meted out the individual's destiny, entering the prescribed details in a ledger. Atropos – the inflexible – the oldest and most terrible of the three, wielded the shears; it was she who decided where to cut, dictating when the individual would die. Alexander's thread was strong, the strands promising fortune and glory, but his life, as Atropos had prescribed, would be short.

The days following the birth were a dangerous time for both mother and child. Many did not survive the first week, succumbing to disease or infection. Pella's Classical cemetery, discovered below the Hellenistic agora and surrounding areas, has provided invaluable insights into the realities of the time. Female burials were twice as common as male, with children accounting for 35–40 per cent of the total number, the majority being babies up to a year old. Infant mortality was shockingly high by modern standards.[52] Many older children were buried with a large number of grave goods, especially terracottas, among them miniature cockerels, pieces of household furniture, nursing bottles, and figurines of wet nurses with babes in arms. The heartache is all too apparent in the possessions laid beside the dead; the Fates had woven sorrowful threads for these children. The fifth-century BC philosopher Democritus of Abdera perhaps put it best: 'The rearing of children is full of pitfalls. Success is attended by strife and care, failure means grief beyond all others.'[53] Alexander was one of the lucky ones to survive.

Rituals and ceremonies helped mark the transformation of the liminal status of the baby into a recognised member of the family unit. Evidence of these customs from Macedonia is lacking, but they probably followed those practised elsewhere in the Greek world. They began moments after birth, the newborn being placed on the ground where it was examined for any sign of weakness. All being well, it was quickly picked up, being considered worthy of rearing, but if it did not cry, if it exhibited any abnormality or even if the family could not afford another mouth to feed, then rejection could follow. The baby would be exposed somewhere outside, placed in the hands of the gods, but this did not always mean death; adoption was commonplace, a practice that furnished many a poet and playwright with a popular plot device.[54] A formal ceremony of acceptance followed on the fifth or seventh day; this was the *Amphidromia*, whereby the baby was carried around the family hearth and a feast given in its honour. The naming ritual usually took place at the same time, or on the tenth day for those that could afford the extra celebrations.[55] Alexander – *Alexandros* in Greek – was a common name in both Epeiros and Macedonia, translating as 'Defender of Men'. Two former Macedonian kings had carried the name: Alexander I, who was one of the most celebrated kings, and Philip's elder brother, Alexander II; it came with its own weight of expectation.[56]

Olympias was fortunate to be part of the royal household, which gave her access to the best physicians in the land. An Akarnanian called Philip, from western Greece, is recorded as Alexander's personal doctor from boyhood. Hellanike – Lanike for short – was appointed wet-nurse. She was a Macedonian woman, sister to one of Philip's courtiers or Companions, Kleitos, a capable warrior. She already had children of her own, Proteas being one of them; from the little we know of him he was a larger-than-life character, and could drink more than any of his peers.[57] Breast milk was seen as the purveyor of strength and aggression for a baby boy and Lanike was probably selected as a wet-nurse for her family's reputation, in the hope that certain qualities would be passed on to Alexander.

The women's quarters encompassed his world during those earliest years. They were usually located on the first floor of the household; it's not known where Olympias lived in Pella, but very probably it would have been the palace's private apartments. A communal courtyard offered an outdoor space where women could sit outside, talk to visitors and work the loom in the fresh air. The children, as in rural communities in modern Greece, were kept under constant supervision, the exploratory wanderings of toddlers guided with a helping hand. The birth of a healthy boy would have greatly improved Olympias' standing in the royal household. As well as dealing with the demands of motherhood, she was also required to acclimatise to life in the Macedonian court. Medea, in Euripides' eponymous play, recounted the challenges that faced a foreign bride on entering her new household: 'We come to new ways of behaviour, to new customs – and, since we have learnt nothing of such matters at home, we need prophetic powers to tell us specifically what sort of husband we shall have to deal with.'[58] Things were probably not so alien for Olympias. Molossia and Macedonia were neighbours, both were ruled by monarchies and the people shared similar beliefs and values.[59] To further ease her transition, she was probably accompanied by her own hand-maidens. Philip's alliance with Arybbas also brought other Molossians to court. One of his bodyguards had a Molossian name, and Olympias' brother, Alexander, later attended the king. Together they formed a Molossian faction in court, representing the region's interests whilst also providing a support bubble for the newest members of the royal family.

In order to ingratiate herself with her new people, Olympias embraced one of the few outlets for female participation in public life: religion. Dionysos – god of wine, fertility, merriment and madness – was a popular god in Macedonia, and was worshipped under a range of different epithets including the False Man, the Savage and the Very Hidden.[60] He also played a role in afterlife beliefs, being the central figure in Orphic cults, the hymns, rites and rituals believed to have been handed down by mythical musician Orpheus. Initiates into his mysteries were buried with small gold tablets placed over the mouth, or elsewhere on the body, admission tickets for a happier abode in the underworld; several of these have been retrieved from Pella's graves, inscribed with the names of the dead – Philoxena, Epigenes, Hegesiska.[61] It is generally believed that Euripides wrote his famous play *Bacchae*, one of the strangest and most terrifying of Greek tragedies, during his stay at Archelaos' court. The descriptions of the Theban women's devotion to Dionysos, their ecstatic and primitive rituals, may well have been influenced by the playwright's experiences in Macedonia.[62] Plutarch, in his *Life of Alexander*, states that all women of these northern climes were addicted to the god's rites and put on extravagant ceremonies, imitating those of neighbouring Thrace, which was also well known for its Dionysian worship. This typically entailed dressing up as maenads (*mainades*), 'the raving ones' – mythical female followers of Dionysos, the women wearing animal pelts and carrying branches or stalks of fennel twined with ivy and sometimes topped with pine cones (*thyrsoi*). Every two years they disappeared into mountain groves where they would perform dances in honour of the god, their hair loosened, dancing to the beat of Dionysiac, hand-held drums, letting out ritual cries of exultation – '*Euoi!*' Poseidippus, a Hellenistic poet and native of Pella, names a Macedonian maenad in one of his epigrams, a teenage girl called Niko, whose early death reportedly plunged the city into grief.[63]

The groups of female worshippers (*thiasoi*) were divided into three, the *Mimallones* (formerly known as *Klodones*), *Bassarai* and

Lydian women.[64] Each of these groups had its own leader and Olympias may have attained such a rank during her time in Pella. After Alexander's death, she was able to gain Macedonian support by appearing to the troops in her maenadic costume, which helped to win them over; there's also some evidence to suggest that she was a tall woman, making her seem all the more impressive.[65] Plutarch relates that she participated in the rites with particular zeal, even providing large tame snakes for her fellow worshippers. They would lift their heads from the ivy and sacred winnowing-baskets, coiling themselves around their ritual staffs and terrifying the onlooking men.[66]

The association between Olympias and snakes is an enduring aspect of her reputation and has been cultivated by authors and film directors, from Mary Renault to Oliver Stone. How unusual this was for the time is another matter. Snakes are mentioned in the *Bacchae*, where they accompany maenadic activity, sometimes worn as garlands and licking the cheeks of their handlers.[67] Their mythical association with Dionysian rites may have influenced contemporary practices in Macedonia; snakes are also mentioned playing a role in the cult of Sabazios – similar to Dionysos' – in fourth-century BC Athens.[68] In antiquity, they were sacred creatures, believed to embody beneficent spirits of the departed, and were symbols of prosperity, fertility and healing. They could be kept as pets, as seems to be the case with Olympias, and were honoured as guardians of the house, helping to keep down mice and other vermin, a tradition still found in some Balkan communities.[69] Terracotta snakes, curled up like Cumberland sausages, have been found in sanctuaries across Macedonia, pressed close to the earth where they could act as messengers to the chthonic deities. Pella's association with snakes continued into Roman times; the satirist Lucian records that during his day they had become something of a tourist curiosity. The city, despite becoming a small and insignificant place, was home to a number of large specimens that were quite tame; they were kept by the local women, and were even said to have slept with children.[70] Lucian believed that it was the predominance of snakes in the region that led to such customs, and that the practice influenced one of Alexander's conception myths, that Olympias had lain with a snake – a god in disguise – and that Alexander was the product.

These stories portray Olympias as mysterious and exotic, a religious fanatic, addicted to weird rites, a lover of snakes. But considering the importance of Dionysian worship in Macedonia, coupled with the likelihood that royal women were heavily involved in its practice, perhaps occupying leading roles, they settle into a less extraordinary context. With a little extra information, even the snake stories do not seem so strange. Olympias' willingness to establish herself in a new society through a religious role must also be considered against the background of the royal household, for she was not Philip's only wife, but rather one of many.

The kings of Macedon could be polygamous and Philip took the practice to new heights during his reign. A fragment from Satyrus' lost biography of the king, written in the third century BC, lists seven wives.[71] For Philip, marriage was a useful means to form and preserve alliances, the high number of brides reflected his expanding influence in both the Balkans and Greece. By the time he met Olympias he already had three, possibly four wives. According to Satyrus, they included the Illyrian, Audata, probably from the family of King Bardylis; Phila, of the ruling house of Elimeia, in Upper Macedonia; and the Thessalians, Nikesipolis of Pherai and Philinna of Larissa, although Philip's marriage to the former is sometimes placed later in the list by modern historians. An Illyrian, an Upper Macedonian, two Thessalians and a Molossian: Philip had an impressive array of trophy wives.[72]

Unlike their contemporaries in many Greek city-states, such as Athens, where women's lives were strictly circumscribed, elite females from the north were afforded a greater degree of liberty. Illyrian queens fought in battle. Thessalians could control vast fortunes and were associated with myths of the first rulers. Molossian royal women acted as regents for their husbands and children.[73] Those from Macedonia have been compared to Homeric queens who were influential in both private and public spheres, perhaps helping to manage the palace during their husbands' absence. On occasion, they may have joined in court banquets, and as Philip's reign progressed, they appeared more often in grand processions and state ceremonies; bedecked in dazzling jewellery and colourful robes, they were the embodiment of regal finery and propagators of the royal line. Much of their lives were unknown and mysterious to ancient writers, therefore it is only at certain times, usually at moments of crisis, that they emerge from the shadows and into the historical record.[74]

The first Macedonian woman to do so was Eurydike, Philip's mother, who was from Lynkestis, a canton in Upper Macedonia.[75] The sources present two differing portraits – the dutiful mother who protected and ensured her children's succession during turbulent times or the adulterous harpy who plotted against her husband and later helped murder her sons.[76] Scholars generally favour the former opinion;[77] the hostile propaganda was likely put out by her court rivals during the contested reigns of her sons. Gygaia, another wife of Amyntas III, is a possible source. She had three sons who emerged as a threat during Philip's early reign; the eldest was murdered while the others fled to Olynthos. Excavations at Vergina (ancient Aigai) have revealed a temple to Eukleia, the goddess of good repute, with statue dedications from Eurydike. Dated to the mid fourth century BC, they have been interpreted as political acts to help overturn her black reputation.[78] She was the prototype for later Macedonian and Hellenistic queens and probably lived well into Philip's reign, the matriarch who all newcomers had to deal with, a distant version of the domineering mother-in-law that looms so large in modern Greek society.

The mix of high-status women in the royal household made it a competitive place. There is no evidence to suggest an official 'chief wife'; the position relied principally on children, the significance of the regional powers the woman represented and Philip's interests, which varied over time. Name changes could signal favouritism or might be used as a means to ingratiate themselves with the king. The Illyrian Audata may have taken the name Eurydike to honour her new mother-in-law on marrying Philip. Olympias, who had also been called Myrtale as well as Polyxena, probably adopted her new name to celebrate Philip's Olympic victory, which coincided with her own domestic triumph, the birth of a boy.[79]

Olympias' main rival for influence in her early years at court was most likely Philinna, a Thessalian noblewoman from Larissa. She had also borne Philip a son, Arrhidaios, perhaps a little before Alexander, but it soon became clear that there was something wrong with him. The ancient sources are vague; 'he was afflicted by an incurable mental illness,' says one historian.[80] Plutarch reports that, as a boy, he had displayed a noble disposition and was seen as gifted until the illness struck; he attributes this development not to nature but witchcraft, 'afterwards Olympias gave him drugs which injured his body and ruined his mind,' he writes.[81]

Belief in the power of magic was widespread in the ancient world. It could be used for protection – children commonly wore amulets to help protect them against the dreaded Evil Eye and a host of malevolent spirits – but also for harm, as instanced by the accusation against Olympias. This rumour found some fasci-

nating context in 1986, when archaeologists discovered a curse
tablet buried with one individual in Pella's Classical cemetery.[82]
It contained a 'relationship spell', composed by a local woman
or someone else on her behalf, that was scored onto a small lead
sheet and placed in the dead man's hand. He was to act as
messenger to the underworld. The woman calls on dark forces
to help rid her of a rival for her partner's love. Driving this act
was fear of abandonment, that she would be set aside and grow
old alone – a terrifying prospect in the ancient world. The tablet
dates to the fourth century BC, to a time when relations in the
royal household were also subject to the conflicting desires of its
occupants, and provides the first evidence of the practice of magic
in Pella. The accusations of Olympias' witchcraft may well reflect
a genuine belief that she was in some way responsible for
Arrhidaios' affliction.

With Arrhidaios sidelined, Alexander became Philip's most
capable son, and his status rose accordingly. By association,
Olympias was able to establish herself at the top of the hierarchy.
Her relationship with Philip is difficult to reconstruct. They had
a second child together a year or two after Alexander, a girl
named Kleopatra, but no more children are recorded, which
suggests that the marriage ceased to be sexual. Renault's reconstruction of their volatile relationship is based on later events,
when Alexander had reached manhood and the introduction of

Illustration of the Pella curse tablet

another wife undermined his and Olympias' position. There is scant justification, however, other than artistic licence, to down-date this conflict to Alexander's childhood. On the contrary, it was essential for Olympias to retain a cordial relationship with Philip in order to secure her own position and Alexander's future. The reality was probably much more benign than that represented in fiction, but it was also one of continual uncertainty. With Philip's ever-expanding state programme, and the risks he took in battle, there was always the potential that things could change in an instant, as so nearly happened in 354 BC, when he took an arrow to the eye during the siege of Methone, another Athenian-controlled port on the Thermaic Gulf.[83] Philip's nephew, Amyntas, was older than Alexander and for many years he may have been regarded as the most likely successor. Then there were the half-brothers of Philip, who had fled to Olynthos and remained a threat. Messages arriving in the dead of night, the silent footsteps of assassins down the palace corridors, the turmoil that came with any king's death, were very real fears. Succession was not formal-ised; it depended on who had the strength and support to grab the opportunity, and was often highly contested. Alexander had to grow up fast.

In this atmosphere Olympias was, understandably, fiercely protective of her children and loyal to her kin. Like Eurydike, she was the subject of character assassination by her later rivals. After Alexander's death, she came into conflict with some of his succes-sors and many slurs and lurid stories circulated. The ancient sources, therefore, present a largely negative portrait of Olympias; Plutarch calls her jealous and vindictive.[84] Antipatros, who administered Macedonia in Alexander's absence, says that she was headstrong, with a sharp temper and interfering ways, in his opinion most unfitting characteristics for the mother of Alexander.[85] She certainly had a ruthless streak, especially when dealing with enemies; murder was part of her repertoire. But in this respect she was no different from the menfolk, although as a woman she was subject to a fair amount of gender stereotyping; ancient writers commonly portrayed powerful women as ruled by desire, fickle and utterly untrustworthy. Her devotion to her children often made her a controlling mother, sometimes overbearing. Alexander apparently berated her constant meddling in his affairs, stating that she charged a high rent for nine months lodging in the womb.[86] Nevertheless, the two shared deep bonds of affection. From Alexander's perspective, Olympias was one of the few people he could trust completely – a single tear shed by his mother had the power to wipe out all of Antipatros' complaining letters.[87] His courteous relationships with foreign women during his reign, for which he was much praised in antiquity, have their likely origin with his mother, and the respect he had for the role she played in protecting not only his interests but his life.

And so, Alexander spent his earliest years surrounded by women – his mother and her handmaidens, nurse, sister and grandmother – learning their stories, revelling in their affections. Philip's various wives probably maintained their own separate residences in and around the palace, but they may have had some limited contact, providing Alexander the chance to form relationships with the other royal children: his half-sister Kynnane, daughter of Audata-Eurydike, Arrhidaios, and his older cousin Amyntas; there were animosities among the wives but perhaps friendships and alliances as well. Philip was an absent father and husband, while despite their varying ethnicities and ambitions, the wives shared common ground; they were all strangers struggling to make their own way in a new world. Like many a competitive mother, Olympias pushed Alexander to be the best he could be, always aware that, should the situation change, he must be ready to take the initiative. His formal education began when he was around seven years old. He had survived the dangers of infancy, and it was now time to leave the world of women and embrace that of men. His Molossian heritage would continue to influence his development, but it was in a Macedonian society that he would have to prove himself.

2.

MEET THE MACEDONIANS

The Vale of Tempe is the most famous and picturesque of the gateways into Macedonia. For those past generations of Greeks who ventured north, away from their hearths and homes, it was a transition point; the eight-kilometre-long gorge, threading its way between mountains and located on Macedon's south-eastern frontier, was a fault line between one land and the next. It is the views of Greeks, primarily those of Athenians – the opinions of outsiders – that prevail in the history books, but they are crucial in helping us understand how contemporaries viewed the Macedonians, and in turn can tell us something about Alexander's identity, because he was part of a distinctive culture, one that was inextricably linked to the geography of his homeland. To undertake the trek through the pass and emerge on the other side is to enter the remnants of his world, and to reimagine the impact it had on ancient eyes.

After journeying across the flats of the Thessalian plain the ground begins to crumple and fold, a seemingly impenetrable barrier of rock rising in front of the traveller. The snaking river Peneios is the best guide; like Ariadne's twine, it leads the way safely through the mountain maze. The agricultural plots strung along either side of the river slowly begin to decrease in size.

Dwindling crop fields turn to orchards, the lines of fruit trees eventually tapering off as the last of the cultivated soil is swallowed up by encroaching bluffs. Many trees, however, still remain. They have found space to grow between river, main road and mountaintop. This thin slice of lush vegetation imbues Tempe with an organic beauty that has changed little over the millennia. It was much celebrated in antiquity, immortalised in poetry and prose; the Roman emperor Hadrian even recreated the rural idyll within his sprawling villa complex at Tivoli in central Italy, a perfect getaway from the day-to-day pressures of running an empire. The area is intimate, cool, and deliciously green. In the morning, mist clings ruggedly to the sides of the gorge like the breath of Zeus, sunsets turning the autumnal trees into a rich patchwork of russets and faded greens. Tempe is a natural wonder of Greece.

One tradition credits Poseidon with creating the pass, prising apart the mountains with an earthquake and allowing the river access to the long-awaited Aegean.[1] It subsequently became sacred to Apollo, who came here to purify himself after slaying the snake-monster Python at Delphi, while Ovid placed the famous myth of Apollo and Daphne in Tempe's vicinity.[2] According to his tale, found in the *Metamorphoses*, the maiden was being hunted down by the infatuated archer-god when, fearing for her virtue, she offered up a prayer to her river-god father, Peneios, imploring salvation. Suddenly her body became numb, bark wrapped her flesh, leaves sprouted from fingertips, toes became roots; she had been transformed into a laurel tree. Apollo caressed the newly formed trunk and could feel the flutter of her heart beneath the bark. 'Since you cannot be mine in wedlock,' he said, 'you must at least be Apollo's tree. It is you who will always be twined in my hair, on my tuneful lyre and my quiver of arrows.'[3] There are still a few specimens to be found along the riverbanks, bright and fragrant, hiding among the stately plane trees that dip their boughs into the Peneios, its ruddy waters gliding like oil towards the sea.

The landscape that lies ahead is different from that elsewhere in Greece.[4] The olive tree – that bastion of Mediterranean culture – begins to disappear, only surviving in a few isolated pockets along the coast. Dense forests, rivers that never fail, mountains and plains now proliferate. It is a self-sufficient land, rich in natural resources, with a climate that is neither entirely Mediterranean nor Balkan but a mixture of the two. On exiting Tempe, the many-peaked Olympos massif dominates the views ahead. A thin strip of land stretches out beneath its shadow, extending north towards the open plains of Pieria and the fertile crescent of Emathia; to the west, hidden behind a screen of mountains, are the highlands of Upper Macedonia, with their fish-filled lakes and expansive plateaus, still frequented by wolf and bear. This is the land that Alexander once called home. This is Macedonia.

To the ancient visitor from the south, it was a strange and exotic place, beset on many sides by hostile peoples – Illyrians, Paionians and Thracians – a middle-land that sat at the nexus of routeways. For much of its history it was an unstable place to live, a wild west of antiquity. The landscape and social conditions had created a people that were, as one contemporary remarked, 'rough and rustic', they called a trough a trough.[5] Many were carpenters and lumberjacks; the region's endless supply of timber had helped build the Athenian navy, and the smell of bubbling pitch and freshly felled pines permeated every corner of the land. Others were shepherds or stockbreeders, while the region's mineral wealth had created a highly specialised group of artisans and smiths that plied their trades in the towns and cities. The Macedonians worshipped the same gods as their southern neighbours. Greek names were common and they shared many of the same Hellenic customs, but there were also differences. The commoners spoke Macedonian, a dialect of Greek with linguistic affinities to Thessaly and north-western

Greece, and was difficult for the untrained ear to comprehend. Their distinctive accent pronounced 'ph' as 'b' – 'Philip' sounded like 'Bilip'.[6] The *kausia* – similar to an oversized beret – was the national headgear, a covering in snowstorms and a helmet in war. Fighting and feasting, hunting and horsemanship were the cornerstones of their culture. It was almost impossible to find a decent slave.[7] Unlike the majority of Greek peoples and city-states, Macedonia had retained its monarchy, the kings continually surrounded by scores of nobles and intimates called Companions (*hetairoi*), an institution straight out of the world of Homer. Their love of wine was legendary, as was their competitiveness. It was a hyper-masculine society where bathing in hot water was banned and reclining on a banqueting couch only permitted after dispatching a boar without the use of a net; killing a man in battle had once been an ancient rite of passage, those who had not achieved the feat being required to wear a halter around their waists.[8] The etymology of the word Macedonian perhaps sums it up best. It can be translated as 'Highlander'.[9] These people were a tough breed.

The Archaic poet Hesiod, in a fragment of his lost *Catalogue of Women*, incorporated the Macedonians within the Greek family tree. He reports that Pieria and Olympos was once the realm of the god Makedon – he who delights in horses – a son of Zeus and Thyia, daughter of Deukalion whose brother Hellen was the founder of the Hellenic race. A later genealogy makes the link more explicit, claiming that Makedon was actually the son of Aiolos, a son of Hellen, and progenitor of the Aiolian tribe of Greeks.[10] But the shifting parameters of Greekness, which varied over time, along with the elastic boundaries of Greece (*Hellas*), coupled with customs and institutions that were often regarded as primitive, as well as a certain amount of mixing with non-Greek peoples, made the Macedonians appear to many outsiders more barbarian than Greek on the cultural scale, and this was exploited for political purposes.[11] The royal family, however, claimed a separate ancestry. They traced their lineage back to that most famous of Greek heroes, Herakles, and ultimately to Zeus.

Herodotus, writing in the fifth century BC, provides the earliest account of the Macedonians' myth, which he had heard first-hand during a stay at the Macedonian court.[12] He reports that three brothers, descendants of Herakles through Temenos (an Argive king), were expelled from their native city of Argos in the Peloponnese. They travelled north, taking refuge in Illyria before venturing into Upper Macedonia where they found work for the local king in a place called Lebaia (Cauldron town). Gauanes and Aeropos, the two elder brothers, took care of the horses and oxen while the youngest, Perdikkas, tended to the smaller stock – sheep and goats. The king's wife was responsible for feeding the workers, but every time she baked a loaf for little Perdikkas it swelled to twice its normal size, a powerful omen. When this had happened several times in a row she decided to consult her husband. It was interpreted as a clear warning from the gods. The three brothers were duly summoned to the royal residence and given their marching orders. But they refused to leave without the wages owed to them. The king was enraged and pointed to a patch of sunlight that was streaming through an opening in the roof, a feature designed to let out smoke from the central hearth. 'There are the wages you deserve!' he cried. Gauanes and Aeropos were stunned – they had poked the bear. Perdikkas, however, was not fazed. Taking out his iron knife he casually scratched a line around the pool of sunlight and began scooping the rays into the folds of his tunic, a symbolic acceptance of divinely sanctioned rule, saying, 'O king, we accept what you offer us.' The three then promptly took their leave.

Soon afterwards, one of the king's attendants pointed out the strangeness of this act and the possible dangerous portents that it foretold. Armed riders were sent to track down and kill the brothers, but they were too late. The fugitives had crossed a river that miraculously rose in spate after them. The horsemen had to give up the chase and the brothers were saved. They continued their journey down into the lowlands and finally settled in a place called the 'Gardens of Midas', on the slopes of Mount Bermion (or Vermion). Herodotus hastily brings his account to a close by stating that they went on to conquer the surrounding territory, Perdikkas becoming the first king, fulfilling his destiny, and founding the ruling family of Macedon. Herodotus called them Temenids, after Perdikkas' descent from Temenos, but they are referred to as Argeads by other sources, a title often preferred by modern scholars and historians.[13] It may derive from Perdikkas' son, Argaios, the name evoking links to the Argive Greeks of the past, or Argeas, son of the god Makedon.

But foundation stories could change over time and were often manipulated to reflect the desires of the people in charge. By Alexander's day the story had shifted to incorporate another founder, Karanos. He also claimed descent from Herakles and Temenos and was slotted into the list of kings before Perdikkas.[14] Following the Delphic Oracle's advice, he reportedly came north with a band of Greeks to colonise a new land. One version of the tale suggests that he settled in Orestis (a region in Upper Macedonia), while another has him venturing into the lowlands where he searched for a suitable capital. The Oracle had told him to trust in the movements of the local goats – animal guides were a recurring theme in foundation stories – and, running from a downpour, he followed one flock as they took shelter in a settlement called Edessa. Karanos took over the site and renamed it Aigai (Goat places).[15] Another tradition, however, credits Perdikkas with the foundation, following his own Delphic instruction.[16] Elements from both founder stories appear to have cross-pollinated in their retelling. They may contain some kernel of truth, perhaps the distant memories of a migration of one band of Macedonians from the highlands to the lowlands, where they sought to establish a territory under a new ruling clan.[17] Despite the confusion among the founding stories the key point is that the royal family could claim an exalted ancestry that went back to Argive Greece, Herakles and Zeus. The claim was a probable creation by the early kings to legitimise their rule, and regardless of whether it was based on any historical reality or not, it was the story they chose to promulgate and which they desired others to believe.

Aigai became the 'hearth' of the Macedonian kingdom, the symbolic capital of myth, history and identity, where all future kings were to be buried. The plural nature of its name – Goat *places* – denotes a collection of loose-knit settlements that congregated around a central hub, where the main public and religious buildings were located. This urbanised centre, dating to the Classical and Hellenistic eras, has been rediscovered by archaeologists next to the modern village of Vergina, on a foothill of Mount Pieria, the acropolis occupying the upper reaches, public buildings laid out on the slopes and terraces below. A sprawling prehistoric necropolis – spread over some 200 hectares – surrounds the northern and eastern parts of the site, dimpled with the excavated remains of hundreds of Iron Age tumuli or burial mounds, dating from 1000 to 700.[18] Archaeologists have discovered that the graves of numerous family members were enclosed under the same mound – their size indicative of status – with clusters or rows of mounds thought to represent different kin-groups or clans. In both life and death these people formed close-knit units. The soil conditions had eaten away the bones and only sets of teeth remained, but their surrounding grave goods survived. Men were buried with iron weapons – knives and swords – emphasising their role as warriors and hunters, and women with jewellery – headdresses, brooches, bracelets, rings and studded leather belts. The remains of sceptres, topped with double axes cut from bronze sheet, accompanied a few high-status females who may have been priestesses – the forerunners of the powerful women of the fourth century BC, such as Eurydike and Olympias. The varying size of the burial mounds and range of grave goods attest to a stable and prosperous society, one that was well-structured with a uniformity of tradition and simple, austere tastes.

The arrival or emergence of the Argeads as the leading clan is usually dated to the mid seventh century BC, although it could have occurred earlier, and was followed by expansion into the surrounding lands. Thucydides picks up the story where Herodotus left off, saying that they began by first defeating and driving out the Thracian Pierians from Pieria (the rich land), and the Bottiaians from Bottiaia (or Bottia), the large fertile plain between the Haliakmon and Axios rivers also known as Emathia (the sandy place). Further conquests followed: the Eordians were expelled from Eordaia, an area of the highlands positioned between Upper and Lower Macedonia, and the Almopians from Almopia, to the north of Bottiaia/Emathia.[19] This expansion, which took place sometime in the sixth century BC, brought new opportunities and riches. The exceptional gold-clad burials from the cemeteries of Archontikon and Sindos, located to the east of Aigai and close to the Thermaic Gulf, are some of the most exciting recent discoveries in northern Greece, and probably belonged to the regional powers that were either forced to relocate or were incorporated into the growing Macedonian kingdom.[20]

Aigai was greatly enriched with the spoils of war, with new and opulent grave goods characterising elite burials from the end of the Archaic period onwards, while those belonging to settlements around the Thermaic Gulf declined in wealth. Macedonian material culture, before and after this time, is said to exhibit a duality in character, both conservative and open to external influences. The Macedonians were staunchly protective of the old ways but also willing to incorporate new fashions into their society as their power expanded, a trait that allowed them to keep hold of their identity while changing with the times.[21]

The stories of Macedon's many former kings must have been well known to Alexander from childhood, their exploits, the legends of their rise and fall, mixing with other myths and folktales in the oral tradition. How, for example, the infant Aeropos had been placed in his cradle behind the Macedonian battle line, the presence of the king making the men fight all the more bravely to defeat an Illyrian invasion. Or the illustrious deeds of his former namesake, Alexander I, who, according to a rather fanciful tradition, had murdered the Persian envoys who came to receive the requisite gifts of earth and water, the symbols of subjugation, and who, despite fighting for the Great King during the Persian Wars of the fifth century BC, had secretly informed the Greeks about their battle plans, later receiving the nickname Alexander the Philhellene – Alexander friend of the Greeks.[22] Then there were stories of the troubled years of Alexander's son, Perdikkas II, who ruled during the Peloponnesian War, the career of the great builder-king, Archelaos, whose palace was still inhabited by the royal family, the long reign of his grandfather, Amyntas III, and the shorter reigns of his uncles, Alexander II and Perdikkas III. The Argead line, it must have seemed, had survived since time immemorial, its longevity and revered origins imbuing the Macedonians with a native reverence for their kings.[23] Right up to Alexander's time, only those that possessed this blue blood could accede to the throne, but colossal pressure also came with the birthright. The king was not just a figurehead. He was expected to lead in battle and during royal hunts, to oversee religious festivals, arbitrate and dispense justice, to control foreign policy and protect those under his rule. There was no written constitution of kingship, but the king was expected to adhere to a set of customary laws or rules (*nomoi*): an ancestral code that underpinned his relationship with the rest of the Macedonians. Councils and Assemblies of his country-men provided the crucial checks and balances on royal power, one of their most important ancestral rites being to acclaim their chosen king. Any breakdown in these relationships, or a failure in kingly duties, could lead to loss of respect, the harbinger of plots and palace coups – a constant threat in a world where others with the same bloodline lingered in the shadows. Young Alexander was expected to be the best proponent of his people – a Macedonian *par excellence* – but also worthy of his royal ancestors. He may have been blessed with an immensely privileged back-ground but he would be expected to deliver if called upon. Luckily, he was fortunate enough to have been born into a time of oppor-tunity. The glorious exploits of Philip, which must have accounted for more than a few bedtime stories, brought new riches to the royal court and afforded Alexander the best education money could buy.

LITTLE ACHILLES

Plutarch states that many people were responsible for overseeing Alexander's upbringing but that one man was in ultimate control and stood above the rest: Leonidas.[24] He was a kinsman of Olympias, an austere Molossian, described by Plutarch as a man of dignity and stern temperament. Philip's wives appear to have been given a considerable say in how their children were to be educated. Kynnane, daughter of the Illyrian Audata-Eurydike, was trained in warfare by her mother – the custom of their homeland – and Olympias' influence is easy to discern behind the appointment of Leonidas.[25] Alexander, despite growing up in Macedonia, would also be raised according to Molossian traditions. It was hoped that some of Leonidas' qualities would be passed on to his ward; emulation and imitation were at the heart of ancient education and Alexander was said to have mimicked his master's manners and even his style of walking.[26] In the Greek world, the *paidagogos* – a conductor of children – was the child's attendant throughout his education, taking him to and from school and overseeing his moral development. The role was often given to a servant of the family. Leonidas was of a higher station but, apparently, he did not shun the title, although he was more commonly called Alexander's foster-father and preceptor, a trustworthy individual who could also protect the boy if the need arose.

Plutarch describes the young Alexander as ambitious and serious, often exhibiting behaviour that was well in advance of his years but also impetuous and violent in other matters, perhaps a retrojection of his later character but one that is not without some likelihood, for there were probably a few temper tantrums before discipline was firmly established. Those involved in his education, and with his early life in general, eventually realised that it was better to persuade rather than to order.

Alexander's education began with a change of surroundings. He was moved out of Olympias' apartments and went to live with Leonidas, presumably elsewhere in the palace or the wider city of Pella. Other boys – his future Companions – were selected to be raised at his side, as was the Macedonian custom.[27] The selection of his inner circle of friends was a royal prerogative, a reward to those children of prominent families. The ancient sources differentiate Alexander's boyhood friends from other Companions by the description *syntrophoi* – 'those reared with' – commonly called 'foster-brothers' by modern historians. They were roughly coeval with Alexander and are thought to have included Leonnatos,

Marsyas, Proteas – Lanike's son – and Hephaistion, who was Alexander's closest friend throughout his life.[28] On reaching the age of education, around the age of seven, they were probably given a new uniform to wear – miniature versions of the traditional clothes of Macedonian men with slight variations, the ensemble consisting of a child-sized *kausia* hat, a short *chlamys* military cloak, a *chiton* or tunic and hard-wearing *krepides* boots, their undergarments and finer clothes weaved by mothers and sisters.[29] Figurines of some Pella boys have been found in the city's western cemetery and are a common find throughout the Hellenistic world. There is one particularly endearing example in the British Museum, with a cheeky grin, curly hair and cloak pulled tight to keep out the cold. One can easily imagine it to be a little Alexander.

Terracotta figurine of a
boy in Macedonian dress,
the British Museum

Leonidas' strict exercise regime was said to have been Spartanesque. He apparently rifled through Alexander's chests of personal possessions, removing any treats that Olympias had sought to smuggle to her son. Alexander later remarked that under Leonidas' charge his breakfast consisted of a night's march, his supper a light breakfast.[30] Leonidas taught Alexander restraint and the necessity of physical endurance, traits that are evident from his later life, but he was less successful in curtailing Alexander's excessive offerings to the gods. On one occasion he remarked, 'Alexander, only when you have conquered the spice lands can you afford to be so lavish with your incense. Until then use sparingly what you have.' When Alexander later achieved this feat he sent sixteen tons of incense back to his old tutor, along with the following message: 'I have sent you myrrh and frankincense in abundance so that you can stop dealing parsimoniously with the gods.'[31] It was a reply that had been a long time in the making, but it was probably Leonidas who had the last laugh: such a quantity of this exotic commodity was worth a fortune.

Leonidas' forced marches were part of a wider programme of physical education that included gymnastics and athletics, activities that took place in and around the wrestling school (*palaistra*) under the instruction of specialised trainers (*paidotribes*). While keeping the children fit and aiding their development it also taught them important life lessons – discipline, competitiveness, and the benefits of hard work – the first steps towards acquiring personal excellence or valour (*arete*), at its core an aristocratic Greek ideal. Alexander also learned to ride and may have acquired some early training in arms, perhaps including the sling, bow and arrow and javelin.[32] But these physical activities only formed one half of his education. As was the tradition in Greek cities such as Athens, he was tutored in a number of liberal skills: reading, writing, some basic arithmetic and music.[33] Philiskos from Aigina is mentioned as his grammarian, who taught him the letters and introduced him to literature. He reportedly advised his student, 'Take care of your reputation; don't become a plague (or a great disaster), bring (peace and) health.'[34] A music teacher, perhaps called Leukippos, was given the task of teaching Alexander to play the kithara, a stringed instrument similar to the lyre, and taught him lyric poetry to accompany it. During one of their lessons he told Alexander to strike a string in accordance with the melody. 'What difference will it make if I touch that one?' Alexander asked, pointing at another. The teacher replied that 'it made no difference to a man destined to be king; it was otherwise for anyone who would prac-tise the art of the kithara.'[35] In addition to these staples of Greek education, Alexander also learnt geometry from Menaichmos, while Anaximenes of Lampsakos gave him lessons in public speaking.[36] It was an educational programme designed to create a rounded individual, both cultured and yet physically tough, who could impress in aristocratic circles and among the common soldiery, a reflection of the qualities and experiences that Philip himself had found so useful in his own rise to power.

There was one figure who loomed larger than any other in a student's world: Homer, known as the educator of Greece. Learning to read and write went hand-in-hand with the introduction to his epics. It is impossible to overstate the importance of Homer to the ancient Greeks. Knowledge of his works was the cultural pass-port of antiquity; if you knew them, you were part of a tradition, part of a much larger world. They encroached upon the youngster's mind from an early age, brought to life through childhood stories and a visual culture steeped in myth and legend. After learning the alphabet, the sounds of the syllables and the spelling of words, came the text.[37] Copying and reciting passages of Homer, with their antiquated vocabulary, syntax and grammar, was a baptism of fire, the modern equivalent of bypassing Beatrix Potter and going straight to Shakespeare. It's doubtful that in the early years of tuition the student actually realised what he was writing down, but such was the hold of these epics on ancient education that they were never replaced and the student, through endless memorisation and repetition, came to know them intimately. Yet learning the texts only formed a part of the Homeric picture, because the tales were also commonly disseminated through a vibrant oral tradition which consisted primarily of recitals by rhapsodes – professional Homeric bards – stitchers of song. They performed at any occasion that provided an audience. Possessed by the Muse, they would stand before the crowd and channel Homer, their actions and changes in voice vividly evoking the characters and events that they described, making the audience both laugh and cry with the power of their storytelling. At some point, young Alexander must have come into contact with Homer's poetry via the honeyed voices of those rhapsodes present at court.[38] Wide-eyed, sitting cross-legged on the floor, he and his friends were taken on an imaginary journey into the distant past. The stories would profoundly shape their respective personalities. Through these experiences they would come to know and love a voice that spoke to them from the depths of time.

To hear the *Iliad* or *Odyssey* recounted in ancient Greek – be it via an eccentric professor, a modern performer or YouTube – is a strange, otherworldly experience. It's almost akin to a religious chant. The ancient verses are constructed from hexameters – lines containing six metrical units or measures known as 'feet'. These 'feet' could either be a dactyl (a long and two short syllables) or a spondee (two long syllables), the last unit always being a spondee. The combination of the two types of feet allowed flexibility while also obeying set forms and rhythms. It was the pacing of the recital that gave the epics a hypnotic power, the words rising and falling with each breath of the performer as the story unfolded. The *Iliad* was more popular than the *Odyssey* and today, no matter the translation or language, the opening lines still shimmer with ancient intensity:

> *Rage – Goddess, sing the rage of Peleus' son Achilles,*
> *murderous, doomed, that cost the Achaeans countless losses,*
> *hurling down to the House of Death so many sturdy souls,*
> *great fighters' souls, but made their bodies carrion,*
> *feasts for the dogs and birds,*
> *and the will of Zeus was moving towards its end.*
> *Begin, Muse, when the two first broke and clashed,*
> *Agamemnon lord of men and brilliant Achilles.*[39]

With these words, the listener is drawn into the world of heroes, into the Late Bronze Age and the flowering of the Mycenaean civilisation in Greece (approx. 1600–1100 BC). The *Iliad* focuses on one pivotal episode that occurred at the end of the ten-year Pan-Hellenic campaign against the Trojans – a war that had been sparked by the affair of the beautiful Helen of Sparta and Paris, a prince of Troy. It is the conduct of Agamemnon, overlord of the campaign, which has nearly cost the Achaian Greeks dear. His requisition of Achilles' Trojan captive, Briseis, has roused the great warrior's anger, causing him to take to his tent instead of the battlefield. It is only the death of Patroklos, Achilles' closest companion, that persuades him to re-enter the fight, and when he does the noble Hektor, prince and protector of Troy, is hunted down and mercilessly dispatched. With him the last hopes of the Trojans dissipate into the blood-drenched plains of the Troad. The epic builds to this intense moment, the final showdown between heroes. The action is fast paced and visceral. Recurring epithets such as the 'swift-footed' Achilles, Hektor 'breaker of horses', 'the wine dark sea' and the citadel of 'windy Troy' become entrenched in the listener's mind, a painting of a thousand strokes taking shape before the audience's eyes. Meanwhile similes of great elegance serve to make incredible moments relatable to the average audience: white dust rises from the battlefield cloaking the soldiers like chaff during winnowing, the Achaians attack the enemy like a pack of wolves, picking off the lambs from a startled flock. But perhaps the most striking aspect of the epic is the brutality of the fighting. For every magnificent hero scything through the enemy's ranks are numerous victims condemned to a grim eternity in the underworld. Blood spurts from wounds, bronze crunches into bone; as death clouds their eyes, armour is mercilessly stripped from their bodies, the victors mocking the fate of the fallen. It is an intoxicating mixture of poetics and the harrowing reality of ancient warfare. Some of those among the rhapsode's audience must have shuddered at the thought of suffering a similar fate in battles to come. Others would have rejoiced at the opportunity for everlasting glory, Alexander no doubt among them.

With sober twenty-first-century eyes, it's perhaps too easy to dismiss these tales as mere fantasy, the words conjured from a brilliant poetic mind, set down on papyrus in the eighth century BC for the world to idolise. But for the ancients the events described were real, as were the heroes and powers of the immortals. This belief made the works of Homer a crucial source of inspiration, especially for children and youths. It was an ancient template that supplied moral guidance as well as a code of honour. For the Macedonians, the Homeric epics contained a particular resonance; values such as bravery, respect, loyalty and good kingship were as relevant in his world as they were in the Late Bronze Age. Alexander, in particular, had a special relationship with Homer's works. They were not only good stories but family history.

Neoptolemos, Achilles' son (also known as Pyrrhos), had settled in Epeiros after the Trojan War and founded the line of Molossian kings. Alexander therefore, through Olympias, could claim Achilles as his direct ancestor. She most likely introduced him to the epics while he was still a child in the women's quarters, and they remained ever-present throughout his education. As an adult, he could recite much of the poems by heart, and during his early campaigns he slept with a personal copy of the *Iliad* under his pillow . . . along with a dagger.[40] He is said to have regarded the work as a guide-book to the military art; 'both a mighty king and strong spearman too' – a description of Agamemnon – was the line he is claimed to have admired most, but it was Achilles that he honoured above all others.[41] Achilles was quicker, stronger, more skilful than the other heroes. He spoke eloquently, could play the lyre, and his prowess in battle, as well as his close relationship with the immortals, commanded instant respect. Peleus' instruction to his son 'to always be the bravest and preeminent above all' is the famous line that encapsulates Achilles' *raison d'être*, words that Alexander would live by as a means to obtain distinction in the competitive world of the Macedonian court.[42] But, as with all the most intriguing figures of veneration, there was a more complex side to Achilles. He could be sullen, stubborn and ruthless, while his rift with Agamemnon, a dichotomy between duty and pride, love and destiny, nearly spelt ruin for the Achaians. These negative aspects of his character, however, also served to make him more accessible, in a way more human. Alexander too had his faults. Although he would also be noted for his desire to walk in the footsteps of Dionysos, to emulate Perseus and imitate Herakles – that progenitor of the Argead line that always formed a central part of the royal identity – it was Achilles who arguably remained the strongest influence in Alexander's early life; he was the embodiment of the heroic ideal, a natural figure of emulation and rivalry, as he must have been for many other boys.[43] His contemporaries understood, and even indulged, the comparison. It was especially cultivated by another of Alexander's teachers: the Akarnanian, Lysimachos, according to Plutarch a man of no general refinement, but because he called himself 'Phoenix' (tutor of Achilles), Alexander 'Achilles', and Philip 'Peleus', he was highly regarded and held second place after Leonidas, his role being closer to that of the traditional *paidagogos*.[44] He later accompanied Alexander to Asia and shared in adventures that would not have been out of place in Homer's epics.[45] But the winning of praise and honour for an achievement (*kudos*) or glory/renown (*kleos*) were redundant ambitions without the means to implement them. Victories required successful armies and it was his father who developed the apparatus that would allow Alexander the opportunity to secure immortal fame. In doing so Philip also created a new Macedonia.

PHILIP'S REVOLUTION

Western Macedonia still feels remote despite its modern transport links. Spring comes late here, winter arrives too early, the plummeting temperatures occasionally bringing 'the cold that kills the birds'. The population is primarily involved in agricultural activities, growing beans – a key ingredient in mountain stews and soups – peppers, crocus, grain and vines, whose sour black grapes produce a heady and distinctive wine. Shepherds and their flocks still roam the pastures, the mountainous slopes in many places picked clean by hundreds of grazing animals, a pack of ferocious guard dogs ensuring their protection against any predatory wildlife. Following the modern Via Egnatia west, one's arrival on the upland plateaus is marked by the power stations at Ptolemaida which, fed by the surrounding lignite quarries, provide electricity for much of northern Greece. The region was also an ancient powerhouse, generating fine horses and even finer fighters including such men as Perdikkas and Krateros from Orestis, Ptolemy of Eordaia and Polyperchon of Tymphaia, commanders who played a crucial role in Alexander's later army. Philip's harnessing of these resources drove his success on the battlefield.

The topography of Western Macedonia, set around the watershed of the Haliakmon river and subdivided by mountain chains, shaped the territory of Upper Macedonia's ancient cantons – Eordaia, which was assimilated into the Argead kingdom early on in its history, Elimeia, Lynkestis, Orestis and Tymphaia; areas that today are roughly equivalent to the regional units of Kozani, Florina, Kastoria and Grevena. The windswept flanks of Pindos – the spine of Greece – form a natural barrier to the west, with Epeiros on the other side, while to the north the cantons once spread into parts of Albania and the Republic of North Macedonia.[46] The Roman historian Livy believed the tougher climatic conditions were reflected in the character of its residents. 'This part of the world is as a whole cold, difficult to cultivate, and harsh; it has inhabitants of temperament like their land,' he writes; they were made all the fiercer by their barbarian neighbours, whose regular incursions schooled them in warfare.[47] As with the coming of spring, archaeological exploration here has lagged behind the coastal lowlands. In 1911–12, Alan Wace and Arthur Woodward described it as an archaeological *terra incognita,* and called on fresh research to provide answers to long-held questions.[48] Their wish has since been answered and a growing number of excavations are providing new insights into highland life.[49] One site in particular has advanced understanding of the region more than any other: Aiani in ancient Elimeia.

In the nineteenth century, antiquarians had noted a number of ancient remains around Kozani, close to the Haliakmon river.[50] A few precious inscriptions – speaking stones – were recorded at Kalliani (modern Aiani), built into the walls of its churches, and

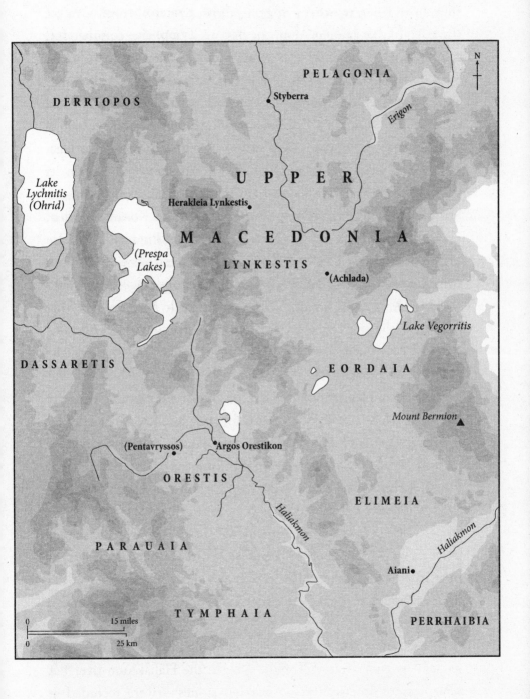

they, in addition to other evidence, allowed researchers to connect the village with ancient Aiani. In the 1960s, Mr Siambanopoulos, a local teacher, took up the investigation. With the help of the villagers and visiting archaeologists, he began collecting together stray artefacts, and among the tattered exercise books and well-worn desks of his primary school a rudimentary archaeological archive began to take shape. He had recognised, along with previous researchers, that the rocky hill of Megali Rachi was a 'hot spot' for finds and was likely to be an ancient acropolis, but the size and character of the surrounding city were still uncertain. Excavations, under the auspices of the 17th Ephorate of Prehistoric and Classical Antiquities, began on the hill in the summer of 1983, led by archaeologist Georgia Karamitrou-Mentessidi. It soon became clear that the area was covered with buildings, the site providing evidence for occupation from the Neolithic to the first century BC. The team have been digging on the site ever since.[51]

The hill is blessed with a number of natural terraces that the ancient architects skilfully exploited for their buildings. The remains of houses have been revealed around the lower levels, their modern names derived from the prevalence of certain features or finds found within them – the House with the Staircases, the House

View from the Aiani acropolis

with the Pithoi (storage jars), the House with the Loomweights. Each property was equipped with a suite of rooms set aside for different activities – workshops, courtyards, living quarters and storage areas – while their foundations were well constructed from rubble-mortar. Some provided evidence of decoration: painted plaster and tiles. Three sets of public buildings have been unearthed on the upper terraces and may have formed part of the agora or the royal complex. They date to the late Archaic and Classical periods (early fifth to the fourth century BC), making them among the earliest monumental public architecture found in Macedonia. Around a kilometre north of the site, archaeologists have located one of Aiani's main cemeteries. It is notable for a number of impressive masonry chamber tombs, sunk into the earth, which also date to the Archaic and Classical eras. Some had their own enclosures, funerary monuments and evidence of cults for the dead. Although robbed in antiquity, fragments of their rich grave goods and decoration have been recovered. These tombs probably belonged to Elimeia's royal family.[52]

Aiani was almost certainly the capital of Elimeia, its urbanised core, surrounded by smaller settlements and farmsteads. It was home to one of Philip's wives – Phila – as well as a formidable cavalry contingent. It possessed all the hallmarks of a thriving and cultivated society that expressed itself in Hellenic terms, with roots stretching back into the depths of prehistory. These discoveries have overturned old ideas that the area was cut off from developments taking place elsewhere in the Greek world.

Further archaeological work in Upper Macedonia has recently identified a number of other similarly rich cemeteries, one near Pentavryssos in the Kastoria regional unit and another at Achlada in Florina, which may be the royal centres of Orestis and Lynkestis – each region appears to have had its own Aiani. They were ruled by independent royal families, many of whom had their own mythical origin stories.[53] At various times, these dynasties were subjects and allies of the Argeads, retaining their native kings, but the ancient sources, before the time of Philip, suggest the relationship was fractious. The historian J.R. Ellis called it one of tension, mistrust and outright enmity.[54] They had suffered from Illyrian incursions and the area is characterised by small forts and citadels built high up in the mountains, to which the inhabitants could flee during times of trouble.[55] It is these unstable circumstances that made alliance with Philip all the more appealing. With his defeat of Bardylis early on in his reign, he had proved his mettle and was subsequently able to win over the cantons to his side. The unification of Upper and Lower Macedonia allowed Philip to incorporate new and powerful communities into his burgeoning state and army. It was the beginning of his revolution, the start of Macedon's rise to prominence.

The history of the Macedonian army prior to Philip is an obscure and inglorious one. There are only a few brief references in the ancient sources: some counter-offensive raids by the Companion cavalry against an overwhelming Thracian host, an ignominious flight before battle against the Lynkestians and Illyrians. Archelaos undertook some reforms, reorganising the cavalry and providing weapons for the infantry, but the army remained small and largely ineffectual, and then came Bardylis' crushing defeat of Perdikkas III where both king and more than 4,000 Macedonians were killed.[56] This figure needs some emphasis. It likely represented the major portion of the army; the recorded number of Macedonian losses was greater than in all of Alexander's major battles combined.

When Philip came to power, rebuilding and improving the army was not only desirable but a necessity. Diodorus Siculus, in the sixteenth book of his *Library of History*, one of the main sources on Philip's reign, reports that he gathered together the Macedonians in various Assemblies; by raising their battered morale with eloquent speeches, he gained support for his ambitious plans for military reform. For too long Macedonia had been a fractured kingdom, unable to hold back surrounding enemies. It was time for a change, time to go on the offensive. Philip, perhaps drawing on experience earned during his time at Thebes, altered the combat units, providing the men with arms, and held constant manoeuvres and training exercises, essentially creating a new Macedonian phalanx or battle line.[57] Other sources provide more information: the heavy infantry was divided into sub-units consisting of companies around 500 strong (*lochoi*), and files, 10, later 16, men deep (*dekades*).[58] Philip initially banned the use of support carriages, and restricted servants to one per file of infantrymen.[59] Forced day marches across three hundred stades (around 50 kilometres) of variable terrain increased their endurance, the men carrying their own military equipment along with cooking utensils and food supplies.[60] Philip also abolished the normal custom of only campaigning for half the year. Winter and summer became the same for him.[61]

The phalanx's main offensive weapon was the *sarissa* – a giant wooden pike 15–18ft (4.5–5.5m) long.[62] When levelled in unison by the infantry an almost impenetrable mass of points, like a porcupine's spines, was presented to the enemy. The length of the *sarissa* far outstripped that of the standard Greek spear and they inflicted terrible damage before their opponents were in range to fight back. Two hands were needed to wield the weapon, and so shields were reduced in size and slung across the shoulder with the aid of a strap.[63] The *sarissa* required incredible strength and skill to wield and so discipline was essential to the success of the phalanx. Philip positioned the most experienced fighters at the front and back of the individual files, forming the tough crusts that kept the rest of the men in check. On the parade grounds of

Macedonia, they practised different formations, changing their alignments to suit various scenarios, sometimes doubling or tripling the file depth, or closing rank to produce a wall of shields, a formation that Philip had apparently learnt from Homer.[64] Commands were executed to the blast of trumpets: *Sarissas* up! *Sarissas* down! The men moved in relative silence, the stamping of feet and the odd grunt of exertion the only sounds to be made. When ready to engage they unleashed an almighty battle cry – *Alalai!* For the enemy it was the noise of impending doom; one Roman general later described the advance of the Macedonian phalanx as the most terrifying spectacle he had ever witnessed.[65] The heavy infantry gained such mastery of their new weapon that they could even use them to clear vegetation while marching, swaying them back and forth in a slashing motion, obliterating any obstacle that appeared between them and the enemy. But good terrain was crucial to the weapon's effectiveness. If they advanced across broken or hilly land then cracks could appear in the line which could be exploited by the enemy. Philip had to be adept at selecting the right topography for battle.[66]

With the incorporation of the Upper Macedonian cantons into the kingdom, Philip was able to create new battalions (*taxeis*) that consisted of around 1,500 men, who fought together with their kinsmen and were often commanded by individuals with whom they were familiar. The pyramids of power remained the same, with the sole exception of the Argead king who now occupied the pinnacle. Philip selected the strongest and tallest individuals from the army to form a new elite corps, 3,000 strong – the Foot Companions (*pezhetairoi*). They could be broken down into smaller groups of 500, and among them was the royal squad (*agema*) that surrounded the king in battle when on foot. They were given the hardest missions and could change their panoplies to suit the occasion. In set-piece engagements they were positioned on the right of the line, forming a crucial link between phalanx and cavalry. Unlike other units, which were levied when needed, their service was probably year-round and they quickly became a highly experienced professional outfit, among the greatest fighters of antiquity. The king was further protected by a select seven-man bodyguard, a position of honour and prestige first recorded under Philip although it probably had earlier origins.[67]

Macedonia had a reputation for the excellence of its horsemen, men who learned to ride before they could walk, delighting in horses like their mythical forebear, the god Makedon. Among the first silver coins of the Argead kings, instituted by Alexander I, was one that bore the image of a mounted warrior on one side, the front half of a goat on the other.[68] The king's Companions made up the core of the heavy cavalry and were supplemented with other troopers of status, their weapons including a lance of sturdy cornel wood (*xyston*) and, for closer encounters, a sabre-like slashing sword (*kopis*) with a razor-sharp edge. The intensity of their training under Philip mirrored that of the infantry, and under his leadership they sharpened their coordination and discipline. They were divided into squadrons (*ilai*) of around 200 individuals with a royal squadron (*agema*), the king's cavalry guard, of extra strength (300–400). Those recruited from Upper Macedonia formed another squadron within the army.[69] At some point the wedge formation was adopted, borrowed from the Thracians and Scythians, and this transformed the cavalry into the shock troops of the army.[70] Despite not having saddles or stirrups, the control that these armed riders were able to achieve was exceptional, their effect on the enemy devastating.

The leaders, positioned at the apex of the various squadrons, would aim their attack at gaps in the opposing phalanx, the charge exploiting the openings, their skills as horsemen allowing them to engage in hand-to-hand fighting, a tactic previously little used by ancient cavalry.[71] But Philip's innovations didn't stop there. He continued to develop the army throughout his reign, adding new specialist brigades such as light cavalry detachments, which included lancers and scouts, skirmishers armed with javelins and slingshot, archers recruited from Crete and Macedonia, mercenary and allied units, as well as creating a small fleet and an engineering corps, whose architects and sappers could bring down the walls of any city. It was this diversity and balance of the army that made the Macedonians so formidable, equally effective in set-piece battles, guerrilla warfare or lengthy sieges. During his first major battle with the Illyrians, Philip could only muster a force of 10,000 infantry and 600 cavalry; by 338 BC that had risen to 30,000 infantry and 2,000 cavalry (including allies).[72] It was this army that would go on to conquer not just Greece, but the furthest reaches of the known world.[73]

These developments had a profound effect on Macedonian society. The army became a legitimate career for many as it moved towards becoming a professional outfit, with plunder and pay providing new forms of income. 'New lands' acquired through conquest were leased or donated to Companions to help further bind the aristocracy to the king. Their estates secured and protected spear-won territory and generated extra forms of revenue which was then subjected to royal taxation.[74] But it was not just the rich who benefited from Philip's state-building programme. He founded many new settlements on his borders, moving around populations and allotting land to the residents, breaking their old ties with previous landlords so that they now owed their livelihood to the king. The ancient writer Justin, who produced an epitome of Pompeius Trogus' now lost Philippic history in the third century AD, says that with these actions he succeeded in making 'one kingdom and one people from large numbers of different clans and tribes'.[75]

The organisation and administration of the kingdom has gained greater clarity through the growing epigraphic record. In his pioneering study, *Macedonian Institutions under the Kings* (1996), the Greek scholar Miltiades Hatzopoulos overturned old ideas that Macedonia remained a tribal kingdom, ruled solely by kings and clans. He has demonstrated that many cities and communities had organs of civic governance, such as Assemblies, Councils and Magistrates, and that Macedonia may have been divided into separate civic territories long before the arrival of the Romans, who are usually credited with this development. Philip, Hatzopoulos proposes, was on the whole respectful of native traditions and sought to integrate existing power structures within his kingdom.[76] The unfortified villages of the Upper Macedonians retained their territorial organisation, which was based around their urban centres and had the same civic apparatus found in the cities of the lowlands. The king was able to communicate with the various elements within the realm through his Companions and *epistatai*, men elected to office in their own communities as representatives of Philip. Attic Greek became the *lingua franca* and royal pronouncements (*diagrammata*) could be widely circulated to publicise policy changes. The organisation of the many disparate elements in the kingdom also made army recruitment a far easier task.

The Companions remained the eyes and ears of the king: his ambassadors, commanders, governors and representatives. Their relationship was celebrated at the annual festival to Zeus of Companionship (*Zeus Hetaireios*), which was perhaps where new members were inaugurated.[77] During his reign Philip expanded the pool of Companions; a contemporary figure of 800 is mentioned by Theopompus, who wrote a history of Philip and stayed at the royal court for a time in the mid fourth century BC. The king's personal retinue, the nucleus of nobility, perhaps numbered 80 to

100 individuals.[78] By extending the position to others, including non-Macedonians, Philip was able to reduce the dominance of the traditional aristocracy. In order to increase loyalty among the most influential members of the Macedonian court, Philip reformed, or perhaps even invented, the institution of the *basilikoi paides* – royal youths or pages.[79] Selected boys attended from roughly the age of fourteen to eighteen. They were recruited from the houses of aristocratic families across the kingdom and sent to Pella, where they were effectively hostages, an insurance policy against revolt. Their official duties included serving the king at dinner parties, attending sacrifices, accompanying hunts, preparing the horses before battle, and guarding the royal bedchamber at night. It was a tough and sometimes demeaning institution, but the benefits far outweighed the negatives.

During their time at court the boys learned key leadership skills and were given access to the inner workings of the state. On graduation, there was the promise of joining the king's foot guard and the ranks of Companions. One of the most exciting recent discoveries from northern Greece now provides an insight into their lives and appearance. In 1994, archaeologists discovered a high-status Macedonian tomb at Aghios Athanasios, to the west of Thessaloniki, its façade richly decorated with painted murals. A feasting scene crowns the lintel, the revellers attended by a number of youths believed to be royal pages, but the most evocative paintings are those flanking the doorway: two near life-size young men, probable graduates of the institution, guard the burial place of what must have been an individual of some importance. They wear Macedonian dress and hold *sarissas*, standing silently in sorrow, custodians of the dead. To visit the tomb, to descend underneath the protective canopy and gaze upon them, is to confront the past and meet members of the ancient Macedonian nobility, the younger generation that played such a critical role in the kingdom's success.[80]

Macedonian guards at Aghios Athanasios

But to fund the redevelopment of Macedonia's infrastructure Philip needed money. Just as he had looked west to secure fresh human resources, he found in the east the means to support them.

With the capture of Amphipolis in 357 BC came the rich hinterland of Mount Pangaion. The Macedonian king retained a royal monopoly on timber and mineral wealth and there was an abundance of both in the region. His ancestor, Alexander I, had controlled the lucrative mines close to Mount Dysoron, perhaps to be identified with Mount Menoikion, near the Strymon, and they reportedly delivered a talent of silver a day to the king's

coffers.[81] Philip desired a similar source of revenue and employed
a number of miners to inspect old workings and locate new ones
– archaeological surveys around Pangaion have so far revealed
over fifty ancient galleries burrowing into the slopes.[82] During
one recorded trip, the workmen descended into an underground
world of vast caverns with rivers and pools of motionless water,
a Jules Vernian scene that sounds suspiciously like the Aggitis
river cave near Drama, where stalactites resembling melted candle
wax hang from the damp vaults, their ghostly images reflected in
the river's course as it worms for kilometres through the rock.[83]
Whether the prospectors found what they were after is not known,
but it was some old workings further to the east that proved the
most bountiful.

In 356 BC, shortly after Alexander's birth, Philip answered a call
for assistance by the inhabitants of Krenides, a colony of Thasos
that had been established some years earlier at the base of Mount
Lekani. The inhabitants were suffering at the hands of the
surrounding Thracians, and so Philip took over the city, renaming
it Philippoi, the first of his self-named foundations. He supplemented the population with new settlers and invested in the city's
infrastructure. Among the buildings dating back to his reign are
the strong city walls and the theatre.[84] He also helped drain the
marshy Philippoi/Drama plain, transforming it into a rural idyll.[85]
Lekani had already revealed traces of gold but the mines were less
productive than they could have been. Philip's miners set about
improving the situation, the workforce greatly increased by
captives taken on the battlefield. The aptly named 'Hill of
Dionysos' revealed godlike riches. It remains unidentified, although
it is believed to be a few kilometres north of Philippoi, but the
ancient sources are unanimous about the benefits it bestowed on
Philip.[86] Diodorus says that the mines brought him a revenue of
more than a thousand talents.[87] This coup would have made him

among the richest men in the Aegean and it underwrote his ambitious plans to bring Macedonia into a new age. During his reign, he struck coins on an unprecedented scale and was the first king to produce gold staters.[88] They became known as 'Philips' – one of the great currencies of the ancient world, their spread across continental Europe would even influence the iconography of pre-Roman coinage minted by the Iron Age tribes, including those in distant Britain. As well as paying for improvements to the kingdom's infrastructure, the money also provided the means to employ a large number of mercenaries, which Philip primarily used to man garrisons and outposts, in addition to offering a ready fund for bribery.[89] Diodorus says that Philip himself claimed that his enlargement of Macedonia owed more to gold than strength of arms.[90] When faced with taking a seemingly impregnable city he would often ask if gold could scale its walls.[91] Alexander slept with a copy of the *Iliad* under his pillow; Philip, apparently, a weighty golden cup.[92]

In regard to relationships with the native Thracians, Philip followed the example of previous Greek colonies that had been planted in the area. As his influence spread eastwards, he established a mutually beneficial relationship where trade and security trumped concerns over land-grabbing newcomers. Philip maintained his dominance through force but then sought to promote stability through a confederacy of alliances that helped to form a buffer zone on the edge of the Macedonian kingdom, set between the Strymon and Nestos rivers. He further secured the region by building a network of forts, some of which have been located along the lower course of the Nestos, eagle eyries positioned high up in the mountains that were connected to each other by line of sight. The effort needed to create them was immense and attests to Philip's considerable investment in the region.[93]

Increases in manpower, mineral resources and new lands powered Philip's revolution. The changes were seismic and were later summed up by Alexander in a speech he delivered to the Macedonian army at Opis, north of Babylon, in 324 BC:

> Philip took you over when you were helpless vagabonds, mostly clothed in skins, feeding a few animals on the mountains and engaged in their defence in unsuccessful fighting with Illyrians, Triballians and the neighbouring Thracians. He gave you cloaks to wear instead of skins, he brought you down from the mountains to the plains; he made you a match in battle for the barbarians on your borders, so that you no longer trusted for your safety to the strength of your positions so much as to your natural courage. He made you city dwellers and established the order that comes from good laws and customs. It was due to him that you became masters and not slaves and subjects of those very barbarians who used previously to plunder your possessions and carry off your persons.[94]

The speech is found in Arrian's *Anabasis of Alexander*, one of the principal accounts of the king's reign. It's debatable whether it is a literary creation, a reflection of Alexander's actual words, or whether, more probably, it represents the general gist of his argument; some elements, such as the depiction of the primitive ways of life in the highlands, are contradicted by the archaeology, but nevertheless it does reflect later perceptions about the seminal role of Philip in building the Macedonian state. It provided Alexander with the platform for future glory and conquest. In more than one way, if there had been no Philip there would have been no Alexander the Great.

These developments did not go unnoticed elsewhere. By the late 350s BC Philip was already known as a man of exceptional talent and his actions were a cause for concern for other peoples. In Athens, among those speaking out against the growing power of Macedon was a young and ambitious politician. He would become Philip's greatest adversary and one of the most famous orators in ancient history. His name was Demosthenes.

3.

GODS, WAR AND WINE

Just after dawn is the best time to visit the Pnyx, the site of the democratic Assembly of ancient Athens. The city is already stirring. Road sweepers make their tours of duty, café owners set out tables and chairs, another busy day in the capital begins. The open-air auditorium occupies a saddle of land between the hills of the Nymphs and the Muses, west of the Acropolis. In the 1950s, the visionary architect Dimitris Pikionis cloaked the entire area in greenery. Stone-paved walkways now wind through mature trees and bushes, the ground carpeted by wildflowers of kaleidoscopic variety – it's a pocket of tranquil beauty surrounded by steaming asphalt roads and concrete high-rises.

Approaching from the nearby Agora, a curved retaining wall appears among the slender pines. It was constructed at the bottom of the slope to create an artificial platform above. The footpaths circumnavigate the large blocks of masonry and lead into the Pnyx, the semi-circular space worn smooth by time and footfall and partially covered in yellowing grass. The speaker's platform (*bema*) projects from a horizontal scarp that cuts across the top of the site; gouged from living bedrock, it is simply known as 'the stone'. The structure visible today dates to c.340 BC but its predecessor, the Pnyx contemporary with Philip's early reign, had the same layout, albeit on a slightly smaller scale, its capacity being generally estimated at 6,000–8,000 people.[1] This empty hillside once echoed with the words of the great orators of the past and among the many topics discussed was the troubling expansion of Macedonian power. The resulting decisions that were made here not only dictated the future of the Athenian city-state but also that of the rest of Greece.

In the same grey morning light that greets many an Athenian day, the ancient citizens would begin to fill the area: the new arrivals taking up their favoured spots, yawning and stretching, complaining about the poor punctuality of the officials; country folk already thinking of home; the most fashionable individuals still chattering away in the nearby marketplace. Once everyone had assembled, a piglet was ritually sacrificed and carried around the boundary of the precinct, its blood purifying all those contained within. The herald then offered up a dedicatory prayer, along with a curse against any speaker who should seek to bring the city into ruin. The Council of Five Hundred had already decided the agenda for the day's meeting. The speakers usually came from a small portion of the population – the regulars. On this occasion, in the summer of 351 BC, when the herald asked, 'Who wants to speak?' Demosthenes stepped forward.

His journey to the speaker's platform had not been easy. He had lost his father around the age of seven and control of the family estate passed to unscrupulous guardians who proceeded to fritter away his inheritance. As a sickly child with a speech defect – he had trouble pronouncing his r's – he was mocked by his peers and given various derogatory nicknames. Short of friends and funds, plagued with bad health, his upbringing was atypical but he did manage to receive an education, and may even have studied under the famed orator Isaeus. On coming of age, he received his much-diminished estate and promptly took his guardians to court, charging them with embezzlement. He eventually won his case, but only recovered a fraction of what had been taken. The experience, however, schooled him in Athenian law, teaching him the importance of rigorous research, preparation, and sound execution. As a result, he gained a reputation as a young man of skill and ambition. He spent some time as a speech writer before focusing on public life.[2]

His previous speeches had not been successful. They were often confused and complicated, more ponderous than persuasive. According to Plutarch, after one particularly bad performance an actor friend followed him home, hoping to pass on some sage advice. Demosthenes complained that he had nearly used up all his physical energy trying to win the favour of the people, alas to no avail. The actor promised to transform the situation and asked him to recite some lines from Sophocles or Euripides, which Demosthenes duly did – an easy task for any educated Greek. The actor then did the same but delivered the words with the artistry of a seasoned performer. The message was simple: content was one thing, delivery another – a true master of public speaking achieved excellence in both. Demosthenes took the lesson to heart. He battled to overcome his speech impediment with a variety of novel exercises: speaking with pebbles in his mouth to perfect his enunciation, strengthening his voice by walking or running uphill, reciting speeches as he did so, and performing in his house in front of a large mirror. When later asked about the key to good oratory he replied, 'Delivery, delivery, delivery.'[3]

He was now in his early to mid thirties, with a wiry frame and a brow that was easily furrowed, perhaps already sporting the receding hairline evident from his later portraits. To his right was the Acropolis, the majestic marble monuments warming with the first rays of the sun; to his left the sanctuaries of Zeus

Demosthenes, Ny Carlsberg Glyptotek

and the Nymphs, women visiting the latter with votive gifts,
hoping to secure divine aid for conception, an easy birth or to
heal a sick child. Directly surrounding him were the faces of
the Assembly members – male citizens old enough to vote, those
aged 18 and over. They had been paid to attend; it was the only
way to guarantee a good turnout in those days. Some were seated
on the floor or on wooden benches with bread and wine ready
to quiet rumbling stomachs; others probably stood, mingling
with friends from the same neighbourhood or village. Once the
session began there would be cheers and jeers, the crowd
reflecting the sympathies of the political parties. The speech
Demosthenes gave in 351 BC was a watershed moment in his
career. It employed a new emotive style of argument with clarity
at its heart, the language relatable to the full range of citizens

in the Assembly, from sophists to sausage-sellers. The topic was one that would come to dominate Greek politics for the next couple of decades – the king of Macedon: it is known as the *First Philippic*.[4]

Demosthenes' preamble was pleasant enough. He explained that he was speaking before the elders because the topic he wished to discuss was not new but that their advice had been far from satisfactory. He then proceeded to his argument: 'Now in the first place, Athenians, there is no need to despair of our present position, however hopeless it may seem. For that which is worst in the days that are past and gone is just what affords the best assurance for the future.' Then came the sting in the tail. 'And what is that? It is that your affairs are in this evil plight just because you, men of Athens, utterly fail to do your duty; since surely, were you so placed in spite of every effort on your part, it would be hopeless to look for improvement.'[5] Demosthenes had decided to go on the attack; there was now fire in his words. One contemporary records that he whirled around the speaker's platform during his speeches, changes of tone and hand gestures probably adding to the impact of his words.[6] To hear them in the flesh must have been awe-inspiring.

Now that he had the audience's attention, he outlined the main problems that were facing the Athenians. First, their own lethargy in protecting their interests outside of Attika, and second the growing threat to the north, the two inextricably linked. Demosthenes believed the inaction of his fellow citizens had directly led to the rise of Macedon. 'But if anyone here, Athenians, is inclined to think Philip too formidable, having regard to the extent of his existing resources and to our loss of all our strongholds, he is indeed right, yet he must reflect that we too, men of Athens, once held Pydna, Potidaea and Methone.'[7]

Athens had technically been at war with Macedon since the

seizure of Amphipolis in 357 BC. As Demosthenes records, Philip had then gone on to root out all other Athenian footholds in the north, depriving them of direct access to the region's natural resources. At sea, his small navy had raided some of their other territories. In one act of barefaced daring, the Macedonians had even captured Athens' sacred trireme – the *Paralos* – during its visit to Marathon. For a city-state proud of its naval power and heritage, this was a most humiliating turn of events.[8] But recently another more troublesome development had occurred. Philip had become involved in the affairs of central Greece.

The Third Sacred War was a decade-long struggle for the freedom of Delphi, home of the Oracle of Pythian Apollo, one of the holiest sites in the ancient world. The Phokians, who lived in central Greece and around Delphi, had seized the sanctuary in 356 BC after the Amphiktyonic Council – the body charged with administering the site and composed of representatives from surrounding Greek peoples – had fined them for tilling sacred land. War was declared the following year. The wealth of Apollo was now being used to fund endless mercenary armies under a line of ambitious Phokian generals. Athens and Sparta, although not in favour of the war, were allies of the Phokians, but neither was in much of a position to help, Athens being embroiled in a separate conflict with a number of rebellious members of their Second Athenian League (the Social War) and the Spartans long since humbled by Thebes. It fell to the Thessalians and Thebans to fight it out with the Phokians, but the former were riven with internal divisions. The tyrants of Pherai, leaders of the Thessalian League, supported the enemy. Philip had already been active in Thessaly early in his reign, building on good relations with the ruling Aleuad family at Larissa and helping to settle a dispute with Pherai. He had married Philinna, and perhaps Nikesipolis as well, during this time. The settlement, however, did not last. The Pherai tyrants – Lykophron and Peitholaos – soon resumed hostilities against Larissa. In 353 BC, Philip was summoned to help defeat them and this brought him into conflict with the Phokians, who dispatched 7,000 men to aid the tyrants; what had been a regional dispute now became a Pan-Hellenic affair.[9] He won an early victory but this led to Onomarchos, the Phokian leader, marching his army into Thessaly. Philip and his Thessalian allies were defeated in two battles, one of which was emphatic.[10] Diodorus records the devastating impact this defeat had on Philip's position: 'he was reduced to the uttermost perils and his soldiers were so despondent that they had deserted him.' To his great credit he managed to rescue the situation; 'by arousing the courage of the majority,' continues Diodorus, 'he got them with great difficulty to obey his orders.'[11] Philip later maintained that he did not flee the battlefield but backed away like a ram, preparing to butt that much harder the next time.[12]

As good as his word, he returned to Thessaly the following year. This time he cast himself as a champion of Apollo, ready to save the god's Delphic sanctuary from sacrilegious enemies. The army marched into battle adorned with laurel wreaths plucked from the god's favoured tree.[13] They met Onomarchos at a place called the Crocus Field, to the south of modern Volos. Forty thousand men fought to the death in the suffocating heat and dust of Thessaly during what has been called the bloodiest battle in Classical Greek history.[14] Philip eventually carried the day, the addition of the Thessalian cavalry to his army proving the decisive factor. He drove the enemy into the sea, killing 6,000 mercenaries and Phokians, Onomarchos among them.[15] Some 3,000 were taken captive and were forcibly drowned as temple-robbers, while their general's body was nailed to a wooden cross as an offering to Apollo. The mass executions must have been a horrific sight, the bloated bodies covering the beach and drifting sombrely in the deep blue of the Aegean.

In the aftermath, Philip liberated Pherai from the tyrants and then campaigned further into Thessaly to subdue other rebellious cities, seeking to unite a fractured region under his leadership. It was likely during this time that he was elected head of the Thessalian League (*archon*) – a position held for life, it gave him the right to mobilise their army, which included their excellent cavalrymen, and placed the region's resources and revenues in his hands. The appointment probably came with the expectation that he would finish off the Sacred War, which still rumbled on. He did eventually lead his army south, but the Athenians who occupied the pass at Thermopylai – the Gates of Greece – barred his way to Phokis and Delphi.

For now, the war remained unfinished business, but his reputation skyrocketed as a result: 'he was held up as the avenger of sacrilege, the champion of religion,' says Justin.[16] Back in Pella a daughter was born to his Thessalian wife, Nikesipolis from Pherai. She was called Thessalonike – 'Victory in Thessaly' – in honour of Philip's achievements, but her mother died shortly after childbirth and Olympias may have adopted the child. She is later mentioned as part of her royal retinue, another sister for Alexander who at this time was still safely ensconced in the women's quarters, yet to start his education.[17]

The Athenians had watched with growing concern as Macedon's influence continued to expand, developments which provided the context for the *First Philippic*. Demosthenes goes on to report that Philip had then campaigned in western Thrace, which was close to the Athenian-controlled Chersonese – the Gallipoli peninsula – which commanded the vital grain route from the Black Sea. The Athenians had formed an alliance with the local Thracian king, Kersobleptes, threatening Philip's new conquests, and his campaign was likely a result of these developments. Illness soon forced him to abandon his activities in the east, alleviating the need for the

Athenians to send out extra ships. The threat, however, still remained. Demosthenes' speech captures the city's decidedly uneasy mood: 'But what are we to think of what is happening now? For my own part I think that for a free people there can be no greater compulsion than shame for their position. Or tell me, are you content to run around and ask one another other, "Is there any news today?" Could there be any news more startling than that a Macedonian is triumphing over Athenians and settling the destiny of Hellas?'[18]

Despite the problems facing the Athenians, Demosthenes was convinced it was not too late for action. He urged the Assembly to shrug off their lethargy and embrace the war with Macedon; to stop fighting Philip like a barbarian boxer, clutching at one area after the blow had been delivered, and to take the initiative. He therefore put forward a two-part proposal. First, he recommended creating a rapid response force that could be quickly deployed to meet any future Macedonian advance, be it against Thermopylai, the Chersonese, Olynthos, or any other place they should target. The second suggestion was to send a guerrilla outfit north. Its purpose was to harry the Macedonians on their own soil, 'to carry on a continuous war of annoyance'.[19] This approach would be pre-emptive and not reactionary. It was a good plan in theory, but the financing was costly, and the Athenians probably had little appetite for further conflict after the debilitating Social War (357–355 BC). Demosthenes ended his speech with a warning: if they did not fight Philip now, while he was still contained in the north, he would soon appear on their doorstep.[20] It was a grim prophecy, one that turned out to be chillingly close to the mark. Still the warning failed to hit home. The herald asked for a show of hands in favour of the motion. After an approximate count, it was clear that, despite the brilliance of the speech, its new style and emotive content, Demosthenes had failed to sway the majority. This was not the end of the argument, however, but rather just the beginning. Over the next few years he would deliver many more harangues against the Macedonian king, making his name in the process. He was convinced that the future of Athens was at stake. He was right.

Demosthenes was not the only one concerned about Macedonian aggression. The Chalkidian League, led by the city of Olynthos, had watched Philip's power grow with each passing year and their proximity soon made conflict unavoidable. Despite an early alliance with Macedon they made overtures to Athens in breach of their existing agreement. On hearing the news, Philip decided to pay them a timely visit, and apparently recounted the fable of War and *Hybris* (arrogance) to the Chalkidian leaders.[21] According to myth, the two gods were the last of the immortals to be paired together. They fell madly in love and became so devoted to each other that wherever *Hybris* went, be it any nation, city or village, War would be sure to follow. It was hardly the subtlest of messages, but then again it had no need to be. Philip had the better army, and he knew it. He withdrew from the Chalkidike but his influence lingered. A certain Lasthenes was seen roofing his house with a gift of Macedonian timber, while Euthykrates seemed to have acquired a large herd of cattle for free. Others returned home with a flock of sheep or stud of horses. Philip's gold was already inside the city walls.[22]

In 349 BC, Philip decided to dispense with threats and invaded the Chalkidike, probably on the pretext that Olynthos had given refuge to his two half-brothers, Arrhidaios and Menelaos (Philip had already eliminated the third and eldest half-brother, Archelaos).[23] He delivered an ultimatum to the city: either they ceased to live in Olynthos or he in Macedonia.[24] His army spread through the region, focusing first on the League's peripheral cities. Some he razed to the ground, others were intimated to submit to his rule,

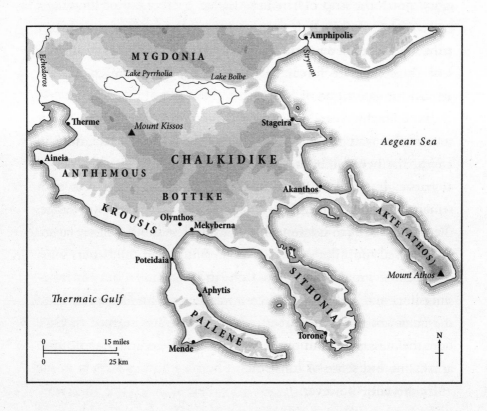

bribery and treachery winning over many more. It was a clever stratagem that aimed to isolate their lead city. By the end of the first year he had subjugated most of the peninsula. Olynthos now took steps to form an alliance with the Athenians. Demosthenes took up their cause, delivering his famous Olynthiac speeches. Rightly observing that the defenders were now fighting 'not for glory, not for a strip of territory, but to avert the overthrow and enslavement of their fatherland',[25] he urged his fellow citizens to rally, which they eventually did. Over the course of the war they sent three separate forces to the Chalkidike, although the last arrived too late to be of any help.[26]

The following year, 348 BC, Philip took the remaining outlying strongholds and fought against the Olynthians in two battles. Defeated, they fell back to their strong-walled city. Today, the archaeological site of Olynthos has an eerie quality. The excavated remains give the impression of a flourishing city suddenly cut to the core, levelled to its stone foundations. Inside the houses, layers of collapsed roof tiles were found covering the ancient floors with evidence of intense burning. Throughout the debris, numerous slingshots and arrowheads were unearthed, many inscribed with the names of the assailants: Philip and some of his generals. One bore the message, 'An unpleasant gift', evidence of the Macedonian army's morbid sense of humour.[27]

In the end, however, it was not their siege tactics that won the day. Demosthenes relates that 500 cavalrymen were betrayed to Philip and soon after, the city itself.[28] The army ran riot, looting, raping, burning. Standing in the carefully manicured site, it's hard to imagine the scenes of carnage that took place: the deafening sound of collapsing buildings, the crackle and roar of rampant fires; soldiers wrestling for the best pieces of plunder, tearing shelves off the walls and smashing open wooden chests. The men, women and children of Olynthos were rounded up and put in chains, ripped from their normal lives and reduced to the status of slaves. Many were sold off to raise further campaign funds; their fate is a reminder that every great story of victory is built upon a mire of human suffering. On that late summer's day in 348 BC the city was destroyed root and branch. Besides a few squatters it was never occupied again. Where houses once stood were now just piles of roof tiles; the open communal spaces – the fountains and marketplaces – were left empty, the sounds of civic life replaced with silence and the occasional moan of the wind raking over the ruins. Olynthos became a ghost. The immediate countryside was left uninhabited until late antiquity, bad memories lingering for centuries. Philip's half-brothers were never heard of again.

News of Olynthos' extinction spread throughout the Greek world. It was a brutal statement that annihilation was also in Philip's arsenal. Alexander would use the same terror weapon during

Olynthos

his own kingship. Despite the brutality of the act it had the intended effect. The Chalkidike became part of the kingdom, new lands were apportioned to Companions and the region never resisted again. For the Macedonians, it was time to celebrate.

CITY OF ZEUS

The philosopher Democritus once said that 'The life without festival is a long road without an inn.'[29] Festivals offered a much-needed break from the drudgery of daily life, a chance to mingle and make merry. They are as important in modern Greece as they were in ancient times, and continue to dominate the calendar, giving structure to the year, now celebrating Christian figures instead of pagan deities. In northern Greece, many festivals retain elements that appear to stretch back to older times, beyond memory and record; they are Gordian knots of tradition, folklore and history. The past can still be felt among the goatskin-clad *Arapides* of East Macedonia and Thrace in January, whose fearsome appearance, their bodies festooned with bells, are believed to banish evil spirits and awaken the spring. Or, during the Carnival at Naoussa, when young men adorned with ghostly white face masks perform martial dances in streets laced with barbecue and fire-cracker smoke. Other festivals are unabashed celebrations of the pagan past, none more so than Tyrnavos' Phallus Festival, near Larissa, held on the first Monday of Lent, where locals parade penises of every conceivable size and material along the streets, beckoning passers-by to kiss their proud creations, the women hoisted onto shoulders to bring fertility, while ribald songs are sung around bubbling cauldrons of spinach soup. Amid the rhythmic beat of drums and haunting notes of wooden flutes, Dionysos' presence still lurks. He continues to lead the fun in phantom form; music and dance last long into the night, the modern-day Bacchants fuelled by wine, tsipouro and ouzo.

The months of the ancient Macedonian calendar were named in honour of the gods, their festivals often coinciding with important dates in the agricultural year.[30] Two festivals were of particular importance: the springtime Xandika, which marked the beginning of the campaigning season – the army taking part in military drills, mock combats and war dances, purified for the battles to come by marching between the dismembered pieces of a slaughtered dog – and the festival of Olympian Zeus and the Muses, held on the first new moon after the autumn equinox, at the end/beginning of the Macedonian year in early October.[31] The modern feast days of the warrior saints George and Demetrios – held on 23 April and 26 October – are the probable descendants of these celebrations, the dates bookending the seasonal migrations of shepherds to and from highland grazing pastures. Archelaos, in the late fifth century BC, had either founded or reorganised the festival of Olympian Zeus and the Muses, turning it into a grand celebration that was focused upon Dion – Zeus' city – located at the foot of Olympos.[32] If Aigai was the hearth of the Macedonian kingdom then Dion was its altar. It was the destination for Philip and his victorious army after the sack of Olynthos.

'Olympos I am! Great of yore, and in the world renowned', begins a famous Greek folk ballad.

The fabled home of the Olympian gods is visible from across Macedonia, a central reference point for all those living in its shadow. Atop its heights stands a great cock's-comb of rock known as the 'Throne of Zeus', where the king of the gods was believed to reside, dispensing thunderbolts, controlling the weather and influencing the affairs of mortals. The Plateau of the Muses spreads out below, named after Zeus' nine daughters who danced and sang for their father's delight, the crisp alpine air ringing with their sweet voices. Olympos was Greece's first National Park and Biosphere Reserve, and is today visited by thousands of tourists each year. Archaeology has revealed that they are not the first people to do so. Between 1960 and 1965, on the Aghios Antonios peak (2,816m above sea level), a number of pottery sherds and evidence of sacrificial activity was found during the construction of a weather monitoring station, along with fragments of sculpture and small marble stelai – three of which were inscribed with the name of Olympian Zeus. They are the remains of a Hellenistic mountaintop sanctuary dedicated to the god. Long before modern explorers and tourists, priests and pilgrims made the laborious ascent in the name of devotion.[33]

The massif's forested eastern slopes, veined with torrents, are dark against the calming green of Dion's open spaces, the close proximity of mountain and city imbuing the site with a special sanctity. Its discovery is linked to one of the founding fathers of Macedonian studies: William Martin Leake, or Colonel Leake as he was known. His four-volume *Travels in Northern Greece* is a masterclass in Greek topography, providing invaluable information about the landscape as it appeared in the nineteenth century, before modern developments took place. He successfully combined military precision with an encyclopaedic knowledge of the Classics and was adept at tracing ancient settlements that had been lost since antiquity.

On a clear December day in 1806, as the rising sun lit the snowy heights of Olympos, Leake descended onto the Pierian plain. On this particular journey, he had just passed the small village of Malathria when he encountered two intriguing low hillocks of earth. He noticed that their unusual shapes most likely foreshadowed the ancient buildings that they now concealed. Leake rightly posited that one was a theatre, the other a stadium.

Nearby he also noted the foundations of city walls and a grave stele or stone, but the dense foliage that had grown up around the ruins hampered further investigation. He recorded the discovery in his journal, stating confidently the identity of the settlement: 'There can be no doubt that here stood the famous Dium, which, though not large, was one of the leading cities of Macedonia, and the great bulwark of its maritime frontier to the south.'[34]

Leake's report marks the re-emergence of Dium, or Dion, in the archaeological record. Excavations began in earnest in 1928, led by the Aristotle University of Thessaloniki. Over the following decades, the city was slowly uncovered along with a number of sanctuaries in its environs. The site's archaeological remains cover a range of periods. The city was developed and walled by the Successor Kassandros and many of the interior buildings date to Roman times, including bathhouses and the magnificent villa of Dionysos with its grand polychrome mosaic representing the god arriving on a chariot drawn by panthers.[35] It was most likely a small settlement during the mid fourth century BC. More important were the sanctuaries to the south, dedicated to numerous gods and goddesses, their weathered ruins still surrounded by an almost exotic abundance of lush greenery and tranquil springs. The sanctuary of Demeter is one of the best-studied examples, where women once came to pray for their own fertility as well as that of the surrounding land. Two small temples were constructed in the late sixth–early fifth century BC. Known as the *megaron*-type, they consisted of small narrow buildings with deep antechambers. Wooden benches once lined their interiors and provided room for dedications to the resident cult statues. Close by were wells, supplying water for purification, altars, and offering tables.[36] The site was further developed in later times but it remained rustic in appearance, which is a feature common to other Macedonian sanctuaries. The construction of monumental temples, like those found elsewhere in the Greek world, seems not to have been favoured in the north.

Alexander was eight years old at the time of the 348 BC festival. A year or two into his education, he already had a reputation for lavishly honouring the gods, much to the chagrin of his overseer, Leonidas. His own religiosity was firmly rooted in his Macedonian background, and he grew up surrounded by seers, purifiers and religious attendants; the smell of exotic incense and the sight of freshly spilled sacrificial blood were common in the Pella palace.[37] Learning the principal rites and rituals was an important part of his upbringing; if he were to become king one day then he would inherit the ancestral position of chief priest, the intermediary between gods and men. Among the many sacred duties were daily offerings, the pouring of libations on entering any city in the kingdom, and presiding over the major festivals.[38] Philip was known for his piety, and fulfilled the ideal for how a king should act in regard to religion. He also demonstrated the benefits that came with exploiting divine links for propaganda purposes. Olympias too passed on her devotion to the gods, Dionysos being a particular favourite. Helping Alexander to discern the will of the gods was the trusted seer (*mantis*), Aristandros of Telmessos. He later became indispensable during Alexander's reign, interpreting omens, the entrails of sacrificial beasts and even analysing his dreams, which in antiquity were believed to reveal the future.[39]

The Dion Olympia were formative events for the young Alexander. They were one of the few occasions when the whole of the kingdom came together, along with embassies from other cities and peoples, and the celebrations of 348 BC were among the most magnificent yet, with Philip presiding and the royal family on show. As with modern festivals, the landscape was transformed. A sea of tents and people sprang up on the lap of Olympos, crowds and stalls were everywhere, thieves operated in the shadows, gambling hives were established around every corner. The focus of activity during the Olympia was the sanctuary of Olympian Zeus. In Hellenistic times it had been delineated by a surrounding wall and colonnades, but its Classical incarnation was more modest, comprising a sacred grove with altars for sacrifices. A lonely metal tower now stands at the western end of the sanctuary providing a bird's-eye view over the flat rectangular space, partially filled with brambles, wild mint and a few youthful plane trees. The river Baphyras bordering its eastern limits.

A royal procession probably inaugurated the festival. The king and his family, Companions and scores of religious attendants led the sacrificial cattle from the city along the sacred way towards the sanctuary. Hymns, music and prayers to the greatest of the gods accompanied the footsteps of the worshippers. On entering the precinct, the ancient pilgrims were confronted with a striking visual display that invoked the history of Macedon – statues of kings, the spoils of war, votives hanging from the branches of oak trees, and numerous stone stelai recording past treaties and oaths. Moving on, the grand monumental altar finally came into view. Its rectangular foundations, 22 metres long, have now been exposed, constructed from limestone blocks and infilled with half-baked bricks. Its humble appearance belies its importance. This was once the most sacred site in Macedonia.

In front of the altar, archaeologists uncovered a number of mysterious stone bases with large bronze hooks, some complete with chunky bronze rings. Once they had been plotted on to a plan of the sanctuary, it became clear that the bases were regularly laid out in rows, some set four metres apart, others with slightly wider spacing; there were thirty-six in all.[40] Their proximity to the altar provided a clue to their function: they were used to tether livestock for the mass slaughter of oxen in honour of Olympian Zeus.

Alexander may well have watched his father presiding over the ritual
– the horns of each animal adorned with garlands and ribbons, a
cutting of their hair thrown into the awaiting flames of the altar.
With a sprinkle of barley grains and water, the final prayer was
uttered and the sacrificial double-axe fell. The beasts were stunned,
their heads then lifted to the sky, as if gaining their consent for
death. Women raised a piercing ritual cry known as the *Ololyge* as
the animals' throats were cut, the sombre sound of the flute accompanying the flow of bright blood that spilled on to the ground. The
carcasses were later hauled up to the monumental altar where they
were skinned and butchered, the thighbones and viscera burnt in
offering, a column of pungent smoke winding its way up into the
heavenly realm of Zeus. The rest of the meat was boiled in huge
cauldrons in readiness for the feasts to follow.

As the sun began to set, torches and lamps were lit, illuminating
the royal tent which was the focus of the celebrations. Philip
presided as the host supreme; hospitality was a sacred duty but
also a means of displaying power and prestige. Macedonian feasts
performed a variety of important functions within society.[41] They
were essential for cultivating bonds between the king, his
Companions and the soldiery, as well as forming new relationships
with visiting dignitaries. Gift-giving was a key element of any
gathering; the king was expected to share his wealth, and such a
custom helped cement new friendships. Diodorus records that
Philip was an attentive host, joining in numerous conversations,
presenting drinking cups to his guests, proposing toasts and
awarding others gifts, his generosity lubricated with Olynthian
booty.[42] He was surrounded by concentric rings of intimates and
royal pages, radiating out from his person in a reflection of the
kingdom's hierarchy. The men, wearing wreaths on their heads and
dressed in all their finery, reclined on wooden couches, similar to
chaises longues, topped with soft furnishings, their façades inlaid

with precious materials and miniature scenes carved in ivory. Favourite courtesans joined them, skilled in cultivating conversation as well as desire. Royal women and their children may have also joined the feasts at certain times, perhaps set apart from the men. Meat was also apportioned to the thousands of other attendees encamped around the royal tent.[43]

During the fourth century BC, actors began to play an important role as ambassadors, men who could speak eloquently and present well. It was a profession that naturally won friends, and Satyros, a comic actor, was one such individual known to have been present at this occasion. Despite the merriment that surrounded him, however, he looked gloomy. Philip prompted him to reveal his troubles and Satyros responded by saying that he wanted to ask the king for a favour but was afraid about what would ensue if he did so. Philip alleviated his concerns, promising to grant whatever he wished. Satyros obliged and said that he knew two of the captive women from Olynthos who had been sent to work on the king's vineyards. They were of good family and marriageable age, and he wished to help them by providing dowries and suitors. Philip consented. It was a fine display of his benevolence.[44]

The blast of a trumpet inaugurated the serious drinking.[45] Macedonia provided many fine vintages, as it still does today, and the apportioning of Dionysos' gift involved much ceremony. The wine was brought to the party in special jugs and then decanted into small buckets which resided at the base of each couch. Attendees could decide on how much water or other ingredients, such as fruit, honey or spices, were to be added, the cocktail tailored to individual tastes. Servants and royal pages were on hand to ladle out the mixtures into cups of precious metal. Many such cups have been recovered from Macedonian tombs and they were often small and dainty, exhibiting a taste for Athenian forms but also barbarian bling. During the Olympian celebrations, a large *krater* or mixing jug may have been used instead of the individual buckets. One very large and fine example (almost a metre tall and weighing 40 kg) has been retrieved from a tomb at Derveni, north of Thessaloniki. Adorned with scenes of Dionysian revels, it hints at the magnificence of the drinking parties that could accompany celebrations dedicated to the gods.[46]

Macedonian feasts and *symposia* (drinking parties) could be as varied as the personnel that attended or the circumstances they accompanied.[47] At certain times, they could be the model of Hellenic sophistication, men talking philosophy, comparing lines of Homer or debating the paternity of heroes, while refined entertainment came in the form of music and dancing boys and girls, but they could also be rowdy affairs with a tough, competitive edge, and none more so than when it came to drinking. Toasts were made with undiluted wine, a perceived barbarian practice, but they were part of the Macedonian culture that emphasised masculine prowess.[48] Both Philip and Alexander were famed as heavy drinkers, as their role required, emulating their ancestor Herakles, the greatest drinker of them all. Competitions were common, a crown being awarded to the victor; death from over-consumption is mentioned in the sources.[49] Freedom of speech, a Macedonian prerogative, could also often lead to alcohol-fuelled arguments and fights; *in vino veritas*.[50] As the celebrations continued well into the night, many would take to their feet to perform native dances such as the *Karpaia*, which acted out the story of a battle between a farmer and cattle rustler, or the martial *Telesias*, undertaken by armed men, while others were said to have mimicked sexual acts.[51] Philip is recorded as being fond of dancing, occasionally leading drunken processions outside the royal tent.[52]

The grand sacrifices to Olympian Zeus and the accompanying feasts were followed by a programme of contests and games which lasted for nine days. They took place in the stadium and the surrounding area and included athletic and equestrian events. A fragmentary inscription from Dion refers to a pentathlon, a long-distance foot race and possible bull hunts, a practice also found in Thessaly, a rodeo-like event whereby the participants would jump from their horses and attempt to wrestle a rampaging bull to the ground.[53] Theatrical performances/contests were also on the schedule and the tradition lives on in the modern festival of Olympos, which takes place each summer with cultural events taking place around Pieria. During this time, Dion's theatre fills once again with people, many bringing their own cushions to ease the passing hours on sturdy wooden bleachers, the smell of perfume and popcorn wafting through the crowd. The actors take to the stage at nightfall and perform the ever-popular tragedies of the great playwrights of the past – Aeschylus, Sophocles, Euripides – or Aristophanes' raucous comedies; old stories set in new contexts. There is an added thrill in attending these performances, as Dion's theatre, in its earliest incarnation, may have hosted productions overseen by Euripides himself – the *Bacchae*, *Iphigenia in Tauris* and *Archelaus* – plays written during his stay in Macedonia, the last penned to honour his royal benefactor, King Archelaos.[54]

Alexander was a great admirer of the playwright's works and learning them formed an important part of his liberal education. He could recite many verses by heart and it was even said that he acted out a scene from *Andromeda* during the last party before his death. When his campaigns took him far into Asia's interior, he found the Classics hard to come by, so he urged his Companion, Harpalos, to send him books; works of the great tragedians were dispatched to the Macedonian front.[55] Throughout his kingship he made sure to find time to indulge his passions, dividing his nights according to a set schedule – rest, state affairs, and the Muses.[56] Witnessing these forms of entertainment at Dion, along with other competitive events, also gave Alexander an appreciation of the importance of celebrations in fostering Macedonian cohesion, as well as in the presentation of royal power, which was as ever-present as Olympos. It was a chance to reward the men after periods of tough campaigning, a time to relax and take stock.[57] He would later name each day of the Dion programme after individual Muses, adding new contests that celebrated the enduring love of the arts that had been fostered throughout his early life. Like his father he had a flair for spectacle and showmanship, later becoming the central actor on the stage of Empire.

Outside Macedon, stories began to circulate about the growing ostentation of Philip's court. The Athenians, who treasured the elevated models of dinner-party sophistication supplied by Plato and Xenophon, enjoyed taking the moral high ground, looking down on the northerners and deriding them for excess and debauchery, even though their own parties often ended in drunkenness and orgies. They helped fuel Demosthenes' anti-Macedonian rhetoric: 'Any fairly decent or honest man, who cannot stomach the licentiousness of his [Philip's] daily life,' he states in his second Olynthiac speech, 'the drunkenness and the lewd dancing, is pushed aside as of no account. All the rest about his court . . . are robbers and toadies, men capable of getting drunk and performing such dances as I hesitate to name to you here.'[58] But these stories were based on the observations of others. Demosthenes would soon get a chance to discover the truth for himself.

WHEN PHILIP MET DEMOSTHENES

Around the time of the Chalkidike war, there had been some talk that Philip was open to the idea of peace with Athens. The destruction of Olynthos, however, brought a temporary halt to the possibility. It was not until a year and a half later, when the actor Aristodemos went to Macedonia to enquire about the release of Athenian POWs, that the idea resurfaced. He returned stating that Philip still favoured reconciliation, and even a potential alliance.[59] The Athenians voted to send an embassy north to begin talks. This decision was influenced by a number of factors intimately connected with current events. The Third Sacred War had by now devolved into a bitter tussle between the Phokians and the Thebans, neither possessing the superiority to force a resolution. Thebes had sent an embassy to Philip asking for support and he provided them with a small detachment of soldiers to aid their fight; although it was not large enough to make much difference, Philip desired the glory of finishing off the war himself, but it was a worrying development for Athens as they feared a resurgence of the power of Thebes, their age-old adversary. Around the same time, the Athenians had passed a decree to garner the thoughts of the rest of Greece, inviting embassies to the city to take part in a conference on the war with Macedon, hoping for a greater commitment to the cause, but it appears never to have taken place and there seems to have been little appetite for further conflict. Philip meanwhile had remained active, venturing once again into Thrace, where he secured some lucrative silver mines and threatened Athenian holdings in the Chersonese. He had also become embroiled in a siege at the Thessalian city of Halos, which had some sort of alliance with the Athenians; the city controlled a vital passage south and brought Philip closer to central Greece. The signs were ominous. There was also the lingering question of the Athenian prisoners and the disconcerting actions of the Phokians, who had recently rebuffed Athenian and Spartan forces sent to help defend the pass at Thermopylai. These elements combined to make peace with Philip the best course of action.

The Athenian statesman Philokrates spearheaded the move to send an official delegation to Pella. Among the eleven elected members of the Athenian embassy were two rising stars of politics: Aeschines, a former actor famed for the strength of his voice, and the youngest member of the group, Demosthenes, who was now nearly forty.[60] They set out from Athens in the late winter of 346 BC. Their herald, who had been sent ahead to secure safe passage, met the embassy at Larissa in northern Thessaly and guided them on the final stage of their journey. They travelled through Tempe, passing Herakleion (a Macedonian border town), Dion, Pydna and Methone, and then rounded the top of the Thermaic Gulf, ending in Pella. At this time of year the land is stark, still awaiting the first bursts of spring, the plough lines of agricultural fields thrown into relief by the low rays of the sun, flurries of snow sometimes blowing down the frost-bitten streets. On this occasion, Philip was making ready to lead his army east, back into Thrace to deal with the troublesome King Kersobleptes. A tented village had probably appeared close to the city, soldiers swelling the population with preparations in full swing. Among the other embassies present were the Thebans and Thessalians, who were petitioning for Philip to resume his role as champion of Apollo and end the Sacred War. The Athenians were eventually led into the palace and presence of the king. Remarkably, we have evidence of what took place next. Both Aeschines and Demosthenes related the event in later surviving speeches, when the two had become bitter enemies, set at differing ends of foreign policy and facing each other in the law courts.[61] They were not written as history and should always be treated cautiously, but under the barbs and slanderous remarks are invaluable glimpses of this incredible moment in world history, when representatives of the most eminent city-state in Greek history came face to face with Philip for the first time.

The Athenians had decided to deliver their speeches according to age, the oldest first. Philip carefully listened to what each man had to say, remembering their points and preparing his responses. Aeschines was second to last. His speech *On the Embassy* outlined his argument. He spoke about the old alliances between Athens and Macedon, reminding Philip that the Athenian general Iphikrates had once saved his life and offered protection to his family following the death of his father. Mention of Amphipolis, the city that had brought the two powers into conflict, was left to the end. Aeschines said that it had not been the Amphipolitans' to lose, it was originally Athenian and arguably was still their property, despite Philip's right of conquest; it was a dubious claim at best. Aeschines had given a composed speech and used his fine voice to good effect. All eyes now turned to the last of the speakers: Demosthenes, already known as one of Athens' most inspiring orators. On the journey to Pella he had boasted to his comrades that his arguments would easily sew up Philip's mouth; everyone expected 'a masterpiece of eloquence'.[62]

They shuffled in their seats, leaning forward in anticipation to hear the climax of proceedings. Demosthenes stepped into the limelight and, with a slight adjustment of his cloak and a darting look at his audience, prepared to embark on his speech. Then something extraordinary happened. One of the greatest orators alive, a man who had made countless speeches in front of thousands in the Athenian law courts and Assemblies, froze. He managed to give a lacklustre introduction before finally falling silent. Philip, playing the magnanimous host, encouraged him to take his time and recall his words but the situation was lost. According to Aeschines, 'Silence followed; then the herald bade us withdraw.'[63] The reasons for Demosthenes' failure remain unclear. His speeches were usually well prepared; one contemporary scoffed that they smelt of lamp wicks, suggesting that he worked hard at them long into the night.[64] His arguments may already have been dealt with by others, leaving him little to say, or perhaps when surrounded by the realities of the king – his court, the wealth and splendour of the occasion – he simply lost his nerve.

Philip consulted privately with his Companions before the Athenians were brought back into his presence. He undertook to answer each point of argument that had been set forth. Demosthenes' failure was courteously glossed over. Amphipolis was undoubtedly mentioned: it belonged to Macedon, and there was to be no exchange. Assurances, however, were given regarding Athenian control of the Chersonese. Philip promised not to set foot on the land while negotiations continued, and he expressed his desire for friendship. His precise aims remain unclear, but it's likely that he had the Sacred War in mind during the talks. Ultimately, he knew that a resolution would only be possible if Athens was neutralised, with a peace and alliance he could bind their hands, further isolating the Phokians before a final offensive.

Macedonian kings had a reputation as a perfidious lot, saying one thing and doing another, double-dealers who exported lies by the shipload. Philip had proved true to the model when he took Amphipolis, promising it to Athens and then keeping it for himself.[65] But such was the mastery of his performance – his sound memory and eloquence – that the Athenians could not help but be impressed and were carried away with enthusiasm for peace. A possible agreement was outlined and a state banquet was later held in their honour. Demosthenes, even though a famous teetotaller, was able to observe first hand 'that they take pride in such hospitality as evidence of wealth and splendour'.[66] For Philip, it was nothing short of a diplomatic coup.

The embassy departed a week later. It was only the beginning of deliberations and they were required to present a formal report to the Council and Assembly in Athens on all that had taken place. They took with them a letter from Philip which echoed his friendly sentiments. During the return journey, Demosthenes talked to his fellow envoys, daring them to make good on relating their favourable impressions of the king to the people; this they duly did, saying among other things that he had an excellent memory, was fair to look upon, and was a great drinker to boot. But Demosthenes had tricked them, and this enabled him to present a more cynical portrait, one that was in keeping with his previous speeches and more favourable to the crowd. He rebutted their arguments by stating that the first quality 'was appropriate for a sophist, the second for a woman, and the third for a sponge, but none of them for a king'.[67]

Their arrival back in Athens was closely followed by three Macedonian ambassadors, Antipatros, Parmenion and Eurylochos, who were among Philip's most trusted men, and whose job it was to accept the Athenian oaths if peace and alliance were agreed. Demosthenes extended them every courtesy, personally entertaining them and putting in a motion to secure the guests front-row seats at the theatre, keen to show that Athenian hospitality could match that of the Argead court. The terms of the agreement, however, were a cause for contention. The crux of the matter was who exactly was to be included. The Phokians, Kersobleptes, and the Thessalian town of Halos, which Philip was still besieging, were not part of the Second Athenian League but had their own agreements with the city-state. A two-day Assembly session on the Pnyx was called to discuss and vote on the proposals. After some back and forth of opinion, it was decided to exclude the non-League allies, the Macedonian ambassadors having undoubtedly made it clear that these were the only conditions that Philip would accept. Macedon and Athens would keep whatever possessions they held at the time, while the Athenians, despite holding onto the Chersonese, were forced to concede that Amphipolis had well and truly been lost. The members of the original embassy reconvened and went north once more, this time to take the oaths of Philip and his allies.

They were slow in their departure, and internal divisions had already appeared. During the journey the others shunned Demosthenes, refusing to take their dinner with him and, where possible, to avoid overnighting in the same lodgings. They arrived back in Pella in May, while Philip was still away in Thrace, reducing Kersobleptes to vassal status, and they were soon joined by many more embassies: Thessalians, Thebans, Lakedaimonians (Spartans), and, intriguingly, Phokians.[68] The full scale of Philip's involvement in Greek affairs became all too evident. The Athenians, who had always considered themselves foremost of the Greeks, were now just one of the many dealing with Macedon.

Alexander was nine years old at the time and it is from these events that we get our first eyewitness account of the boy. Aeschines records that during their stay in Pella, the prince made an appearance as part of the after-dinner entertainment. He played the kithara, suggesting that he was already a proficient player, recited verses and debated with another boy who is sadly not identified, probably one of his foster-brothers with whom he was being raised. Although he was too young to take part in the drinking and conversation, his presence was a conspicuous display of the culture of the Macedonian court and the sophistication of the royal family. The embassy took notice of the boy's talents, and he was later discussed in Athens. Demosthenes had apparently made some lewd jokes at Alexander's expense – it was the beginning of a hostile relationship between the two – and Aeschines was accused of trying to seduce him. Despite his youth, Alexander was already being talked about outside Macedonia.[69]

When Philip returned to Pella he immediately set about preparing to march south to finish off the Sacred War. The Athenian embassy was given an audience once again, and this time Demosthenes was the first to speak. He gave a more assured performance but it was a sycophantic display, some of his colleagues hiding their faces in shame as he related all the good deeds he had done for the Macedonian ambassadors. Word had apparently reached Philip about some of the slanderous comments he had made to his fellow Athenians, and Demosthenes did his best to correct them, 'I did not say that you are beautiful, for a woman is the most beautiful of all beings; nor that you are a wonderful drinker, for that is a compliment for a sponge, in my opinion; nor that you have a remarkable memory, for I think such praise belongs to the professional sophist.'⁷⁰ Aeschines followed, and he addressed some of the larger issues at play regarding the fate of Phokians. He implored that it was only the leaders who should suffer punishment, and that Philip should not allow the Thebans to profit. The king's response was vague; he was playing a dangerous diplomatic game, hosting private talks with the various parties, carefully manoeuvring himself into a position of primacy. Through his Companions, numerous promises were relayed. Aeschines, was led to believe that Philip would follow his advice, while contrary assurances were probably given to the Thebans and Thessalians. There was an air of uneasiness and uncertainty surrounding the whole affair. Demosthenes began to cast a more discerning eye over the situation and became fearful for the future.

Philip kept the Athenians at Pella until he was ready for the campaign, stating that he needed their help to resolve the situation at Halos. He agreed to return their prisoners taken at Olynthos and elsewhere before the summertime festival of the Panathenaia, but until then they remained in his custody, although Demosthenes managed to pay the ransom for some of them, a good deed that he would make much of in the future.⁷¹ Philip also delayed giving the oaths needed to ratify the peace until he reached Pherai. By then it was too late for any reversals. The peace became known by the name of its lead member: Philokrates. The terms were inscribed on stone stelai and set up in Athens and Macedonia.

The embassy sailed back to their city having been away for more than two months. They delivered their report to the Council, Demosthenes apparently airing his concerns, saying that the delays had been costly and allowed Philip time to expand his position of power. He urged them not to give up Phokis or abandon Thermopylai. An Assembly was held the next day whereby another courteous letter from Philip was read out, apologising for the delays and giving assurances about his willingness to do the city a good turn. Aeschines also helped to put the people at ease, relating what he believed to be Philip's plans, and asserting that Athens would benefit from his actions. They moved a decree that the peace and alliance should be extended to Philip's descendants, also agreeing to help the Amphiktyons should the Phokians fail to surrender Delphi. Yet another embassy was convened to relay this latest development to Philip; this time Demosthenes made his excuses and did not go, while Aeschines may have feigned illness to ensure that his rival could not persuade the Assembly to go back on their decisions.

Philip's secret negotiations with the Phokians had paved the way for his advance into central Greece. They surrendered Thermopylai on his approach, the general Phalaikos withdrawing his 8,000 mercenaries, and the remaining Phokians quickly capitulated.[72] The Sacred War ended without further bloodshed. Athenian hopes of a lenient punishment for their allies were crushed when Philip placed the decision in the hands of the Amphiktyonic Council, which was loaded with hostile parties. The Phokian cities were split up, their membership of the Council revoked and heavy fines levied until Apollo's wealth had been restored, but in reality, it could have been much worse: the Oitians, who were among the Council's members, had wanted to kill all Phokian men of military age.[73] The Athenians felt duped and the peace was unpopular from the start. The agreement had produced no tangible benefits,

Amphipolis had been lost, their Phokian allies had been destroyed, Theban power, far from being curbed, was now back in the ascendancy and Philip had won control of the Thermopylai pass. For a time, they even thought their city under threat from a Macedonian attack; a decree was passed to evacuate the countryside and strengthen the surrounding forts. Further assurances from the king alleviated their immediate concerns, but the aftermath led to bitter feelings in the city. Divisions among the original embassy members began to widen. Demosthenes quickly distanced himself from the peace, his anti-Macedonian rhetoric finding a welcome audience; it soon made him the most influential man in the city.

As a reward for his role in ending the war, Philip was handed the two Phokian votes on the Amphiktyonic Council, giving him a future say in the affairs of mainland Greece, as well as the privilege of *promanteia*, the right to consult the Oracle first, bumping the Athenians from the top of the list.[74] In some capacity he also presided over the Pythian Games at Delphi, which had not been held for almost a decade, an event that the Athenian officials decided to boycott.[75]

A symbolic procession made the lengthy trek up the towering Phaidriades, the shining rocks that form the spectacular backdrop to the sacred city of Delphi. The Phokian weapons were thrown into a chasm, the war was over.[76] As the iron clattered and clanged into the depths, the Amphiktyons could reflect on the sorry state of the sanctuary. The treasuries stood empty, the temple of Apollo dug up in the search for hidden treasure; even the famous golden tripod that commemorated the Greek victory over the Persians at Plataia in 479 BC had not escaped destruction. It had been melted down, used to buy more mercenaries; only the distinctive serpentine column of bronze – nine metres tall and inscribed with the names of the defenders – remained standing.[77] The trophy's shattered form, its finery wrenched apart, could easily be seen as a metaphor for the fractious nature of the city-states. Together they could resist the strongest of tyrants and achieve glorious things but, more often than not, their inherent animosity towards each other kept them apart, and could even lead to horrifying acts that wounded the very heart of *Hellas*. Philip's experience dealing with the different powers would be invaluable in the years to come. The great renown that he had won during the Sacred War added to his rising status.

Back in Pella, Alexander was growing up in a changing world. Macedon now played a leading role in Greek affairs, Philip had become the most powerful individual in the Balkans and Greece. As he neared the end of his elementary education Alexander played the kithara for his father at a symposion. According to Plutarch, Philip became concerned. 'Are you not ashamed to play as well as that?' he said.[78] Alexander was clearly spending too much time on music rather than other manlier pursuits, and he is not mentioned playing the instrument again. His military training would intensify over the coming years. The riches of the royal court continued to attract the finest men of the age and the next stage of his life would become famous for new friends, among them antiquity's greatest thinker, and one extraordinary horse.

4.

FRIENDS

When Alexander was around eleven years old the Thessalian horse-dealer, Philoneikos, came to the Macedonian court.[1] He brought with him an exceptional specimen, a Pharsalian stallion valued at an astronomical thirteen talents.[2] The king and his entourage, which included the young Alexander, went down to the nearest pasture to appraise the beast. The horses of Classical Greece were small by modern-day standards, only rarely reaching fifteen hands in height, but they were stocky, with barrel-like bodies, thick necks and small elegant heads.[3] The Thessalians, with their large arable estates and renowned cavalry, had succeeded in breeding Greece's finest. Philoneikos' animal, probably bay or chestnut coated rather than black, was notable for its large size and noble spirit.[4] It had already been broken in, but, on this occasion, was skittish, rising up on its hind legs and refusing the royal grooms close enough proximity to mount. After a number of failed attempts Philip grew angry, believing the horse too wild to ride. He ordered it to be led away. Alexander thought differently. 'What a horse they are losing and all because they don't know how to handle him, or dare not try!' he complained, making sure he was within earshot of his father. Philip held his tongue for the time being, but Alexander went on making his scorn known to everyone around him. Eventually, Philip snapped. 'Are you finding fault with your elders because you think you know more than they do, or can manage a horse better?'

'At least I could manage this one better,' said Alexander.

Philip turned to his young son, probably with a mixture of apprehension and disbelief. 'And if you cannot?. . . what penalty will you pay for being so impertinent?'

'I will pay the price of the horse,' Alexander cockily replied.

A chuckle rippled around the crowd. How could the boy be expected to succeed where more experienced handlers had failed? Was he mad or really that arrogant? But Plutarch, who provides the fullest account of the story, reveals the secret source of Alexander's confidence. He had spotted what no one else had – the horse was shying at its own shadow. Alexander approached, probably not rushing to its side as Plutarch records but moving slowly and cautiously, so as to not threaten the animal, following the advice recorded in ancient equitation manuals.[5] When he was close enough, he managed to take hold of the bridle-rein and turned the horse to face the sun, away from its fretful shadow. It took a little time to settle, Alexander followed its movements, running alongside for some way, soft words and caresses cooling its heated spirit. Carefully setting aside his *chlamys* cloak, he waited for the right moment. Then, in one quick effortless motion, he mounted and gathered in the reins, all the time making sure not to tear at the horse's bit. Once sure that he had gained the horse's trust, he raised his voice and urged him on with a swift kick in the sides. They took off, boy and beast, for their first ride together. Philip and his Companions were uneasy, scared for the lad whose fall would not just be a blow to his confidence but could cause painful injury. Their fear abated when they saw Alexander handling the horse with great skill before, making the proper turns, he raced back to the waiting crowd. They cheered the young prince and

Philip was said to have actually shed tears of joy. When Alexander dismounted he kissed him and said the prophetic words, 'My boy, you must find a kingdom which is your equal. Macedonia is too small for you.'

The bet being won, Philoneikos got his money, the fee perhaps being paid not by Philip but Demaratos of Corinth, an aristocrat visiting from the Peloponnese who was on friendly terms with both father and son.[6] Thessalian horse breeds were branded with different marks identifying the region they came from. The Centaur was linked with those produced from around Larissa, the Axe with Pherai. Alexander's new horse was probably named after the Pharsalian sign of the ox-head that was burned into his side – Boukephalas.[7] He remained Alexander's equine companion throughout his life, the start of their relationship as incredible as their later adventures. He was by all accounts a remarkable animal. Once adorned with his regal finery he would allow only Alexander to mount him. When he was kidnapped by hostile tribesmen near the Caspian Sea, Alexander threatened to wipe out the entire population unless he was returned unharmed, which he duly was. Boukephalas reportedly lived for thirty years, enduring the hardships of march and battle, carrying his master to the ends of the known world. He died in 326 BC on the banks of the Hydaspes (Jhelum) river in modern-day Pakistan, worn out with age and toil. Alexander was deeply grieved by the loss. He held a funeral for his beloved horse, leading the procession himself, and a city named in the animal's honour – Alexandria Boukephala – was built around the tomb.[8]

This anecdote reveals many insights into the young Alexander – his consummate horse-riding abilities from an early age and an understanding of animal psychology, his tremendous self-belief and willingness to take risks on the large stage. It also provides a rare glimpse of Philip and Alexander's relationship – it is one of youthful exuberance rewarded with fatherly pride. It was, perhaps, the first sign that he was no ordinary child. Plutarch says that Philip, on observing his son's potential, 'would not wholly entrust the direction and training of the boy to the ordinary teachers of poetry and the formal studies, feeling that it was a matter of too great importance'.⁹ He had found Alexander an exceptional horse, he would also provide him with an exceptional teacher.

Stageira, in the Chalkidike, occupies a rocky double-hilled promontory on the eastern side of the peninsula, north of Athos. It was founded by settlers from the island of Andros in the seventh century BC and was a prosperous city in the Archaic and Classical eras.¹⁰ The site faces towards the sea, the main source of trade and communication for so many of the region's Greek colonies, and is surrounded on all sides by cascades of forested green that flow down the steep slopes, plunging into the Aegean with a few protected beaches of burning sand in between. Clouds of dusky butterflies inhabit the shaded woodland fringes, nightingales sing in the thickets, and it is hard not to be instantly charmed by the setting. Dense vegetation made archaeological work difficult, extensive excavation not taking place until the 1990s. Nine successive seasons of digging have subsequently located the main buildings and infrastructure of the settlement. The site has now been made visitor friendly with creosoted wooden walkways and information boards.

Ancient buildings await around every corner, set among the bushes that thrum with the rasping chorus of cicadas. The settlement's layout recalls modern villages and towns of the Greek islands, with walls grafted onto rock, winding streets of paved stones and incredible views of the sea – civilisation in harmony with the natural beauty of the surroundings. Some Classical houses have been exposed to the east of the agora, terraced into the slope with a narrow alley scoured down to the bedrock running between the properties, overlooked by venerable olive trees. The best-preserved house had its own sheltered courtyard leading onto the kitchen and men's dining room. The upper storey boasted magnificent views south along the wild coastline, a scene once replete with vignettes of ancient life – women praying at the sanctuaries set on the promontory's edge, fishermen hauling in their daily catch, citizens shuffling off to Council meetings while children played in one of the many idyllic coves, collecting sea urchins and crabs. It was in a house like this, in 384 BC, that Aristotle was born.

Aristotle was one of antiquity's most brilliant minds. He wrote over a hundred and fifty treatises on everything from cosmology to politics, meteorology to the soul, animals to the arts; he was

Aristotle, Athens Archaeological Museum

just as comfortable picking apart the plot of a tragedy as the innards of a cuttlefish. He was the third link in the chain of great minds of the Classical age – Socrates, Plato, Aristotle – and among his most famous teachings was the need to strive for moderation in all things, the 'Golden Mean' as it was later known. He once wrote that 'All men by nature desire to know', but what sets him apart from his lofty predecessors was his empirical approach to topics.[11] He was a great amasser of information, cataloguing and classifying all that he saw in the world around him. Philosophy means 'the love of wisdom' and Aristotle was its embodiment.[12]

He spent his early years in Stageira and may have also visited Pella where his father, Nikomachos, a prominent physician, had served at the court of Amyntas III; Aristotle's life was to be forever intertwined with the affairs of Macedon. It was perhaps at his father's side, among the blood and guts, fevers and fits, that a passion for the inner workings of life was nurtured. But Aristotle was not to follow Nikomachos' path; his parents died while he was still young and Proxenos from Atarneus took over his guardianship. At the age of seventeen he was sent to Athens, to the Academy – an extraordinary community dedicated to higher learning, headed by the renowned philosopher Plato. It was a move that would come to define his life. He stayed for a further twenty years, earning a reputation for his voracious thirst for knowledge; he became known as 'The Reader'.[13] Natural sciences, astronomy and the collection of proverbs were some of the subjects that formed his early studies; towards the end of his tenure he took to teaching a course on rhetoric.

But in 348/7 BC everything changed. The Chalkidike war flooded Athens with refugees, stirring up animosity towards the Macedonians. Stageira had been caught up in the fighting and was sacked by Philip in 349 BC; slingshots inscribed with his name and those of his generals have been found on-site.[14] For Aristotle, a man with family links to the Argeads, Athens became a dangerous place to stay. Around the same time Plato died and there was little to keep Aristotle in the city, so he decided to relocate. The court of Hermeias – tyrant of Atarneus and Assos – on the coast of Asia Minor in modern-day Turkey, was his destination. He had met Hermeias at the Academy where they became close friends, and he later married his adopted daughter or niece, Pythias. After his lengthy stint studying at the Academy, this was a time for active field-work. He joined a community of philosophers at Assos and may have helped draw up new laws of governance. At nearby Lesbos, he stayed with another fellow intellectual, Theophrastus, who shared Aristotle's fascination for the natural world. Together, at the inland lagoon of Pyrrha (Kalloni), the two indulged their passion, interrogating the local fishermen, dissecting the daily catch and roaming the shores for specimens, the research becoming part of their respective works on zoology and botany.[15] In 343/2 BC, the invitation for Alexander's tutorship arrived from Macedon.

Philip was no stranger to the world of philosophy. It was said that during his time as a hostage in Thebes he came into contact with the principles of Pythagoras.[16] Plato had also sent one of his Academic pupils, Euphraios, to the court of Perdikkas III – Philip's older brother – to aid him with his early kingship. Euphraios' presence was not wholly appreciated by the majority of Macedonians. It was said that he organised life within the inner circle in a pedantic fashion – only those individuals who understood geometry and philosophy could dine with the king. His stay, however, did have one key benefit for Philip. Euphraios persuaded Perdikkas to give his younger brother a piece of territory to control, probably around Amphipolis. It was this act that allowed Philip to establish his credentials as a leader and to build loyalty in the army; he was, therefore, perfectly placed to take control when Perdikkas was killed in battle against the Illyrians.[17] Philip remained an admirer of Plato and reportedly paid him honours at his death, but it was probably Aristotle's links with the Macedonian royal family rather than his Academic background that made him the favoured candidate to be Alexander's tutor.[18] Philip secured his appointment with a noble and appropriate fee for his services.[19] He also agreed to rebuild his home town of Stageira, perhaps on further petition from Alexander.[20] Archaeologists have traced a late Classical wall on the north-eastern edge of the northern hill that dates from this time. It delinated an area slightly smaller than the city's former boundaries, and is an indication that, despite the new investment, Stageira's heyday was over. It was deserted by the end of the first century BC.[21]

The coming together of the young Alexander and Aristotle is an extraordinary occurrence. Some have thought it too good to be true, but it is true, although romance has the habit of overwhelming the rather meagre facts.[22] Part of the problem is that later ancient writers looked back to this moment, colouring it with new significance in the light of the grand achievements of both individuals. But at the time, Alexander was just a young prince, thirteen or fourteen years old, and Aristotle a wandering philosopher in his early forties; neither was famous. The relationship was probably only of interest to those directly involved.

Plutarch records that it was not at Pella that Alexander was to be educated by Aristotle but at Mieza, on the slopes of Mount Vermion that rises on the western edge of the Emathia plain. The remains of the ancient city are now set within an intensive fruit-growing region. Peaches, nectarines, apricots, grapes and apples ripen here with Atalantian speed; the summertime roads rumble with aged 4x4s stacked high with the latest produce, the satisfied song of plump blackbirds rings through every orchard. Among the rich palette of colours it is green and blue that predominate. Homer called it 'lovely Emathia', today the locals know it as a paradise.[23] Plutarch, who is the only ancient author to connect Aristotle and

Alexander with Mieza, goes on to say that Philip assigned master and pupil the sanctuary of the nymphs – the Nymphaion – for their studies near Mieza. In Plutarch's day, during the second century AD, tourists were still shown the stone seats and shady walks of Aristotle's school.[24] It was rediscovered in the mid 1960s by Photios Petsas, at Isvoria, close to the Arapitsa river, perhaps the ancient Astraios, where Macedonian fishermen once caught trout by using artificial flies, the first historically attested people to use the technique.[25] It consists of a large outcrop of volcanic rock that had been worked back by human hand, with a number of caves set along its length. Between the back wall and pooling springs of looking-glass transparency, there was space for some basic structures, primarily a stoa or covered walkway that was attached to the rock face and supported by Ionic columns. The discovery of a decorative terracotta roof gutter provided a fourth century BC date. Whether visiting in the spring, when the countryside is set alight with the purples, pinks and whites of blossoming fruit trees, or in the autumn, when shrivelled leaves fall like snow on the earthen paths, the Nymphaion never loses its ability to bewitch. The nymphs may have departed, but sitting amid the wild figs, the fallen fruit adding a fermenting tang to the air, it's easy to conjure the ghosts of Alexander and Aristotle – the squeak of sandals under the shaded walkway, boys sleeping in caves, philosopher and prince setting the world to rights on a hot and humid afternoon.

There remain, however, some nagging concerns. Not with the identity of the site as a Nymphaion – that seems almost certain – but with the theory that it functioned as Aristotle's school. It's inescapable that it closely resembles an ancient quarry; there is one area of deep excavation and even some roughed-out blocks yet to be prised from the bedrock. Other similar quarries have since been found dotted around the slopes of Vermion; the mountain provided a ready source of building material and was

The Nymphaion at Mieza (Isvoria)

duly exploited. But before Philip there was a distinct lack of monumental buildings in Macedonia. It seems likely, therefore, that the quarrying activity dates to his reign and the great projects he inaugurated, funded by the spoils of war. The covered walkway came later, and in all probability the Nymphaion did not exist during the mid 340s BC. It is also generally accepted that Alexander and Aristotle were not alone, and that other boys, the prince's foster-brothers, were also present.[26] Where did they eat, exercise and train? In other words where is the infrastructure? Where is the reality that must always be sought beneath the romance? These questions have recently led to another candidate for Aristotle's school to emerge.

In the 1970s, excavations took place a couple of kilometres north-east of the Nymphaion, between Kopanos and Lefkadia close to the core of ancient Mieza. A colossal public building complex was discovered among the orchards, occupying an area some 300 x 150 metres.[27] It was constructed over numerous levels that were terraced into the slope; in its lower reaches was a grand entranceway, its interior corridor lined with a false façade of semi-columns, while a ramp led upwards towards a small temple-shaped building and a Doric stoa with mosaic floors. On the level above was a large peristyle or courtyard building, with suites of banqueting rooms occupying the north and west wings, richly appointed with bronze door fittings, Doric pillars and marble thresholds. A small theatre was later revealed further to the south-west.

The complex dates to the second half of the fourth century BC and has been identified as a sanctuary to the healing god Asklepios, located in the ancient agora of Mieza. But recently, archaeologist Angeliki Kottaridi has been reconsidering the evidence. She noted that a series of oblong rooms, adjoining the peristyle building, look remarkably similar to known Hellenistic barracks, and that the architecture closely resembles that found in Macedonian palaces. Kottaridi believes that this grandiose structure was built by Philip and that it was no agora sanctuary but a new school for the royal pages, a state-funded facility that provided the infrastructure necessary to train and educate the elite youths of Macedon, the real backdrop to Alexander's stay at Mieza.[28]

The complex was destroyed in the first decades of the third century BC, a likely result of the Celtic invasion recorded at the time, and Mieza never really recovered, although it remained sparsely populated into the fourth century AD. Kottaridi suggests that it was the destruction of the school that led to Aristotle being associated with the nearby Nymphaion, which was chosen because of its aesthetic appeal and surviving architecture, a connection perhaps fostered by the locals in order to please visiting Roman tourists. Only more digging will bring confirmation of these ideas but it remains a fascinating new direction for Macedonian archaeology. Moreover, it prompts a reconsideration of Alexander's secondary education, one that is more in keeping with the context of the time.

Philip, it was said, had the highest respect for education, a statement that is supported by the army of tutors that surrounded Alexander from an early age and the important role of the royal pages during his reign.[29] With his increasing conquests and alliances, he expanded the institution, perhaps incorporating influences from places such as Thebes, Sparta and Athens. It was designed to transform aristocratic boys into men – men who could be of benefit to king and kingdom – and combined liberal studies with a tough physical regime that prepared them for life in the army. It became the Sandhurst or West Point of its day.

The gymnasion was the focus for higher education in the Greek world. Athens, for example, had three such public facilities. They were magnets for the city's youth who went there to practise athletics, meet friends and pursue love interests – they've been called the leisure centres of the ancient world.[30] Thanks to their situation outside the walls, the open countryside and surrounding groves provided space for relaxation as well as horse training and muster points for the army. Sophists and philosophers followed the youngsters, keen to earn some money or attract new pupils. One of these gymnasia was located at the Academy, and Plato lived in its vicinity, another was at the Lyceum, where Aristotle taught on his return to Athens in 335 BC. The Mieza facility has many elements that parallel those found in other gymnasia and appears as a prototype for similar complexes found in later Hellenistic royal cities. It was a single architectural conception, the buildings providing accommodation, training and teaching areas for the boys, the spaces embodying Greek educational ideals for adolescents – fitness of the body continued to go hand-in-hand with that of the mind. Mieza was well placed to function as a new

school for the pages, carefully removed from the twin capitals of
Aigai and Pella but within a short ride of both. It offered ample
space for their training and benefited from cooler summer temperatures; it may also have doubled as a countryside retreat for the
royal court.

Scholars have attempted to reconstruct the various stages that
comprised this cultural and educational institution.[31] It has been
suggested that the selected sons of Macedonian noblemen started
the programme at fourteen or fifteen. They were pages for four
years, the final year comprising personal service to the king.[32] At
eighteen they became *ephebes*, spending a further two years training
and forming the royal foot guard of the king on state occasions.
On turning twenty they were enrolled in the army at the springtime Xandika, taking their oaths of allegiance and later joining
the ranks of Companion cavalry or other prestigious units. Such
was the success of this programme that it prompted one ancient
writer to reflect: 'never before that time did Macedonia, or indeed
any other nation, produce so rich a crop of brilliant men.'[33]

The size of the Mieza complex may hint at the number of boys
that participated in the programme under Philip. Most of the
archaeological remains have been backfilled for their protection,
but as you walk across the site something of its enormous scale
can be grasped. Each of the eleven banqueting rooms discovered
so far could hold seven couches, with two people sitting on each;
the simple arithmetic suggests there was space for over one hundred
and fifty diners. This number tallies with references in the ancient
sources which suggest fifty boys to a year group, the oldest boys
being attached to the king's retinue.[34] Although Alexander is never
mentioned as participating in the programme it seems highly likely
that he did, and during the Hellenistic period it became common
for royal children to serve as pages.[35] However, as Philip's most
capable son, he was fast-tracked through the system, taking up his

first position of responsibility at sixteen. With these considerations, previous ideas of an idyllic youth spent with only his close friends under the direction of Aristotle vanishes, replaced by a much more nuanced picture, with potentially over a hundred and fifty boys training alongside him in a school alive with specialist staff, cooks, grooms and attendants. Aristotle's presence at the Macedonian court has long overshadowed the physical aspect of Alexander's upbringing, which focused on horse-riding, conditioning of the body and other skills that were transferrable to the military arena. Leonidas had supervised this side of his physical education from boyhood, with long marches and meagre rations, and it would continue at Mieza.

THE BODY

The study of gymnasia and their role within Macedonian society has undergone rapid advancement in recent years.[36] Two inscriptions in particular have proved of exceptional value in providing a flavour of their organisation – the gymnasiarchical law of Beroia (modern Veroia) and the ephebarchical law of Amphipolis. Both date to the late royal period and are attributed to decrees put in place by the penultimate Macedonian king, Philip V. [37] During his reign (221–179 BC) he faced growing pressure from the expansion of Roman power into Greece and the Balkans. He used gymnasia at a grassroots level to recruit and train the next generation of troops. The laws are incredibly detailed and outline the different age groups which attended: *paides* (14/15–18), *ephebes* (18–20) and *neaniskoi* (20–30). The gymnasia come across as strictly regimented spaces; no slaves, drunks, or men of vulgar trades were allowed entry. It was forbidden to exercise in another facility and there were three reviews a year to monitor each attendee's progress. The gym master (gymnasiarch) was in ultimate control, and had the power to impose fines and even flog those that fell out of line. The most important date in the calendar was the Hermaia or festival of Hermes, who along with Herakles was a patron of gymnasia. Prizes were awarded for discipline, diligence, good physical condition and victories in foot and torch races. Sadly, the part of the Beroia inscription dealing with the training of the *paides* has not survived, although javelin throwing and archery are mentioned as daily exercises for the older *ephebes*. The Amphipolis law provides more detail. It outlines the ephebic programme, which may have been similar to that of the *paides*. Sessions took place twice a day, from sunrise to sunset with a break for lunch, and were overseen by the gym master's specialist staff. In the morning they were taken out into the countryside to practise horse-riding, archery, javelin throwing, the use of slings, and stone throwing, while in the afternoon they returned to the gym to repeat the same exercises, with the exception of horse-riding. No liberal studies are mentioned; by this time Macedonian education was purely militaristic and was designed to quickly produce fighters who could be called on to defend their cities and kingdom.

Those who have studied the texts have drawn attention to similarities that exist between the laws and descriptions of education, both real and idealised, in the works of Xenophon, Plato and Aristotle.[38] Philip V, it seems, was using the lessons of the past to help shape his policies. He was also an admirer of his Macedonian predecessors, on one occasion requesting a special edition of Theopompus' *Philippic Histories* for his personal reading.[39] There is the tantalising possibility that these epigraphic records contain echoes of the regime undertaken by the royal pages in the mid fourth century BC, which finds some corroboration in references to Alexander's tough militaristic upbringing; 'it is universally acknowledged that from his childhood he was well versed and trained in the art of war,' says Polybius, a Greek historian writing in the second century BC, while Plutarch adds that Alexander 'trained himself always to be formidable in arms'.[40]

During their adolescence, the boys probably also gained some knowledge of tactics and the history of warfare. In the fourth century BC, literary compilations filled with examples of good generalship began to widely circulate, along with specialised military manuals that dealt with aspects as diverse as how to survive a siege and wartime financing.[41] Group fights and mock battles, a practice attested in both Sparta and Crete, may also have played a role, along with ball games such as *episkyros*, where two opposing teams of around twelve to fourteen players would attempt to push the ball over the goal line of their opposition – perfect training for army cohesion. Alexander is later recorded as being a keen ball player.[42] Athletics continued to be practised and festivals such as the Hermaia and Dion's Olympia provided stages for the boys to win individual acclaim among their peers. A growing collection of inscriptions dated to the fourth century BC attests to the importance of foot and horse races in Macedonia, which probably marked the graduation from one age group to the next. These contests formed one of the many rites of passage that marked the route to adulthood.[43]

It was a tradition among the Argeads to take part in Pan-Hellenic games. Alexander I had been the first to do so. He gained consent to participate in the Olympics by proving his Greekness to the ruling authorities, recounting the story of Perdikkas I and his descent from the Argive Temenos. Herodotus says that he came joint first in the foot race.[44] Archelaos and Philip also entered their horses and riders in the equine competitions, winning a number of races. But Alexander, although reportedly a fast runner, was not so keen to take part. He later countered the suggestion by saying he would only do so if he could have kings as his fellow competitors, his reasoning being that the contest was unfair because 'it was one in which a victory would be over commoners, but a defeat would be the defeat of a king.'[45] His unwillingness to enter or even attend such Pan-Hellenic events may be a reaction to his father's interest in athletics, especially wrestling, and his intimidating record at the games.[46] Plutarch says that although Alexander held many athletic contests among his army during his reign, along with competitions in hunting and fighting with staves, he took no interest in offering prizes for boxing or the pankration – a no-holds-barred form of wrestling. Plutarch prefaces this information with the statement that Alexander actually disapproved of athletes as a whole.[47] This claim may seem a little paradoxical considering his patronage of numerous games but there had long been sceptical views on career athletes, with their seemingly gluttonous body-building diets and tailor-made regimens. These hostile views intensified in the fourth century BC with the growing divide between 'professional' athletes and soldiers. Athletics was by now moving into the realm of pure entertainment with many dedicating their lives to competing at the games, becoming the sports stars of the ancient world. This naturally provoked resentment and rivalry between the two professions, one seeking renown on the battlefield, the other on track and field.[48] Alexander would always favour the former. Indeed, it was said that he desired a very particular type of fame, not that of a victorious athlete or eloquent speaker, but one that came with leading a life extraordinary, one drenched in glory, like the heroes of old.[49]

The various physical activities in which the boys partook succeeded in creating tough individuals whose skills could be readily transferred into battle. Arms training accustomed them to handling weapons, athletics helped condition the body, while mock fights and ball games developed teamwork. Horse-riding too remained an important part of their time at Mieza, preparing them for their role in the cavalry, the boys racing across the Emathian plain, practising attack formations which took rigorous training to perfect, the drumming of hooves sounding like distant thunder as Alexander and Boukephalas learned the skills necessary to lead the charge.

Mieza's many exquisite Macedonian tombs, for which it is famous, are a lasting testament to the area's history in producing formidable warriors. The interior of Lyson and Kallikles' is adorned with frescoes depicting numerous panoplies of arms – swords, shields, greaves, helmets and cuirasses. The so-called 'Kinch' tomb revealed one of the most detailed images of a Macedonian cavalry-man ever found, captured mid-gallop by the painter, about to skewer an enemy foot-soldier. But the most magnificent tomb in Mieza is that of the Judgement, discovered in 1954 and subsequently restored. It can be visited today, concealed inside a metal building which has a passing resemblance to an aircraft hangar. Its painted façade evokes a palace of the dead; a battle frieze believed to depict fighting between Macedonians and Persians runs across the upper storey. On either side of the doorway are painted figures. A deceased warrior is depicted in military dress, with spear in hand and white cuirass with purple trim. Hermes, who guided the dead to the underworld, stands beside him. The man's life is in the process of being judged by Aiakos, the god responsible for deciding the fate of those from Europe, and Rhadamanthys who did the same for those from Asia. A possible candidate for the tomb is Peukestas, a Companion of Alexander who had saved the king's life in India and was honoured by being appointed an eighth bodyguard. He was originally from Mieza and may have returned later in life to his home town, where he was eventually buried. The dual images of the judges reflect a life spent straddling continents, the legacy of Macedonian military supremacy.

THE MIND

Aristotle's Macedonian pupils must have been somewhat different to those from the Academy or the court of Hermeias; boisterous, competitive, all dressed in the uniform of aristocratic boys – *kausia*, *chlamys* and *krepides* – perhaps already physically imposing, as straight and tall as *sarissas*. Alexander, who inherited his father's compact frame, must have looked small in comparison. Conversely, from the boys' perspective, Aristotle was probably not what they were expecting. His biographers record that he had a penchant for finger rings and wore elaborate clothing and shoes – a dedicated follower of ancient fashion – although his surviving portraits makes him look more like a gruff than a dandy. Some sources suggest that he spoke with a lisp and the thinness of his legs was apparently matched by the smallness of his eyes.[50] He strongly appreciated the value of a good education, with natural ability, study and practice being the keys to success. When asked how the educated differ from the uneducated, he is said to have replied, 'as much as the living from the dead'.[51] But, at the same time, he was rather dismissive of the youth of his day. 'Now the young are by character appetitive and of a kind to do whatever they should desire,' he writes in his work on rhetoric, 'they are irate and hot-tempered and of a kind to harken to anger . . . they think they know everything and are obstinate.'[52] 'The roots of education are bitter, but the fruit is sweet' was apparently one of his favourite sayings, surely the musing of a teacher who had endured his fair share of tricky pupils. Discipline was needed in order to stop their wits from going wool-gathering.[53] Another recorded piece of advice suggests that he had little time for those who were slow on the uptake. When once asked about how students could best make progress in their studies he replied, 'By pressing hard on those in front and not waiting for those behind.'[54]

It's not known how many boys were taught by Aristotle at Mieza, perhaps only the inner circle around Alexander or those that could be lured away from their exercises in the gymnasion. Considering Alexander's costly education up to this point, he was unlikely to have been one of the stragglers, and it's easy to imagine him being the class know-it-all, keen to prove himself better than his peers, and perhaps even his new master. The *Alexander Romance* plays with this idea. The prince rebuked Aristotle as he went around the pupils, asking what favours they would bestow on him when they inherited their fathers' positions. 'Are you already asking me about things that will happen in the future,' replied Alexander, 'when you have no certainty about what will happen tomorrow?'[55] Although such stories are literary fiction, the two may not have seen eye-to-eye on many things. In their later lives they certainly had different opinions about a range of issues, including relations with barbarians, the best way to live – for Aristotle it was the life of quiet contemplation, for Alexander that of action – and the nature of the divine. One fragment from a lost work on philosophy reports that the prince grumbled to Philip about his master, scorning his discourses that refuted Nikagoras, a tyrant of Zeleia, and his claim that he was the incarnation of the god Hermes – Alexander evidently thought differently – a rare insight into his early religious outlook.[56] However, the bond between pupil and master in antiquity was a special one, and there is no reason to disbelieve that their relationship was amiable, even one of affection. Plutarch, always keen to stress Alexander's philosophical side, says that he came to love and admire Aristotle, in some ways more than Philip, because whereas one had given him life, the other taught him how to lead a noble life.[57]

Those wanting to experience something of the essence of these Aristotelian lectures need look no further than the philosopher's surviving corpus, which takes up a sizeable chunk of shelving in any bookshop or library. Unfortunately, none of his public works, greatly admired in antiquity for their charm and eloquence, have survived; what remains, estimated to be only a fifth of what he wrote in his lifetime, is believed to represent his lecture notes. They can be rough and endlessly test the concentration – the eighteenth-century poet Thomas Gray likened reading them to eating dried hay.[58] The modern reader is faced with the same challenges as his ancient pupils who listened to their master as they strolled around the school's shaded porticos. It is easy to get distracted, especially when we lack the opportunity to ask the additional questions that may have clarified any discussions. Nevertheless, those willing to endure and to follow the train of argument are rewarded with moments of incisive and original thinking. In the context of the fourth century BC they were bold, challenging and, in many places, extraordinary. This practice of walking and talking was to define the Aristotelian approach to philosophy. He and his successors were known as Peripatetics, which comes from the Greek 'to walk around'. According to one tradition, the idea had originally been conceived in Macedonia. Diogenes Laertius, who wrote a life of Aristotle, mentions that while Alexander was recovering from an illness he was joined by his teacher on his daily walks, and the two discussed a range of topics to help pass the time, the movement of the body proving conducive to stimulating the mind.[59]

What exactly was on the Mieza curriculum has long been an issue for debate. The period is not directly referenced in any of Aristotle's surviving works. Plutarch, in his *Life of Alexander*, mentions ethical and political doctrines, which is a fair guess. The stepladder to becoming a virtuous man was a fundamental

Aristotelian concern; his surviving treatises the *Nicomachean* and *Eudemian Ethics* are among his most enduring works. The study of politics, too, is to be expected. During his lifetime, Aristotle organised the collection of over one hundred and fifty city-state constitutions, as an aid to understanding the machinations of different types of government. That subject was more relevant than ever in the light of Macedon's entrance into wider Greek affairs. They complemented his famous work, the *Politics*, in which he interrogates the different constitutions in a masterclass of political philosophy. The bulk of this material is believed to have been produced during his residency at the Lyceum (335–323/2 BC), but it undoubtedly reflects a lifetime's worth of research and interest, and one late source attributes Philip and Alexander as the original funders of the research.[60] How much the pupils took on board is another matter. Aristotle once wrote that 'a young man is not a fit person to attend lectures on political science, because he is not versed in the practical business of life from which politics draws its premisses and subject-matter.'[61]

One of Aristotle's Athenian rivals provides a precious contemporary insight into another subject that was practised at Mieza. Isocrates was an aged teacher and head of a prestigious school in Athens that specialised in public speaking. He preached the benefits of his own educational system – designed to train young men for the realities of political and civic life – while pouring scorn on the Academics who, in his view, prattled away the day on theoretical matters. In around 342 BC, he wrote a letter to Alexander, couched in highly diplomatic language and with the bitter flavour of sour grapes; Philip's choice of an Academic associate as Alexander's tutor rather than one of Isocrates' followers, such as Theopompus, who also spent time at the Macedonian court, probably explains the context.[62] In the letter Isocrates urges Alexander to give up eristics (arguing a topic from both sides) in favour of his own approach to rhetoric. What exactly Alexander made of this is not recorded, but it must have been flattering to know that his education was a source of interest to the leading minds of the age.

Isocrates, however, had failed to appreciate the value of this practice in Macedonian society, where freedom of speech between king and countrymen was a prized asset. Debating a topic from both sides of the argument trained the mind in the art of deliberation. It allowed the student to weigh up the pros and cons of any subject, enabling him to make an informed final decision. It also fostered competition, each youth wanting to claim victory, and was an important part of Aristotle's approach to rhetoric which aimed to combine wisdom with oratorical eloquence.[63]

Eristics evidently remained popular with Alexander and his friends and they continued the practice during their time in Asia. During one drinking party, Kallisthenes, Aristotle's relative and the campaign's official historian, was invited to attend. The men were making their own entertainment and when the communal cup came around to him, he was bidden to speak in praise of the Macedonians. Kallisthenes gave a rousing speech, which was such a success that he was given a standing ovation, the men throwing their garlands at him in honour. Alexander was pleased with the performance but thought the challenge too easy, quoting a line from Euripides' *Bacchae*: 'A noble subject, it is easy to speak well!'[64] He then gave Kallisthenes a harder and more dangerous task. 'But show us the power of your eloquence . . . by a denunciation of the Macedonians, that they may become even better by learning their faults.' Kallisthenes acquiesced, but this was not Mieza; around the room were a now hardened set of warriors. Aristotle apparently said that he lacked common sense, and Kallisthenes momentarily forgot who he was dealing with.[65] He launched into a bitter harangue against the Macedonians. Faces dropped in stunned silence. What really got their blood boiling was Kallisthenes' assertion that it was only division among the Greeks that had allowed Philip to rise to power, reciting the proverb 'But in a time of sedition, the base man too is in honour.'[66] Kallisthenes, Alexander declared, had given proof, 'not of his eloquence, but of his ill-will towards the Macedonians'. His days were numbered.

A few other subjects can also be added to the Mieza curriculum with some certainty. Plutarch mentions the healing arts, a conclusion based on some letters that described Alexander coming to the aid of his Companions with suggestions of treatments and regimens.[67] The letters on which Plutarch drew may not have been genuine – unbeknown to him, many forgeries circulated among the epistolary corpus – but they probably embellished an existing tradition. That Alexander had some knowledge of medicine was to be expected. A Macedonian king was responsible for the health of his people both in peacetime and war; he was also the direct intermediary with the healing gods. Illness and injury were commonplace and it was prudent to know the curative properties of certain plants.[68] An early interest may also have been fostered by Philip the Akarnanian, a physician who was the guardian of his health from boyhood, as well as Olympias who was always concerned about the well-being of her son.

There could be no more appropriate place to study medicine than among the foothills of Mount Vermion. Its rich diversity of floral species made it a pharmaceutical wonderland; it was once known colloquially as the 'Gardens of Midas' – a name connected with the Phrygians who were believed to have occupied the area in the distant past – and it has retained Nature's golden touch.[69] Aristotle, along with his colleague Theophrastus, who accompanied him to Mieza, continued their biological research in this bountiful setting. They mined the root cutters and herb collectors for information, observing and describing the different species that they found on their expeditions, perhaps passing on what they had learned to those around them.[70]

Today, many plants continue to flower under the Emathian sun, 'the hands of the gods' as one ancient physician called them, each with its own properties and a myriad of uses, their roots entangled in myth and history.[71] Yarrow (*Achillea millefolium*) was known as Achilles' plant: its haemostatic properties could help staunch blood flow, a most useful herb in times of war with battle wounds aplenty. Basil thyme soothed stomach aches, sage combated fevers, boiled sow thistle was good for the kidneys, and ironwort or mountain tea (*Sideritis scardica*) combated winter colds. Much of this plant lore has been retained by modern-day residents of northern Greece. The walls of Aristotle's school may have long since crumbled, but the natural world surrounding them has remained resolute. Despite the intensive fruit cultivation in the area, it is here that ancient wisdom continues to live on, to grow and flourish.

The study of literature, that mainstay of ancient education, would also have continued under Aristotle's tutelage. He, like Alexander, admired the great Athenian playwrights, believing tragedy to be the highest art form, and Mieza had its own theatre to host visiting productions, where the texts came alive on stage. It was discovered in 1992, to the south-west of the public building complex. Built in the early Hellenistic period, it was remodelled by the Romans, but some bronze coins of Philip and some fourth century BC pottery sherds hint at an earlier, more rustic incarnation, perhaps comprising just a grassy hill for the audience to sit on, with a few wooden structures, a dedicated space for cultural events.[72] On the night of the last full moon in August, modern productions of the Classics are performed here once again, the lines of Aeschylus, Sophocles and Euripides echoing around the hillside and escaping into the fruit trees.

Homer too retained his position of primacy in the syllabus. The students would already know the epics well, some being able to recite large sections, but it was now time to interrogate them, to debate their meaning and tease out their moral lessons. Critiquing Homer had a long history and many intellectuals had found fault in the works, citing their various inconsistencies and falsehoods, pulling them apart to the point of irrelevance. Zoilos of Amphipolis, known as the scourge of Homer, was one of them. Plato, despite having a deep affection for the *Iliad* and *Odyssey*, refused them a place in his idealised *Republic*, believing them misleading for the city-state's youth. Aristotle saw things differently; he was an ardent supporter and applied his usual scientific rigour to the works.[73] He believed that poetry should not be subject to the same criteria as other arts; any falsehoods or moments of fantasy in the text were admissible if they successfully built the sense of drama. He also implored readers to consider the context of the time, one that was different from their own. With these points, recounted in his *Poetics*, he successfully swept away the old arguments. It was surely an approach that found favour with Alexander and there is a tradition that it was Aristotle who provided him with a special edition of the *Iliad*, the same copy that he kept under his pillow in Asia.[74] During Alexander's time at Mieza, the epic must have taken on new relevance as, following Philip's recent successes, talk began to circulate about another Pan-Hellenic campaign in Asia.

THE PROMISE OF PERSIA

After the Peace of Philokrates and the end of the Third Sacred War, Isocrates had published an open letter to Philip. It called upon him to unite the Greeks in a joint crusade against their age-old enemy: Persia. The fifth century BC Persian Wars, and the desecration of Greece's holy places, had never been properly avenged and Isocrates believed the new peace offered an opportunity for the city-states to band together once again, to bury their bitter rivalries and bring further glory to *Hellas*; 'if you succeed,' he wrote, 'you will cause your own reputation to rival that of the foremost men of history, while if you fall short of your expectations you will at any rate win the good will of all the Hellenes – which is a better thing to gain than to take by force many Hellenic cities.'[75]

The Persian Empire was a land of fabulous wealth and exotic wonder. The Achaimenid Great King, along with his regional governors or satraps, controlled a huge swathe of the known world, from Egypt, the Levant and Asia Minor, across Iraq and Iran – the Persian heartlands – to Central Asia and eastwards into the Indus valley. From the rising sun unto its setting, it was said, the Great King could claim to be lord of all men.[76] Despite popular Greek views which portrayed the Persians as effeminate and under the heel of despotic kings, theirs was a prosperous and largely stable empire, not one that was in decadent decline, as some ancient writers suggested.[77] The dichotomy between East and West was also not so clear cut as is often envisaged.[78] The coast of Asia was the location of many Greek cities and there was a regular exchange of people, goods and ideas across the Aegean. The Great King had acted as arbitrator and guarantor of a previous Hellenic peace, and his court continued to attract a range of Greeks – from entertainers to doctors – with many mercenaries finding gainful employment in the Persian armies. In fact, more Greeks fought against Alexander than for him during his Asiatic campaign.[79]

The Macedonians had a complicated relationship with Persia. For around thirty years, in the late sixth to early fifth century BC (512/11–479 BC), they had been subjects of the Great King, a vassal state of the Persian Empire. They were probably known to their masters as *Yauna takabara*, 'Greeks with shields for hats', a reference to their *kausias* or wide-brimmed *petasos* sun hats, and some scholars have suggested that the development of the Macedonian royal court was heavily influenced by eastern models.[80] Whether this was the case or not, the Persian Empire offered many useful lessons for ambitious leaders on how to administer and control new lands and peoples. Philip, early on in his reign, had a pact of peace and alliance with the Great King, Artaxerxes III (Ochos), but following the end of the Sacred War, he began to entertain ideas of a Persian campaign, apparently independently of Isocrates.[81] Philip knew his history, and Polybius records that he drew confidence from the examples of previous Greek armies that had ventured into Persia, including the famous exploits of Xenophon and the 10,000, and the campaigns of the Spartan king Agesilaos II in the 390s BC.[82] 'From both of these facts,' says Polybius, 'Philip perceived and reckoned on the cowardice and indolence of the Persians as compared with the military efficiency of himself and his Macedonians.' But Philip was also acutely aware that stability among his neighbours was a prerequisite before any military action could take place.

Whilst Alexander was busy training and studying at Mieza, Philip set about strengthening his frontiers. He took a large army into Illyria, devastating its cities and countryside, while a major battle was fought against King Pleuratos in which Philip emerged victorious but suffered another injury in the process, this time a broken collar bone.[83] He is then mentioned in Thessaly, removing more troublesome city tyrants and reorganising the region, placing its administration under four tetrarchs.[84] In Epeiros, Arybbas was forced to relinquish his throne. Olympias' brother, Alexander, who had been groomed for the role at the Macedonian court, took his place as king, and he and Philip extended Molossian control further south, towards Ambrakia.[85] In the late 340s, Philip was able to concentrate on subjugating Thrace and began pushing his way towards the Hellespont, the ancient bridge between Europe and Asia. With these achievements, a war with Persia became more likely.

From boyhood, Alexander had been fascinated by Persia. He had read Herodotus and Xenophon, and admired the deeds of Cyrus the Great. It was his keen understanding of the Persian Empire, its administration, networks, and policies towards subject peoples, that would eventually allow him to replicate the success of previous Great Kings, and secure his own conquests. In Pella, according to Plutarch, Alexander had once met and conversed with Persian envoys. Rather than enquiring about the Hanging Gardens of Babylon or the jewel-encrusted golden vine found within the royal palace of Sousa, he asked them about the length of their roads, the size of their army and about the Great King himself. Plutarch says that the envoys were duly impressed by the young prince, 'and regarded the much-talked-of ability of Philip as nothing compared with his son's eager disposition to do great things.'[86]

These were not the only Persians to visit Macedonia. In the late 350s BC, the fugitive satrap Artabazos had sought refuge at Pella.[87] He was accompanied by his many sons and daughters, said to number twenty-one in all, along with his extended family which included the Rhodian commander Memnon.[88] Alexander's future would be intimately connected with this noble family. Memnon and Artabazos' son, Pharnabazos, were key commanders in opposing his invasion of Asia Minor. Memnon's wife, Barsine, became his royal mistress and bore him a son – Herakles. Artabazos himself, for a time, was appointed satrap of Baktria. The Persian contingent probably stayed in Pella until the mid to late 340s BC and must have been a regular sight in the Macedonian capital during Alexander's youth, a ready source of information on exotic customs and news from the East. It was Mentor, Memnon's brother, who eventually enabled the family to return to the Persian fold. He had fought for the Great King in a campaign against the rebellious Egyptians and shown himself worthy of his trust and confidence. He was subsequently responsible for inflicting a wound that was sorely felt in Mieza.

It concerned Hermeias – Aristotle's father-in-law and tyrant of Atarneus and Assos – who had recently rebelled against Persian authority. Artaxerxes, shortly after reconquering Egypt, set his sights on reclaiming control.[89] In 341 BC, Mentor set a trap. He invited Hermeias to a conference between the two powers. Hermeias, perhaps favouring his intellectual side over a strongman's pragmatism, went along. He was promptly arrested and sent to Sousa in chains. In a contemporary speech in Athens, Demosthenes reports that Philip's 'agent' had been seized and that all the Macedonian preparations against the Great King would be laid bare.[90] This is the first mention of a connection between Philip and Hermeias, a relationship perhaps mediated by Aristotle, probably in the hope of an alliance for the war to come. Hermeias was tortured for information but in a final letter to his friends he stated that he had held his tongue and done nothing unworthy of philosophy. His loss hit Aristotle hard and he was moved to write a poem in his honour:

Virtue, you who bring many labours for the race of mortals, fairest quarry for a man's life, for the sake of your beauty, maiden, even to die is an enviable fate in Greece, or to endure cruel unresting toils: such a fruition, as good as immortal, do you bestow on the mind, better than gold or parents or soft-eyed sleep; on your account noble Herakles and the sons of Leda endured much in their exploits, (hunting?) your power; in their desire for you Achilles and Ajax went to the dwelling of Hades; and on account of your dear beauty the nursling of Atarneus left desolate the rays of the sun. Therefore he is glorified in song for his exploits, and the Muses, daughters of Memory, will exalt him to immortality, exalting the majesty of Zeus, god of hospitality, and the privilege of secure friendship.[91]

The theme of the poem – the striving for personal excellence or virtue (*arete*) – was the central premise of ancient Greek education. It's what drove the heroes of old, their efforts to attain this highest and most elusive quality, justifying their inclusion in myths, poems and songs; it continued to be the ideal for all schoolchildren as well as adults, be they philosophers, statesmen, soldiers or generals. The quest for virtue was the quest for immortality in public consciousness – the body may die but the name lives on. The significance of the poem cannot have been lost on Alexander, who strived to equal the deeds of the heroes. Like Achilles before him, he would look east to win fame and fortune.

Aristotle also uses another word in the poem that the later historian Arrian would use to define Alexander's inner drive to do and see new and extraordinary things: *pothos*, an ardent desire or longing. It was *pothos* that made him climb the Gordian acropolis to examine the fabled Gordian knot, *pothos* that drove his decision to found the city of Alexandria in Egypt, *pothos* that made him send an expedition to explore the Caspian Sea; the single word embodies both his intellect and the far-reaching curiosity that must have been cultivated by Aristotle.[92] It was perhaps at Mieza that his eyes were opened to a much wider world; one that was not set in stone but constantly evolving, a world awaiting fresh discoveries, where his *pothos* could have free rein.

Developments in astronomy, geometry and mathematics, along with existing Egyptian and Babylonian wisdom, had allowed Greek intellectuals to map out a theoretical concept of the world in the

sixth century BC.[93] Texture and topographical details were added
to the *oikoumene* or inhabited lands by later writers, primarily
drawing on accounts of travellers and explorers. It was soon postulated that the world was not flat but spherical, an idea that Aristotle
supported.[94] He further divided the globe into five climatic zones
and envisaged the *oikoumene* as stretching around the earth's surface,
from the pillars of Herakles – the promontories that flank the
straits of Gibraltar – in the west to India in the east, the two
points separated by the outer ocean. But, despite these advances,
many blanks on the map still remained, especially towards the
liminal areas of the *oikoumene*, which were yet to be properly
investigated and were said to be occupied by strange races of men
and weird creatures. Aristotle could therefore theorise that the
outer ocean could be seen from the heights of the Hindu Kush.[95]
It was an idea that Alexander would later put to the test. But when
he recrossed the mountains in 329 BC, on his way to India, there
was no ocean in sight. It must have then dawned on him that the
world was far bigger than he had been led to believe.

His *pothos*, along with more pragmatic aims to bring peripheral
areas of the Persian Empire under his control and secure his rear,
probably forced him onward. The outer ocean would prove a fitting
culmination to his eastern campaigns. His soldiers, however, did not
share his ambitions. At the Hyphasis (Beas) river in northern India,
they finally declared that they had had enough. The fighting in India
had been brutal, and the onset of the monsoon quickly washed
away their resolve. There were rumours of ever more terrifying and
warlike peoples ahead; it was time to turn back. Alexander gathered
them together and gave a speech to rouse their ambitions. 'Yet if
any one longs to hear what will be the limit of the actual fighting,
he should understand that there remains no great stretch of land
before us up to the river Ganges and the eastern sea. This sea, I
assure you, will prove to be joined to the Hyrcanian [Caspian] sea;

for the great sea encircles all the land.'[96] For Alexander, world's end was tantalisingly close, but his men were not persuaded. They looked down at the ground like guilty schoolchildren, evading the piercing glance of the king's eyes. 'Exertion and dangers are the price of deeds of prowess, and it is sweet for men to live bravely, and die leaving behind them immortal renown,'[97] Alexander continued, calling on the values that many had learned as youngsters, but it was of no use. Too many had died, not just in battle but of disease, their weapons were rusting, their clothes in shreds. It was time to go home. Alexander took to his tent in a sulk, declaring that he would go on alone if they would not change their minds. He continued to make sacrifices to ensure a safe crossing, but the omens turned out to be (conveniently) unfavourable. Finally he announced to his commanders that he had decided to turn back. Twelve huge altars were erected on the banks of the Hyphasis, apparently along with a bronze tablet inscribed with the words, 'Here Alexander stayed his march'.[98] It was said that later, while conversing with the court philosopher, Anaxarchos, about Democritus' theories of an infinite number of worlds, Alexander lamented that he could not make himself master of even one.[99]

COMPANIONS AND PASTIMES

Alexander was not alone in benefiting from Aristotle's wisdom. His foster-brothers were with him, and shared in the same dreams and ambitions. It was probably at Mieza that he also formed new friendships with other royal pages, individuals who would rise to prominence during his reign and help him extend the boundaries of the Macedonian Empire. Men such as Perdikkas of Orestis, who was given the ring of power on Alexander's death;

Lysimachos, Seleukos and Ptolemy, who would go on to carve out their own Hellenistic kingdoms; the Cretan Nearchos, admiral of his fleet; the brothers Laomedon and Erigyios from Lesbos; and Harpalos of Elimeia, Alexander's later treasurer. Many became known for their competent leadership and acts of bravery, Perdikkas leading the charge in a battle against the Thebans, Lysimachos wrestling a lion, Seleukos manhandling a wild bull that had broken free from its ropes, Erigyios killing an enemy leader in single combat.[100] But it was Alexander's relationship with another boy that remained the most important throughout his life. Aristotle defined friendship as one soul dwelling in two bodies. For Alexander that saying came closest to the truth with Hephaistion, his most trusted confidant and Companion.[101]

Hephaistion is a difficult character to reconstruct from the historical record; he is rarely given many column inches.[102] He seems to have been an ambitious individual, charming and cultured but at times fiery and divisive, in many ways similar to Alexander, although he was apparently taller and more striking. According to one famous tradition the Persian Queen Mother mistook him for the king. (Alexander reportedly averted embarrassment by saying, 'You are not mistaken, mother; for this man too is Alexander.'[103]) He never failed in any mission assigned to him and his status aroused much envy among the other Companions. Most importantly of all, he was unflinchingly loyal and had Alexander's complete trust, being privy to his innermost feelings, his ambitious designs and changeable moods. On one occasion when Alexander was silently reading a confidential letter from Olympias, Hephaistion, lying next to him, quietly put his head beside Alexander's and began reading too. Alexander could not bear to stop him and placed the seal-ring on his lips to ensure secrecy.[104]

There was a tradition in antiquity that Hephaistion also shared direct correspondence with Olympias. She had apparently grown jealous of his continued favour and wrote him a stinging epistle laden with threats. He felt sure enough in his position and friendship with Alexander to answer her forcefully, even using the royal 'we' when referring to himself: 'Stop quarrelling with us and do not be angry or menacing. If you persist, we shall not be much disturbed. You know that Alexander means more to us than anything.'[105] If genuine, they are the only words we possess of Alexander's right-hand man. His death in 324 BC sent Alexander mad with grief.

The ancient sources are not explicit about whether their relationship was or had been sexual.[106] Achilles and Patroklos may have been the model; the exact nature of the heroes' relationship was still debated in the fourth century BC, although many believed it had its source in passion, and it is uncertain to what extent later writers played with this comparison.[107] But if Alexander and Hephaistion were at some point physically intimate there would have been nothing unusual about it. Same-sex relationships were common in the Greek world, often existing between boys and men where they would serve an educational purpose, the young learning from the old. They were strictly controlled by social *mores* which varied from place to place. In Elis and Boiotia, male lovers could be of the same age and there is some indication that this was also the case in Macedonia, where relationships are attested among the royal pages.[108]

However, sexuality was one of key areas that could be exploited for hostile propaganda and it was often used by writers to suggest moral depravity on the Macedonians' part. Theopompus, for example, depicts the Argead court as a sort of brothel, with men, both clean-shaven and bearded, having sex with each other and surrounded by male prostitutes, suggesting that they were more 'Courtesans' than 'Companions'.[109] Others attest to Philip's various liaisons with young men, but this could just be slander and, in reality, it is unknown whether the Macedonians were any looser with their sexual practices than other communities in the Greek world. Modern sensibilities have also hindered the debate and made such subjects controversial. An academic conference in 2002, held in Thessaloniki, featured a talk on Macedonian homosexuality, but advance publicity caused an uproar among some locals, and policemen were quickly deployed to stop protests from turning into a full-blown riot.[110] Oliver Stone's *Alexander*, which portrayed Alexander going to bed with a Persian eunuch, prompted a group of Greek lawyers to threaten the director with a lawsuit. Such reactions say more about modern society than the ancient, where the terms 'gay', 'bi' or 'straight' did not exist.

In general, though, when it came to sex, Alexander appears to have been a man of restraint.[111] Those who later sought to promote hostile views of the king tried to turn this aspect of his reputation against him. Theophrastus actually spread the rumour that he was impotent.[112] According to the philosopher, Olympias and Philip had shown some early concern with their son's apparent lack of a sex drive, hiring a saucy Larissan courtesan – Kallixeina – to stir up his libido. She may have succeeded in claiming Alexander's virginity, although this feat is also attributed to Pankaste, another courtesan from Larissa, as well as Barsine.[113] Nonetheless, Alexander did go on to take three wives: Rhoxane, a Baktrian noblewoman, and two royal Persians, Stateira and Parysatis.[114] Plutarch records that Alexander is once said to have remarked, 'that it was sleep and sexual intercourse which, more than anything else, reminded him that he was mortal', the need for both being seen as weaknesses of human nature, an indication, perhaps, that he could not live without either.[115] But it was another pastime that consumed his interest more than any other – hunting. It was not only a court institution but a rite of passage. Alexander, like all Macedonians, was required to prove himself an able huntsman – the sport was ingrained in society, stamped onto their coins, painted on their tombs, and stitched in river-pebble mosaics.[116] His passion for the sport is recorded across the ancient sources, where he is reported to have exhibited the same fearlessness that he did in warfare. The famous Alexander Sarcophagus from Sidon, currently housed in the Istanbul Archaeological Museum, depicts the king in battle on one side and on the hunt on the other; they were the twin beacons that communicated royal strength and authority.

Walking up into the foothills of Mount Vermion, it doesn't take long for the marching lines of fruit trees to be steadily overcome by rich deciduous woodland. A canopy of beech trees soon closes out the sun, the terrain now covered with moss-covered boulders and rushing streams. In Macedonia, the visitor is never far away from such pockets of true, untouched wilderness. It was much more extensive in antiquity, the forests descending further towards the plain and the reed-fringed lakes, the ideal habitat for boar and deer. It was a hunter's paradise and special game reserves – the king's private property – were to be found across the land.

Alexander and his friends had probably started hunting from the beginning of their elementary education. Birds, hares and foxes were the early quarry on which they developed their skills, while as they grew older they proceeded to more dangerous beasts. The first boar kill without the use of nets was necessary for full acceptance into adult society; only then could an individual recline on a couch during a feast – a feat that Alexander's Successor, Kassandros, had failed to achieve by the age of thirty-five, despite being an able huntsman.[117] When or how Alexander took his first boar is not recorded, but the ancient writer Xenophon wrote a treatise on hunting and it remains the best guide for imagining these incredible events that were as dangerous as they were thrilling.[118]

On entering the hunting grounds, one of the accompanying dogs would be loosed to pick up the scent. They were the indispensable allies of the hunt, bulky Molossian mastiffs and swift, slender-bodied Lakonian hounds being the favoured breeds. The animals were well-trained, equally adept at hunting men as game. Philip reportedly used them to track down scattered enemies in the mountainous countryside of Thracian Orbelia.[119] Alexander, like many other young Macedonians, would have had a number of such pets from childhood, and two of his later dogs are recorded: Triakas, given to him by a satrap in Asia, and Peritas, known as 'The Beast of India'.[120] Just like Boukephalas, Peritas had a city named after him.[121] With the abundance of game in Macedonia it wouldn't take long for a scent to be picked up.

The hunters, either on foot or on horseback, followed the lead hound, perhaps also accompanied by more experienced huntsmen and attendants. Alexander would have led from the front as they moved through the stillness of the wood as silently and effortlessly as early morning mist, the covering of damp leaves and beech mast absorbing the sound of their tread. As they neared the quarry more signs of the boar's activities could be discerned: broken branches, trees rubbed bare by tusks; they were close. The hound was brought to heel and tied up so the plan could be set. The hunters scouted the perimeter around the lair, identifying natural features in the landscape that presented good catch points and cover. Alexander whispered his commands, marshalling his team accordingly. The hunt provided many skills transferrable to the arena of warfare; it was the closest thing to battle. They then took up their positions, each with his favoured weapon, the double axe, javelin or spears of varying length – Xenophon mentions that the best spears for boar should have blades fifteen inches long with stout teeth at the middle of the socket to help them lodge in the creature's flesh.[122] There was time for a brief prayer to Apollo, Artemis and Herakles the Hunter before the action, and part of the spoils would be given as an offering if they were successful.

When all were ready, the hounds were unleashed, their frenetic bodies disappearing into dense thickets which were impervious to wind or rain. The shrill barks and sound of snapping jaws were soon accompanied by the startled squeals of the boar. Suddenly, over a hundred kilos of twitching muscle, tipped with deadly tusks, exploded from the undergrowth, the beast's deep-set eyes ablaze, a mixture of fear and anger. Its stunted legs and squat build enabled deadly bursts of speed; it could easily toss aside a man as if he were made of straw. With no nets to help ensnare the beast, the hunters relied on teamwork and the training of their hounds to direct the boar towards the killing ground and lead huntsman – Alexander. Honour was at stake here. He would be given the first chance for the kill, but on a hunt, anything could happen. With the beast out in the open, confused and disorientated, a well-aimed javelin could bring it down, otherwise the longer spears came into play. These required the hunter to get dangerously close, a true test of courage. Xenophon describes the technique needed for the death strike when hunting on foot: legs apart, body turned to the left, spear held out in front, the left hand gripping the shaft tightly, the right hand ready to drive the point home, eyes, at all times, fixed on the boar's head and those deadly tusks.[123] Speed, skill and nerve were essential on approach, the pounding of the heart by now drowning out all other sounds, adrenaline flooding the body, making it ready for fight or flight, those few split seconds before impact must have been terrifying. The target was the neck area, but every hunter knew that a quick sideways jerk of the boar's head could easily knock the spear out of the hand. At that point there was no choice but to fall to the floor and pray that those tusks did not cause a fatal injury, for the boar's wrath against its aggressor was terrible. With any luck the hounds would keep the beast pinned down and the aim would be good, the spear thrust home with all the power the hunter could muster. With a deafening squeal and collapsing legs, hounds tearing at its flesh, the boar's strength quickly gushed away, a blow of a double axe severing the last vestiges of life from its crippled hulk. Alexander, like every Macedonian, would never forget his first boar without nets.

Such experiences helped create strong bonds between Alexander and his peers. During their time at the royal school these noble youths, selected and removed from their own families, formed an extended clan that revolved around the prince. They learned together, trained together, slept together, ate together and played together. As the seasons passed, the years turning on their axle, they came into the flower of youth, their bodies strengthening, their heads filling with new ideas about the world. Meanwhile, outside the bounds of the school, Philip remained engaged in his Thracian wars, but with the king's prolonged absence came new opportunities for Alexander. In early autumn 340 BC, he was summoned back to Pella. Education was one thing, experience another. It was time to put into practice all that he had learnt.

5.

CAMPAIGN

At the age of sixteen, Alexander was appointed regent of Macedon and keeper of the Royal Seal.[1] The post involved him in the day-to-day running of the kingdom and came with a mixture of public, administrative and military duties – it was his first taste of real power. Among the words of wisdom that Philip reportedly passed on to his son was to associate with the Macedonians so as to win their favour, a far easier task when another ruled.[2] Philip had managed to gain a reputation for being accessible and considerate with his countrymen; it was one of his qualities that they came to admire most. This may not have always been the case.[3] An elderly woman had, according to one story, sought to petition him only to be constantly put off by his reluctance to engage, a lack of time his common excuse. 'Then don't be king,' the woman had snapped.[4] Philip quickly changed his ways.

Now it was Alexander's turn to deal with the masses. If he wanted to emulate his father, he would have to give regular audiences and answer the flood of written petitions that flowed into the palace each day; the seal-ring was used to sign all official correspondence.[5] It was not the most glamorous of duties but it provided an opportunity to build on the Aristotelian lessons he had learned at Mieza. Reliability and consistency of judgement were important traits for any ruler, and could only be learned through experience.[6] Fortunately, he was aided in his decision-making by a group of seasoned advisors, the invaluable Companions of his father who were accustomed to delicate matters of state. They could provide on-the-spot advice or be dispatched to the problem's source in order to investigate further. Antipatros was one of Philip's most accomplished and experienced men, a staunch supporter of the royal family and someone who could be trusted with governance in his absence. He was a learned man, a man of famed sobriety – a rare exception in Macedonia – who wrote a history of Perdikkas III's Illyrian wars, and befriended numerous intellectuals of the age, including Isocrates and Aristotle. Philip is said to have claimed that he slept safely while Antipatros was awake.[7] His whereabouts during Alexander's regency are difficult to pin down – at one point he is recorded in Thrace, another at Pella – but it is probable that the two spent a good deal of time in each other's company.[8] Olympias may also have played an advisory role, albeit in an unofficial capacity. Freshly reunited with her son, she could provide precious behind-the-scenes information concerning the designs and manoeuvres of various court cliques. The support of both individuals remained crucial throughout Alexander's early life.

In order to strengthen his position at court, Alexander, perhaps taking his father's advice a little too far, began to distribute lavish gifts to certain Macedonians. His generosity earned him a reprimand from Philip. 'My son, whatever line of reasoning gave you this idle expectation to make you think that people whose love you forced with money would be loyal to you?' he may have written in one letter.[9] Olympias would say something similar when he was king, stating that it was wrong to elevate his Companions to an equal rank of wealth. But Alexander did not count among his friends those who refused his gifts and, in reality, he was following the example of his parents.[10] Philip, it was said, had bought more of Greece than he conquered.[11]

Despite the considerable authority that the regent was able to wield, the Macedonian king remained the true power. He continued to handle all the big issues of the day, directing state policy from wherever he happened to find himself, be it palace, guesthouse or tent, and one of Alexander's principal duties was to ensure that supply and communication lines between king and capital remained open. Sound administration was just as important as military glory and Alexander became known as a gifted marshal. By the autumn of 340 BC, when he took up the regency, Philip had been away for over two years campaigning in Thrace. The period is scantly recorded in the ancient sources and hence is all too often glossed over in the history books, but these years were of crucial importance, not only for the development of Philip's foreign policy but that of the army as well. The conquest of Thrace represented a monumental challenge; it was much larger than Macedonia and home to a multitude of warlike tribes. It tested the army to the limits but, in doing so, prepared them for Alexander's later Persian invasion, familiarising the soldiers with guerrilla tactics and the besieging of formidable coastal strongholds. It was also the Petri dish that bred new mechanisms of Macedonian control – the beginnings of empire. Archaeological discoveries in the eastern Balkans and the development of Thracology (studies on Thrace) are now providing some perspective on these achievements, as well as insights into the enigmatic Thracians themselves – a people that provided Alexander with his first experience of warfare.

THRACE – THE FINAL FRONTIER

Bulgaria's National Museum of History is located in the Boyana suburb of Sofia. It was originally built as a luxury residence for the State Council of the People's Republic of Bulgaria, when the country was a one-party Socialist state. The totalitarian building, with its squat, brown façade, was designed to fit comfortably into the surrounding Mount Vitosha National Park; in the autumn, the intense auburns and yellows of the forest mantle the complex like a golden fleece. The interior has retained its former grandeur, the visitor welcomed onto polished stone floors, chandeliers hanging like snowdrops from wooden coffered ceilings, while staircases mimic the tumbling of waterfalls; huge rear windows frame the mountain vistas, breathing the natural world into the first floor's ceremonial hall. There is one very special display room nearby, special not so much for its architecture – there are far more impressive rooms in the building – but for its contents. Packed into a narrow, oblong hall are numerous glass cases; they fringe the walls and populate the interior, their contents sparkling under the halogen lamps suspended above them. This is the Thracian Hall, and it contains one of the most extraordinary collections of ancient metal artefacts in the world.

The experience of exploring the room is cumulative, each display case building on the last. There are silver-gilt appliqués with relief depictions of hunting, forgotten myths and battles between wild beasts; elegant silver bowls with protruding belly-buttons; silver drinking horns terminating in the front halves of a galloping horse or the placid face of a deer; wide-eared vessels and tear-shaped jugs; exquisite necklaces and golden pectoral plaques. One earring, composed of a tiny figure of Nike riding a chariot, requires the help of a mounted magnifying glass to appreciate its finery. The visual assault of artistic brilliance makes its final coup in the centre of the room, where the incredible Panagyurishte treasure resides – nine elaborately decorated feasting vessels of twenty-three-carat gold, undimmed by millennia spent beneath the earth.

The hall's objects, recovered from buried hoards and unplundered tombs, testify to the Thracians' mastery of decorative metalwork, especially toreutics – the art of carving or embossing relief designs onto their products. They incorporate influences from surrounding regions – Scythia, Greece, Macedonia and Persia – and were most likely the products of royal workshops. Today, their true value lies not in the weight or quality of the metal but the depictions they bear. The Thracians were a non-literary people and left no histories or narratives in their own words; it is primarily through art and archaeology that they now live on. Within this room, among the glittering array of their ancient treasures, the heartbeat of Thracian life can be experienced.

Thrace roughly encompassed today's Bulgaria and parts of Romania, north-eastern Greece and European Turkey. To the north it extended beyond the Danube to the Carpathian Mountains; to the south as far as the Aegean coast, the horizontal lines of the Rhodope and Stara Planina or Balkan mountain range (ancient Haimos) carving up the interior, the Thracian plain lying between. Bitter in winter and sweltering in summer, it was described to the travel writer Patrick Leigh Fermor as 'all flies and dust'.[12] Their world was one of sacred mountains with rock-cut sanctuaries, mist-damp forests and open grasslands; the general populace lived in scattered villages with houses dug into the ground, while the numerous kings occupied sturdy tower residences. It was the preferred retreat of Ares (god of war) and home to the cold North Wind.[13]

Thrace was not a nation in the modern sense of the word but rather a patchwork of different tribes, of which there may have

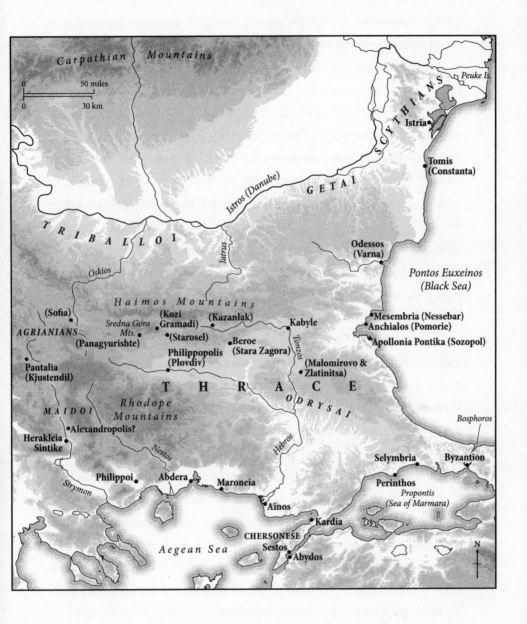

been as many as forty. Herodotus believed that the Thracians were the biggest 'nation' in the world, next to the Indians.[14] They were said to have resembled their gods with their blue eyes and red hair. Noblemen were adorned with tattoos, those that lived by war and raiding being the most honoured in society.[15] The Thracians shared many similarities with the Macedonians, both in the structure of their society, which revolved around the rule of hereditary kings, and their culture of warfare, feasting, hunting and gift-giving, although here it was customary for the king to receive rather than to offer gifts.[16] They had once inhabited large parts of Macedonia before they were pushed further east by the early Argead kings. Militarily they could be formidable but their chronic lack of cohesion prevented them from becoming 'invincible', as Herodotus suggested in his *Histories*.[17] This idea had turned out to be rather prophetic as, in 429 BC, during the Peloponnesian War, the Odrysian king Sitalkes achieved the seemingly impossible and united many of the disparate tribes. His army was said to be 150,000 strong, a third of which consisted of cavalry. They invaded and devastated Macedonia before returning to their own lands laden with booty. It was an outright demonstration of power and might, a history lesson of which all subsequent Macedonian monarchs must have been all too aware. The Odrysians remained the predominant power in the mid fourth century BC.[18] They formed a supra-tribal state controlling much of Thrace south of the Haimos mountains. One particularly rich grouping of burial mounds belonging to their kings and nobility has been identified in a valley between the Sredna Gora and Stara Planina ranges, near the town of Kazanlak. A small number of tombs have been opened to the public; their granite-lined entranceways lead to small, well-constructed masonry chambers, many resembling domed beehives. There are estimated to be around 1,500 burial mounds in the general vicinity, their rotund profiles set against fields of pasture and cultivated rosebushes. Just like Egypt, Bulgaria has its very own valley of kings.

Philip had started to whittle away the Odrysians' holdings in his campaigns of 356, 352 and 347–6 BC, starting with their coastal territories, Macedonian influence creeping eastwards like an untended vine. Kersobleptes, one of their kings, had been subjugated, but not for long. He soon started to cause trouble again, attacking some Greek cities and ravaging their territories. Diodorus records that Philip marched east in 342 BC to help defend the cities, but there were surely other motives at play.[19] Thrace, with its considerable natural resources and position at the crossroads of Europe and Asia, was a valuable prize for any would-be conqueror. The hall's many gold and silver objects testify to the riches that were on offer. The Odrysians, however, would not give up control easily.

There is one find, positioned at the end of the Thracian Hall, that confronts the visitor with an elite, possibly royal, warrior from this time, a contemporary of Philip and Alexander, probably one of the many who faced them on the battlefield. He was discovered in 2005, near the villages of Malomirovo and Zlatinitsa in southeastern Bulgaria, buried in a tumulus that had been in use since prehistory.[20] His jewellery denoted his social importance – a wreath of golden olive leaves and fruit still crowned his head, an image of the goddess Nike was pinned to the front. Twenty-nine gold appliqués found nearby are believed to be the remains of a diadem, while on the little finger of his left hand he wore a chunky gold signet ring. Placed around him, along with other precious belongings, was a variety of weapons – a curved sword, knife, seven spears, and two groups of arrows, their shafts, quivers and accompanying bow having long since decayed. But what really stands out about this burial is the man's armour. It has been conserved, reassembled and put on display in a rectangular glass case. This

Thracian warrior went to battle in flamboyant fashion; his bronze helmet was in the Chalkidike style, crested with a fearsome three-headed snake, a pectoral guard slung around his neck, his upper body encased with an innovative corselet of iron scales, enabling flexibility and protection during the fight. An astonishing silver-gilt greave (displayed separately) adorned his left leg, and bore the embossed face of a sullen-looking goddess at the knee. Two of his favourite horses, sacrificed by the graveside, were found during excavations. His appearance echoes Homer's description of the mythical Thracian king Rhesos, who travelled to Troy with his snowy-white horses and finely wrought armour of hammered gold, fit for an immortal.[21] Many other splendidly adorned individuals, members of the local aristocracy, likely fought alongside him on horseback. They were also supported by some of the best light infantrymen in the ancient world, known as peltasts after their oval or crescent-shaped *pelte* shields; expert guerrilla fighters, night raids and ambushes were their favoured mode of attack, a curved dagger and numerous spears the weapons of choice. They were said to have fought like caged beasts, bellowing a hymn to the Titans before battle, collecting and displaying the heads of the slain as trophies of war. The Greeks often hired them as mercenaries and their skills would later earn them a place of great respect in the Macedonian army.[22]

Philip adapted his tactics to deal with the Thracian style of warfare. Instead of relying on his heavy *sarissa*-based infantry, he used skirmishers, slingers, archers, mercenaries and cavalry.[23] By splitting his manpower into columns, each under the command of an experienced general, he could assault numerous tribal territories simultaneously. Several battles were fought, not all were successful. On one occasion, when he was being pursued by the Thracians, he ordered the men at the rear to stand and fight as the rest of his army took to their heels. During another, he sent ambassadors to a hostile Thracian city for talks. Once the enemy had been assembled to hear their words, Philip ordered the attack.[24] The ancient sources only give us these few fragments of information, but archaeology is starting to provide more depth to the story.

A previously unknown Odrysian stronghold has recently been discovered in central Bulgaria, at the south-eastern foot of Kozi Gramadi (Goats' Cairns) Peak, 1,113m above sea level in the Sredna Gora mountains.[25] Impressive ashlar walls encircle a space of 3.4 hectares, protected on two sides by steep gorges and surrounded by dense deciduous forest. Access was controlled through a single tower-gateway and inside were distinct areas for residential and commercial activity. At its core was a monumental rectangular building which may have been utilised as a treasury. In the surrounding environs a religious sanctuary, a small settlement and burial grounds have also been traced.[26] On the foothills below, near the village of Starosel, a concentration of important cult monuments (tumuli and temples) can be more easily visited. The entire area was once a substantial centre of Thracian power.

The compound was short-lived and has been dated to between the beginning of the fourth century BC and the 340s. The cause of its demise was discovered during its excavation: numerous iron arrowheads and over a hundred and fifty slingshots, some bearing the names of Philip's generals.[27] The majority of them were found clustered on a low hill, some 200 metres east of the fortress – this was evidently where the Macedonians set up their siege operations, and the finds may represent unused ammunition. They concentrated the assault on the main entrance, their superior firepower having the inevitable result. The defenders were overcome and the site was burnt to the ground. The forest soon closed in, the indifference of nature once again proving the archaeologists' boon. Similar assemblages of slingshots are starting to be recovered from other mountainous strongholds across Bulgaria, providing archaeologists with the opportunity to plot the Macedonian army's movements.[28]

Philip probably began his campaign by moving from the Aegean coastline up the ancient Hebros (Evros/Maritsa) river, where he set about subjugating the main settlements of the Thracian plain. Demosthenes, in a speech delivered in the spring of 341 BC, mentions Philip besieging such places as Drongylon, Kabyle and Masteira, enduring toil, harsh winters and the utmost dangers.[29] He then moved into the mountains to stamp out the last vestiges of resistance. It was a gruelling operation and he was forced to call in reinforcements from Thessaly and Macedonia.[30] The hardships he endured nearly cost him his life. He had fallen dangerously ill during the winter of 342/1 BC, but he eventually recovered and went on to defeat Kersobleptes and his co-ruler Teres: Odrysian dominion was replaced by Macedonian. Afterwards, Philip moved across to the Propontis, where the pinch points of the Hellespont or Dardanelles controlled access between the Aegean and the Black Sea. Some of the region's Greek cities had reneged on their alliances and were promptly besieged. Sometime in late 340 BC, word reached Pella about a rebellion among the Thracian Maidoi. A portion of the army had remained in Macedonia to be used on just such an occasion. Alexander could have delegated the response, but that was not his way. Hungry for action, he marshalled his men and set out for Thrace.

ALEXANDROPOLIS

The Maidoi once occupied the middle reaches of the Strymon or Struma valley in south-west Bulgaria, two or three days' march from Pella.[31] The river's blue-tinged waters slide effortlessly through open grasslands, winding between gravel banks lined with lofty poplars and around small sandy islands, freshly exposed in the hot summer months. Wild forests descend from the edges of the nearby Pirin mountains. According to Aristotle, Paionian bulls (European bison) could once be found on the western borders with Paionia. They were hunted for their meat and hides, which when stretched out covered a seven-seat dining room.[32] This was the setting of Alexander's first recorded military action, perhaps where he killed his first man, another important rite of passage for the young Macedonian.

The campaign provided Alexander with an introduction to military life and all it entailed – the gathering of intelligence, the process of establishing camp, and general army logistics. As with his other regency duties, he would have been accompanied by veterans for whom the business of war was second nature. Plutarch, our only source for this mission, does not provide much detail on what happened next but Alexander appears to have had little trouble in subduing the Maidoi. He took their main city, drove out the rebels and settled a mixed population in their place. It was renamed Alexandropolis – Alexander's city – the first of many such foundations that would bear his name from Egypt to India.[33]

Alexandropolis is yet to be identified on the ground – it was not one of his more successful settlements and soon vanished from the historical record – but there are a few ideas about its lost location. Close to the spa town of Sandanski is perhaps the most promising. A protruding hill at the nearby village of Laskarevo provides a similar topographical feature to other Macedonian foundations in the region, such as Philippoi and Herakleia Sintike (recently discovered near Petrich).[34] It was previously thought by some scholars that by renaming the city after himself Alexander was rebelling against his father, but the idea has rightly been rejected.[35] It is much more likely that he was following Philip's example, probably with his permission, and in doing so he exhibited an understanding and attentiveness to Macedonia's new foreign policy that was rapidly evolving under Philip's kingship.

In Thrace, Philip pioneered a multifaceted approach to consolidating his newly won territory. Those tribes that could be wooed with the benefits of alliance were folded into the Macedonian framework, others, tucked away in remote mountains ranges, were easily bypassed and kept their autonomy.[36] Philip focused his efforts on the settlements of the interior. Those that resisted his advances were conquered and resettled with a mixed community of Macedonians and Greeks. They likely included such sites as Pautalia (Kyustendil), Philippopolis (Plovdiv), Beroe (Stara Zagora) and Kabyle – which functioned as the fetters of Thrace. The army were able to fortify them within a matter of weeks but such activity has proved difficult to trace in the archaeological record; evidence from the fourth century BC usually lies buried deep under a multitude of later occupation layers.[37] At Kabyle, however, archaeologists have identified stone towers and fragments of encircling walls that fortified the acropolis, and which have been tentatively associated with the early phases of Macedonian control.[38] They overlie areas of earlier Thracian religious activity – which may be a coincidence, the elevated sanctuaries also providing the best place to police the surrounding land, or may represent a symbolic display of the new authority. Such a process may well have taken place at Alexandropolis.

The settlers either replaced the upper strata of Thracian society or formed the nucleus for new foundations. Theopompus suggests that these people were not of the highest moral character and that one of Philip's Thracian cities was known as 'Degenerateville', where he had collected together those 'accused of degeneracy . . . sycophants, false-witnesses, and professional prosecutors, and other degenerates to the number of two thousand'.[39] Philip's Thracian settlements, it seems, had a certain reputation in antiquity – the

A possible Macedonian tower at Kabyle

original 'Sin Cities'. Despite the opportunities that resettlement offered the new residents, the increasing distance from their home-lands may have caused some resentment. Justin describes the feelings of those forced to abandon their homes during Philip's population transfers of the 340s: 'The evacuees looked wistfully now at the tombs of their forefathers, now at their ancient family deities, now at their houses in which they had been born and had themselves produced children, sorrowing at one moment for their own fate, for having lived to see that day, and at the next for that of their children, for not having been born after it.'[40]

The new families and garrisons of soldiers were forced to make the best of their new situation. Some of the settlements took the name of their former homes – Emathia or Beroe. They brought with them their gods, customs and taste for Hellenic culture, the creature comforts of home, and thereby became vehicles for the spread of Hellenism into new and foreign lands, a process that would continue under Alexander as he went east. These settlements formed a principal aspect of Macedonia's early imperialism, but they were only part of Philip's grand design. To strengthen his grip on the region, he built forts and guard-posts to protect the main mountain passes and the precious coastal road, providing new investment for some of the Greek cities: Abdera, for example, was founded on a new site during his reign, ushering in an era of prosperity.[41] This spider's web of cities, defences, control points and alliances helped consolidate Philip's hard-won conquests. A tithe was then imposed on the population, a welcome source of new revenue for the royal coffers.[42] Under Alexander a Marshal of Thrace is recorded – he was appointed to administer the region, to collect taxes and levy troops – and this post too may have had its origins with Philip.[43] The Thracians were incorporated into the swelling Macedonian army, providing cavalry and light infantry. What is now becoming clear from the archaeology is that when Alexander invaded Asia he did so with the Macedonian model for expansion already firmly established.

PEACE NO MORE

Alexander's swift actions in Thrace successfully re-secured the Macedonian rear as Philip continued his operations around the Propontis (Sea of Marmara). He had moved into the area earlier in 340 BC. The Athenian cleruchs or settlers on the Chersonese had been troubling his ally Kardia and raiding into Macedonian-controlled territory, causing an escalation in hostility between the king and Athens. Their antagonism had forced Philip to escort his fledgling fleet, which probably transported his siege train, along the Chersonese coastline.[44] Distrust reigned on both sides. The Peace of Philokrates was now hanging on by a thread.

It was probably shortly afterwards that Philip sent an open letter to the Athenians communicating his dissatisfaction with the current state of affairs.[45] In it, he set forth a series of complaints about their recent conduct, stating, 'you must not be surprised at the length of the letter, for I have many charges to prefer, and it is necessary to put them all clearly and frankly.'[46] Among the cited 'infringements' of the peace were their kidnapping of Nikias, a Macedonian herald, the ongoing dispute over ownership of the Aegean island of Halonnesos, and the recent developments in the Chersonese, where Amphilochos, one of Philip's ambassadors, had been imprisoned and tortured. There was also a rumour of an Athenian embassy to Persia whose aim was to incite war between the two powers. But 'the crowning absurdity', as Philip put it, was their refusal to engage in new talks about the prospect of amendments to the peace. The letter is matter-of-fact, diplomatic, but behind the carefully chosen words is the shadow of immense power. It ends with the ominous paragraph, 'Such are the complaints I have to make. As you were the aggressors and, thanks to my forbearance, are making still further attacks on my interests and doing me all the harm in your power, I shall defend myself, with justice on my side, and, calling the gods to witness, I shall bring my dispute with you to an issue.'[47]

The peace agreement of 346 BC had started to unravel shortly after the end of the Third Sacred War. A few years later Philip had sent an embassy to Athens, led by his friend Python of Byzantion, to suggest alterations to the peace, with the possibility of extending it to other Greek city-states – a Common Peace. Aeschines had supported the idea but Demosthenes and his supporters were now all too aware of the dangers in trusting the king's words, and the embassy was rebuffed.[48] Shortly after, Philokrates was accused of taking bribes from Philip during the previous embassies to Pella; he fled before the case was brought to trial, a response that many took as a sign of guilt. A similar charge of treason was levelled against Aeschines, but he managed to secure an acquittal, if only by thirty votes. It was, however, a pyrrhic victory and drastically reduced his political influence, although he would remain an advocate of peace for the rest of his career.[49] It was indicative of the anti-Macedonian feeling that prevailed in Athens in the late 340s, spearheaded by Demosthenes who had become the city's leading orator – the 'cock of the walk'.[50] He had distanced himself from the peace soon after its agreement, and regarded it merely as a stopgap before a resumption of hostilities.[51] Once again, the Pnyx shuddered with his further tirades against Philip as he accused his fellow Athenians of being like men who have drunk too much mandrake juice, stupefied and unwilling to act.[52] Philip, he argued, was already at war with Athens. He called the Assembly's attention to a growing number of case studies that, he believed, laid bare Philip's imperial ambitions. They included his interventions in the affairs of many Greek city-states, including Megara, Messenia, Elis and Euboia. His influence, Demosthenes claimed, was spreading like a virus, infecting even those who thought themselves at a safe distance.[53] But it was his continued actions around the Chersonese and surrounding coastal territories that were the most worrying development.

Demosthenes had already realised that Philip was too powerful to fight alone. In a speech known as the *Third Philippic*, dated to 341 BC, he called on the Athenians to rally the other Greek cities to his cause. Philip, he said, was 'not only no Greek, nor related to the Greeks, but not even a barbarian from any place that can be named with honour, but a pestilent knave from Macedonia'.[54] He labelled all those who sympathised with the king as corrupt, stating it was 'better to die a thousand times than pay court to Philip'.[55] He sped around Greece and the Aegean trying to garner support. One of his trips was to Byzantion, modern-day Istanbul.[56]

Athenian relations with the Byzantines had soured since the Social War of the 350s, when they had successively rebelled against the Second Athenian League. They had since, along with other cities in the region, gone over to Philip's side. But Demosthenes was able to play on their concerns over the king's growing power. They subsequently ditched their Macedonian alliance and the Athenian Assembly sent forty ships under the command of Chares to help aid resistance around the Chersonese and Propontis.[57]

Perinthos, one of Byzantion's closest allies, was the first city that Philip had besieged, early in the summer of 340 BC.[58] It occupied a narrow neck of rock surrounded by the sea and linked to the mainland by an isthmus only 200 metres wide. It has been identified as Marmara Ereğlisi in European Turkey. Among the modern buildings only a few segments of the city's two circuit walls survive – one protecting the upper city and acropolis, the other the lower city. It was flanked by two natural harbours and could be easily resupplied from the sea.[59] The Perinthians' confidence in their formidable defences meant that not even Philip's gold could scale their walls. Nevertheless, they must have watched the approach of the Macedonian army with dread – thirty thousand men, with an array of siege machines, filling the landward approaches to the city, fresh from success against the Thracians. They were surely aware of the fate of those who had resisted Philip before, especially the Olynthians. Diodorus, probably drawing on a fourth century BC history written by Ephorus, provides a detailed account, perhaps because it represented a watershed moment in the history of warfare.[60] The historian Guy Griffith described it as the first great siege of the Macedonian era.[61]

On arrival, Philip's engineering corps began to assemble their vast array of siege machinery. The battering rams, housed in wooden sheds, were duly assembled and marched like giant tortoises towards the city gates. Scaling ladders were put at the ready and siege towers, said to be 80 cubits (around 37 metres) tall, threw the city's walls into shadow – they loomed above the Perinthian defences, allowing expert archers, slingers and artillerymen to play Apollo, raining down missiles on the enemy from up on high. Below the ground, Philip's engineers were also busy. Sappers had the tricky task of trying to undermine the walls and towers. If they dug too shallowly the tunnel could collapse on the diggers; too deep and they would not succeed in bringing down the constructions above.

The Macedonians' efforts soon began to bear fruit and a section of the Isthmian wall was pulled down, but they were frustrated by the Perinthians, who had managed to throw up a secondary wall. The defenders' resistance was fuelled by the Byzantines, who were able to resupply them from the sea. Philip's fleet was largely reduced to the sidelines. Undeterred, the Macedonians pressed for another breakthrough on land. The men were split into divisions and assaulted the city in relays, day after day, night after night.[62] There was no respite for the defenders; the enemy's resources seemed limitless. News of Philip's operations soon spread across the Propontis and into Asia. The Great King, Artaxerxes III (Ochos), had also grown increasingly concerned with Philip's expanding power and wrote to his coastal satraps to provide rein-forcements.[63] The Perinthians and their allies proved equal to the Macedonians' tenacity, and the grim slogging match continued. Philip kept up the morale of his men by promising rich rewards: 'the hope of profit steeled them against danger.'[64] When a breach was made in the walls, catapults, which unleashed Titan-sized arrows, helped clear the battlements. A detachment of soldiers, most likely the Foot Companions – Philip's elite infantry corps – then pushed their way through the opening. Brutal hand-to-hand fighting ensued. The bodies soon started to pile up. With a Herculean investment of labour and hard fighting, they finally managed to overcome the second Isthmian wall, but the city's layout now came to the defenders' rescue. The houses were packed closely together; tier upon tier of them rose up towards the acropolis, resembling from afar the seats of a theatre. Whenever the Macedonians succeeded in perforating the defences, the Perinthians simply blocked up the alleyways and used the lowest circuit of houses as the next makeshift city wall. The siege dragged on with no end in sight.

By the autumn of 340 BC, around the same time that Alexander took up his regency, Philip made the decision to extend his operations along the coast. He divided his army, sending a detachment east to attack Selymbria (Silivri) while he went on with another sizeable force to Byzantion.[65] It was against this backdrop of events that war was finally declared between Macedon and Athens. The precise chronology of events remains unclear – there are conflicting accounts – but it was an audacious Macedonian mission that was either the first action or cause of the war.

The Black Sea grain ships were now gathering at the northern mouth of the Bosphoros, at a headland known as *To Hieron* – the sacred place – a large religious complex that once occupied the Kavak Point, on the Asian coast.[66] It was an inviolate site; one tradition ascribed its foundation to Jason and the Argonauts, and generations of sailors had gathered here to pray to Zeus of the fair winds, hoping for a successful onward journey through the tricky currents of the Bosphoros.[67] The Athenian general Chares was in charge of protecting the flotilla but he was soon called away to a meeting with the Persian satraps. He probably assumed that the religious sanctity of the site, along with the remaining warships, would keep them safe until his return. It proved a costly act of negligence. Philip immediately took the initiative. He sent his own fleet across the straits to seize the cargo ships but was unable to capture them on the first attempt. He then landed a special amphibious force on the Asiatic shore. Under the cover of darkness they made a lightning attack and succeeded in seizing the entire flotilla, said to consist of 230 ships. He spared 50, those that did not belong to the Athenians, and plundered the rest, the raid netting 700 talents' worth of cargo and captives – an escapade that even the Argonauts would have been proud of.[68] He apparently later justified this piratical act by saying that the ships and their supplies were destined for those he was besieging at Selymbria.[69] On hearing the catastrophic news, the Athenians symbolically smashed the inscribed stele bearing the terms of the Peace of Philokrates. Athens and Macedon were once again at war.

Philip, meanwhile, set up his siege operations at Byzantion. Its inhabitants were well known as being *bons vivants*, a pleasure-loving people famed for their parties and fondness for drink; a contemporary of Alexander derided it as being the armpit of Greece.[70] One of the foremost men in the city, Leon, was known for the girth of his belly; Philip, according to one late source, had attempted to buy him but could not afford the price.[71] The Byzantines were no strangers to sieges, and their walls were of great size and strength. They abandoned their surrounding territory and, like the Perinthians, trusted in their defences. Philip first threw up a stockade across the headland and then bridged the Golden Horn, securing a valuable land route to the Black Sea. The captured ships from the grain fleet were broken up, the timber used to assemble new siege machines, while a temple to Hades/Pluto was dismantled to provide further building material.[72] Little of the narrative of the siege is known except that it was a time of great innovation for the Macedonian engineering corps. Their lead designer, the Thessalian Polyeidos, put a new type of siege tower – the *helepolis* – into use, and scholars have theorised that it was during this period that the torsion catapult, which had probably been under development for some time, began to be deployed with more success, the tightly wound sinews able to launch arrows and stones with greater force than their mechanical predecessors.[73] It was later said that Philip counted these tools of warfare among his greatest treasures.[74]

Such was the Byzantines' faith in their walls and sea power that, at first, they refused Athenian aid. Their spirits were further buoyed by a victory over the Macedonian fleet, whereby they forced their opponents to retreat into the Black Sea.[75] The Athenians, still eager to help, appointed an austere general called Phokion, nicknamed 'the Good', to take another forty ships north. Phokion was a more trustworthy individual than Chares, and this time the Byzantines accepted Athenian help. Together they managed to further frustrate Philip.[76] Even the local dogs were against the aggressors and sounded the alarm during one night-time attack.[77] The stalemate continued throughout the winter and into the following spring. Macedonian forces were now spread across the northern Propontis and Bosphoros, a massive enterprise and a clear indication of their military might and ambition. But victory was not forthcoming; the Persian mercenaries supplied to Perinthos eventually compelled Philip to raise the siege of that city. and he also abandoned Byzantion soon after.[78] Some agreement may have been reached with the defenders, helping to break the deadlock.[79] It was around this time that Alexander joined his side. Justin says that he was summoned 'to receive his initial training under his father in the field'.[80]

When exactly Alexander arrived on the scene is difficult to place. Justin includes the detail within a larger summary of Philip's final actions in the Propontis. It's tempting to think that he witnessed some part of the siege operations. Such an experience would have given him an early appreciation of the skills and resources needed for such endeavours. He would later inherit the expertise of the engineering corps and their new innovations. Polyeidos' students, Diades and Charias, would accompany him into Asia. Combining new developments in siege technology with his 'fiery and resourceful determination', as one scholar put it, Alexander would become the most accomplished besieger in ancient history.[81]

Philip had not seen his son for nearly three years. Alexander had changed in that time. He was no longer the same boy who had been scolded for being too proficient with the kithara. The early promise he had shown taming Boukephalas had been developed by his numerous trainers; the wisdom of Aristotle had nurtured his intellect; he had already proved himself a capable regent. The so-called *Alexander Itinerary*, a short account of the king's reign produced in the fourth century AD, provides one of the most evocative descriptions of Alexander and lends itself well to imagining the youth who now confronted Philip.[82] His hair, the anonymous author writes, was said to be thick and swept back and away from the face, a fashion that reflected his love of riding at speed. He had a prominent forehead with a somewhat aquiline nose and sharp expression. He was of medium stature, like his father, with slim limbs but with a body knotted in muscle. In combat he showed great coordination and speed, being a tireless runner and hurling spears with excessive force. Other descriptions attest to the melting gaze of his eyes, and that he was fair skinned with a ruddiness around the face and chest; his body apparently exuded a sweet smell, perhaps betraying an expensive taste in spice and fragrance, while he was quick in movement and harsh in voice.[83] He may already have been sporting the ragged sideburns that appear in later portraits, a fuzz of facial hair adorning his young cheeks, although most often he was clean shaven. It was said that, overall, he possessed a natural beauty, but also that there was something alarming about his appearance.[84]

Dio Chrysostom, a Greek writer working during the Roman Empire, likens the young Alexander to a pedigree puppy that cannot bear being left behind when his master goes out hunting.[85] Philip, he said, tried to discourage his son from joining him on campaign but with no luck; Alexander could not hold himself back.[86] The prince may well have been accompanied by some of his friends, perhaps the other pages who were taking up their final year of training at the king's side. This group of noble youths came east to learn the realities of life on campaign, a life for which they had been trained since boyhood.

TO THE DANUBE

With the failure of the Perinthos, Selymbria and Byzantion sieges, Philip needed to restore the morale of his troops. He set his sights on the Scythians, who had established a foothold around the Danubian Delta and the lands to the south; the Athenians would be dealt with when more favourable circumstances allowed. Before he could move north, however, he needed to extricate his fleet from the Propontis. He did so by delving into his general's playbook. A letter addressed to Antipatros in Pella was allowed to fall into enemy hands. It reported that Philip was heading back into Thrace to deal with an uprising and that Antipatros was to join him as soon as possible. The 'fake news' distracted the Athenians and they withdrew their own fleet from the area. The Macedonian ships slipped silently and unmolested back into safer waters.[87]

The army's probable route towards the fair-flowing Istros, or Danube, lay along the coast of the Black Sea, once called the 'inhospitable' sea by the Greeks. But, with their increasing knowledge and colonisation of the area, the name had softened to become instead the 'hospitable' sea – *Pontos Euxeinos*.[88] It took them past the Greek cities of Apollonia Pontika (Sozopol), Anchialos (Pomorie) and Mesembria (Nessebar), settlements set on rocky fingers of land that jut out into the sea, perched like steely-eyed herons above water that once bubbled with fish. Today, this is an area of intense modern development, with holiday apartment blocks rising along the sandy stretches of beach. Storks occupy the procession of lamp posts that line the slick modern road; from their pillars of solitude they preen and observe passers-by with the detachment of stylite monks. Philip had probably been active in the region earlier during his Thracian campaign – some Macedonian slingshots have been found along the coast, and a number of mass burials discovered at Apollonia Pontika may be connected with military action.[89] Polyaenus, a Macedonian writer who composed a book of stratagems in the second century AD, describes an unsuccessful siege of a place called Karae, which may have been on the Black Sea, but otherwise no further details are known.[90]

Continuing north, the great wooded mass of the Stara Planina soon divides the Bulgarian coastline, the land rising, its eastern extremities cut off by the sea, to form a series of perilous cliff-lines. The modern city of Varna (ancient Odessos) lies on the other side of the mountains. An intriguing story from a fourth century AD writer called Jordanes records that Odessos was occupied by the Goths or Getai – one of the most powerful of Thracian peoples – led by the local king Kothelas. On Philip's arrival, an embassy of holy men issued forth from the main gates, dressed in white, playing harps and chanting hymns. Their fearlessness in the face of a superior army unnerved the Macedonians.[91] A diplomatic solution averted bloodshed. The residents may have shrewdly decided to pay Philip to move on.[92]

The region north of Odessos, stretching away to the Danube, is now called the Dobruja and is divided between Bulgaria and Romania. It is a flat landscape, a lonely landscape. In winter, the dark ploughed soil swallows up the night. Hordes of crows settle

on a scatter of denuded trees, a sinister foliage that caws and flaps
in the damp morning air. Even in the spring and summer months
it cannot relinquish its feeling of isolation. The Roman poet Ovid
is partly responsible for colouring first impressions. He was exiled
here in AD 8 after incurring the wrath of the emperor Augustus.
At Tomis – Romanian Constanța – he wrote his *Tristia* (Sorrows)
and *Pontic Letters*. In them, he commits his grief to papyrus – the
indignity of being wrenched from his adoring social circle and
sent to a place 'no fortunate man should visit'.[93] He was now
surrounded by uncultured locals – rustic Greeks, Scythians, and
Getai – a population of 'harsh voices, grim faces'.[94] His descriptions
of the land reflect his innermost feelings of abandonment: the
perpetual winters and barbarian incursions on this outpost of
empire, the lonely creak of a nomad's wagon occasionally breaking
the bleak silence as it rolled across the frozen waters of the Danube.
For Ovid, being exiled here was the closest thing to dying.

Philip, a far more pragmatic soul, saw the value in the region.
The grain harvest was significant, and by removing the Scythian
presence he may have wished to gain some control over its trade.
The Danube also offered a readymade border that would help him
secure northern Thrace. Ateas – the Scythian king – had dealt
with Philip before. When the Macedonians were invested in operations around Byzantion, he had requested their help. An enigmatic
king of the Histrianoi, probably based around the Danubian Delta,
had been causing Ateas problems.[95] A promise of adoption, making
Philip heir to the Scythian-held territory, was made to sweeten the
deal. Always keen to expand his influence, Philip duly obliged and
sent a detachment of soldiers north, but in the meantime the king
of the Histrianoi died. Ateas quickly backtracked and the
Macedonians were turned away. They took with them an insulting
message. It stated that the Scythians were superior to the
Macedonians and had never asked for their help in the first place;

what was more, Ateas already had a son and was in no need of another heir. Philip countered by asking for funds to help support his siege of Byzantion – considering the poor reception his envoys had received, it was the least Ateas could do. None, however, were forthcoming. It provided the perfect excuse for a new campaign.

Philip attempted to conceal his designs from Ateas for as long as possible. He sent messengers ahead to explain the army's seemingly hostile movements. Philip, they said, was not marching north for war, but rather to fulfil a religious obligation. During the siege of Byzantion, he had promised to set up a bronze statue of Herakles at the mouth of the Danube and was now intent on fulfilling his vow. Ateas was not to be duped. The wily old king saw straight through Philip's ploys. He replied that he would not permit the army to enter his territory but offered to set up the statue on their behalf; if they ignored his commands he would destroy the statue and melt it down to make arrowheads. The Macedonians, unflustered by such threats, continued their march.

As they closed in on the enemy, there must have been growing talk about what lay in wait for them. The Scythians were famous mounted archers, the women often fighting alongside the men. It was said that they drank out of the skulls of their enemies, and that they purified themselves by inhaling hemp, which made them howl in delight. They were drinkers of fermented milk, trouser-wearing barbarians, but warriors of great renown. For those that knew their Herodotus, the stories of the Persian Great King Darius I must have been familiar. He had invaded Scythia in 513 BC but found it impossible to engage the enemy in battle; they simply drew the Persians further into the wilderness, making hit-and-run raids whenever the opportunity arose. In the end Darius was forced to make a humiliating retreat.[96]

Philip had no such problem in forcing a confrontation. The prize was control of the land and cities around the Danubian Delta and Ateas was loath to relinquish control. The battle took place somewhere south of the river, the Macedonians facing a Scythian army consisting of both infantry and cavalry. They were arrayed in their characteristically flamboyant colours, flaming reds and bright blues. Many of the nobles wore double belts with elaborate buckles, their weapons including tough composite bows and short swords wrapped in thin gold plate. Attached to the horses' bridles were grim reminders of their riders' savagery – macabre scalps of the slain that fluttered disconcertingly in the wind. Ateas led the army into battle, which was some feat considering he was in his nineties.[97] He is perhaps depicted on a small collection of silver coins discovered around the Black Sea coast in the twentieth century, charging full pelt, bow drawn.[98]

The valour and determination of the Scythians was said to have exceeded that of the Macedonians, but that could not save them. Ateas was killed and Justin says that Philip won the battle by cunning.[99] The Roman historian Frontinus, however, suggests that it was discipline that proved the key factor.[100] Philip, he writes,

Ateas coin

stationed his most trustworthy cavalry at the rear and ordered them to execute any member of the Macedonian army who attempted to flee. Death at the hands of the enemy was preferable to that of their comrades and they succeeded in routing the Scythians. Alexander's role during the battle is not recorded, but he may have been among the cavalry charged with keeping order. The victory failed to produce much silver or gold besides that which could be stripped from the dead, but Philip was rewarded with other spoils: twenty thousand women and children were captured, along with an equal number of thoroughbred mares and a large herd of cattle.[101] The rest of the Scythians probably retreated across the Danube and the Getai were placed back in control of the region. It was probably around this time that Philip took a sixth wife, the enigmatic Meda, a daughter of the local Getic king Kothelas, whose dowry consisted of a large number of gifts, another trophy wife to add to the royal collection.[102]

The army, slowed down with their living and breathing booty, then started their long march back to Macedonia, probably setting out west along the course of the Danube. But this part of the return trip was to be fraught with danger. The homeward route took them through the territory of the fearsome Triballoi, who are variously described as being of Illyrian or Thracian extraction. They demanded a share of the Macedonian plunder in return for safe passage. Philip, naturally, refused. The decision nearly cost him his life. In the ensuing battle he was badly wounded, injuring his hand and taking a spear in the thigh that was delivered with such force that it killed the horse beneath him.[103] Everyone thought he was dead, and in the confusion the Triballoi made off with the majority of the Scythian plunder.[104] The army then made their desultory way back to Pella. Philip was to be lame for the rest of his life, but Alexander tried to keep up his morale by saying, 'Be of good cheer, father, and go on your way rejoicing, that at each step you may recall your valour.'[105] Despite the hardships, their experiences on the campaign trail had brought them closer together.

Alexander had had a busy few years, being appointed regent, founding his first settlement, and fighting against the Maidoi, Scythians and Triballoi. He would soon face another set of intimidating opponents. The war for Thrace was over, the war for Greece was just beginning.

6.

THE ROAD TO CHAIRONEIA

During Philip's absence in Thrace, the Amphiktyonic Council of Delphi went about their business as usual, administering the affairs of Apollo's sanctuary and holding two meetings a year – one in the spring, the other in autumn. But there was much festering resentment among the Council members, a hangover from the last Sacred War combined with age-old animosities between city-states. At the autumn meeting of 340 BC, the Lokrians of Amphissa, a city to the west of Delphi, charged the Athenians with impiety and attempted to levy a fifty-talent fine against them.[1] The nature of the offence was pretty innocuous. The Athenians had made the mistake of dedicating some shields – old spoils from the Persian Wars – at Delphi's new temple of Apollo before it had been consecrated, but it was the caption added to the dedication that was the real source of trouble, it read: 'The Athenians, from the Medes [Persians] and Thebans, when they fought against Hellas.'[2] The words were ill-chosen and reminded all those who visited of a dark period in Theban history when they had 'Medised', being allies of the Great King. The impiety charge was probably an attempt by the Amphissians to gain favour with their Theban friends.

Aeschines was among the Athenian envoys sent to Delphi, and no sooner had he begun his defence against the charge than an

Amphissian, described by the orator as 'a scurrilous fellow . . . a man of no education', interrupted him and launched into a long list of grievances against the Athenians.[3] Aeschines was forced to listen to the insults with growing exasperation. When his chance for a rebuttal finally arrived, he used his superior oratorical skills to turn the tables on the accusers. From the meeting place in lofty Delphi, positioned high above the coastal plain of Kirrha or Krisa – Apollo's land – he pointed out to the Council some Amphissian buildings that were clearly encroaching on the sacred soil, an illegal act. Moreover, they had walled the sacred harbour, which it was forbidden to use, and were said to be collecting revenue from incoming goods.

The next morning the Council members and some young Delphians descended onto the plain to take a closer look. Aeschines was proved right, and the party despoiled the harbour and burnt down the offending buildings. The Amphissians, however, were not prepared to be silent bystanders. They suddenly appeared in full battle armour, seizing some Amphiktyons and scattering the rest. Afterwards, it was decided to organise a special Council meeting to discuss the matter, which was to take place at Thermopylai before the next official gathering in spring. The resolution was agreed upon by the Athenians, despite Demosthenes speaking against the idea in the Assembly. He saw the potential problems of getting involved with the dispute: the Thebans would naturally defend the Amphissians and this could bring Philip and his Amphiktyonic allies into a new war. If Thebes were destroyed then Athens could soon follow. And so he decided to use a crafty piece of constitutional trickery to get his own way. He entered the Athenian Council Chamber, ejected the non-members, and found an inexperienced drafter to word a new motion. It stipulated that envoys were only to be sent to regular meetings of the Amphiktyonic Council, thereby excluding this special meeting. With the Assembly winding down, when many, including Aeschines, had already returned home, he managed to ratify the motion, turning it into a popular and binding decree. Neither the Athenians nor the Thebans, therefore, were present at Thermopylai when a new Sacred War was declared against Amphissa. A Thessalian called Kottyphos was placed in charge of the Amphiktyonic forces, Philip still being away in Thrace at the time. They had no trouble in subduing the Amphissians. Their leaders were exiled and a heavy fine was imposed, the full amount of which was due before the Council meeting in autumn 339 BC. But by the appointed repayment date, there was still no money in sight and the Amphissians had recalled their exiled leaders. The Council now turned to Philip, who had recently returned to Macedonia, and invested him with the generalship of their army in order to settle the dispute.

The opportunity to march south was well timed. Philip had recovered from his leg wound and the new Sacred War offered a smokescreen behind which he could manoeuvre against the Athenians. Alexander, now established in the army, would accompany him, but his relationship with Thebes was a cause for concern. The powerful city-state, leader of the Boiotian League, was his ally but they sympathised with Amphissa, and had recently expelled the Macedonian garrison at Nikaia, which controlled the crucial Thermopylai pass.[4] The Thebans' wariness of Philip's ever-growing power and influence had started to produce visible signs of resistance. The situation was precarious and had to be handled with care.

Philip decided to circumvent Thermopylai. Instead, he led his army into central Greece via a harder and less frequented route which ran between Mount Kallidromon and Oiti. Access to this 'back door' was made possible through his alliances with the surrounding peoples and the dismantlement of Phokian power that had taken place during the last Sacred War. The Macedonians, their ranks constantly enlarged with the arrival of allied contingents, then established a base camp at Kytinion in Doris. From here, there was a direct passage south to Amphissa via the Gravia pass. To the onlooker, it must have seemed that Philip only had the resolution of the Sacred War in mind, that there was no cause for concern for the Athenians as yet. But then he unexpectedly swung eastwards and occupied Elateia in Phokis, close to the borders of Boiotia and only three days' march from Athens.[5] It was a clear indication that Philip sought to settle both wars in the immediate future. The news sent the Athenians into panic.

At dawn the following day the citizens hastily assembled on the Pnyx, arriving well before the presiding Councillors.[6] Many had suffered a sleepless night as fear spread like wildfire between the neighbourhoods of tightly packed houses and narrow streets. Once everyone had gathered, the latest intelligence was related to the crowd and the herald then asked his customary question, 'Who wishes to speak?' There was silence among the thousands of citizens, sitting, standing, crouching, craning, all looking at each other in desperation. The herald repeated his question again and again, the words failing to incite a response. There was nervous chatter now as a myriad of restless eyes began to seek out the same man in unison – not a general, but the orator who had foreseen the growing menace to the north, who had delivered speech after speech against Philip from this very place. In their darkest hour, the Athenians turned to Demosthenes. He finally rose from his seat and appeared at the rostrum like a divine epiphany in Greek tragedy, ready to rescue the day. He observed correctly that Philip's relationship with the Thebans was in a fragile state, hence his halt at Elateia rather than pushing through Boiotian territory towards Attika. There was no time to rally their other allies; they must persuade their age-old enemy Thebes to join them against Philip. Only together could

they hope to defeat him. The freedom of the Greeks would hinge on the Athenians' ability to persuade.

Demosthenes urged his fellow citizens to banish their fear, and suggested that every man of military age, and all the cavalry, were to march out to Eleusis, on the road to Thebes, in order to show the world that the city-state was now on a war footing, ready to come to their neighbour's aid if called upon. Ten ambassadors must also be quickly dispatched to Thebes. Most important of all, they must not ask for any favour but simply offer their help, no strings attached. Demosthenes' proposals were accepted with unanimous applause; of course he was among the ambassadors sent north. He was not only Athens' foremost orator but also a Theban *proxenos* – an honorary representative of the city; his relationship and understanding of the Theban mentality would be crucial to the mission. They were a belligerent people, not easily swayed; the Athenians disparagingly called them 'Boiotian pigs'.[7]

By the time the embassy reached Thebes, Philip's men were already there – some representatives of his Amphiktyonic allies and selected Companions, the party led by Amyntas (perhaps Philip's nephew) and another called Klearchos.[8] A special Assembly was convened on the Theban acropolis – the Kadmeia – to hear what both sides had to say. The Macedonians, as allies, were allowed to speak first. They stated that the Boiotians should show gratitude to Philip for all the good turns he had done them and should punish the Athenians for their past injuries. Underneath the layers of eulogy, perfumed words and flying accusations was a simple ultimatum: either allow the Macedonians free passage through their land, and, if they so desired, join in the plundering of Attika, or renounce their alliance and declare themselves enemies. The route of least resistance must have seemed like the most sensible option.[9] Demosthenes now took to the floor, the fate of Athens hanging on the success of his words. He did not freeze, as he had done in Pella all those years ago, but delivered a speech so impassioned, so brilliant, that the Boiotians cast aside all other considerations. Their courage and honourable ambition was kindled and suddenly burst into a fire of patriotism and defiance as they threw their lot in with Athens.[10] Or, at least, that is how Demosthenes described the event. The truth of the matter, however, is not as straightforward as he would have us believe.

In the mid-2000s, part of a previously lost speech from Hyperides, who also took part in the embassy, was discovered in a medieval codex.[11] *Against Diondas* recounts an alternative version of events where the Boiotians did not make up their minds on the spot but rather took time to deliberate on the matter. They planned to send an embassy of their own to Philip, primarily to discuss the fortress at Nikaia, which the Amphiktyons were demanding should be handed over to the Lokrians. Meanwhile, they explored a possible alliance with Athens and put forward terms that were heavily weighted in their favour – the Athenians were to recognise the legitimacy of Thebes' claim to the whole of Boiotia, take on the bulk of wartime expenses, and place themselves under Theban leadership for any land-based campaign.[12] They probably expected the usual back and forth that characterised ancient negotiations, allowing them extra time to consider their options, but they had drastically underestimated the fear of the Athenians, who promptly accepted the terms and marched their army to Thebes to cement the alliance. It was, therefore, probably the swift arrival of the Athenian troops, and not Demosthenes' speech, that made them renounce their alliance with Macedon.[13] How Philip reacted to the news is not recorded: disbelief probably, anger almost certainly. Diplomacy had failed and he was to be forced into action.

The Greek coalition acted with admirable speed, occupying key strongholds that guarded the passages south before Philip was able to respond. The Gravia pass, which controlled the road towards Amphissa, was manned with 10,000 mercenaries and placed under the command of the gullible Chares and a general called Proxenos. Another force was established at Parapotamioi, where the river Kephissos entered Boiotia, effectively barring the only alternative route south. Both forces settled in to spend a long winter around the folds of Mount Parnassos.[14]

This was Alexander's first experience of a winter campaign. He was able to observe first-hand the role of the king in keeping up morale, but also the disciplinary actions that were needed to keep the army in check. On one occasion, Philip was forced to take drastic measures when two of his officers – Aeropos and Damasippos – smuggled a female harpist into camp. He responded by exiling both men, a heavy penalty for a harmless misdemeanour.[15] He had also earned a reputation for strictness among the attending royal pages, punishing those who did not perform their duties adequately or took a slack approach to obeying orders. According to one ancient writer, he had once whipped a youth for breaking ranks, and even executed another for taking off his armour without permission.[16] Alexander too would later earn a reputation for severely punishing derelictions of duty.[17]

As winter started to give way to spring, the deadlock did not thaw and so Philip, once again, decided to delve into his general's playbook. Chares had bought one of his tricks on the Propontis; could he be fooled again at Gravia? A fake letter to Antipatros was allowed to fall into enemy hands. It stated that Philip was postponing his invasion due to a revolt in Thrace. The retreat was carefully organised; as the waving *sarissas* receded into the distance the soldiers occupying the pass relaxed their guard. A few days later, Philip attacked.[18] He burst through the pass and defeated the mercenary force. Within a day, the Macedonians were at Amphissa and the Sacred War was brought to an end. The Athenian/Theban defensive alliance pulled their troops back from Parapotamioi to Chaironeia.[19]

Two clashes between the Macedonians and the Greeks are alluded to by Demosthenes around this time – a battle by an unnamed river and another during the winter, the Athenians apparently proving themselves capable fighters, admirable in their discipline, equipment and determination.[20] A possible summary of the first battle comes from a tenth-century AD compendium of strategies and provides more detail.[21] The year was long remembered as being especially wet and the night before the engagement the Greeks managed to secretly flood an area of ground that lay between the two sides.[22] On the following day, the Thebans orchestrated a feigned retreat. Luring the opposition's cavalry into the trap, they succeeded in capturing many men and horses who became bogged down in the mire. It may have been this setback that led Philip to seek further diplomatic solutions. Demosthenes responded by threatening to imprison anyone who suggested the mere possibility of peace and managed to keep the coalition together.[23] All roads now appeared to lead towards a final and decisive battle; it was to take place at Chaironeia, in August 338 BC, where the future of Greece was to be decided.[24]

THE LION OF CHAIRONEIA

Boiotia's flat plains and strategic position in central Greece made it a common setting for ancient confrontations; the Theban general Epameinondas had called it 'the dance-floor of Ares'.[25] The coalition forces had chosen Chaironeia due to its protective mountains that narrowed the Kephissos valley into a slight bottleneck. To the north, across a chequerboard of fields, Mount Akontion frames the skyline, the Kephissos river and nearby railway line running close to its base, trains occasionally flashing past its dappled side. The village of Chaironeia occupies an enclave of the Thourion hills to the south, characterised by a collection of russet-roofed houses stretching along the main road, with court-yards containing scrawny chickens and dilapidated farm machinery. The buildings are overlooked by the rocky Petrachos, the ancient acropolis, a theatre resembling a giant's bite-mark sunk into its base. It was the birthplace of Plutarch, who spent much of his life here, opening a school for the sons of his friends and producing an incredible range and multitude of works. Despite its distance from the main centres of culture, he refused to leave his beloved Chaironeia, lest it become smaller still.[26] During his research for the *Life of Alexander* he was able to draw upon the area's oral traditions, but his account of the battle of Chaironeia is still woefully brief. In this sin, he was not alone. Other ancient writers failed to provide further information.

In June 1937, the British historian Nicholas Hammond came to Chaironeia to investigate the battlefield. He was a Cambridge graduate and had already spent a year traversing the Pindos moun-tain range, following lost roadways, identifying archaeological sites, recording inscriptions and doing his best to avoid the shep-herds' fearsome guard dogs, not always successfully. His knowledge of the Greek language and landscape would later make him a valuable asset to the Allied forces operating in Greece during the Second World War: an expert in explosives and wireless operation, he was parachuted into Nazi-occupied territory to liaise with the local resistance fighters, and he returned to the Pindos, living among the wild places he had come to know as a student. He eventually reached the rank of lieutenant colonel, receiving the DSO and Greek order of the Phoenix for his efforts.[27] Yet he is best known as a prodigious scholar who had a special interest in ancient Macedonia and Epeiros. Throughout the course of his

career he wrote over 130 articles and 15 books, including the
seminal three-volume, *A History of Macedonia*, parts of which
were authored by fellow scholars Guy Griffith and Frank Walbank.
Other historians had previously offered their own interpretations
of the battle of Chaironeia but they remained controversial.[28]
Hammond attempted to reconcile the surviving scraps of written
evidence with a more detailed examination of the site's topography;
his account has subsequently found its way into the majority of
history books that deal with the battle, and remains the most
plausible reconstruction.[29]

Hammond, as other researchers had done, positioned the Greeks'
right wing at a Macedonian burial mound or *polyandrion* (a
communal grave) situated next to the Kephissos river, where it
was commonly believed some of the most intense fighting took

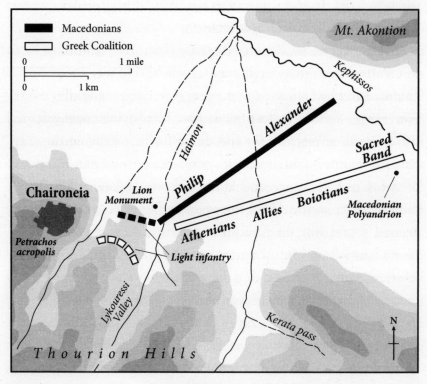

Chaironeia battle plan

place. From here he projected the battle line diagonally across the plain, a distance of around two kilometres, to the Lykouressi valley, just to the south-east of Chaironeia, where Plutarch reports the Greeks had their base camp. It was protected by the fortified Petrachos to the north-west while also covering the Kerata pass to the rear, a useful evacuation route that led across the hills to Lebadeia (modern Livadia). Plutarch called the stream issuing from the Lykouressi valley the Haimon (blood stream), but believed its earlier name was the Thermodon. It crossed the plain towards the Kephissos, and Hammond postulated that it played a key role in the battle, as its name change indicated.[30]

He placed the Athenians on the left, the allies in between and the Boiotians, the Thebans among them, on the right, close to the Macedonian burial mound. The Thebans, under their general Theagenes, were given overall command of the phalanx.[31] The coalition likely also had a sizeable cavalry force but they appear to have played no serious role during the fighting, and their location during the battle remains unknown. The Athenian generals, Chares, Lysikles and Stratokles, also helped in marshalling their own men.[32] Demosthenes was somewhere within their serried ranks, who were deployed in their respective tribes, his shield emblazoned with the words 'Good Luck' in golden lettering.[33] He had done fine work in helping to marshal the defence; Achaians, Arkadians, Corinthians, Euboians and others had joined the anti-Macedonian alliance.[34] Admiring the breadth of their forces, and remembering their victory over the Macedonian cavalry only a few months before, the men remained in good spirits, but that could not make up for the reality that they were bereft of skilled leaders. They had no Iphikrates, Epameinondas or Pelopidas. Philip had the edge in generalship.

The formation of the Macedonian line is more clearly attested. Alexander was positioned somewhere on the left wing. In Plutarch's day an oak tree next to the Kephissos and the fringing marshland was associated with the place he pitched his tent the night before battle.[35] It's likely that he was placed in charge of the Companion cavalry. Although only eighteen years of age he had already gained a reputation as a fighter of valour and swiftness, but in order to temper his inexperience he was surrounded by a number of seasoned generals, among them perhaps the capable cavalry commander, Kleitos the Black, and Parmenion as well, who probably had overall command of the left wing.[36] Philip had once said that the Athenians were lucky to find ten generals to elect each year, he had only ever found one – the aforementioned Parmenion.[37] This was to be a stern test for Alexander, an act of faith on Philip's part. Opposite him were the best fighters in the Greek army, which included the crack infantry unit the Theban Sacred Band, said to have been composed of 150 pairs of male lovers who believed that Love was the only invincible general.[38]

Philip himself occupied the right wing, the traditional posting for the Macedonian king, and was accompanied by his 'picked men', most likely the Foot Companions. They would fight on foot and were supported by the royal pages and recent graduates, the latest crop of young spearmen, among whom were Alexander's boyhood friends. Other units were ordered as the situation demanded, the core of the sarissa-bearing phalanx, some 9,000 men, occupying the centre of the line while divisions of light infantry, archers and slingers protected the flanks.[39] There is no mention of the Thessalian cavalry but they were most likely present, perhaps held back in reserve or positioned alongside the Companion squadrons. The Macedonians and their allies are said to have numbered more than 30,000 infantry and 2,000 horse.[40] Their considerable number represented the manpower that had been marshalled from both inside and outside Macedonia, a reflection of Philip's past twenty years of conquest. Diodorus asserts that they had the numerical superiority; Justin, however, states that the advantage lay with the opposing Greeks.[41] The sides were probably evenly matched.

The Macedonian preparations would have been completed well before battle; the terrain scouted, knives, swords, spears and arrows all sharpened. Philip, his Companions and other allied leaders had made their plans. Orchestrating their collective forces required great discipline and coordination; quick orders, clear directions and timings were of crucial importance if they were to emerge victorious. Philip, perhaps like Alexander before the epic battle of Gaugamela in 331 BC, may have instructed his commanders 'to urge each man in the moment of danger to attend in his own place in the line to the requirements of order, to keep perfect silence when that was necessary in the advance, and by contrast to give a ringing shout when it was right to shout, and howl to inspire the greatest terror when the moment came to howl; they themselves were to obey orders sharply and to pass them on sharply to their regiments, and every man should recall that neglect of his own duty brought the whole cause into common danger, while energetic attention to it contributed to the common success.'[42]

The men must have passed an uneasy night, nerves gathering in the darkness as the watches slipped by. Under torchlight Philip and a select group of followers had probably sacrificed to the gods of the place. Apollo, Herakles and Zeus were all worshipped in Chaironeia, and were among the Macedonians' favoured immortals; Aristandros and other seers were on hand to read their designs in the warm entrails.[43] Before the clash they would watch the skies for further omens of success; the Argead kings believed an eagle swooping from the clouds and simultaneous strikes of lightning were sure signs of victory, that Zeus was on their side.[44] The Greeks, on the other hand, had been plagued by disturbing signs from the gods in the run-up to battle. Celebrants of the Eleusinian Mysteries, while purifying themselves in the sea, had been attacked and killed by a shark.[45] The Delphic Oracle had uttered dire prophecies; Demosthenes accused her of being bribed by Philip, but the Athenians' sacrifices had also been ill-omened. He urged the men to ignore these signs, stating that great leaders of the past had regarded such things as a pretext for cowardice and that the dictates of reason must be followed.[46]

The Macedonians deployed at dawn, arraying themselves against the Greek line, the men emptying their bladders and drinking some wine, a balm for the nerves, before taking up their positions. Today, the Petrachos acropolis provides one of the best vantage points of the battlefield, an ordinary stretch of ground where extraordinary events occurred. Slowly, the outline of Mount Akontion begins to glow a rosy red. The local farmers are already up, their tractors and 4x4s rattling down the dirt tracks that fringe every field, the drowsy chirp of crickets soon accompanied by birds awakening for the new day. As the sun clears Akontion, pale yellow rays flood the narrow, burnished plain. The cool morning air is a luxuriant that will not last, the light teasing out the corrugated plough soil and dense tangle of cotton plants; an arsenal of sprinkler guns imperceptibly pirouette on their metal bases, arching their precious jets of water over the summer crop. On that fateful August day, over two thousand years ago, the plain would have bristled with the weapons of some 60,000 men, and it is only from a position of height that the modern spectator can get some sense of this awesome spectacle: the dance floor of Ares filled with detachments, battalions, rank and file, the stage set for the bloody ballet to come. On the ground, the men would only have been aware of what was within their field of vision. They did not have to worry about the grand plans; their job was simply to obey orders, to kill and avoid being killed.

The battle likely began among the light infantry and skirmishers who tried to dislodge each other from the flanks, slings, javelins and arrows taking some early casualties – the usual prelude to the

The battlefield of Chaironeia

main engagement. A full-throated rendition of a *paian* – a sacred hymn in honour of the gods – was then sung by both sides as the men called on the immortals to aid their cause, the bellowing unison of voices inspiring confidence in themselves and each other. Trumpets inaugurated the Macedonian advance. Hammond believed that their speed had been prearranged, and that the right wing slowly began to extend out in front of the rest of the line, so that the Macedonians were marching obliquely against the defenders.

Peering over their mass of shields, the Greeks gazed upon the Macedonian advance. The thicket of iron spikes pointed to the sky, yet to be lowered into position; the sound of stamping feet drumming in their ears, sweat began to gather under their cuirasses, the spears feeling slippery in their hands. The shouts of their commanders echoed down the line, words to rouse passion and steel courage. The ancestors of the Athenians had once beaten back the Persian hordes; the Thebans had bested the fearsome Spartans. There was much cause for optimism, but the army that was marching towards them was a different prospect – a well-drilled and highly experienced force that practised a new type of warfare, one that was both more advanced and more adaptable than traditional hoplite-based tactics.

Another blast of the trumpet and the *sarissas* were lowered, levelled directly at the Greeks. The points of innumerable spears projecting out from the front of the line, the Macedonians' grizzled faces just visible through the forest of wood and iron, the most fearsome warriors surrounding Philip – the Foot Companions – probably armed with the same panoplies as their enemies: swords, spears and large shields. The ominous battle cry *Alalai!* then erupted from their ranks, the Greeks answering in kind, man screaming at man as if they were separated by mountaintops. Xenophon, writing about another fourth-century BC battle, describes the actions that accompanied the crunch of impact: the men, 'Thrusting shield against shield . . . shoved and fought and killed and fell. There was no shouting, nor was there silence, but the strange noise that wrath and battle together will produce.'[47] Diodorus, who provides the only summary of events, says that the fight was hotly contested for a long time, many falling on either side, so that for a while the struggle permitted hopes of victory for both. Hammond believed that a stratagem recorded by Polyaenus should be attributed to this time, whereby Philip yielded and carefully began withdrawing his right wing.[48] The Greeks opposite had their blood up now. They took the bait and pursued, the Athenian general Stratokles urging his men to push the enemy back to Macedonia.[49] Philip, saying that the Athenians didn't understand how to win, moved his men backwards and to their right, closing their ranks and extending the line, the centre drawing in reinforcements to ensure that no gaps emerged. Its aim was to loosen the coalition's formation and to draw their left wing away from the rest of the line. Philip also believed that the longer the battle lasted the more it would favour his own men, who were fitter and more experienced.[50] Hammond estimated that they retreated some 150 metres, a manoeuvre which probably took them less than half an hour to execute.[51] Alexander, at the head of the Companion cavalry and astride Boukephalas, patiently observed the scene: his wing still slowly advancing, the line flexing like a discus thrower's arm. He was waiting for a moment, the moment that underpinned Philip's master plan, the moment that promised victory. As predicted, the advance of the Greeks began to drag their line across to the left. Those opposite Alexander, however, remained in position so as not to expose their flank. A tear appeared in the middle of the line, either between the divisions of Greek allies or where they joined the Boiotians. Alexander charged towards the opening.[52]

The cavalry's spears smashed against the hoplite shields, some horsemen fighting on with the broken ends of their weapons, others reaching for the razor-sharp *kopis* sabres secured to their sides. This was a new type of cavalry encounter, more like a mounted infantry battle than the usual long-distance hit and raid tactics that the Greeks were accustomed to. The horses had been exceptionally well trained not to flinch at the danger; they wheeled, reared and rammed those around them, horses entangled with men, the Companions raining down blows on the enemy as death came from above.[53] Alexander, it is said, was the first to succeed in rupturing the enemy line, striking down many and urging Boukephalas deeper into their ranks, severing the Greek forces into two, the Companions around him also fighting with distinction, all the time opening up more gaps.[54] Meanwhile, Philip had retreated to some slightly higher ground which Hammond identified with the raised banks of the Thermodon/Haimon stream.

The final phase of the plan now came into effect. The trumpets sounded the general advance. The Greeks took the full force of the Macedonian phalanx.[55] Whetted steel parted flesh, bellies split open like ripe pomegranates, the ground was coloured black with blood and gore, the air reeking with the smell of shit and sweat. Battle frenzy gripped some, the dead and injured dropping to the ground, quickly replaced by those stationed behind. The Companion cavalry had by now succeeded in routing much of the Greek centre and right wing, putting many to flight, but the Sacred Band remained, holding steadfast to their position, probably battling a division of the *sarissa* phalanx. Alexander gathered his men together and made ready to make another charge, perhaps shouting the words that he would later use against the Persians: 'Let us charge once more Macedonians, once more nobly!' Plutarch says that he won acclaim for his actions, being the first to break the ranks of the Sacred Band.[56] They were eventually surrounded and cut to pieces. Those defenders at the centre and on the left suffered similar casualties and were forced back towards the Lykouressi valley. Those that did not flee were annihilated. The Thermodon's waters ran red from the fighting. Victory belonged to the Macedonians.

The battlefield was strewn with the human wreckage of war. Under the scorching August sun, lifeless bodies blistered and burned, the victors stripping the dead while physicians and those with some knowledge of healing arts set about attending to the wounded; the restless spirits of the dead wandered the plain, 'the earth stained with blood, friend and foe lying dead side by side, shields smashed to pieces, spears snapped in two, daggers bared of their sheaths, some on the ground, some embedded in the bodies, some yet gripped by the hand.'[57] This is how Xenophon describes the scenes accompanying the aftermath of combat, and so it must have been at Chaironeia too. More than a thousand Athenians had perished, the Boiotians losing a similar number, perhaps their allies as well; the Theban Sacred Band had been all but wiped out. Philip later encountered these elite Theban warriors lying where they had fallen, surrounded with the broken shafts of *sarissas*; he shed tears, stating, 'A curse on those who imagine that these men ever did or suffered anything shameful!'[58] – perhaps a reference to their famed homosexuality that others had used as a means of slander.[59] Two thousand Athenians and many Boiotians had been taken prisoner during the battle, while the rest of the army managed to escape via the Kerata pass and regrouped at Lebadeia. Demosthenes was among them. He had stood honourably at first but he was no fighter; during his getaway, he had apparently caught his cloak on some brambles and, without looking behind, cried, 'Take me alive!'[60] Philip did not pursue. The victory had been decisive, the Greek resistance decimated, but according to Plutarch, he would later shudder at 'the power and the ability of the orator who had forced him to hazard his empire and his life in the brief span of a single day'.[61]

The Macedonians chose a location next to the Kephissos for their funeral rites. The huge earthen burial mound (roughly 7m high and 70m across) is now covered with black cypress, the tree of the dead. It was excavated by Georgios Sotiriades at the beginning of the twentieth century.[62] Underneath, he discovered the remains of a large funeral pyre, a congealed mass of ash, bone and half-burned logs, some 10m in diameter and in places 75cm thick.[63] No figures for the Macedonian dead are given but the size of the pyre indicates that it was no small number. The bodies had been incinerated by the intense heat, leaving only fragments behind. Two large crates of charred human remains were retrieved from the site, along with a collection of iron weapons laid at their side – *sarissas*, javelins, swords and knives, some of which are now on display in the local museum.[64] The offerings were simple. There was no gold or silver, only the everyday objects that accompanied an army on campaign – a few coins, some ceramics and an amphora of wine.

The Macedonian burial mound at Chaironeia

Philip presided over the ceremony; the burial of the war dead
was a royal duty. Speeches were made, sacrifices offered, the army
parading in honour of their fallen comrades.[65] The palm of bravery
was the highest accolade, awarded to the individual who fought
with the greatest distinction. Alexander would later win the palm
in Asia, but it was probably Philip who won it here as he was
given overall credit for the victory.[66] Diodorus' account of the
battle, which tends towards the romantic, portrays father and son
competing with each other for the glory of winning the day.
Alexander, he says, was set on showing Philip his prowess in battle,
yielding to none in the will to win. He had succeeded in proving
himself, not just as an able warrior but also a leader of skill and
courage – it was a clear sign of things to come. Many more prizes
were likely given to other individuals who had performed admi-
rably, the gifts helping to strengthen morale while reinforcing the
central importance of honour within the army.[67] As the pyre was
kindled, trumpets sounded, the men raising their battle cry, some

throwing their own offerings onto the heap of bodies as the column of black smoke rose into Boiotia's laden air, the pungent smell of burning flesh filling their nostrils.[68] Feasting and funeral games probably followed. Afterwards the army worked together to heap earth over the remains of the dead. The Macedonians did not erect trophies; it was the battleground burials and associated rituals that lasted, both in local memory and the physical landscape.[69]

At the entrance to the village of Chaironeia, on the other side of the valley, is the site of another mass grave. It is marked by a colossal statue of a lion, its rigid gaze transfixed on the Macedonian mound to the north-east. During excavations in 1880, 254 skeletons were discovered in a rectangular enclosure around the statue's base, the men neatly buried in rows, 'a phalanx of the dead' as one historian called it.[70] The number of the deceased roughly corresponds with the 300 of the Sacred Band and the tomb is commonly ascribed to them. The records of the excavation are incomplete, although some of the original drawings of the skeletons and mass grave have recently come to light.[71] The lead archaeologist died shortly afterwards and his notes have been lost. Six crates of bones were reportedly sent to the Archaeological Museum in Athens but they have also disappeared. A small collection of remains, however, has survived to be studied, a miscellany of bones believed to represent twelve to eighteen individuals. They provide a snapshot of the brutality of fourth century BC warfare, and the terror of the Macedonian war machine in action.[72]

Out of the ten sets of cranial remains all except one show signs of trauma. Three skulls have evidence of sword cuts delivered from above, which is consistent with a cavalry attack; one of them bears the puncture wound of a spear's butt spike. The warrior, fallen to the ground, appears to have been trampled by the advancing Macedonians, where someone took the time to make sure death was certain. Another died from the blow of a large blunt object, probably the rim of a foot soldier's shield, which was rammed upwards into his face, separating it from the braincase. The skull of 'Gamma 16' is the most horrific: the straight cut of a sword sliced across his forehead, a backhanded flash of a cavalryman's blade as he charged past the defender, the man's face nearly sheared clean off. Numerous hacking injuries to the legs and some severed feet suggest that the bodies were mutilated after death, evidence of a gruesome dismembering of the slain. It is easy to get carried away with the romance of these ancient battles: the glorious deeds of the victors, the slick choreography that Hollywood films have made famous, the past often sanitised with our growing distance from it, but these bones bring us closer to the reality – the chaos, desperation, harrowing injuries, mutilations and shuddering acts of violence that accompanied every Macedonian victory.

After the duties to the dead had been fulfilled, Philip celebrated with his men. It was a much-needed release from the nerves and hardships that had been his constant companions since the campaign began. Elated by the mixture of wine and victory, he led a *komos*, a drunken procession, through the Athenian prisoners of war. One of them, the orator Demades, rebuked him for his insensitivity. He is said to have remarked: 'O King, when Fortune has cast you in the role of Agamemnon, are you not ashamed to act the part of Thersites?'[73] Thersites was the most despicable character in the *Iliad*, 'ill-favoured beyond all men who came to Troy', and moreover he was lame in one leg; considering Philip's limp, an outcome of the wound suffered at the hands of the Triballoi, the insult was exceptionally well aimed and succeeded in cutting him to the quick.[74] He cast off his garland and instantly changed his demeanour. Justin, however, records an alternative tradition, where Philip shrewdly concealed his joy at victory, neither laughing at dinner nor allowing games to be played, using no garlands or perfume: 'as far as he could, he conquered without making anyone feel that he was a conqueror.'[75] This version is perhaps to be preferred as it is consistent with his general magnanimity towards the Athenians during his reign. Nevertheless, he did at some point strike up conversation with Demades who, along with his own envoys, was sent to Athens to begin peace talks.

The city had fallen into despair on hearing the news from Chaironeia. Women could be seen crouching in doorways, desperately asking passers-by for news about their loved ones, while the Athenians' hopes came to rest with the men over fifty, who had been exempt from military service. They could be seen shuffling around the streets with their cloaks pinned double around them, a new sense of purpose in their aged step. The depleted Assembly hastily voted for a series of drastic measures in preparation for what they believed to be an imminent Macedonian attack – slaves were to be freed, resident foreigners (*metics*) made citizens, and exiles recalled. One contemporary would later claim that to see the Assembly support such acts would surely have stirred any spectator and moved them to tears over the sorrows of Athens.[76] Every man in the city was set to work, either digging ditches or making palisades, in the expectation of a siege. The women and sacred objects were evacuated to the Peiraieus – the port of Athens – and pleas for aid were sent out to their nearby allies. But their fears turned out to be unfounded. Demades, on his arrival, let them know that Philip desired peace.

The Athenians charged Phokion, Demades and Aeschines with finding out what exactly the terms entailed. They headed back to Boiotia, but, realistically, they were in no position to negotiate. Philip was lenient, allowing them to keep the freedom of their democracy. There were to be no Macedonian garrisons, and their fleet was to remain intact; he did insist, however, that the Second Athenian League be disbanded, although they were allowed to keep control of some of their island holdings. In these measures Philip exhibited a sound understanding of the source of Athenian power; by removing their hegemony over the Aegean and thus reducing the revenues accrued from tribute-paying islands, he was cutting the legs out from beneath them. They were almost certainly also forced to recall their settlers in the Chersonese, who are not heard of again. The Athenians accepted the terms. They could have been much worse, especially when viewed alongside the treatment of Thebes.

Philip treated his treacherous allies harshly, putting a price on the Theban prisoners of war and even ransoming the bodies of their dead.[77] The city's leading men were either exiled, some finding refuge in Athens, or beheaded, while a new government of three hundred pro-Macedonian personnel replaced the former democracy. Their leadership of the Boiotian League was revoked and, as an extra indignity, two thousand Macedonian soldiers were garrisoned on the Kadmeia. But Philip didn't stop there. To further limit their influence, Oropos, a Theban-controlled city on the border with Attika, was given its independence, and the Boiotian cities of Plataia, Orchomenos and Thespiai – previously destroyed by Thebes – were rebuilt and repopulated.[78] They were to act as a permanent safeguard against any possible return of Theban dominion. Why exactly Philip spared Athens a similar fate remains unclear. He may have wished to assume control of their sizeable fleet, the invasion of Persia being still on his mind, but it was perhaps a concern for his own reputation that ultimately lay behind the decision. He was all too aware of the venom and bile that had been expended by orators like Demosthenes in depicting him as a monster. Philip reportedly said, 'I try both by my words and by my deeds to prove that they are liars.'[79] Some of his Companions had pushed for more drastic punishments, such as garrisons, but he 'preferred to be called a good man for a long time rather than a master for a short time'.[80] A preoccupation with his public persona was a trait he shared with his son.

As a further sign of his good will towards the Athenians, he released their prisoners of war, although he was annoyed when they asked for the return of the personal possessions seized by the Macedonians. 'Does it not seem to you', Philip said to his men, 'that the Athenians think they have been beaten by us in a game of knuckle-bones?'[81] The dead were also to accompany the living back to their homeland. With Philip's consent, they had been retrieved from the battlefield, divided (where possible) into their respective tribes, and most likely cremated. They were to be escorted by a special Macedonian embassy, which included Antipatros, a Macedonian nobleman called Alkimachos, and Alexander.[82] His trip to Athens, the only one he ever made, is not recounted in any detail by the ancient historians but the experience must surely have affected him. His education had been steeped in Athenian culture; the city was the birthplace of theatre, and the leading light in philosophy and political oratory – its list of famous names, from Theseus to Themistokles, ran longer than Homer's catalogue of ships. The recent events at Chaironeia, however, made it a sensitive time for a Macedonian visit. The city's mood must have been decidedly sombre. The statesman Perikles had once likened the loss of young citizens in battle to spring being taken out of the year.[83]

The embassy had work to do, securing oaths and allegiances, but there must also have been the opportunity for Alexander to explore and satisfy his renowned curiosity. Like that of a modern tourist, his itinerary probably included the must-see sights – the richly adorned Agora, packed with shops, noticeboards, law courts, stoas and statues – sculptures of Philip and Alexander were soon to be added to the collection – and perhaps, considering Alexander's interest in philosophy, a trip to the Academy. It may have been in the grounds surrounding the gymnasion that Alexander raced against a famous sprinter, Krison, a story recounted by Plutarch, although he was apparently indignant that the champion appeared to slacken his pace as not to embarrass him.[84] And then, of course, there was the Acropolis – the crowning architectural glory of Athens. It is visible from every part of the city, the eyes constantly drawn up to its precipitous flanks that blush pink in the morning light – the domain of gods and birds.

Today, the long walk up towards the propylaia – the ancient entrance – adds to the expectation of what lies within the snug-fitting walls; the small but exquisite temple of Athena Nike peeping over the side, the grand staircase disappearing between marble columns as the city stretches out below, Helios' rays dancing on innumerable windows, car bonnets and asphalt roads. A colossal bronze statue of Athena Promachos, the goddess with shield and spear standing 30ft (9m) tall, once greeted the ancient visitor, though sadly only a faint impression of the base remains. The Acropolis was the centre of her cult in Athens. She had won the mythical contest for the city's patronage, beating the sea god Poseidon by providing the residents with an olive tree, far more useful than Poseidon's gift of a salt-water spring. The oddly shaped Erechtheion temple held her most sacred image, a wooden statue that was believed to have come straight from the heavens, but the most magnificent edifice was the Parthenon, Classical Greece's largest temple. It was built entirely of snow-white Pentelic marble that had softened into a creamy-yellow over time; the joins between the masonry blocks were so exact that not even a knife blade could penetrate, the sculptural adornments and architectural decorations picked out with brightly coloured pigments, now long faded. Inside was the Athenian sculptor Pheidias' masterpiece, the gold and ivory statue of Athena Parthenos (Athena the Virgin), standing 11m high, in her hand a human-sized figure of Victory.

All of these monuments had risen from the flames of Persian destruction. The holy centre of Athens had been sacked in 480 BC by the Great King Xerxes and his innumerable hordes. Its regeneration, following the Greek victories at Salamis and Plataia, marked the beginning of an Athenian Golden Age. The significance of the site to the collective Greek psyche was not lost on Alexander. He would later send three hundred panoplies of Persian arms to be dedicated here, along with the inscription, 'Alexander son of Philip and the Greeks, except the Lacedaemonians [Spartans], set up these spoils from the barbarians dwelling in Asia.'[85] The temple absorbed and monumentalised his achievements, just as it had done for the Athenians. He left the city after, having been made an honorary citizen, taking oaths of allegiance back to his father, dreaming, no doubt, of the opportunities that the future would bring.

A FAREWELL TO ARMS

That winter, the Athenians staged the funeral of their war dead. It took place outside the walls in the *Demosion Sema*, the public cemetery of Athens, which was located within the Kerameikos district, named after the neighbourhood's many ceramics workshops and described by the historian Thucydides as the 'loveliest suburb of the city'.[86] The Kerameikos archaeological site, which preserves part of the ancient cemetery, is sunk amid the modern cityscape. On a chilly, grey winter's morning it is an ideal place for a walk. Dark rain clouds sail across the washed-out sky with the stately elegance of triremes at sea. Replica funeral stelai and sculptures have replaced the originals, and the walker is haunted by their depictions of sorrow, final farewells captured in marble. Sisters Demetria and Pamphile look out vacantly from beneath the pediment of their grave relief, playing with their veils in a

timeless moment of uncertainty. Nearby, Dexileos has been immortalised in the heat of battle, riding his horse over an enemy.
Epigrams accompany some of the images of the dead. Eukoline's,
now housed in the on-site museum, reads:

> *This woman had a name*
> *connected with Ease.*
> *Now she lies in the earth and shares*
> *The fate common to all.*[87]

That above the stele of matronly Ampharete is one of the most
poignant. She is shown cradling her lost grandchild in one arm,
the baby wriggling in delight as she shows it a toy bird:

> *I hold here the beloved child of my daughter,*
> *which I held on my knees when we were alive*
> *and saw the light of the sun,*
> *and now, dead, I hold it dead.*[88]

The *Demosion Sema* begins two hundred metres beyond the
remains of the Dipylon gate, lining the road to the Academy. It
was the widest road in the city, in some places reaching just over
forty metres in width, a grand boulevard of the dead where the
great and the good of Athens, along with those killed in battle,
were laid to rest at public expense; an evocative display of both
the city's history and its ideals.[89] Only a small section of the road
survives today, along with a few masonry tombs; they are well-
constructed, imposing. Casualty lists were once displayed alongside
them, detailing the names of those contained within. The
Chaironeia war dead were buried somewhere beyond the limit of
the archaeological park, the epitaph bearing the line 'Never to fail
and ever to succeed belongs to the gods.'[90] The second century AD

traveller Pausanias records that their tomb was to be found near those killed at Amphipolis, Delion in Boiotian Tanagra, Thessaly, Cyprus, and during a sea battle at the Hellespont.[91] It may well be discovered in the future, but for now, the exposed northern part of the site is the closest one can get to where – the Athenians believed – Greek freedom was buried.[92]

Two days before the funeral, a tent was erected where the ashes of the dead were displayed, enabling the families to pay their respects. The main ceremony began with a procession before dawn. Ten cypress wood coffins, one for each of the city's tribes, were transported to the cemetery on wagons. They were accompanied by a train of mourners, while an eleventh bier followed, dressed but left empty. It was for those missing in action – the original unknown soldiers.[93] Demosthenes, despite the catastrophic defeat and his central role in bringing about the conflict, was elected to give the eulogy. On his return to Athens he had helped them prepare for the siege, and he would later be honoured for his services to the city with a crown, so he still had the people's respect and trust.[94] The Athenian general Lysikles had not been so lucky. Following the defeat at Chaironeia, the orator Lycurgus labelled him 'a living monument of our country's shame and disgrace', and he was duly executed.[95]

The eulogy was probably given by the side of the graves, before they had been backfilled. As the sky began to lighten, Demosthenes took to the platform that overlooked the crowd, many perhaps sitting on bleachers temporarily erected for the event; the congregation a mass of heartbreak, runny noses and numb hands. The eulogy followed a set format. Demosthenes recounted the dead's noble ancestry, their bravery in battle, the virtues of democracy and the mythical stories of the ten tribes that incentivised their thirst for honour. He then summed up:

It is a grievous thing for fathers and mothers to be deprived of their children and in their old age to lack the care of those who are nearest and dearest to them. Yes, but it is a proud privilege to behold them possessors of deathless honours and a memorial of their valour erected by the State, and deemed deserving of sacrifices and games for all future time. It is painful for children to be orphaned of a father. Yes, but it is a beautiful thing to be the heir of a father's fame. And of this pain we shall find the deity to be the cause, to whom mortal creatures must yield, but of the glory and honour the source is found in the choice of those who willed to die nobly.'[96]

It is not among his most brilliant of speeches; the constraints of tradition weighed heavily on his words. He ended the eulogy simply and abruptly, as was the fashion: 'and now. . . having spent your grief and done your part as law and custom require, disperse to your homes.'[97] Demosthenes believed that the soul of Greek freedom had died with these men; with their loss, 'all the old-time radiance of the Greeks is sunk in gloom and profound obscurity.'[98] After his duties had been fulfilled, he took a step back from the limelight, continuing to propose decrees but no longer in his own name.[99] The future of the city was entrusted to others.

All eyes were now focused on Philip. He had control of Greece. The question was, what was he going to do with it?

7.

RECONCILIATION

The Epigraphical Museum in Athens contains over 14,000 inscriptions – a dizzying array of decrees, laws, treaties, voted honours and financial disclosures, an enduring testament to the Greeks' love of bureaucracy, an archive set in stone. Inscribed stelai, of varying size and completeness, line the edges of the museum's main halls, each bearing painted-on reference numbers, with more fragmentary blocks placed on sturdy shelves above. EM 7146 and 7182 are particularly relevant to the events that followed Philip's victory at Chaironeia, and are two parts of the same stele, once set up on the Acropolis. The script is in poor condition; a step-ladder and a strong beam of raking light are needed to tease out the worn impressions of the stonemason's chisel. Precise reconstructions of the text have proved tricky, but the first fragment is believed to read:

> Oath. I swear by Zeus, Earth, Sun, Poseidon, Athena, Ares, all the gods and goddesses: I shall abide by the peace (?); and I shall neither break the agreement with Philip (?) nor take up arms for harm against any of those who abide by the oaths (?), neither by land nor by sea; nor shall I take any

city or guard-post nor harbour, for war, of any of those participating in the peace, by any craft or contrivance; nor shall I overthrow the kingdom of Philip or his descendants, nor the constitutions existing in each state when they swore the oaths concerning the peace; nor shall I myself do anything contrary to these agreements, nor shall I allow any one else as far as possible.

If any one does commit any breach of treaty concerning the agreements, I shall go in support as called on by those who are wronged (?), and I shall make war against the one who transgresses the common peace (?), as decided by the common council (*synedrion*) and called on by the *hegemon*; and I shall not abandon . . .[1]

The inscription breaks off, but the text that does survive, battered and barely decipherable to the naked eye, represents a seminal moment in ancient history, the culmination of Philip's vision for the future of Greece – the establishment of what is now known as the League of Corinth.

The groundwork for this settlement was laid in the weeks and months following Chaironeia. After dealing with Thebes and Athens, Philip turned his attention to the other regional powers. The remaining anti-Macedonian city-states surrendered to him as he marched south, individually coming to terms with the new master of Greece.[2] A natural reordering of local governments took place in his wake, with pro-Macedonian factions rising to prominence. Garrisons like that established at Thebes were also carefully positioned at a few other key locations: Ambrakia in western Greece, Corinth, and probably Euboian Chalkis as well.[3] The Lakedaimonians, led by the city of Sparta, had not joined the

Greek coalition at Chaironeia. They had long since been humbled
by Thebes, but with the recent defeat of the Thebans, many
Peloponnesians began to fear a return of Spartan dominion. Some
city-states had already started to sympathise with Philip, and they
now appealed to him to enter their lands, embracing the king as
their new protector.[4]

The Macedonian army's movements in the Peloponnese are not
easy to trace; there is only a thin trail of breadcrumbs to follow.
Pausanias, in his second century AD *Guide to Greece*, mentions the
remains of Philip's camp at Nestane, on the northern borders of
Arkadia, as well as a spring that was named after him.[5] In the
agora of Megalopolis, further to the south-west, the residents
dedicated a newly erected stoa to the king which probably held
his statue, suggesting that he had paid a visit.[6] Alexander was most
likely with the army during this time.[7] At Gortys, a day's travel
north of Megalopolis, the local people preserved the tradition that
he had dedicated a breastplate and spear to Asklepios at the city's
sanctuary, and they were still there in Pausanias' time.[8] That
Alexander made the trip cannot be securely known – the dedications could have been sent by others – but such an experience fits
with what we know about his curiosity and medicinal interests.
There were other sights too that must have made an impression
on him, as well as Philip, during their time in the south. The grave
of Epameinondas, a famous Theban general, lay on the route
through Arkadia, as did the magnificent temple of Athena Alea at
Tegea, which was said to have housed the withered hide and tusks
of the mythical Kalydonian Boar. At the spring outside its walls,
Herakles had reportedly violated the maiden Auge. The Peloponnese
was the arena for many of the hero's exploits, such as the killing
of the Nemean lion and the Stymphalian birds, stories that
Alexander had grown up with. He and his father were now
following in the footsteps of their illustrious ancestor.[9]

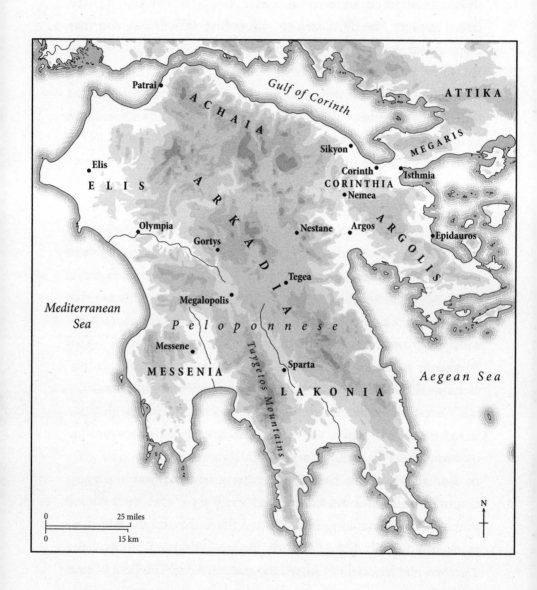

The primary objective of their campaign was the Spartans. According to Plutarch, Philip wrote to them asking whether he should enter their territory as friend or foe. 'Neither,' was the famed reply.[10] He subsequently ravaged their land, cutting the crops and trees, burning homesteads; Lakonia's borders were then reordered in favour of his allies.[11] It was only when all disputes were settled, probably towards the end of 338 BC, that Philip called the Greeks together at the Corinthian Isthmus to establish the League. The Lakedaimonians refused to take part, 'thinking that what was not agreed on by the cities but imposed by a conqueror was not peace but servitude.'[12]

The grand meeting probably took place at the sanctuary of Poseidon at Isthmia, the site occupying a sea-girt ridge overlooking the Saronic Gulf.[13] Every two years, Greeks from far and wide came here to celebrate the Crown Games of Isthmia. It was one of the four on the Pan-Hellenic circuit, along with the Olympics and the Pythian and Nemean Games. The athletes, glazed in olive oil, competed for wreaths of wild celery, the games being held in honour of the boy-hero Melikertes-Palaimon. The sanctuary itself was heavily robbed in antiquity but the foundations of Poseidon's temple can still be seen. It was once fronted by statues of the sea god and his associates, the sacred ground dripping with brine-soaked imagery. Set among the umbrella pines that the ancient geographer Strabo mentions as a notable feature of the site are also the ruins of a theatre, shrines, caverns for ritual feasts, and a starting gate from the original stadium.[14] The sanctuary's infrastructure catered for large crowds and made it a suitable place for the meeting. The Greeks now came together not in celebration of the games but at Philip's behest. Demosthenes was not among the Athenian delegates, although he may have stood for election as one of their representatives. The Assembly wisely overlooked his candidacy, for such an act could have easily been construed as defiance against the new arrangement.[15]

The exact nature of the League of Corinth is still debated but essentially it was an organisation charged with keeping a new Common Peace between the Greeks, an idea that Philip had been toying with since the late 340s BC. He and his advisors, Aristotle perhaps among them, knew their history and sought to incorporate lessons from the past in order to establish a more lasting settlement.[16] A Council of the Greeks (*synedrion*) was created as the decision-making body. They could pass judgements and act with relative autonomy; meetings were held annually and took place wherever the Pan-Hellenic Games were being held that given year.[17] Philip was elected *hegemon* or chief executive as the guarantor of the peace, the iron hand beneath the velvet glove. On the face of it, the League of Corinth offered freedom, but in reality it was a mechanism of Macedonian control. The oath, a sacred pact, bound the city-states and peoples of Greece together. They swore to uphold the Council's decisions and not to make war on each other or on Philip and his successors. If any reneged on the peace, they would face a powerful coalition spearheaded by Macedon. The second fragment in the Epigraphical Museum bears the names of some of the members, among them Thessalians, Ambrakiots, Phokians, Lokrians, Malians, Perrhaibians and Oitians, as well as those from the islands – Samothrace, Thasos, Zakynthos and Kephallenia. Next to the names are numbers which probably represent the votes allotted to each party on the Council and their military obligations, which were dictated by their respective sizes.[18] Together, the two marble fragments resound with the many voices of the ancient Greeks, all declaring in unison an end to the internecine wars that had dominated their history. Philip was at his diplomatic best during the League's formation, and steps were taken incrementally to build the organisation and elect officials. It was probably at a subsequent meeting, held in spring 337 BC, that he revealed the next stage of his grand plan: there was to be an offensive alliance between the members, who together would launch an invasion of Persia.[19]

It was sold to the Greeks as a war of revenge, payback for the Persian destruction of their holy sites in 480–79 BC. The endeavour would help galvanise the disparate communities into a single entity, with peace to be sealed in Persian blood. The Corinthian Isthmus was an appropriate setting for the proposal, as a Hellenic alliance had been formed there during the Persian Wars, and Philip was able to tap into the memories of the past in order to strengthen support for his bid.[20] As with the Sacred War, he fashioned himself as a champion of the gods, fighting on their behalf in order to gain the goodwill of the Greeks. The Council voted for war; they probably had little other choice. Philip was elected commander-in-chief of the operation, and each member state was then instructed to levy troops and to put preparations in train.[21] Beneath the façade of pious retribution lay Philip's true ambitions. The desire for such a campaign had been a long-term goal. The conquest of Thrace and the settlement of Greek affairs, although worthwhile in their own right, were necessary precursors for any serious expedition to the east. The Persians had already declared their animosity towards Macedon by sending troops to help protect the Propontic cities while they were under siege, and Philip may have wished to put an end to their meddling in Greek affairs once and for all.[22] The extent of his ambitions remains unclear, but they may have aligned with those proposed by Isocrates in his open letter to the king, which had been circulated after the Peace of Philokrates – in other words to conquer the entire Persian Empire. If that turned out to be impossible, to annexe Asia Minor, from Kilikia to Sinope, would be acceptable, or, at the very least, to liberate the Ionian cities of the region.[23] After the battle of Chaironeia, Isocrates, then ninety-eight, picked up his pen once more and sent a final letter to Philip urging him to take up the fight: 'Be assured that a glory unsurpassable and worthy of the deeds you have done in the past will be yours when you shall compel the barbarians – all but those who have fought on your side – to be serfs of the Greeks, and when you shall force the king who is now called Great to do whatever you command. For then will naught be left for you except to become a god.'[24] Isocrates would never get to see the manifestation of his lifelong dream – he died shortly after writing the letter – but his carefully chosen words suggest that, along with Philip's many other possible motivations for the Persian campaign, the striving for everlasting fame was perhaps the strongest.[25]

The timing of the campaign was to be opportune. The Great King, Artaxerxes III (Ochos), had recently died. His son Arses (Artaxerxes IV) had succeeded to the throne but the early years following accession were often troubling times for new monarchs, the instability playing into the hands of enemies.[26] Philip, however, did not rush into the campaign. He had been away from Macedonia for over a year and the army needed some rest and time with their families. It was also too soon to say whether the League of Corinth would prove a stable solution to the affairs of Greece. An advance expedition was planned for the following spring in order to secure a bridgehead for the main invasion, which was to take place the year after. But before Philip left the Peloponnese, he found time to commission a unique monument that enshrined his achieve-ments and broadcast the Argeads' new status as leaders of the Greeks. It was built in one of the most sacred precincts in the Hellenic world – the Altis of Olympia – and became known as the Philippeion.

Philip had already used the Olympics as a useful propaganda tool. His horse and chariot teams had won the illustrious olive wreath in the past, and he had minted special coins to mark the occasions. The Elians, who controlled the site, had accompanied the Macedonians into Lakonia and had been rewarded in the form of new territory stripped from the Spartans; they now reciprocated and granted Philip permission to build a monument within Zeus' sacred boundary.[27] The famed sculptor Leochares was hired to undertake the project, probably with the intention of having it complete for the IIIth Olympic Games, in 336 BC.[28] Following the modern tourist trail, it is now among the first buildings to be encountered on entering the walled Altis. It occupied an exalted location, close to the Prytaneion that held the victory banquet for the Olympic victors, the precinct of the hero Pelops, the Hill of Kronos and the temple of Hera. For a long time only the two concentric rings of foundation stones were visible, along with a few of the remaining marble architectural fragments, but in 2005 the German Archaeological Institute completed a partial restoration of the circular façade, recapturing something of its original grandeur. On top of the three-stepped marble podium are some reassembled Ionic columns, crowned with a section of curving entablature. They once encircled a *tholos* chamber which housed life-size statues of the Argeads arrayed on a semi-circular base. Philip's image is believed to have been placed in the centre, opposite the doorway. His father, Amyntas III, and mother, Eurydike, were probably on his left, Alexander and Olympias on his right. Pausanias tells us that they were made from ivory and gold – chryselephantine – a combination that had divine connotations for the Greeks. Pheidias' colossal Olympian Zeus, set up in the sanctuary's main temple, was of the same material.[29]

For those who had never seen the Argeads before, had only heard of the numerous victories that had allowed their previously fragile kingdom to strengthen and grow, this was their first introduction. It told them everything they needed to know – what they looked like, the various members of the royal family, past and present, and their willingness to communicate their newfound power in Greece.

The Philippeion at Olympia

This dynamic statue group was carefully selected. Philip's elder brothers, both kings before him, were not shown, nor were his other wives or children. Alexander and Olympias were given a position of prominence in the royal line-up, a reflection of their status in the continuum of Argead power. By this time Plutarch tells us that Philip was excessively fond of his son. Following the success at Chaironeia, he rejoiced to hear the Macedonians jokingly refer to Alexander as their king and Philip their general. This story may well contain some truth, as Justin records that Philip issued orders that he not be addressed as 'king of Greece', a term unpalatable to the Greeks, but as 'general' instead.[30] The good-natured state of the relationship between father and son, however, would not last. Fresh from attaining new heights of adoration, it took an ugly turn.

BREAKDOWN

The problems, it was claimed, had their source in the women's quarters.[31] Philip had so far married six times. Of these royal wives Nikesipolis had died shortly after giving birth to Thessalonike and it is unclear which of the others, aside from Olympias and probably Meda, were still alive, but Alexander's position had long made his mother the most influential among them, and she had the most to lose in any shift of favour. Sometime in 337 BC yet another wife entered this fragile domestic environment. Kleopatra was a young Macedonian of noble birth and the niece and ward of the Companion Attalos; Philip had reportedly 'fallen in love with the girl when he was past the age for it'.[32] Athenaeus, writing in the early third century AD but drawing on an earlier biography of Philip, says that when he brought Kleopatra into the royal family, 'he wrecked his entire life.'[33] The proposed marriage stirred up a hornet's nest of anxieties, jealousies and insecurities among the wives, Olympias foremost among them. Kleopatra was clearly perceived as a dangerous threat to the established order.

Marriages in the ancient world were arranged. They were not matters of the heart but were made with reproduction and social standing in mind. Although there is no reason to think that Philip had not fallen in love, there were most likely other reasons behind the match. First of all, a new and young wife represented the best chance to sire more sons. Philip's track record, as far as is known, was not prodigious – two sons (Alexander and Arrhidaios), one of whom (Arrhidaios) was not fit for power, and three daughters (Kynnane, Kleopatra and Thessalonike). Considering Alexander's new and important role in the army, he was probably destined to accompany Philip to Asia. Although this is only speculation, it is difficult to imagine that he could be persuaded into staying behind.

The many wars to come would inevitably put both king and prince at risk, and a concern for the future stability of the royal house may have been pushed by the Companions. They would take a similar approach with Alexander when he became king, urging him to marry before leaving for Asia.[34] It is also important to consider Kleopatra within the context of Philip's general marriage policy. Each of his previous six wives had been taken for some political advantage, and it is likely that this latest match also served some wider purpose.

In a little over twenty years, Philip had transformed Macedon. His state and army building policies had strengthened the kingdom beyond all recognition and fostered a new sense of ethnic pride and identity among its population. But these developments had also undermined the power of the old aristocratic families and may have led to some lingering resentment. Philip, it seems, had purposefully avoided taking a Macedonian wife so as not to favour any one family. Now he either felt secure enough in his position or compelled to do so, perhaps in an attempt to heal internal divisions within the kingdom, a symbolic action to put the Macedonians first in whatever passed for the marital bed.[35]

The combination of Philip's romantic favouritism for Kleopatra, along with the presence of a new and influential Macedonian faction within the royal family, goes some way to justifying Olympias' concerns. To add insult to injury, Arrian suggests that Kleopatra changed her name to Eurydike on her marriage to Philip.[36] Such name changes were common among the royal women but this one had great significance. The original Eurydike, Philip's mother, may have recently died, and Kleopatra's adoption of the name could have easily been interpreted as an ambitious move by the new wife to occupy the matriarch's former position of influence. Alexander's loyalty to his mother probably made him unsympathetic to the wider political and social concerns that Philip was having to deal with, the prospect of another male heir also stoking his paranoia. Father and son quickly became embroiled in bitter quarrels.[37] With the prospect of another prolonged absence from court, Olympias' position was as crucial as ever; Alexander would fight to keep it so. The stakes were high, and when combined with age-old fears of the usurpation of power and the fluidity of court favour, tempers quickly began to come to the fore.

Matters reached a head at the wedding feast. After the ceremony, a simple affair whereby a loaf of bread was cut with a sword, both spouses eating some of the food, the drinking and feasting began.[38] Everybody was already well into their cups when Attalos, uncle and guardian of the bride, rose to give a toast. He called on the Macedonians to ask the gods that the new couple might produce a legitimate successor to the kingdom. The words were ill-chosen. Alexander, half-Molossian, fearlessly protective of his mother and already sensitive to his position, reacted immediately. 'And what about me, you wretch!' he shouted. 'Do you take me for a bastard?' In a rage, he threw his cup at Attalos. Philip, according to Plutarch, intervened, drawing his sword not against Attalos but Alexander. Fortunately, he was in no state to fight and tripped and fell before he could get close enough to use it. Alexander mocked him, saying, 'Look now, men! Here is one who is preparing to cross from Europe to Asia; and he is upset in trying to cross from couch to couch.'[39] It was an explosive episode. Philip's actions cannot be merely brushed aside as a drunken mistake; they were most likely the culmination of his son's tiresome resistance to the changing world around him. Alexander and Olympias immediately left the court, a self-imposed exile; their honour and status being called into question, they headed to Epeiros. Philip made no immediate conciliatory gestures to heal the breach in the royal family, and resentment festered on both sides. Philip and Alexander's relationship was never really to recover.

LIKE FATHER LIKE SON

From childhood, Alexander had regarded his father with a mix of admiration and resentment. He was a natural role model and they had grown close during their campaigns together, but with Philip's successes, there was also the concern that it would be he and not Alexander who would equal the deeds of the heroes of old. 'Boys, my father will anticipate everything,' Plutarch has the young Alexander saying to his friends, 'and for me he will leave no great or brilliant achievement to be displayed to the world with your aid.'[40] After the Attalos incident, his future suddenly became uncertain. Everything that he and his mother had been working towards was now in doubt. In exile, admiration inevitably gave way to intense feelings of resentment and rivalry. For the rest of his life Alexander would retain a sizeable Philip-shaped chip on his shoulder. An obsession with outdoing his father's achievements was born and, despite the colossal scale of his own conquests, that chip remained. The insecurities ran deep. They were brought out into the open during one of the most controversial events of his later life.

It took place at another party, this time in the Asian citadel of Marakanda (Samarkand) in 328 BC, some ten years after the drunken argument with Philip. Alexander's conquests, up to this point, had almost defied belief. He had defeated the Persians in every pitched battle and assumed the title, 'king of Asia'. He had pushed north, into the Baktria and Sogdiana, to secure the upper satrapies of the Persian Empire. but the local chieftains had begun to fight back. The previous year had been tough as the army battled to overcome numerous insurgents. In a moment of light relief, a feast was given in honour of Dionysos' sacred day and the drinking was heavy. Alexander's youthful self-restraint had slowly been worn

away by years of constant warfare; wine, often safer to drink than
water, was being consumed in larger quantities. He was surrounded
by his friends and court flatterers, and as part of the entertainment
they delighted in hearing verses composed by one of the poets.
The subject matter, however, was not to everyone's taste – the
content lampooned the Macedonian generals who had recently
been defeated by some of the rebels. The veterans among the party
were not impressed by the king's favourable reaction.[41] Kleitos the
Black, in particular, took offence. He was one of Philip's men; his
sister, Lanike, had been Alexander's childhood nurse, whom it was
said he loved as a second mother.[42] Under Alexander he had occupied some prestigious posts, commander of the royal cavalry
squadron and then joint head of the Companion cavalry, but age
and ill health may have recently caught up with him and influenced
Alexander's decision to appoint him satrap of Baktria and Sogdiana.
Such an appointment could either be seen as a great honour or a
demotion, and it is probable that Kleitos saw it as the latter. As
the party wore on, some of the flatterers began to claim that
Alexander's deeds were greater than the heroes of the past, the
Dioskouroi (Kastor and Polydeukes) and Herakles among them.
Kleitos, reclining on a nearby couch, began to grumble to those
around him, saying that it was the Macedonians who had won
the victories, and without them the king was nothing. The conversation then moved on; now it was Philip's own achievements that
were belittled in favour of Alexander's. The Roman historian
Curtius, whose *History of Alexander* is another key source on the
king's reign, gives a particularly lurid and detailed account of the
boasting; Alexander, he records, began to say that the famous
victory at Chaironeia had been his work, and that his father, out
of jealousy, had taken all the glory. He also relates a further episode
for which we have no other account, that he had saved his father's
life when a fight broke out between the Macedonians and some

Greek mercenaries in the army. Philip had fallen off his horse and, despite feigning death, was in mortal danger, Alexander had apparently protected his body with his own shield, slaying all those who approached. Philip, it was claimed, had never admitted that he owed his son his life.[43] Kleitos, hearing all, began to raise his voice, defending Philip and attempting to take down Alexander's ego a peg or two. The king's wide-eyed glare became fixed on his old friend, trying to discern his every word through the background noise, the wine mixing with anger to create a terrible and ultimately lethal cocktail. Kleitos was scratching at a sensitive wound, that timeless division between the young and the old.

The dispute turned into heated argument, Kleitos airing his own resentment at his new appointment. At this point Alexander may have asked him to leave, but he remained on his couch until his friends began to forcibly move him towards the door. Kleitos now played his trump card. He had saved Alexander's life during the first battle in Asia and decided the moment was ripe to remind him: 'This very hand, Alexander, saved you then!' he cried in anger.[44] Alexander reacted; an apple may have been thrown. The king leapt up and began looking around for a sharper weapon than just fruit. The other guests intervened, and both men were restrained as the insults began to flow freely. Ptolemy and Perdikkas held Alexander around the waist as others hid the available arms for which he was desperately seeking. He cried out in Macedonian dialect, in that distinctive harsh voice of his, to summon the guards and sound the trumpet in alarm, as if a coup were under way. The trumpeter suddenly found himself at the centre of an impossible situation and much to his credit did nothing, despite Alexander striking him for his disobedience. His friends tried to calm the king's temper. 'But his ears were closed, deafened by wrath.'[45] Some accounts say that Kleitos was manhandled from the scene, Alexander screaming out his name after him, 'Kleitos!' But just when disaster appeared to have been averted, Kleitos wrestled himself loose and returned. Arrian has him saying, 'Here I am, Kleitos, Alexander!'[46] Plutarch says that he quoted a line from Euripides' *Andromache*, 'Oh, how wrong the custom is in Greece!' – a lament delivered by Peleus to Menelaos, scorning the bad habit of generals who took sole credit for military victories.[47] Whatever the exact words, they were to be his last. Alexander grabbed a *sarissa* from one of the guards and ran him through.[48]

This event, more than any other in Alexander's life, reveals the complexity of his character – one moment brilliant, magnanimous and charismatic, the next, impetuous, jealous and violent. He never forgave himself for losing his restraint. The act was not honourable or virtuous – he had killed a guest and friend at his own table, it was an almighty stain on the reputation that he held so dear. Although it is often claimed that he inherited the darker side of his personality from Olympias, whom Plutarch calls a jealous and vindictive woman, there is an equal argument that Philip too possessed such traits.[49] Justin says that Alexander surpassed him in both good qualities and bad.[50] The Kleitos incident has clear parallels with the wedding feast in 337 BC. Alexander was very much his father's son, and despite the scale of his own achievements the ghost of Philip continued to haunt him.

EXILE

It would have taken the royal entourage around a week to make their way across Upper Macedonia and into Epeiros, their route dependent on their departure point – which was presumably either Aigai or Pella. The Pindos formed the natural boundary between one land and the next; there were various passes through the mountains but none of them was easy. Their use was dictated by the size of the group travelling and the time of season, details that are unfortunately lacking.[51] One of the oldest and most frequented routes goes via Metsovo, a stone-built Vlach village famous for its smoked cheeses and woodworking craftsmen, set high up in the clutches of Pindos. The modern Via Egnatia motorway follows its course, avoiding the often snow-choked Katara (or Accursed) pass by a new tunnel driven through the rock. The road then descends into Epeiros.

There is a type of Greek folk song that captures the raw essence of the region. It is known as *Skaros* – a shepherd's song originally played to flocks that grazed by night during the hottest summer months.[52] Recordings of the music begin with a brooding clarinet, the notes ascending and descending, the hypnotic sound awakening visions of Epeiros in the listener's mind.[53] The landscape takes shape, the melody mimicking the warble of a songbird, the burble of a mountain stream, the soft patter of rain. Violin strings shiver in the background, echoing the pulse of insect life high in the meadows; clarinet and violin later exchange solos, the differing rhythmic layers producing new wondrous images of pastoral bliss. Close your eyes and you can almost hear the contented sounds of the sheep and goats as they tug at the dew-fattened grass, their orchestra of bells carrying on the breeze; Pan himself could not have composed a more haunting tune, a national anthem to Nature. The music fits the landscape as snugly as a pair of lambskin slippers.

This was Olympias' home. There were no large cities like those elsewhere in Greece, the Molossians lived in a network of unwalled villages that spread over steep mountain and narrow plain. Family dwellings were clustered together around a communal courtyard; the ties of kinship were strong, monumental stone buildings were still a novelty.[54] The culture, traditions and ancestry of the royal Aiakid line had been impressed on Alexander from a young age.

He was a child of both Molossia and Macedonia, and it was to the former that he now turned in this time of uncertainty.

Passaron, the Molossian capital, was probably their intended destination. It is now believed to occupy the same location as Ioannina's castle, located on the shores of Lake Pamvotis.[55] Olympias' brother, Alexander, was reigning king of the Molossians. The arrival of his sister and nephew on his doorstep put him in an uncomfortable situation. They were family but he owed his position and enlarged territory to Philip. He apparently resisted Olympias' entreaties to make war on Macedon but gave her safe sanctuary; whether the same was offered to Alexander is not recorded. The young prince now faced one of the biggest decisions in his life and may well have sought divine advice to help him make up his mind.

Although there is not a single reference to Alexander consulting the Oracle of Zeus Naios at Dodona it must have happened, either by proxy or directly. The Oracle was said to be the oldest in Greece and was Molossia's most sacred site. Olympias, during Alexander's later absence in Asia, was involved in its administration, on one occasion reprimanding the Athenians for adorning one of the sanctuary's statues without her permission. She was privy to a special relationship with the resident gods and could have easily facilitated access or prompted her son to visit.[56]

The sanctuary lies in a secluded valley south of Ioannina, overlooked by the 'hundred springed' Mount Tomaros. It was greatly embellished in the Hellenistic Age. The theatre, which could hold some 17,000 people, is one of the largest in Greece. Zeus was believed to occupy a sacred oak tree which he shared with a goddess called Dione, from where they provided pilgrims with divine advice through the rustling of leaves and the cooing of resident doves. The original oak tree was destroyed in the third century BC but another has since been planted within the remains of the encircling sacred house, and tourists leave coins in the depression of a nearby stone block as modern offerings. Questions were inscribed on lead tablets and handed over to the resident priestesses; excavations have discovered over 4,000 of them, a selection of which are currently on display in Ioannina's Archaeological Museum.[57] Some asked whether to be a soldier on sea or land, if their wife would bear more children, or if the harsh winter was due to someone's transgression. The priestesses interpreted the will of Zeus, observing the oak tree, its movements and sounds, providing simple yes or no answers which were sometimes scored onto the back of the lead sheet. The pilgrims left the sanctuary with the confidence that only communication with the gods can inspire. Alexander, whether divinely advised or not, decided to head north, into Illyria. The period draws a blank in the historical records. His motivations, whether it was sanctuary or an alliance that he sought, are not mentioned, nor how long he was away for. It was likely an episode that he had no wish to remember, which explains the silence in the existing accounts of his life.

The sacred house and oak of Dodona

It was an old friend of both father and son who eventually managed to heal the rift in the royal family. Demaratos of Corinth, who had paid for Boukephalas all those years ago, had recently returned from Sicily and now paid a timely visit to Pella. Philip asked him how the Greek city-states were adapting to the new arrangements. 'It is all very well for you to show so much concern for the affairs of Greece, Philip,' Demaratos replied. 'How about the disharmony you have brought about in your own household?'[58] His words brought Philip to his senses. No matter the wounded pride and battered egos, it made no sense to leave Alexander out in the cold. Especially with the Persian campaign looming, he was too dangerous to be left behind. Demaratos managed to reconcile father and son and Alexander was brought back to court. It had not been an easy negotiation; Justin says that he was barely persuaded to return by the entreaties of his relatives.[59] Olympias' reinstatement was likely part of the agreement, although it is unclear whether she returned to Macedonia or stayed on in Epeiros.[60]

Curtius, in his account of the fatal feast with Kleitos, records an event that may relate to this time. Alexander, he reports, when boasting about his achievements and ridiculing Philip's, is said to have claimed 'that after the campaign which he himself had made without Philip against the Illyrians, when victorious he had written to his father that the enemy had been routed and put to flight; and that Philip had nowhere been present.'[61] Philip was apparently away on Samothrace at the time, perhaps inaugurating the Hall of Choral Dancers. The passage raises many questions. If it can be trusted, it may relate to an Illyrian campaign that took place either before or after his exile, or it could reflect some spin on Alexander's part, whereby he depicted his time in Illyria as still fighting for Macedonian superiority.[62] The options are as tantalising as they are impossible to substantiate.

No sooner had Alexander been brought back into the fold than he committed another serious blunder. According to Plutarch, who is the only ancient writer to record the incident, the prince was informed of a marriage that was being arranged between his half-brother Arrhidaios and the eldest daughter of Pixodaros, a dynast and satrap from Karia on the coast of Asia Minor.[63] Pixodaros had initiated the proposal, sending the actor Aristokritos to Macedonia as an envoy. A rare gold coin of the Karian king was found among the looted grave goods from a tomb in Aigai, providing some possible archaeological evidence relating to the embassy.[64] For Philip, Arrhidaios was a small price to pay for what could be a most valuable alliance for the campaign to come but, behind the scenes, Olympias and Alexander's friends fanned the prince's paranoia, suggesting that Philip aimed to confer more power on his disabled son and that he might even be groomed as his successor. Arrhidaios was not capable of holding any office; the fact that Alexander believed the rumours gives some sense of the insecurity he was feeling at the time. He took the audacious decision to secretly counter the marriage proposal and sent his own actor friend, Thessalos, to Karia, offering himself as the proposed husband instead of Arrhidaios. Pixodaros, as can be imagined, was delighted with the news; Alexander was a far better catch. Philip soon found out and was furious, whereafter the marriage plans collapsed. He confronted Alexander in his chamber, taking Philotas, Parmenion's son, perhaps a friend turned informer, as a witness. Philip upbraided his son for his meddling, saying that he was unworthy of his position if he wished to become the son-in-law of a barbarian king. Thessalos was arrested in Corinth and put in chains, while Alexander's other friends – Ptolemy, Harpalos, Nearchos and the brothers Erigyios and Laomedon – were exiled. Alexander's position at court was dealt another severe blow, and he was now more isolated than ever.[65]

Third-century AD gold medallions of Olympias (top left),
Philip II (top right) and Alexander the Great (bottom)

Views of Macedonia after exiting the Tempe pass

Warrior's helmet with gold mask from Sindos

Aghios Antonios Peak, Mount Olympos. The location of a Hellenistic
mountaintop sanctuary dedicated to Olympian Zeus

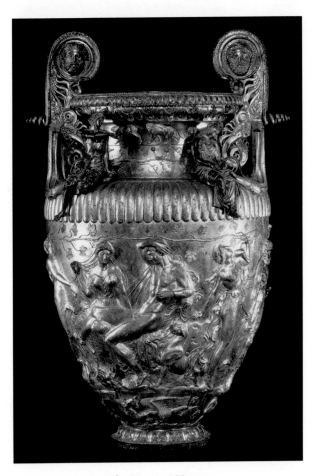

The Derveni Krater

The Panagyurishte treasure, Bulgaria

The Lion of Chaironeia

Aigai (Vergina)

Entrance to the Museum of the Royal Tombs of Aigai, Vergina

Reconstruction of Tomb II's façade, Vergina

Golden larnax from Tomb II's main chamber, Vergina

Reconstructed shield from Tomb II's main chamber, Vergina

Diadem from Tomb II's antechamber, Vergina

Gorytos from Tomb II's antechamber, Vergina

The marriage into the Karian dynasty may have never happened, but a number of other weddings that did take place around the same time enabled Philip to consolidate relations within the royal family. His nephew Amyntas was wed to Kynnane, his warrior daughter by Audata-Eurydike. She had already proved herself in battle, taking part in a previous Illyrian campaign where she succeeded in killing one of their queens and putting other enemies to flight.[66] The marriage undoubtedly elevated Amyntas' status as another eligible successor who could take power should Philip die. They had a daughter together, Adea, who was trained by her mother in warfare and would emerge as a key figure after Alexander's death. In order to reaffirm ties with Epeiros, Alexander's sister Kleopatra was also given to the Molossian Alexander; uncle was to marry niece. This last marriage took place in October 336 BC and was combined with the end-of-year festival of Olympian Zeus and the beginning of the Persian campaign. Philip was still experimenting with new forms of royal ceremony and the guest list was considerable, with friends and envoys coming from across Greece. It was one final grand party before the business of war began again. The ceremonial capital of Aigai hosted the event, with a recently constructed palace at its heart. The story of its rediscovery and restoration is among the most exciting in Macedonian archaeology, providing the opportunity to reimagine the celebrations in all their glory. The building affords a rarefied aperture into the past and the events that marked both the culmination and the extinction of Philip's reign.

PART TWO

THE KING
(336–323 BC)

8.

THE FINAL ACT

In the middle of the nineteenth century, the French archaeologist Léon Heuzey arrived in Greece. He was only in his mid-twenties, but had already developed a keen eye for antiquities, alert to the lumps and bumps that denoted subsurface ruins and quick to spot reused ancient material in modern buildings. As a member of the French School in Athens, he began to take an interest in the lands beyond the northern boundaries of the newly formed kingdom of Greece, which at that point only extended as far as Thessaly. These areas were still under Ottoman control and had yet to be properly investigated. It was where the most exciting discoveries might be made.

In spring 1855, on one particular journey into Macedonia, Heuzey met an educated priest who informed him of some ruins at Palatitsia, a small village at the base of Mount Pieria, close to where the Haliakmon river emerges onto the coastal plain of Emathia.[1] Heuzey had passed within a short distance of this village before, but had never heard any rumour of ruins. The name, however, intrigued him; it translates as 'little palace'. Willing to take a chance on the priest's information being valid, he left his colleagues behind and hired a guide to lead him into the unknown.[2] As they approached Palatitsia, the middle section of the Pierian foothills receded and the landscape revealed itself: forests and mountainous vegetation, dense as boar-hide, descending to the banks of the Haliakmon river, where flocks of geese splashed in the water honking as if in delight, fields of corn and sesame appearing as islets of cultivation among beautiful elm groves. Villages and red-roofed farmsteads were dotted here and there, surrounded by a maze of fences and hidden paths, rutted with the hoof prints of buffalo and ox. Heuzey knew the area as *Roumlouki*, 'Land of the Rum' – Rum or Romans being what the Ottoman Turks called Orthodox Christians living under their rule, although in this instance he used the term in the narrower sense of Greek speakers, in contradistinction to the 'Bulgarian' speakers of Slavochoria further to the north. The people living here, in the shadow of the Pierians, considered themselves the direct descendants of the ancient Macedonians, and Heuzey recorded that under the men's sheepskin jackets and tight-fitting turbans were the still visible signs of their illustrious heritage – long oval faces with straight noses, deep-set, almond-shaped eyes, their features expressive and intelligent. The women, he observed, had a proud and refined beauty. They took on statuesque poses as they carried earthenware jugs around the villages; in the fields, they stood upright on their rickety carts, reaping the corn with a scythe in one hand while holding the reins of their horses in the other, their stance reminding Heuzey of Nike riding her chariot. He was instantly enraptured by the countryside, later writing: 'Nowhere else has nature been brought alive in this way by the movement of agricultural life more freely and more nobly.'[3]

The locals were enthused by Heuzey's interest and guided him around Palatitsia, as well as the nearby hamlets of Koutles and Barbes (later synocised and renamed Vergina). 'The three villages are full of ancient remains,' he excitedly writes in his account of the visit, 'the churches and most of the houses are literally built with fragments of ancient monuments.'[4] The source for much of this salvaged material, so the locals informed Heuzey, was a small plateau situated between Palatitsia and Koutles. He set out to investigate.

It was an incredible moment for the young Frenchman as he climbed the hill, finally emerging from the surrounding trees into a clearing that he recalled was spread out like a village square. The entire area was covered with ancient masonry – mouldering walls, broken columns, decorative relief elements and a sea of terracotta tiles, all scattered pell-mell across the plateau. At its eastern end stood a decrepit monastery church dedicated to the Holy Trinity; an inscription testified to repairs in the fifteenth century, but it had long since fallen out of use. On closer inspection, Heuzey found that it had grown almost organically from the building beneath it. He guessed that the underlying ruins belonged to a grand temple dated to the time of Alexander's Successors. The priest had not been lying about Palatitsia: 'I recognized,' Heuzey wrote, 'not without astonishment, that the discovery that almost escaped me had to be by far the most interesting of my entire trip.'[5]

His find was greeted with amazement back in France, and he returned to the site in 1861, this time as the leader of a special scientific mission sponsored by Napoleon III. The team concentrated their efforts on the eastern side of the plateau and succeeded in recovering much of the ancient building's original plan. After forty days, however, the relentless attacks of the local mosquitoes proved too much. One member after another had succumbed to malaria and Heuzey decided to curtail the project, the team retreating to their frigate anchored in the nearby Thermaic Gulf. The season's work had come to a premature end, but plenty had been achieved. The discoveries were published in 1876, the weighty tome enhanced with beautiful drawings, reconstructions and plans

courtesy of Heuzey's invaluable colleague, H. Daumet. The excavations had changed Heuzey's mind as to the function of the
building. He rejected his original hypothesis that it was a temple
and proffered instead that it was a grand royal residence, perhaps
a holiday retreat for the kings and queens of Hellenistic Macedonia
– it was the first great discovery of Macedonian archaeology. At
the time, he believed the city to be Balla, a rather insignificant
place rarely mentioned in the ancient sources.[6] It was not a
comfortable identification, there were reservations, but it stuck
nonetheless. That was until 1968, when Nicholas Hammond
suggested that this was not Balla but none other than Aigai, the
ancestral capital of ancient Macedon, an identification accepted
today.[7] Further excavations followed at the palace after the Second
World War, and by the 1970s it had been fully exposed, but many
questions remained – its precise date, phasing and appearance. In
2007, the local Ephorate embarked on an ambitious restoration
project, hoping that renewed study would provide some answers.
For well over a decade, concealed behind the foliage, the site has
been undergoing a metamorphosis. Floors have been conserved
and relaid, walls rebuilt, the building's disembodied pieces supplemented by modern prostheses of mortar, titanium clamps and
new volcanic stone blocks, the excavations supporting a redating
of the monument to the time of Philip. It was here, in October
336 BC, that he staged his grand celebrations – an event that
combined the marriage of his daughter Kleopatra to Alexander
the Molossian, the festival of Olympian Zeus and the beginning
of the Persian campaign.

The palace of Aigai is now in its final phases of completion,
with sections opening to the general public. This remarkable structure has much to tell us about the king and the way he wanted
to be represented.[8]

That autumn, the various roads and routeways that linked Aigai with the rest of Macedonia, as well as the lands beyond, became thronged with people; statesmen, musicians, athletes, soldiers, merchants and many others descended on the city. Philip had invited all of his guest-friends from the Greek cities and asked his Companions to do the same; he wanted to be seen as amiable to all, worthy of his new position as *hegemon* of the League of Corinth. Certain notable individuals, as well as representatives from the various city-states, brought with them gold crowns to be awarded to Philip. Athens followed suit, although, unsurprisingly, Demosthenes was not among their ambassadors. The herald's announcement of the award ended with the declaration that anyone who plotted against the king would find no protection in their city.[9] Some would have felt obliged to attend – it was politic considering the new prominence of Macedon in Greek affairs – others had made the journey simply to enjoy the convivial court atmosphere and to make the most of the royal court's legendary generosity. There were to be lavish sacrifices, musical contests and, of course, lots of feasting and drinking. Philip had long recognised the importance of such festival events for self-promotion and morale. This occasion represented another leap forward in magnif-icence, a great celebration to inaugurate the great war to come.

Aigai was, above all, the city of tradition, where Macedonian history and ancestry was writ large in its monuments. Hundreds of prehistoric burial tumuli greeted the visitors. This long-venerated patch of ground, crowded with ancestors and the remains of the mighty dead, spoke of the longevity of the Macedonians and the Argead ruling family. Just outside one of the main gates was a group of extraordinary female burials, one perhaps recently built for Philip's formidable mother, Eurydike, who is believed to have died in around 340 BC. Inside, her ashes were interred in a precious casket and placed on an elegant marble throne, its backrest painted with a scene from the underworld – Hades and Persephone charging forward in their chariot to collect the remains of the dead.[10] Further uphill, the agora, sanctuary of Eukleia and theatre, recently constructed and on the same alignment with the palace, part of Philip's grand designs to bring the old capital into a new age, provided spaces to gather and take in the surroundings, a place to catch up with old friends or experience the festival atmosphere. The crowd consisted of Macedonians, Greeks and other peoples, many wearing straw hats to keep off the October sun, some of whom may have chosen to enjoy a picnic in the theatre or to peruse the merchants' wares on pop-up stalls. The most important guests were invited to the post-wedding banquet and had one last journey to make.

The palace's vast dimensions dominated the city and surrounding countryside; it was three times larger than the Parthenon, and coated with a thick layer of bright white stucco that must have shone like glass in the midday sun. Its large podium rose above the theatre, while a balcony fronted the northern side, providing the royals with unrivalled views across the Emathian plain, the Pierian foothills gently curving away to the east, and the Thermaic Gulf winking in the distance. Visitors entered via the eastern side which was designed to impress. It's now estimated to have been two storeys high, flanked with Doric stoas. The monumental entranceway protruded slightly from the rest of the façade, and was framed by a pair of large double-sided Ionic pillar-columns. Above was a row of smaller half-columns and alternating false windows, crowned with a triangular pediment. The entire building was capped with a terracotta-tiled roof, terminating in palmette antefixes that pierced the Macedonian sky; rich reds and deep blues complemented the façade's relief elements, breaking up the pure white stucco covering. The architect may have been Pytheos, famous for designing the great Mausoleum of Halikarnassos – one of the seven wonders of the ancient world.[11]

The palace of Aigai

On entering the palace, the visitors passed through a series of cavernous antechambers, the final one guarded with heavy-set Macedonian doors at least a foot thick. As they did so, they moved towards a square of light. An enormous open-air peristyle courtyard occupied the heart of the structure. Unlike other courtyards, which were often purely decorative, this was a functional space, used to accommodate large Assemblies or extra guests at royal banquets. The building was organised in a similar way to aristocratic houses, but here the scale was monumental. The blueprint followed sound geometric principles – the 'charm of the measure' was to be found in every nook and cranny.

One of the first rooms to be encountered was a circular *tholos* chamber, similar to the Philippeion in Olympia, positioned between entrance and courtyard. Inscriptions found within the room mention *Herakles Patroos* (Herakles the ancestral god). It was most likely a sacred space with a cult statue dedicated to the Argead's famous ancestor. Its position at a critical juncture of the palace layout was no accident; Philip wanted all new arrivals to remember the royal family's lineage, the hero's legendary exploits and, perhaps, to invite comparison with his own achievements, a new Herakles made flesh.[12] This room, along with a suite of adjoining offices, were the atypical spaces in the palace. The rest were seemingly given over to one purpose and one purpose only: entertainment.

Walking around the courtyard, the visitors passed banqueting room after banqueting room. Some of the finest were paved with river-pebble mosaics and tessellated marble pieces; one of the most striking aspects was the use of red and ochre dye for the mortar flooring. The walls of the rooms were likely also to have been decorated with bright colours. Life in the palace was rendered, not in black and white, but in glorious, sometimes gaudy technicolour; paintings, statues, spoils of war, and hides from vanquished beasts probably completed the finery of the surroundings. Those asked to recline in the banqueting rooms on the southern wing must have taken a moment to marvel at the mosaics laid out before them. One features an exquisite floral scene, its central rosette surrounded with spiralling tendrils and four flower maidens positioned at the edges. Another depicts Zeus in the guise of a bull abducting the maiden Europa, she who gives her name to the continent of Europe. This scene had particular significance. Theopompus famously claimed, 'Europe had never born such a man as Philip, son of Amyntas.'[13] On the eve of the Persian campaign, with conquests in a new continent beckoning, the king may have sought to style himself as the Lord of Europe. His daughter by Nikesipolis had been called Thessalonike, in honour of his victory in Thessaly; when his new wife Kleopatra-Eurydike bore him a baby girl, she was named Europa.[14]

The scenes were extraordinary. The banqueting rooms filled with laughter, music and dancing, the smell of roasted meat wafting through the air, servants rushing to and fro from the service quarters – attached to the main building at the western end – emptying piss-pots and ensuring there was a steady supply of wine, while the royal pages struggled to serve the many guests. The courtyard filled with more couches, ribbons and freshly cut boughs of greenery adding to the ambience of celebration. The men, from the Peloponnese to the Balkans, talked politics, philosophy, art and warfare, in the palace at the heart of a new world order.

Philip was in his element. He was probably to be found in a tripartite complex – two banqueting rooms and a shared antechamber – positioned opposite the main entrance. These were the largest rooms in the palace and testify to the scale of Argead regal splendour. It's been estimated that their ceilings were double height, around 11m high. The antechamber was faced with five Ionic pillar-columns, and perhaps additionally lit by openings in the eastern wall above, it may have functioned as a throne room. There was space enough for at least thirty couches in each of the adjoining banqueting rooms; with two diners to a couch, the rooms could accommodate 120 reclining guests, though many more could have been fitted into the antechamber if needed. The king, sitting atop a luxurious couch with plump purple cushions, sampled the cellar-fresh wine in exquisite cups of precious metal, sharing stories with his closest Companions and enjoying the entertainment – a stirring word from a poet or the caress of a talented courtesan. The marriage between the Molossian Alexander and his daughter Kleopatra had gone off without a hitch, there had been no drunken arguments. It was another ingenious piece of diplomacy from the king, reaffirming the ties between Molossia and Macedon. Prince Alexander was somewhere among the crowd, probably close to his father, his own circle of friends drastically reduced since the Pixodaros affair. But his split from Philip was in the past and the royal family put on a public front of unity, even if there was some lingering resentment among its members.

Fortunately for Alexander, Attalos was not present. Along with Parmenion, he had led an advance force of some 10,000 soldiers into Asia earlier that spring. Their mission was to secure the Hellespont crossing, to create a bridgehead for the later invasion and to start liberating the Greek cities, depriving the Persian fleet of key strategic harbours in the process.[15] Wanting to enter the war with the gods' approval, Philip had sent an enquiry to the Delphic Oracle about whether he would succeed in conquering the Persian king. He received the following reply: 'Wreathed is the bull. All is done. There is also the one who will smite him.'[16] It was an ambiguous answer, as was often the case with oracles, but Philip chose to interpret the message in a favourable manner. As far as he was concerned, the Great King was the sacrificial bull and he the one that would lay him low.

The intended victim was no longer Artaxerxes IV (Arses), but a new king, Darius III (Kodomannos). His predecessor had been assassinated earlier in 336 BC; the man said to have been responsible was a treacherous eunuch called Bagoas, who also killed off all other male children in the royal line. Seeking a ruler who could be more easily manipulated, Artashata – satrap of Armenia and a descendant of an outlying branch of the Achaimenid royal family (also known as Kodomannos) – had been installed on the throne. He was famed for his bravery and had apparently killed a Kadousian champion in single combat. Soon after his elevation, during which he adopted the name Darius (III), he had been wise enough to do away with Bagoas, but it was too early to tell what sort of king he would be.[17] As the festivities wore on, the rooms a-chatter with the prospects of the war to come, Philip asked an actor friend, Neoptolemos of Skyros, to recite some poetry relevant to the Persian campaign. He rose from his couch and with his fine actor's voice gave a rendition of the following lines:

Your thoughts reach higher than the air;
You dream of wide fields' cultivation.
The homes you plan surpass the homes
That men have known, but you do err,
Guiding your life afar.
But one there is who'll catch the swift,
Who goes a way obscured in gloom,
And sudden, unseen, overtakes
And robs us of our distant hopes –
Death, mortals' source of many woes.[18]

The words were chosen to rebuke the wealth of the Persian Great King, suggesting that someday his fortune would fail. Philip was delighted and, in conjunction with Delphi's prediction and perhaps some early news about the expedition force's first victories, he was buoyant about the chances of success. Little did he know, however, that he had wrongly interpreted the meaning of the oracle. The end was near. Somewhere within his own ranks was another who had a knife. It was not the Persian who was to be the sacrificial bull, but Philip.

Pausanias of Orestis had a personal grudge against the king. He had been a court favourite of Philip's and, supposedly, one of his lovers, but he had been replaced in the king's affection by another youth, coincidentally also called Pausanias. On campaign in Illyria, the scorned lover had made life uncomfortable for the new favourite, calling him a hermaphrodite among other slurs.[19] The insults soon proved too much to bear. During a major battle with the Illyrians, probably in 345 BC, the second Pausanias was fighting among the royal foot guard and decided to die in heroic fashion. In the thick of the action he jumped in front of Philip and took all the blows that were aimed at the king; his valiant death was a last attempt to cleanse his besmirched name. The incident was widely discussed and Attalos, with whom the dead Pausanias was friendly, decided on retribution.[20]

It probably took place several years later, after the marriage between Philip and Kleopatra-Eurydike, which facilitated Attalos' rise in status. He invited the surviving Pausanias to a drinking party and plied the young man with unmixed wine. When he was no longer in control of his senses, Attalos handed him over to the muleteers, the lowest of the low. They gang-raped him.[21] On his recovery, Pausanias petitioned Philip, demanding justice. The king found himself in an awkward situation; it was inevitable that he would side with his new father-in-law, but he tried to mollify Pausanias' anger with gifts and a promotion in the royal bodyguard. Pausanias' honour, however, could not be bought. He was now set on taking action, not against the man who had ordered his rape and since left for Asia, but against the king and former lover who had denied his entreaties for justice. Now all he needed was the right moment to strike.[22]

Before sunrise the following day, the theatre began to fill with people. Neoptolemos was to be involved in proceedings again, this time in a new stage production retelling the myth of Kinyras, a mythical king of Cyprus.[23] The earthen bank (or *koilon*) where the audience sat was stepped with receding levels, and probably held tiers of wooden benches with narrow corridors of cobbled stone subdividing the various sections, a wooden superstructure, built on the western side, perhaps completed the symmetry of the seating.[24] Only the first row of seats was made of stone; it was likely reserved for the upper echelons of Macedonian society and provided space for 100 individuals, perhaps the king's inner circle of Companions.[25] In all, it is estimated that the theatre could hold around 3,000 people. The orchestra was far larger than the modest seating necessitated; it was a multi-purpose arena for political, religious and theatrical spectacle, but it still felt intimate, as if you could reach out and touch the performers. The audience huddled together in the dark, pulling their cloaks tightly around them in an effort to ward off the autumnal chill, waiting for the festivities to begin. Slowly the stars above began to fade, the morning sky undergoing its Protean change, turning from a silvery-grey to orange to the first hints of azure. Like a pinch of Egyptian blue added to an artist's wash, the natural complexion of day was revived, the sun warming the misty Emathian plain, the stage set for one of the most dramatic events in ancient history.

The surviving accounts of what happened next, provided by Diodorus and Justin, are based on two earlier and distinct histori-ographical traditions which differ in their retelling.[26] Diodorus provides the most detail – his version is romanticised, its reliability questioned, but it is also the most memorable. He writes that the parade formed at dawn, most probably outside the palace. The

The theatre of Aigai

royal party shrugged off the excesses of the night before and then began their descent towards the theatre, musicians, religious attendants and performers leading the way, with lavish displays of every sort. A guard of young spearmen brought up the rear, protecting the king and his friends; their triumphal entrance was to be the prelude to the day's festivities. A small courtyard at the eastern side of the theatre allowed the members some time and space to carefully coordinate their arrival. The procession then emerged into the orchestra, greeted by the audience with appropriate pomp and ceremony, the atmosphere rising with the sun. Among them were statues of the gods, richly decorated and wrought with great artistry. The twelve Olympians were all represented, but in addition there was a thirteenth statue. It was of Philip: he had enthroned himself among the immortals. The audience was whipped up into fever pitch by the extravagant scenes. Philip bade his friends go ahead while the guards kept their distance. The king wished to enter the theatre protected by goodwill alone. He was appropriately dressed for the occasion, wearing a white *himation* or wrap with a golden wreath adorning his head – 'Wreathed is the bull'; black-bearded, perhaps already sporting a few greys, one eye blinded and walking with a limp, he bore his visible scars with pride, his person unifying all those traits that marked him out as an exceptional ruler: fearless in battle, eloquent in speech and skilled in diplomacy, a champion of the gods and protector of his people. He was in his mid-forties and at the height of his power. As he made his triumphal appearance, praise and congratulations showered down upon him.

Under the gaze of gods and men, he took a moment to acknowledge the crowd, basking in the glory of the occasion. It was then that disaster, suddenly, and unexpectedly, struck. Pausanias, who was among the royal bodyguard, took out his Celtic dagger, rushed the king, and drove the blade deep into his ribcage.[27] Philip fell to the floor like a sacrificial victim, his white robe stained with a hideous crimson. The wound was fatal, the king was dead. The actor Neoptolemos was later asked what amazed him most in the work of the great tragedians, Aeschylus, Sophocles and Euripides. He replied that none could compare with the drama of Philip's murder.[28]

The theatre descended into chaos. The scenes of jubilation, the cheers and deafening applause that accompanied Philip's entrance, swiftly turned to screams of dismay and faces frozen in shock. The royal guard of young spearmen acted immediately, one group pursuing the fleeing assassin, the other racing to the fallen king.[29] The orchestra became thronged with jostling bodies, those Greek ambassadors invited to the celebrations perhaps already looking to make a sharp exit. Macedonian successions were usually messy affairs, it was best not to linger. Justin reports that Prince Alexander and Alexander the Molossian had been given the honour of walking by Philip's side during the parade. Diodorus doesn't mention them in his account, but they were probably eyewitnesses to this traumatic event, although according to his alternative version Philip was struck down in the corridor leading to the orchestra before he emerged in front of the crowd. It is impossible to know what must have been going through young Alexander's mind. He had seen his father killed in cold blood only a few metres away and had been powerless to save him. Arrian, who provides some additional information on the aftermath of the murder, says that his supporters promptly rallied to his side, suggesting that they may have feared for his safety, and that it was uncertain if the full extent of the plot had been revealed. Alexander the Lynkestian, a seasoned general from the highlands and son-in-law of Antipatros, was the first to proclaim his support for the new would-be king. He strapped on a cuirass and, along with the royal guard, escorted his namesake to the security of the palace, perhaps on Antipatros' orders. With Attalos and Parmenion away in Asia, Philip's faithful steward was the most influential man at court.[30]

HAIL ALEXANDER!

The minutes and hours that followed the assassination were of paramount importance for Alexander and his hopes of kingship.[31] His recent rift with Philip had been widely known but the two had been publicly reconciled, and, if Justin can be trusted, Alexander had been given the honour of marching at his father's side before entering the theatre. Philip had clearly designated him as the chosen successor and had long associated his son with royal power, both during his regency and on campaign. This was a Macedonian custom but political reality could often overcome the wishes of the former king.[32] Plutarch reports that Philip, on hearing about Alexander's concerns that he was having children by other women besides Olympias, took his son aside and said, 'Well then, if you have many competitors for the kingdom, prove yourself honourable and good, so that you may obtain the kingdom not because of me, but because of yourself.'[33] Confidence and self-belief was never a problem for Alexander, but his youth meant that he was not universally respected. He had to gain enough support among the leading Macedonians to reach a critical mass that would sweep all other rivals away and secure the throne. It was Antipatros who proved the crucial agent of power. He had known Alexander since he was a child and was aware of his abilities. He too strapped on his cuirass, arming himself as an attendant of the new king. His choice had been made.[34]

A Macedonian Assembly was formed in the theatre ready to perform the customary rite of acclamation.[35] It had been decades since the last ceremony and, with Philip's death, all of the victories, alliances, friendships and treaties evaporated, despite the sworn oaths that applied to his descendants. For those unhappy with the new arrangement it was a chance to rebel; the coming weeks would be fraught with troubles and challenges. The Companions were acutely aware that a capable successor was needed. Macedon was only as strong as its king.

Antipatros led Alexander into the theatre and gave a long speech, filling the Macedonians with favour towards the youngster. After he had finished it was Alexander's turn to perform. Apparently, he judged the situation well, winning over the sceptics in the crowd with a tactful speech, saying that the king had changed only in name, and that the state would be run on principles no less effective than those of his father's administration. He further exempted the Macedonians from all state obligations, primarily taxes, with the important exception of military service, a shrewd public statement that did much to win over hearts and minds. His many lessons in rhetoric were finally paying off.[36]

Philip's body had yet to be recovered from the theatre and it was perhaps now that the ring of power was slipped from his dead finger and given to Alexander. Spears were beaten against shields, the men bellowing out his name in unison, acclaiming their new king – *Hail, Alexander!*[37] They then swore a sacred oath that from now on they would share the same friends and enemies.[38] Sacrifices sealed the allegiances. This was the moment that Alexander had been preparing for his entire life; all the training, education, royal duties and campaign experience had been accrued with this ultimate goal in mind. The timing was premature, the circumstances turbulent, but he had attained the position for which he had long dreamed, despite being only twenty years of age. The kingship was his.

After the ceremony, the Assembly was given permission to leave the theatre. Philip's body was handed over to those entrusted with preparing the customary rites before burial.[39] Alexander then summoned the Greek embassies that were still in Aigai for an audience, imploring them to maintain the loyalty that they had shown his father. At the same time, he ordered an immediate mustering of the army. More speeches were probably given, and they marched between the ends of a slaughtered dog to purify themselves after the recent bloodshed. Alexander sought to instil discipline within the ranks with constant drilling and tactical exercises, as Philip had done on coming to power all those years before. The army would be sorely needed in the weeks to come.[40]

The accession of a new monarch was bound up with a number of other rituals that aided the transition of power, among them the royal funeral and the prosecution of those responsible for the king's death. These were sacred duties and Alexander was expected to perform them adequately.[41] Philip's body was displayed within the palace for the symbolic *prothesis*, where friends and family came to pay their final respects to the dead. The blood had been washed off his lifeless skin, oil and perfume rubbed into his corpse and the king dressed in fine robes. The royal women undertook the preparation and sang dirges to the dead while they did so. His body guarded by his closest friends as mourners filed by.[42] It was common in the Greek world for burials to take place on the third day after death, but considering Philip's status and the costly preparations needed for the funeral, the process may have been extended beyond normal parameters, as was the case for Homeric heroes. Meanwhile, below the city, at the intersection of slope and plain, the pyre of fir trees began to take shape, and the tomb's construction also started. The funeral was to be the most magnificent Macedon had ever seen, a tribute to the immensity of Philip's achievements.[43]

Pausanias had been captured shortly after the murder. According to Diodorus, he was running to his waiting horses at the city's gate, but caught his foot on a trailing vine. The royal guard of young spearmen, Alexander's friends Perdikkas and Leonnatos among them, were on him as he scrambled to his feet, skewering him like a captured boar.[44] Another tradition, preserved on a few scraps of papyrus – fragments of a lost work on Alexander – suggests that he may have been taken alive; regardless, he was promptly executed, his body nailed to a wooden cross and publicly displayed.[45] This regicide was not a unique event in Macedonian history. It was said that more kings had been killed at the hands of their own people than those of the enemy. In a world where honour, respect and reputation were the central values of society, not even Philip could escape that most powerful of human emotions – the need for revenge.[46] The timing of the assassination was telling, one public humiliation payback for another. Aristotle, who may have witnessed the event, wrote that the sole motive for murder was Pausanias' personal grievance, but other ancient writers attest that suspicion spread to other suspects. Conspiracy theories abounded as much in antiquity as they do today.[47]

The sons of the Lynkestian nobleman Aeropos, perhaps the same Aeropos who had been exiled by Philip before the battle of Chaironeia, were quickly implicated as co-conspirators.[48] Arrhabaios and Heromenes were arrested and sentenced to be killed at Philip's tomb.[49] Their guilt was widely believed at the time but the lack of clarity in the historical sources make it difficult to be sure about the extent of their involvement, or whether it was merely a fabrication to purge rivals. They may have had a claim to the throne through a possible outlying branch of the Argead royal family.[50] One of the most confusing elements is that Alexander the Lynkestian, another son of Aeropos, was among the accused, but he was pardoned for being the first to proclaim his support for the new king. Many scholars have seen within this episode some tension between Upper and Lower Macedonia, the highland nobles, unhappy with being subject to the Argead king, finally taking action through the agency of a disgruntled court follower. Alexander's sparing of his namesake could be seen as a necessary concession in order to keep some stability between the various factions; the Lynkestian was also the son-in-law of Antipatros and his influence may have lain behind the decision.[51] It was customary in such matters to also kill off the sons of the condemned. One of Arrhabaios' sons fled to Asia to join the Persian forces, but another remained faithful to Alexander and was spared – one of his first acts as king was to go against established tradition.[52] It is, perhaps, indicative of the fragility of the situation that he found himself in. The tightrope of power was a difficult one to walk, each step had to be taken with care and with due consideration for the possible repercussions.

It was later said that Persian gold had helped drive the dagger into Philip's ribs; apparently the Great King Darius had claimed credit for organising the conspirators.[53] Philip's death effectively stymied the invasion plans, and Persian involvement in the plot is attractive but far from certain. Alexander may have invented the story as a means to further justify his later campaign against the Persians. It was also natural that ancient writers would cast some suspicion on Alexander and Olympias. With the benefit of hindsight, it is easy to see that they had most to gain from Philip's death.

Plutarch records that Pausanias had approached Alexander to bewail his humiliation at the hands of Attalos, a situation with which the prince must have sympathised. He is said to have replied, 'The giver of the bride, the bridegroom, and the bride,' a line from Euripides' *Medea*, implying that not only Philip be killed but also Attalos and Kleopatra-Eurydike.[54] The darker sides of Alexander's personality – jealousy, insecurity and rampant ambition among them – are evident from an early age. The official explanation for the murder is also rendered suspicious in attributing blame in particular to Attalos, Alexander's known enemy. His recent rift with Philip and covert meddling with Pixodaros are also indicative that he was unhappy with his position. The killing of one's relatives was not an uncommon occurrence in Macedonian dynasties. However, the location of the assassination, the confusion that followed, and the fact that Alexander may have feared for his own life, suggest that he was as unaware of the plot as Philip. None of his contemporary rivals accuse him of being involved and their silence does much to exonerate him.

Whether Olympias had some hand in the events is harder to dismiss. Plutarch recounts that she had added her own exhortations to Pausanias' anger, even inciting him to the deed. Justin says something similar; that Pausanias had been suborned by Olympias and that Alexander was also aware of the plot.[55] Her whereabouts at the time of Philip's murder are uncertain; she was either still in Epeiros or at Aigai, though Alexander's elevation to king quickly brought her back to prominence. Justin's version of events is full of scandalous details. He writes that Olympias crowned Pausanias' crucified body with a golden wreath and later took care to attend to his burial, erecting a tomb and ensuring that offerings were to be made to him every year, and concludes by stating, 'all this was done so openly that she appears to have been afraid that the crime might not be clearly demonstrated as her work.'[56] This account smacks of the hostile propaganda that circulated after Alexander's death and the ensuing wars of the Successors, in which Olympias played a key but ultimately unsuccessful role. That she performed such actions is hard to credit. They directly undermined Alexander's position, which was heavily reliant on Philip's memory and friends. There is not enough evidence to turn rumours into fact, although some suspicion will likely always remain.

Olympias' treatment of Kleopatra-Eurydike is more securely attested. At some point over the following year, when Alexander was away from court, she took the opportunity to rid herself of her court rival. Justin says that she forced her to commit suicide, having already murdered the baby at her breast.[57] Another writer states that she killed mother and child by dragging them over a bronze oven filled with fire.[58] These may be exaggerations that played on the stereotypes of the vindictive queen, but she was undoubtedly responsible for their deaths. Alexander, on hearing the news, was said to be angry with his mother's actions. As a royal widow, Kleopatra-Eurydike was under his protection, and it did not reflect well on his new role as head of the Argead family.

Meanwhile Attalos remained in Asia, where he was in joint command of around 10,000 men. He had acquired great popularity in the army, being of easy bearing and ready to grant favours. Parmenion was there as well, reportedly devoted to Alexander, but, away from court and yet to swear allegiance, his loyalty could easily have been doubted. While Attalos lived he was a natural focus for opposition and Alexander decided to send one of his friends, Hekataios, along with some soldiers to Asia. When an opportunity presented itself, they were either to kill Attalos or bring him back to Macedonia alive.[59] He had been eliminated by 334 BC. Eurylochos, another prominent Macedonian nobleman, shared the same fate. According to Justin, Alexander also arranged for the murder of his half-brother, Karanos, whose existence is not recorded in any other source. Some believe that he was a newborn son of Kleopatra-Eurydike, but her married life was short and it's unlikely that there was time for another birth after Europa. If he is not a fiction, Karanos may be an illegitimate son of one of Philip's concubines.[60] Alexander's incapable half-brother Arrhidaios was not suitable for any position of command and was spared.

Amyntas, Philip's nephew and Alexander's cousin, was a more real threat. Plutarch appears to associate him with the treacherous Lynkestian brothers, stating in his *Moralia* that when Alexander became king, 'All Macedonia was festering with revolt and looking towards Amyntas and the children of Aeropos.'[61] Plutarch may be guilty of compressing events, but it is possible that Prince Amyntas was somehow involved in the plot to kill Philip. He had been passed over as king while still young, and a later attempt against Alexander's life is mentioned by the Roman historian Curtius.[62] His movements are difficult to trace. A fragmentary inscription discovered in Boiotian Lebadeia lists 'Amyntas, son of Perdikkas, king of the Macedonians' among those who visited the Oracle of Trophonios, where pilgrims sought to commune with the dead.[63] Its dating is uncertain, but if it follows Alexander's accession and can be trusted (the inscription has since been lost, hampering further analysis), then Amyntas was calling himself king and seeking to press his claim, perhaps with the backing of embittered Boiotians. He had connections in the area, being made a *proxenos* or guest-friend of the newly liberated Oropos after the battle of Chaironeia.[64] One of his allies may have been a son of Antiochos, also called Amyntas, who was awarded the same honour at the same time, their names appearing together on an inscription from the Amphiareion of Oropos. This second Amyntas fled to Asia at some point after Alexander's accession and later acted as an agent for Alexander the Lynkestian, who in 334 BC apparently turned traitor, seeking the Great King's backing in order to dethrone his namesake. The charges against the Lynkestian may have been invented, or perhaps the highland general had come to regret his decision to champion the prince following Philip's death. These scattered pieces of evidence suggest a possible triangulation of opposition against Alexander in his first years as king, represented by the two Amyntases and the Lynkestian brothers – another conspiracy theory to add to the many – but Alexander's later actions add some plausibility to the claims, since they were all eventually eliminated. The Lynkestian Alexander, arrested during the Persian campaign, was after some time in chains put to death; Prince Amyntas was probably dead by the summer of 335 BC, when his wife, Kynnane, was promised to another.[65]

The sources tend to depict Alexander's early kingship as a reign of terror, slaughtering all who posed a threat; such blood purges accompanied many an accession. The reality is probably more complicated.[66] Alexander appears to have dealt with his rivals when circumstances allowed and when he felt more comfortable in his position. Yet Plutarch's comment that he received the throne when the kingdom 'was exposed to great jealousies, dire hatreds, and dangers on every hand' is no exaggeration.[67] It is against this background of insecurity that Philip's funeral took place. It was not only a chance for Alexander to honour his father and predecessor, but to bind the Macedonians together under his new rule. The ancient sources do not provide much detail about the event; it has fallen to archaeologists to bring this pivotal moment in Alexander's life back into focus.

9.

RETURN OF THE KING

The *Megali Toumba*, or Great Tumulus, was situated on the western edge of Aigai's cemetery. Its massive dimensions – some 12 metres high and 110 metres in diameter – dwarfed the surrounding tumuli, and, later, the loose-knit houses of Vergina; Léon Heuzey called it the finest burial mound in Macedonia.[1] A depression had appeared on its flattened crown at some point in history, and the Frenchman believed that it was caused by the collapse of a man-made structure buried beneath. He did not attempt its excavation but prophetically observed that, 'as in the subterranean tombs of Egypt and Etruria, there is more than a selection of ancient objects for us to recover; there lies the life and a history of an entire people awaiting our discovery.'[2]

The tumulus' investigation is intimately connected with one of Greece's most famous archaeologists: Manolis Andronikos. He had first visited Vergina in 1937 as a student of Konstantinos Rhomaios (another key figure in the site's history), later becoming superintendent of the Emathia region. He spent nearly all his summers excavating at Vergina and could usually be found perched on the edge of the trench, a peaked cap set on his head, a steady flow of cigarettes from his pocket. His rather sullen eyes, set behind a large pair of glasses, stared down into the earth or examined some freshly uncovered find, one hand occasionally rubbing his grey goatee, reminiscent of a French philosopher at thought. He effortlessly combined professionalism, knowledge and experience with a deep reverence for the past. The discoveries he made at Vergina conferred on him instant celebrity status in Greece. Streets have subsequently been named after him, while his portrait has featured on postage stamps and, most recently, a commemorative two Euro coin. When he died, in March 1992, Thessaloniki's flags flew at half-mast. His funeral was attended by thousands of people, including the Greek Prime Minister.[3]

Andronikos, like Heuzey before him, was drawn to the *Megali Toumba* and the possibilities it concealed. It had produced its first finds during the Greek Civil War (1946–9), when a detachment of soldiers used the raised ground as a defensive position. They fortified it with trenches and uncovered fragments of some broken grave stelai in the process. It was the first hint of things to come, but Andronikos had to wait until 1952 to begin his own investigations. At first, he postulated that the tomb was to be found within the body of the tumulus and sank some trial trenches into its centre and south-western side.[4] He was able to confirm that it was man-made, but only a few pottery sherds were retrieved, providing a Hellenistic construction date. Despite the disappointments of that first season, 'The secret of the Megali Toumba', as Andronikos called it, had taken hold of his imagination, and was to occupy his thoughts for the next twenty-five years.[5]

Other research projects around Vergina kept him away from the tumulus for the next decade. He returned in 1962 and 1963, this time opening a large trench, 35 metres long, from the eastern side towards the centre. More fragments of broken grave stelai emerged although there was still no sign of a tomb. He began to consider the possibility that it lay not within the overburden but beneath the original ground level. Evidently a much greater investment of time and manpower was needed if there were to be any hope of revealing the tumulus' secrets.

In 1976, Andronikos was back at the site, this time with a mechanical digger and driver. The central 'crater' trench was expanded, the aim being to open a large area from which the archaeologists could plumb the original ground level the following season. During the work, more fragments of broken grave stelai began to appear, but this time in a much larger quantity. When reassembled, they brought the total number to around nineteen, many bearing names of the dead, details of relief decoration, and even painted depictions.[6] They dated to 350–275 BC and Andronikos believed that they came from the surrounding cemetery. Whoever had built the tumulus had evidently found them broken and reused them to aid the mound's construction, yet the cause of their violent destruction remained a mystery. The size of the monument, coupled with the considerable resources needed for its completion, suggested a royal enterprise, but there was a problem with this idea. At the time, it was still believed that Aigai, burial place of the Argead royal family, was to be located at Edessa, further to the north. When Nicholas Hammond put forward his Aigai–Vergina theory, during a conference in Thessaloniki in 1968, Andronikos had responded by saying, 'I would be happy if I really were the excavator of Aigai, even without knowing it. But I can't believe it.'[7]

After the dig had finished, Andronikos returned to Thessaloniki to ruminate on the matter. He recalled that the Long Walls of Athens had been similarly constructed from grave monuments destroyed by the Persians in 480 BC, but he was at a loss to connect any historical event with the cemetery's destruction. He reached for Hammond's first volume of *A History of Macedonia*, which had been published in 1972. In it, the British historian had gathered together many of the historical sources that dealt with the region's various archaeological sites. His entry for Aigai–

Vergina immediately struck Andronikos as being of vital importance. It sent him scrambling for his copy of Plutarch's *Life of Pyrrhus*.

Pyrrhos, a Molossian king who was involved in the wars of Alexander's Successors, came to Aigai in 274 BC with a band of Celtic mercenaries (variously called Gauls or Galatians). Plutarch recounts that Pyrrhos 'captured Aigai, where he treated the inhabitants harshly and left a contingent of Gauls who were campaigning with him to garrison the city'. What the barbarians did next was of key interest for Andronikos. Plutarch continues that, 'As a race, the Gauls possess an insatiable appetite for money, and they now dug up the tombs of the rulers of Macedon who are buried there, plundering the treasure and insolently scattering the bones.'[8] Andronikos saw in this written testimony an explanation for the shattered grave stelai that he had been considering for the past twenty years. He believed that the desecration had not been limited to the royal tombs but also extended to the wider cemetery. 'The light shed by Plutarch's text unlocked all the joints of my thought,' he wrote in his memoir, 'now everything was illuminated, became simple and self-evident.'[9] It followed, therefore, that he was not excavating an unknown Macedonian settlement, but none other than Aigai – the ancient capital of the Macedonians. Hammond was right! Moreover, the tumulus' size and construction, erected as it was after the catastrophic plundering of the cemetery, suggested that it might well be hiding one of its kings. When he published these ideas in his regular newspaper column and a scholarly journal, expectations for the next season skyrocketed as a result, bringing fresh hopes but also added pressure.[10]

Andronikos' team started again in the last days of August 1977, the mechanical digger eating away more of the tumulus' mass. The pine trees that had been planted in the 1950s fell away one by one, the dust and sand sticking to the archaeologists' bodies as they oversaw the work, their eyes riveted on the ground, ready to pick out any signs of ancient activity or loose artefact. The excavations were once again focused on the centre of the tumulus, where Andronikos believed the tomb to be hidden. The first discovery was a heap of unworked stones that had been laid horizontally to form a flat level; there was some evidence that it had walls and was around 20 metres long and 3 metres high. It was originally thought to be a capping that concealed a tomb below but this turned out to be a red herring; it was actually a simple masonry core around which the Hellenistic mound had been built. After thirty-five days of work, and the removal of 18,000 cubic metres of earth, the team succeeded in revealing a good amount of the ancient surface. Five trial trenches were then sunk into the ground in the hope of hitting a subterranean construction.[11] They all proved to be sterile, nothing but virgin soil. After twenty-five years of waiting, Andronikos found himself sitting on the edge of the crater trench, staring into the desperate void with his head in his hands. It was already October and there was no sign of any tomb. Some of Andronikos' university colleagues began to mock him. 'Manolis, when you find the tomb, let us know,' said one of them.[12]

This major disappointment, however, did have one benefit. It forced Andronikos to consider a layer of marble and stone chippings uncovered in a second trench that had been opened up from the south towards the centre. It suggested building activity somewhere nearby, close to the periphery of the tumulus. The layer thinned out towards the east but continued to the south-west, so another trench was opened up further to the west to pick up the trail and provide an access ramp for the following season. Things immediately appeared more promising here. In the embankment a smaller and older tumulus was discovered; its original covering of red earth made it stick out from the sand, gravel and pebble layers of the later Hellenistic tumulus. It was on 11 October 1977, with morning hastening towards another stifling afternoon, that the digger fell silent. It had advanced some 10–20 metres into the great tumulus and the workmen and archaeologists began gathering around the freshly exposed area – the sure sign of an interesting development. They had discovered the top of a mud-brick wall, its western face bare but the top surface and eastern side coated with coarse stucco. It was a rough construction, unlikely to be a tomb, but it was the first building to be found and was the cause for some excitement.

The team continued to expose the surrounding area and developments now came thick and fast. Nine metres to the north they came upon a patch of burning with remains of bone, ash and broken pottery, evidence perhaps of sacrificial activity. They predated the Hellenistic mound and had been deposited in the second half of the fourth century BC, around 340. Underneath was another mud-brick wall which was soon identified as a continuation of the one they had already found. A second sacrificial area was discovered nearby and then, to the south-west, the limestone foundations of another building. It was square in shape, almost ten metres across, and later excavations into its foundations revealed a number of marble architectural fragments that had once been part of its superstructure. It was thought to be a heroon – a shrine for the worship of the dead – and was positioned at the edge of the earlier tumulus. It had been destroyed in antiquity but suggested that whoever was buried nearby was of some importance.[13] Almost adjoining it, set at a deeper level indicating that it may have been built first, was another structure – a rectangular masonry box capped with several large slabs of volcanic rock. It was a tomb.

After days spent staring at sand and gravel the team could hardly believe their eyes, but the discoveries didn't stop there. That strange mud-brick wall they had originally encountered was in fact attached to another tomb, much larger and grander than the first. This curious wall, as it turned out, had been constructed above the tomb's façade as a parapet to hold back the earth of the tumulus above. These last days of the dig, as is often the case with excavations, proved to be the most exciting. In the space of a day, the feelings of disappointment and dejection were replaced with optimism and the promise of more finds to come.

The smaller tomb (Tomb I) was the first to be entered. It had been robbed in antiquity; the vandals – most likely the Gauls – had first tried to hack their way through the west wall before giving up and, turning their attention to the flat roof instead, they broke one of the central stone slabs and slipped inside. The exterior openings had allowed a large quantity of earth to fall into the space, but sometime before the great tumulus was raised above, the holes were blocked up with field stones by some considerate locals. Andronikos simply removed these stones from the top in order to gain access. His eyes, at first, were fixed on the ground, where among the soil there were scattered bones along with some broken ceramics. After a few moments, he lifted his head to examine the walls. They were painted: a rich blood-red for the lower register, a blue band decorated with griffins and flowers in the middle and then, on the white upper parts, something extraordinary – beautifully painted mythical figures. 'It was immediately obvious that that tomb robbers had done their job thoroughly,' wrote Andronikos about the discovery, 'but simultaneously, we could see they had left us the most precious item in the tomb; the magnificent and captivating painted decoration.'[14] It is rare for ancient Greek paintings to survive, and here was the work of a master. His rough outlines were incised into the plaster when still wet, the layers of paint applied with a free and flourishing elegance. The scene was a popular one and related to the myths of the underworld. Hades has erupted from his subterranean domain, his chariot pulled by a team of immortal white horses; in his arms he clasps his prize, the maiden Persephone who, only a few seconds before, had been gathering flowers with her friends in a blissful meadow. The artist chose to depict the moment of capture; Persephone, with flailing hair, stretches out braceleted arms in hope of salvation, her face set in a chilling expression somewhere between shock, terror and the impending certitude of her fate, her body stiff with fright. One of her fellow maidens is shown on the floor next to the wheels of the chariot, breasts bared, a solitary hand held up in front of her face in protection but also a haunting final farewell. The rich purples of their cloaks, the matching auburn hair of Hades and Persephone, and the red and brown of the chariot, appear as flashes of bright colour from the ghostly white background. Hades' eyes are implacable; with Persephone in one hand, a sceptre and the reins in the other, he urges his horses onwards, their course guided by swift-footed Hermes – Conductor of Souls – towards the House of Death, the realm of dust and darkness, their final destination. On the eastern wall, Demeter, Persephone's mother, is depicted sitting on a rock, her perfumed robes drawn tightly around her, covering her body and ambrosial hair, framing a grief-ridden face. Traces of other goddesses, probably the three Fates, appear on the southern wall, a reminder that destiny is set from birth, the underworld the final resting place of all. The paintings discovered during that season of 1977 are among the undoubted masterpieces from the ancient world.[15]

Thoughts soon turned to possible occupants. The richness of the decoration suggested someone affiliated with the royal house. The excavation of the interior revealed a few damaged grave goods that had escaped the robbers' notice – an ivory comb, a broken marble shell, perhaps used to pour libations, and fragments of gold and bronze. The lack of any associated male items, such as weapons, made it probable that the tomb once belonged to a woman. The pottery dated it to immediately after 350 BC and

The Abduction of Persephone from Tomb I, Vergina

one of Philip's wives is likely: Phila of Elimeia or Nikesipolis of Pherai are good candidates. But the skeletal material recovered from the tomb has long confused the question. Originally it was thought there were remains of three individuals: a woman, a baby and a man.[16] But a recent cataloguing of the bones, during which some misplaced skeletal material was discovered, has brought the number of identified individuals to seven (one man, one woman, four infants and one newborn child), the human bone mixed together with those from animals. The tomb was clearly used as a charnel house after its original desecration, a practice that is well known in Aigai and elsewhere in ancient Macedonia. This contamination of the primary burial, which may no longer be present, means that, for now, the original occupant of Tomb I must remain a mystery. It provides a pertinent case study of the limitations that must be accepted when dealing with any burial pillaged in antiquity.[17]

The excavation of the second, much larger tomb (Tomb II) took place concurrently with the investigation of the first. It was of a different construction and design, a distinctive type of burial monument known as the 'Macedonian tomb' – a subterranean structure characterised by a barrel-vaulted roof with a façade resembling a temple or house of the dead, approached by a sunken road or *dromos*. The general architectural form is believed to have come into existence around the middle of the fourth century BC. The team set about revealing the tomb's façade and quickly started to uncover an elaborate colour and decoration scheme. The cornice was painted in red and dark blue with white palmettes set along its length. As they continued down they came across its most stunning feature – a large painted frieze, 5.56 metres long and 1.16 metres high.[18] It was far more detailed than the frescoes in Tomb I but time and localised soil conditions had done much damage. As conservators began to carefully peel away the dirt, the image, like a photograph developing in the dark room, began to emerge. It was a hunting scene, with animals and men depicted in mellow tones of grey, white, brown and green; a composition of unparalleled skill, the most magnificent painting ever found in Macedonia, or anywhere in Greece for that matter. It was a just reward for the team's hard work and further emphasised the importance of whoever was buried within.

Funds were now rapidly running out and there was only time for a few days' further excavation. The looting of Tomb I had prepared the archaeologists for the possibility that this structure too had been plundered. That was the norm with Macedonian tombs: fifty-one had so far been discovered and all but one, whose contents were poor and insignificant, had been desecrated.[19] It was the usual practice of the grave robbers to gain access via the roof, then smash their way out through the main doors, arms laden with treasure. Andronikos hoped to expose the tomb's entrance. If it had been looted, as was suspected, the doors would no longer be in their original position, and he would be able to appraise the state of the interior before wrapping up the dig.

The team continued their work, revealing the rest of the entablature, which was also highly decorated with another painted cornice beneath the frieze, and below that alternating blue triglyphs and white metopes contained within bands of red. The weekend was now approaching and Andronikos was required to attend a meeting in Thessaloniki, so he left his two assistants, Stella Drougou and Chrysoula Saatsoglou-Paliadeli, in charge. While away he received an unexpected phone call from the site; as there was only one phone in Vergina it suggested some urgency. 'Who's calling?' he asked. 'It's Stella,' came the reply, 'Professor, we've found the door.'

This didn't strike Andronikos as unusual – they had expected to find the door, albeit probably smashed and lying on the ground. He couldn't understand why Stella would phone him with such news.

'Listen,' she continued, 'the door is still intact.'[20]

The gravity of the revelation left Andronikos dumbfounded. There was now a very good chance that the tomb had never been discovered by ancient robbers. He rushed back to the dig to take a look for himself. A rough limestone wall had been constructed in front of the doors, a measure taken by the ancient builders to stop the weight of the tumulus pressing upon the entrance. A small gap had been left below the lintel from which the doors could be seen. Andronikos wrote about the thrill of this discovery in his 1984 publication about the dig: 'It was almost unbelievable; the door of the tomb, two intact wide marble leaves, stood *in situ*. Had they never been forced? Had the tomb robbers left the tomb unplundered? Even though it seemed like a dream, it was nevertheless reality. Now when I reflect on it I think that this is still the most deeply moving moment of the excavation.'[21]

Andronikos' curiosity, along with concerns about the tomb's security, made further investigation necessary, and he managed to obtain some extra funds to continue digging. It was still far from certain that the tomb had managed to evade robbers. They may have entered and left a different way. In order to find out, the team now set about further revealing the tomb's vault. They quickly came down onto a layer of mud-brick, ash and burned remains. Andronikos thought that it might belong to a funerary altar, but later changed his mind when two melted swords, the head of a *sarissa* and pieces of horse tack were discovered. He realised that it was the remains of the funeral pyre, collected together and spread on top of the tomb's vault before it was covered with the original earthen tumulus. A section of the front part of the vault had already been excavated; its exterior had been plastered with a thick layer of stucco with no signs of disturbance. Expectation mounted as the back end of the vault was found to be similarly untouched. The thieves had never discovered the tomb.

The news of these discoveries had long since escaped the confines of the excavation, attracting the local press. All eyes were now on Andronikos as he prepared to enter the tomb and confront the past.[22]

The opening took place on 8 November 1977. To gain access to the burial chamber the team focused on removing a key stone of the vaulted roof, a trick they had picked up from the ancient tomb robbers. An iron clamp attached to a pulley was rigged up in order to lift the block free. It took two attempts to do so, while Andronikos waited patiently for his first fabled views of what lay inside. The events told in this book's prologue record those incredible moments of discovery. The intact main chamber and its time capsule of finds vindicated Heuzey's premonition about the tumulus' potential to reclaim the history of the Macedonians; that one of the richest burials ever consigned to the earth had evaded detection all this time was nothing short of a miracle. Perhaps this was a sign that it had long been revered and protected by the local populace.

After Andronikos' colleagues had also taken a look inside, each patiently queuing up to await their turn, a ladder was lowered into the dark interior. Andronikos was the first to go down, the opening so tight that he had to keep both arms by his side. He immediately felt both the elation of a scientist and the guilt of a desecrator, though 'of course the first cancelled the other out', he later remembered.[23] Many of the grave goods were no longer in their original positions, the result of earth tremors and the decay of the organic furniture. The box-shaped marble sarcophagus, close to the back wall, contained the deceased's ashes and formed the locus of the chamber. Andronikos later theorised that a wooden couch had been positioned in front of it. Fragments of ivory, glass and gilded pieces that once decorated its façade had long since dropped onto the floor as the wooden frame disintegrated, among them the tiny portraits which Andronikos believed repre-sented Philip and Alexander. Some of the weapons found in the general vicinity of the sarcophagus, including two iron swords, the cuirass and helmet, may also have once been placed on the couch, perhaps on stands. A table laden with symposion vessels – eleven of silver, two in bronze and six in clay – had been placed next to the couch, which was reduced to a dark fan-shaped stain on the ground; two of its northern legs had given way first, sending the items tumbling towards the northern wall where they remained. In the south-west corner was a bronze bathing set, along with a unique silver-gilt diadem and the remains of what later turned out to be a richly decorated shield. After everything had been photographed in situ and the inner door supported by wooden scaffolding, the team began to pack up the items for their safe removal, the sheer quantity of artefacts necessitating the use of milk and detergent boxes to make up for the shortfall in containers. They made for a peculiar procession as the team members brought them out into the open, their eyes still filled with ancient riches and newfound wonder.

Throughout these first days of work the sarcophagus remained untouched, still tightly sealed shut, and Andronikos suspected that it probably contained the chamber's most precious treasure. When he felt that the time had come, he descended into the tomb with a few chosen colleagues to open it up. They gathered around the sarcophagus and proceeded to lift the lid. Andronikos' instincts had been right: housed inside the marble box was a stunning golden ossuary – a larnax – made of twenty-four-carat gold and weighing almost eight kilos. It was a breathtaking piece of ancient craftsmanship, with embossed floral decoration around its sides, attached glass-paste florets and lions'-paw feet. Emblazoned on top was the symbol of a shining star or sun. A common motif in Greek art, it quickly became known as the Vergina Star or Sun.

They carefully laid the larnax on the floor and then opened it. 'Our eyes nearly popped out of their sockets and our breathing stopped,' records Andronikos, 'there, unmistakably, were charred bones placed in a carefully formed pile and still retaining the colour of the purple cloth in which they had once been wrapped. In one corner lay a very heavy gold wreath, now folded, which had covered them. We shut the valuable casket, covered it, and placed it in an inner corner of the chamber.'[24]

The team returned to the surface to recover from the thrill of the discovery. Andronikos soon began to drift away from the others. He was starting to process all that he had seen, going over each piece of evidence in turn as a working hypothesis about the identity of the dead man began to emerge. The grave goods suggested royalty, and they appeared to date to around the third quarter of the fourth century BC. 'Everything indicated that we had found a royal tomb,' Andronikos later wrote with excitement, 'and if the dating we had assigned to the objects was correct, as it seemed to be, then . . . I did not even dare to think about it. For the first time a shiver ran down my spine, something akin to an electric shock passed through me. If the dating . . . and if these were royal remains . . . then . . . had I held the bones of Philip in my hands? It was far too terrifying an idea for my brain to assimilate.'[25]

And yet the tomb had one final revelation: an antechamber, which up to this point had remained unexplored. The team held out little hope that it contained anything of interest, such spaces were usually empty. Not wanting to prise open the interconnecting marble doors that linked it to the main chamber, Andronikos sought to remove one of the stones from the partition wall instead. On 21 November, he put his head through the opening and gazed upon an unexpected sight: directly in front of him was another sarcophagus, a secondary burial.

Raising his eyes to the vault, following the beam of his torch, he saw that the chamber was finished to a higher standard than the first. The plastering had been completed and painted, white for the lower parts and red for the upper. Where the vaulted ceiling met the wall, there was, an ornamental moulding, with a decorative band of rosettes beneath that ran around the chamber; nails were affixed along its length, suggesting that objects and textiles had once hung from the walls. A scatter of small golden discs, bearing more star/sun bursts, could be seen among the lumps of fallen plaster. They had probably been sewn onto a lost fabric canopy or baldaquin erected over the sarcophagus, its deterioration causing the gleaming droplets to rain onto the ground.[26] Andronikos managed to wriggle through the hole and tiptoed into the centre. He first examined the outer door, which was leaning slightly inwards but appeared stable. He then turned his attention to the internal door behind him, which led to the main chamber. 'The threshold', he wrote, 'was packed – a spear, alabastra, a Cypriot amphora and, in the left hand corner, between the jambs and the door, a curious gold object with

dainty decoration and relief scenes.'[27] Andronikos recognised it
as a *gorytos*, an elaborate golden quiver that held both bow and
arrows – the prestigious weapon of Scythian mounted archers.
Among the rotten remains of wooden chests and boxes were
other armaments: a pair of gilded greaves, the left one taller and
wider than the right, a crescent-shaped pectoral, several iron
spearheads and the golden fittings of a leather cuirass. More ivory
and gilded elements were found in front of the sarcophagus and
Andronikos guessed that they belonged to another couch.

The team opened the sarcophagus the next day. It was covered
with more organic remains, the wasted skeletons of flowers and
grain, while a crumpled gold-myrtle wreath lay on the floor
nearby.[28] Remarkably, it contained another gold larnax, slightly
smaller and plainer than the first but stamped with the same star/
sunburst design upon its lid. The most exceptional aspect of the
find, however, was waiting inside. Unlike the first larnax, the gold
and purple cloth that wrapped the bones was still preserved; once
unravelled and conserved it revealed a floral motif of acanthus
leaves stitched in gold thread, another unique find. Squeezed next
to the cremated bones was a folded golden diadem – a mesh of
delicate branches and tendrils, with flowers and palmettes springing
from the undergrowth on coiled golden stems, a miniature bee
and bird's nest depicted among the tangle of sparkling verdure.
The workmanship was stunning; it is undoubtedly the finest piece
of jewellery ever discovered in Macedonia.

The objects provided more information about the tomb as a
whole but also posed new problems for its interpretation. The
grave goods in the antechamber were an odd mix, with elements
common to both female and male burials. Preliminary investigation of the bones revealed that they belonged to a young
female, believed to have been in her twenties at the time of
death.[29] Andronikos thought that the individual may have been

one of Philip's wives. He considered that the weapons may have belonged to her, but favoured the interpretation that they were the king's instead, an overflow of his grave goods.[30] The ante-chamber discoveries were a fitting end to what had been an extraordinary season.

Following a short press release on the finds, a conference was organised to take place on 24 November in Thessaloniki. During the run-up to the event, Andronikos spent many sleepless nights going over the evidence, clarifying the reasons that lay behind the identification of the deceased in the main chamber as Philip. Instinct was to be tempered with the strict methodology of academic consideration. On the morning of the conference he still had reservations about going public with his thoughts, for some of his colleagues had doubts over the identification. He informed the Greek President and Prime Minister about what he wished to say and they urged him to make good on his convictions.[31] Andronikos followed their advice. In front of a packed-out auditorium he related the discovery, placing emphasis on the finds and the miracle of their survival. The identification of the deceased was the elephant in the room and Andronikos did not ignore it: 'basing my judgement on firm archaeological evidence,' he summed up, 'I believe I have the right to claim this tomb as that of Philip II.'[32]

THE TWO PHILIPS

Andronikos' theory soon came under scrutiny from the academic community. This was to be expected and was indeed necessary – every hypothesis needs to undergo peer review. That it represented a royal burial found almost unanimous consensus. The remains of the extraordinary pyre covering the vault, the richness of the grave goods, not to mention the size of the tumulus and its location in what was now believed to be Aigai – the burial place of Argead kings – all reinforced such a conclusion. Based on the finds, Andronikos dated the burial to 350–325 BC, but others subsequently argued that the evidence failed to allow for such a tight chronological framework. There has been a push and pull over certain artefacts, the skeletal material, and even the construction date of the tomb itself, with many trying to down-date it to the end of the fourth century BC. This brought in the possibility that the tomb did not belong to Philip, but rather to his son, Arrhidaios.

The incapable Arrhidaios was elevated to the throne after Alexander's untimely death at Babylon in 323 BC. He took the name Philip (III) and later shared the kingship with Alexander's infant son, Alexander IV. They were mere puppets in the power struggles that soon engulfed the Macedonian Empire and didn't last long. Both were eventually murdered. Arrhidaios-Philip was buried in Aigai sometime after late 317 BC along with his wife, Adea-Eurydike, daughter of Kynnane.[33] The two Philips were the only Macedonian kings reported by the ancient sources to have been buried there during the mid to late fourth century BC; hence both were possible candidates for Tomb II.[34] To further complicate matters, they were close in age at the time of death – both were in their forties – and were buried only nineteen years apart, a time frame that makes dating extremely difficult. The female in the antechamber was also a cause of contention. Andronikos proffered that it was Kleopatra-Eurydike, Philip's last wife, but others favoured Adea-Eurydike.

In the years since the discovery two camps have emerged, each championing a different Philip, in a battle for identity waged across numerous academic journals and publications.[35] Archaeological knowledge of ancient Macedonia has, in many ways, been trying to catch up with the debate. Some of the early arguments for dating were based on artefacts that lacked a large enough comparative database to be assured, while the chronologies were somewhat fluid and could quickly change on the basis of new finds or interpretations. Various analyses of the bones were also plagued with inconsistencies; one identification was supported, then another. Recent studies, however, along with the emergence of long-awaited reports on some of Tomb II's assemblages and artwork, have strengthened Andronikos' original conclusions.[36] But perhaps the most persuasive point in favour of his hypothesis lies not in any one element, but rather in the overall magnificence of the tomb and its contents. This is not the burial of a weak king whose reign was short and of no consequence, but of an individual who eclipsed all those that had gone before, the greatest king buried on Macedonian soil.[37] It seems almost certain that it belongs to Philip II.

ENTERING THE SHADES

The museum/shelter of the royal tombs of Aigai now houses the monuments and finds once concealed by the *Megali Toumba*. The entrance lies off a pedestrianised road on the eastern edge of Vergina, lined on one side by a procession of cafés, tavernas and souvenir shops, on the other by the site's iron-railed compound. The archaeological remains are hidden under a reconstituted earthen mound, grassed over and fronted by a large gravel forecourt. Clumps of rosemary and oleander drape themselves over the two walkways that lead into the structure's innards, one an exit, the other an entrance. The sloping passages, lined with honey-coloured ashlar blocks, allow for a steady descent; darkness becomes almost total, it feels like entering the underworld. The space comprises four contiguous hexagonal rooms with floors of granite-coloured marble, the architecture evoking that of a crypt.[38] The eyes take a few moments to adjust; people wander around with hands behind their backs, while conversation is conducted in hushed voices. This is no ordinary museum or archaeological site but an experience.

A selection of grave stelai are the first exhibits to be encountered. They stand erect in the pale glow of overhead spotlights, resembling stalks of asphodel stretching out into the sepulchral gloom. Sixty-seven were found in all during the excavations. They still bear the visible scars of their destruction at the hands of the Gauls; now pieced back together again, they act like an ancient greeting committee, introducing the visitor to the former citizens of Aigai – the athletic Antigonos, the family group of Kleonymos, and the so-called Madonna of Aigai, whose dream-like face and shawl of red and orange would seem equally at home in an Orthodox church. These were the people who could once be found strolling around the agora, haggling over the price of a bushel of wheat, visiting the city's shrines or attending the theatre, their lives set against the backdrop of the sulking Pierian mountains and the grandiose architecture of the royal family.

Continuing on the clockwise museum circuit, venturing deeper into the darkness, the spectral shape of the heroon appears, a cube of earth and volcanic blocks set beyond the sunken remains of another tomb, that of 'the free-standing columns', discovered in 1980. It was heavily plundered in antiquity, and only the burial chamber's foundations and fronting portico have survived. The box-like Tomb I is set in the heroon's shadow. Enlarged photographs of the 'Abduction of Persephone' mural have been set against the museum's back wall, allowing visitors to appreciate the finery of the paintings that remain hidden away in the protective darkness of the tomb.

An interior partition divides the southern part of the museum from the space dedicated to Tomb II's contents. A large glass case contains neatly ordered piles of charred, melted and fragmented finds. At first there seems little to get excited about, but what they represent is truly extraordinary – the remnants of one of the most spectacular funeral pyres known from antiquity. Visitors huddle around the display, their faces illuminated by the under-lights as if the pyre were still smouldering, yet to be extinguished by time and libations; gazing upon the seared remains it's almost possible to hear the crackle and roar of the conflagration, to feel the heat of the ancient spectacle. Incredibly, archaeologists have been able to postulate the pyre's form and construction from some of the preserved elements. The layer of mud-bricks found deposited over the barrel vault is thought to come from the podium. Collections of sizeable iron nails, bronze door fittings and an ornamental lion-headed knocker suggest that it resembled a house or funerary temple, perhaps even a combustible copy of the final tomb.

The offerings were as numerous as they were diverse, their sorting and identification the result of hours in the conservation lab with tweezers and microscopes – food and drink, weapons, an elaborate chryselephantine couch, clothes, jewellery, strigils, incense and perfume. The bones of dogs and horses, along with their bridle fittings, suggest that the king's animal companions were also added to the groaning pyre. Standing back from the display, the visitor gets some sense of its awesome scale. It was heroic, Homeric, in its proportions, recalling the pyres of Patroklos, Hektor and Achilles, as well as of Herakles, who burnt himself on Mount Oiti before ascending to Olympos.[39]

This was the main event in the king's funeral, which according to the *Alexander Romance* was attended by 'all the people of Macedonia'.[40] Beforehand, after a period of lying in state, a ritual procession was formed – the *ekphora* – where the body was moved from palace to pyre, the royal train consisting of many attendants, family and friends. Some perhaps had cut their hair short in mourning. The women, ashen faced, beat their breasts in lament. This solemn event caused many to reflect on the irony that the torch lit for the daughter's marriage was being put to her father's pyre.[41] As the mortuary house began to glow red, olive oil and unguents made the fire spit and flare. Philip's body and the items positioned around him, all that he could ever need in the next world, were consumed in the blaze. His spirit was now free to make its onwards journey 'from here to there', as it was called.[42] Coins placed over his eyes were to pay Charon, ferryman of the dead. Philip's induction into mystery cults, such as that of the Samothracian Great Gods and probably Orpheus' as well, had provided him with the necessary directions to find a peaceful resting place. The wooden superstructure collapsed, the grand design reduced to dust and ash, the congregation's grief dying with the flames; the ceremony had a cathartic effect on all those gathered around.

Soon afterwards the king's remains were collected, washed in wine, wrapped in a royal textile and placed in a gold larnax, ready to be interred in the tomb when it had been completed. It was to be accompanied by an exceptional collection of grave goods, Philip's most prized possessions. The majority of the museum's remaining space is given over to the objects recovered from the main burial chamber, along with those from the antechamber. Some have required years in the conservation lab, others, such as those wrought in silver and gold, required nothing more than a good clean to be exhibited; each one has its own biography, a different story to tell. Every visitor has their own favourite piece or assemblage, items that leave an indelible mark on the imagination. For some, it's the bathing apparatus, a complete set rendered in bronze and now endowed with a stately patina of verdigris. They call to mind the opulent bath-times described by Homer, where the heroes would strip off their clothes, heavy with dust from the road or blood from combat, and ready themselves for the feasts to come. One of the associated tripods is much older than the other items, a dotted inscription on the rim proclaiming 'I am from the games of Argive Hera.'[43] It dates to the second half of the fifth century BC and is most likely a family heirloom, emphasising the longevity of the Argeads' athletic prowess and Argive connections.

For others, it's the silver symposia vessels that linger on in the memory; they make it possible to picture what it was to drink and converse with the king, in all the finery and ceremony of such occasions. The couches with their reassembled façades of ivory, glass and other decorative elements are the most surprising objects. Philip's couch bears a hunting scene like that shown on Tomb II's painted frieze, and comprises fourteen figures on foot and horse-back. Their hands and limbs, preserved in ever-white ivory, emerge in relief from a gilded background, their clothes coloured with bright pigments. Among them are the portraits that Andronikos believed were those of Philip and Alexander. They undoubtedly resemble known depictions of the pair, but there are reservations; other faces in the composition have similar features, and there is repetition in both form and style from a growing corpus of ivory figures recovered from the decayed couches of other Macedonian tombs. They may just be stock depictions from the artist's or guild's repertoire.

Standing rigid in the centre of the space, encased in glass, is arguably the most evocative representation of the king – a pair of greaves, cuirass, helmet, sword and shield, reassembled in full battle array. Together they form the ghost of Philip, outlined in gold and iron, one of the finest panoplies ever made. The attention to detail is remarkable, from the miniature helmet on the sword's pommel to a small gold plate bearing the club of Herakles – an Argead talisman – that was affixed to the reverse of the shield. It is a visceral representation of his power and prestige, the work of a master armourer, a fitting panoply for the man who had built the Macedonian army.

There is a strong Pan-Hellenic theme to some of the finer elements of the decoration. Athena's face emerges from beneath the shadow of the helmet's crest, while on the side of the cuirass she is represented on another small golden plate, the pose reminiscent of her chryselephantine statue in the Parthenon. Her presence on the armour probably went beyond her usual role as goddess of wisdom and battle strategy. In Homer's *Iliad*, she supported the Achaians against the Trojans, an obvious divine mascot for Philip's Persian campaign. The entire set may have been expressly designed with that goal in mind. This idea finds some collaboration with the theme represented on the shield's face. It took five years to reassemble, and when originally discovered in the tomb it was nothing more than a heap of ivory, glass and gold.[44] At its centre, surrounded by inlaid rings of decoration, is a piece of 3D art: two ivory figures, eroded by time, emerge from the golden background, a man about to slay a woman, probably Achilles subjugating the Amazonian queen Penthesileia – Greek triumphing over Barbarian. Philip had planned to lead his men into Asia with Hellenic ideals in the vanguard.

The gold larnax that once held his cremated remains is displayed at one end of the museum space, opposite that from the antechamber, the 'his and hers' set glowing seductively at each other across the darkness. Philip's golden wreath, a radiant profusion of oak leaves and acorns, was originally folded and placed beside his bones. It is now suspended above his larnax. Perhaps the same wreath that he wore on the fateful day of his assassination. There is burning on one side and some loose acorns and leaves were found among the pyre remains on the tomb's vault; it had evidently been snatched from the flames by some brave soul before it could be consumed. The same action was performed with the ceremonial shield, evidence of some unknown funeral ritual.

Philip's bones were well preserved compared to other known cremations. The king's body may have been wrapped in some fire-retardant cloak or lain on an incombustible surface within the pyre.[45] Those responsible for gathering his remains had done a thorough job; even the malleus bone from the middle ear, one of the smallest in the human body, was retrieved.[46] They were placed in the larnax in an anatomically correct order, with cranium on top and longer bones below.[47] Along with fragments of the royal textile and wreath, traces of a composite material, containing the white pigment, Egyptian Huntite, have been detected on the bones, perhaps all that is left of a religious or death mask placed on top of them.[48] Examination of the skeletal material has provided some interesting details about Philip's appearance and health. Estimates of height range from 5ft 2in to 5ft 6in (160–170cm); he was not a tall individual, even by ancient standards.[49] Schmorls nodes discovered on his lower vertebra are indicative of intensive horse-riding. Much attention has been given to the skull in an effort to locate the arrow wound he suffered at Methone, but its fragmen-tary and heat-warped state has made conclusions difficult. There are signs, however, that he suffered from recurrent infection, perhaps sinusitis, which could have resulted from some facial trauma. The only wound identified with certainty was the healing mark of a small blade on one of his left finger bones; such a wound is listed in the ancient sources as being among Philip's known injuries.[50]

Analysis of the female's remains from the antechamber has proved a harder task. They are more fragmentary, suggesting that the cremation occurred under different circumstances, most likely separately; her magnificent diadem had also been rescued from the flames and shows some damage and scorching. There is still an active debate as to the individual's identity. Kleopatra-Eurydike, the Getic Meda, or even an unknown Scythian wife, have all been proposed.[51] Her estimated age at death has varied with different examinations, ranging from the early twenties to, most recently, around thirty-two years of age.[52] Numerous Schmorls nodes have been discovered on her vertebrae as well, suggesting she led an active life. She had suffered a bad injury in youth, a healed compression fracture being identified on her left tibia. Such an injury can cause leg shortening, atrophy or lameness and may explain the different size and shape of the greaves discovered in the antechamber, the left being shorter and slimmer than the right in order to accommodate the differing proportions of her legs. If they do belong to her then the other weapons may as well. This link between the bones and the panoply, especially the gilded *gorytos* – the weapon of a mounted archer – have been put forward in support of the Scythian identity, perhaps a daughter of the fallen king Ateas. However, such items could also be attributed to Meda. Her people, the Thracian Getai, shared the same mode of warfare with their Scythian neighbours, the women perhaps also fighting alongside the men. During Ateas' reign both groups occupied the Dobruja region and this may have led to further cultural exchange and possible intermingling between the populations. The Getai had a strong belief in an immortal afterlife, where they would join the divine Zalmoxis in the hereafter, and the wives were said to have sacrificed themselves upon the death of their husbands. Meda may well have taken her own life after Philip's murder, later being honoured with a cremation pyre in royal fashion.[53] Yet those who refute the strength of this evidence and the new estimate of her age maintain that Kleopatra-Eurydike, Philip's last wife, who was likely in her early twenties when she died (sometime before 334 BC) is the favoured candidate. In this case the grave goods are explained as belonging to Philip, booty from the 339 BC campaign, and could account for the later date of the antechamber's decoration. Debate will probably continue for some time yet.

The tomb in which these remarkable artefacts were discovered lies at the bottom of a wooden staircase, just off the main hall. Its façade is visible behind a plexi-glass screen, the doors, flanked with Doric pilasters, have never been opened. With each step down the creaking stairs the subjects of the painted frieze begin to emerge, though like a newspaper's front page that has partially rotted away, the story is still there albeit only in ghostly form. Binoculars or a sharp pair of eyes are needed to appreciate the minute details. Bare trees framed by rocky slopes recall the Macedonian mountains in winter. A tall square pillar surmounted with three statues, along with a garlanded tree, suggests a sacred grove and/or a royal game reserve. The composition is designed to be viewed from the left to the right, the trees and broken landscape dividing up the narrative and its figures. Together they reflect the overall story of the hunt.[54]

Starting on the left, among the rocks and trees, are wild animals and hunters, depicted in heroic nudity and dutifully aided by a number of hounds. A deer has already been captured, a boar is being finished off. The figure in the centre of the frieze is mounted on a bay horse, wearing a belted purple *chiton* and laurel wreath. He has a spear raised in readiness for what lies directly to the right, the royal quarry, the mountain lion – as unbelievable as it may seem to us today, these beasts could once be found in ancient Macedonia.[55] It has been surrounded by hunters and hounds; one youth, dressed in *chlamys* and *kausia*, levels his spear at its neck, feet apart in bracing position, another hunter behind the beast readies his double-headed axe for a fatal swing. The lion is already bleeding from its wounds, but remains undefeated. It snarls in defiance, staring up at a horse and its rider that are rearing above him, the man's spear ready to be driven downwards as hunter and hunted lock eyes. This is the culmination of the scene; the mature individual, bearded, his face in profile, is thought to represent Philip, the king captured in a last moment of glory. His marginalisation to the right side of the painting is at odds with his rank and predominant role in the hunt, but is explained by the identity of the youth on his bay horse in the centre of the composition. Behind him a boar lies defeated on the ground, while his attention is now focused on the lion, the next target. Hunting, that age-old allegory for status in Macedonian society, is being displayed with a purpose here. The figure is most likely Alexander. If correct, this is the earliest depiction of him that has survived from antiquity. He has already successfully completed his important rite of passage – the killing of a boar without nets – and, although still young, is ready to take on the lion. In this context, the painting can be viewed as a political statement, designed to strengthen his early rule. He was honouring his father and predecessor, but at the same time emphasising his readiness and qualifications for kingship.

It is with these interpretations that the royal tombs and their priceless treasures take on new meaning. The grandeur of the pyre, the rituals of the royal ceremony, the banquets and games that followed, were all officiated by Alexander, and were among his first acts as king. The funeral was carefully orchestrated and had the characteristic stamp of flamboyance that would remain with him throughout his reign. To stand on the wooden platform above the ancient ground level, faced with the profile of the tomb, is perhaps to occupy the same spot as the young Alexander in 336 BC. The hastily finished main burial chamber, which was never properly decorated, probably draped with purple curtains to hide the unadorned plaster, may suggest some anxiety on his part; speed was necessary for the final rituals so he could get on with dealing with the kingdom in turmoil.[56] As the last of the grave goods were interred inside, the marble doors of the main chamber pulled shut, a bronze wedge falling into place to lock them for eternity, he must have considered the enormity of the challenges that lay ahead. The sense of history in this dark and humid space is palpable.

It may have been on this occasion that the two Lynkestian brothers – Heromenes and Arrhabaios – were executed.[57] Two skeletons were found during the excavations nearby, also covered by the red earth of the original tumulus. Their graves were simple and did not contain any goods; they probably represent the bodies of the convicted accomplices. The antechamber's completion was afforded the luxury of time, allowing the finer painted decoration to be finished before the interment of the royal female.[58] The pyre

Tomb II, Vergina

remains were collected and spread atop the tomb's vault, its façade and painted frieze perhaps remaining visible for some time before the earthen mound swallowed it up. What had been created for the benefit of the living now belonged to the dead. A heroon-shrine was later erected beside the tumulus to facilitate a cult of the deceased.[59] The greatest king Macedonia had ever known was gone, but all that he achieved, and the dream of a Pan-Hellenic expedition to Persia, did not follow him into the darkness of Tomb II. Alexander was intent on following his father's plans. First, however, he had to prove to his fellow Macedonians, as well as the rest of the Greeks and Balkan peoples, that he was fit to lead. The situation following his accession was still precarious. He had yet to eliminate his rivals at court, and the Greek cities were already showing signs of dissension. The Illyrians and Thracians were also threatening to throw off the Macedonian yoke, and yearned for the rule of their native kings. Alexander's counsellors urged him to give up on the Greeks, to win over the barbarians through bribery or territorial concessions and to abandon his father's designs; the stability of the kingdom should be his primary concern.[60] But Alexander was not the type of ruler to give up hard-won gains. He would start his reign as he meant to go on, with quick, decisive action and a monumental dose of self-belief.

MEGALI TOUMBA POSTSCRIPT

But before leaving the *Megali Toumba* to pick up Alexander's story, there is one final surprise: a third unlooted royal tomb, 'the tomb of the prince', as it is now called. It was discovered in 1978 and lies at the end of another subterranean staircase. The recovered grave goods, placed in the last of the museum's display cases, include more bathing and symposium vessels, strigils for athletics, the remains of a couch bearing Dionysos cavorting with his companions, and an array of weapons. The cremated remains of the individual were found inside a silver *hydria*, a golden oak wreath hung around its neck. Examination of the bones revealed that they belonged to a teenage boy, aged around thirteen or fourteen. The dating of the tomb and its artefacts suggested that he died in the late fourth century BC, and archaeologists and scholars generally agree that it belongs to Alexander IV, Alexander the Great's son who was murdered in 309 BC by the Successor Kassandros. His death brought an end to the Argead dynasty which had ruled Macedonia since the beginning of the kingdom's history. An old legend had foretold the event: Perdikkas I, it was said, had decreed to his successor that all his descendants should be buried at Aigai, and so long as this tradition was followed, their family would remain in power. Alexander the Great was eventually entombed in Egyptian Alexandria. The thread was broken.[61]

Alexander never met his son, who was born after his death. Half-Macedonian, half-Baktrian, he embodied the ideals of his father who had attempted to unify a wide and diverse empire under his rule. The grave goods suggest that the boy had already started his secondary education, learning the arts of warfare and practising athletics, brought up in the Macedonian manner, but as long as he lived he was a threat to those who coveted the throne. Even Alexander's memory and royal bloodline could not protect him. He, along with his mother Rhoxane, was secretly murdered at Amphipolis. His later burial was probably overseen by the new Antigonid dynasty that took power after the fall of Kassandros.[62] Afterwards, they sought to repair the damage caused by the Celtic mercenaries by burying the royal tombs under a giant mound. Its design echoes one of Alexander's plans that became widely known after his death, a new burial monument for his father Philip that was to rival Egypt's Great Pyramid in size.[63] It never reached those ambitious heights, but it succeeded in protecting its secrets until the twentieth century when it finally emerged once more into the light of history, heralding not only the return of the king, but a revolution in Macedonian archaeology and the knowledge of its buried past.

10.

ALEXANDER IN CHARGE

In Athens, Demosthenes was the first to hear about Philip's demise, the message being delivered by scouts of an Athenian general – Charidemos – who was active in the north. Ever the opportunist, he used it to further his own reputation, this time by depicting himself as a man favoured by the gods.[1] He declared that they had communed with him in a dream, and to him alone they had revealed the future: Athens would soon receive some great stroke of fortune. The news of Philip's murder soon 'miraculously' vindicated the truthfulness of the dream. Many of the Athenians rejoiced and offered up sacrifices in thanks, while the Assembly voted the assassin Pausanias a posthumous crown.[2] The sober-minded Phokion the Good, however, urged caution and reminded his fellow citizens that the army that had beaten them at Chaironeia had only been weakened by the loss of one man.[3] Demosthenes cast aside such concerns. Philip was dead, one of the king's own men had done what no enemy army had been able to achieve; it was time to celebrate. He set up a shrine to Pausanias and even though his daughter, his only child, had recently died, he took to the streets adorned with garland and white robe, revelling in being 'cock of the walk' once more.[4]

Demosthenes had begrudgingly acknowledged that Philip,

while alive, was a leader of some talent, but when it came to
Alexander he wildly underestimated his abilities.[5] He considered
him to be no immediate threat, a mere boy. No stranger to
nicknames himself, Demosthenes called him Margites – a comic
fool from poetry, a parody of a Homeric hero. He chose to
conveniently forget his role at Chaironeia, instead dwelling on
those first impressions from Pella many years before, when the
Athenians had been entertained by his kithara playing and debates
with another boy. Demosthenes used this rhetoric to rally support
for rebellion, suggesting that Alexander was content to saunter
around Pella observing the omens. He would never stir beyond
Macedon's borders, or so claimed the orator.[6] In order to gain
new allies, letters began to pass between him and Attalos in Asia
– Alexander's most dangerous enemy, who was still alive and
active – and the Great King Darius III, who instructed his satraps
to provide Demosthenes with funds to finance an uprising.[7]
Around this time, other city-states also began to agitate for
independence. Alexander was aware of these developments and
was anxious to stop a full-blown revolt before it was too late.[8]
As soon as he was able, he marched south with his army.

The Thessalians had for the most part kept faith with Philip,
and they would do the same with his son, but they needed some
persuading.[9] It was probably at the Pan-Thessalian sanctuary of
Athena Itonia, near modern Philia, that they gathered to hear what
Alexander had to say. His skills in rhetoric were needed once more.
He drew attention to their shared descent from Herakles and
Aiakos, and to the benefits that Philip had bestowed on them, and
by raising their hopes with kind words and rich promises he
succeeded in winning them over. They acknowledged him as their
new leader and handed over control of state revenues, taxes and
military forces, as well as backing his bid to become the *hegemon*
of the League of Corinth. When Alexander continued his march

south, he did so knowing that the feared Thessalian cavalry were on his side.[10] At the sanctuary of Demeter at Thermopylai, he secured the second pillar of Macedonian control of Greece – the support of the Delphic Amphiktyony. By now news of his movements had spread to the rebellious cities, some of which were having second thoughts about their actions. One by one embassies arrived asking for forgiveness; others needed further prompting.

Alexander entered Boiotia with his army in full battle array. After Philip's death, the Thebans had voted to expel the Macedonian garrison installed on the Kadmeia and refused to recognise Alexander as the new leader of the Greeks. But they experienced a drastic change of heart when they gazed upon the thousands of soldiers encamped outside their city's walls. With memories of Chaironeia still fresh in their minds, they submitted without the need for any further bloodshed. Athens soon followed suit. They sent a belated embassy to Alexander to apologise for their tardiness in acknowledging him as their leader. Demosthenes was among the envoys, but he lost his nerve halfway to Thebes and fled back to Athens. Aeschines reminded him of this embarrassment in a later speech, calling him 'useless in peace and war alike!'[11] Alexander received the remaining Athenians with good grace and released them from their fears. They conferred upon him honours greater than they had Philip.[12]

The lightning tour of Greece was capped off at the sanctuary of Poseidon at Isthmia, where representatives of the remaining Greek city-states gathered to swear their allegiance to Alexander, just as they had done for Philip a few years previously. The Lakedaimonians once again refused to take part, stating that it was their tradition to lead not to follow.[13] He was formally recognised as *hegemon* of the League of Corinth, guarantor of the Common Peace and new commander-in-chief of the Persian expedition.[14] Within a matter of weeks, he had reversed a dire position.

Philip's achievements, the result of many years of diplomacy, war and hard-fought peace, had been kept intact. It was now winter and the army prepared to return home. But there is one last story about Alexander's time in the environs of Corinth that cannot be ignored – a meeting with one of the ancient world's most eccentric characters. He was nicknamed 'the dog', often slept in a ceramic storage jar, and was famous for his savage, caustic wit. He was Diogenes of Sinope or Diogenes the Cynic, as he is better known.

The encounter was among the best-loved tales from antiquity, stressing the stark differences in life and values of the two individuals. Diogenes was apparently sunning himself next to his mobile home when Alexander and his entourage arrived. He approached the philosopher and asked if he wanted anything. 'Yes,' replied Diogenes, 'stand a little out of my sun.' Reflecting on this spectacular snub, Alexander, according to Plutarch, later joked about the event with his friends, and mused, 'if I were not Alexander, I would be Diogenes.'[15]

Alexander meets Diogenes statue, Corinth

On his way back to Macedonia, Alexander made a detour to Delphi. The Pythia's former pronouncement – 'Wreathed is the bull' – had been tragically fulfilled, and it was now time for a new prediction regarding the fate of the Persian campaign. The royal party made the trek up to the sacred city but arrived on an inauspicious day, when the Pythia was not in attendance at the temple. Alexander sent for her but she refused to come forth. He managed to track her down, and proceeded to forcibly drag her towards the tripod from which the oracles were delivered. As he did so the Pythia cried out, 'You are invincible, my son!' Alexander had the answer he desired.[16] Plutarch, once again, is the only ancient writer to preserve the story and there are problems with it. A very similar tale is attributed to a Phokian general during the Third Sacred War, and there are also parallels with the exploits of Herakles, who attempted to seize the tripod after the Pythia refused him an audience; it is unlikely to be an accurate reporting of Alexander's visit.[17] Any prophecy that he did receive remains a mystery. Justin cryptically mentions an oracle that had foretold a plot against his life from within Macedonia, which may refer to his cousin Amyntas' bid for power, but it is unknown if this came from the same consultation.[18] Alexander may have learned from his father's bitter experience and decided to keep the answer to himself.

Back in Macedonia, the new king was able to consolidate his position and make plans for the future. With affairs now settled in Greece he could afford to concentrate on his barbarian neighbours. The Thracians were unsettled, the Illyrians and Triballoi restless; they would have to be humbled before any Persian expedition could take place.[19] Alexander gave himself an entire campaign season to deal with these issues. It was a chance to prove himself as a military leader in his own right, to win over the remaining doubters in his ranks, and to re-secure the Balkan territory that his father had spent so much time and effort in acquiring. Revenge was also a particularly strong motivator. The Triballoi had defied Macedon in 339 BC, nearly killing Philip in the battle for Scythian booty. Alexander was most likely present on that occasion. He now had the chance to right that particular wrong.

WHIRLWIND IN THRACE

Amphipolis had been one of Philip's first and most important acquisitions, captured in 357 BC. With it came the rich natural resources of the surrounding countryside as well as control of a major crossroads and port. He had invested in the city, adding a new neighbourhood and establishing a royal mint within its walls; public and private land was reapportioned accordingly, to loyal citizens and faithful Companions.[20] Its position close to the eastern borders of the kingdom made it the ideal base for expeditions into Thrace, and so it remained under Alexander. It was here that he made his final preparations for his first campaign as king.

The archaeological site of Amphipolis is vast. The hilltop city, cradled by a languid bend of the river Strymon, has an impressive set of outer fortification walls stretching for some seven kilometres. To the south the waters dissolve into the Aegean, the nearby lagoons pink-lined with flamingos. Inside, only small pockets of the ancient city have been revealed. The visitor must embark on an archaeological safari, across dew-damp grass and scrub-studded hillsides, in search of the solitary brown signs that accompany some of the uncovered structures – a few houses, a well-preserved gymnasion from the Hellenistic period and a scatter of sanctuaries. Many of the antiquities harvested from the area and its surrounding cemeteries reside in the on-site museum, the compact display spaces filled with a range of artefacts that proclaim Amphipolis' former prosperity. The discovery in 2014 of an elaborate Hellenistic tomb beneath the Kasta burial mound, to the north of the city, attracted worldwide attention and attests to the large amount of money that flowed into the city after Alexander's Asian conquest.

That spring in 335 BC, Amphipolis became a hive of military activity. Horses were readied for the march, supplies gathered, the altars of the gods, Artemis Tauropolos being the most important, freshly bloodied and smoking with newly made sacrifices. A sizeable army had been assembled for the campaign to come – a precise figure is not provided by the ancient sources, but around 20,000 men seems likely.[21] Among the various units were heavy infantry battalions, the elite Foot Companions, cavalry squadrons, archers and light-armed troops, including those from the Agrianians (a Balkan people who remained loyal to Alexander). Engineers and a range of artillery accompanied them, while a small flotilla of ships was to meet the army at the Danube, Alexander's intended destination. It was a diverse and mobile fighting force, tailored to combat the unique challenges that the barbarians presented.

The springtime Xandika festival, which inaugurated another year of warfare, had probably already taken place. Alexander led the procession for the first time, the weapons of his father carried in attendance along with those of former Macedonian kings. The mountain passes had by now started to clear of ice and snow, the roads hardening under the lengthening days, the seas calmed by the changing of the seasons. He would not be accompanied by the kingdom's two most seasoned generals – Antipatros and Parmenion, who remained in Macedonia and Asia Minor respectively – but he was still surrounded by experienced individuals, including the seven-man royal bodyguard, inherited from his father, and numerous battle-hardened Companions. Alexander would have to temper his own impulses with their advice, although tradition holds that he trusted in his own judgement above all else.

As king, Alexander became the intermediary between his people and the gods, daily offerings and prayers helped keep their favour. While on campaign, every endeavour had to be crossed-checked with their designs, either through divination of animal innards or the observance and interpretation of omens. Chief amongst his religious attendants was Aristandros of Telmessos. Dressed in white, head veiled, and holding the sacred branches, he often guided Alexander through the complexities of communication with the immortals. Aristandros had known him since he was born, and had a keen understanding of the king's ambitions, often proffering readings that were in tune with his wishes. The will of the gods framed Alexander's actions but rarely dictated them.

In his royal duties, he could now rely on a capable secretary called Eumenes, whom Philip had head-hunted during a stay at Kardia, and a selection of eager royal pages and clerks who organised the world around him. Those friends exiled after the Pixodaros affair were recalled, although they, along with his other boyhood Companions – the ever-faithful Hephaistion, the flashy Leonnatos – would have to await their chance to move up the military ranks. Perdikkas, however, gained an early promotion; at some point in 335 BC he assumed command of the heavy infantry battalion from Orestis and Lynkestis. Philotas, son of Parmenion, who was probably slightly older than Alexander, was to lead the Companion cavalry, a prestigious post that perhaps was awarded in return for his father's loyalty. The hierarchy remained essentially the same as it had been under Philip but there is reason to believe that Alexander, shortly after becoming king, took the decision to extend the name 'Companions' (*hetairoi*) to the rest of the Macedonian heavy infantry and cavalry. It was a savvy political decision; with more men sharing in the royal Companionship Alexander evidently hoped to increase loyalty among the ranks. The original Foot

Companions, the 3,000-strong elite unit created by Philip, was renamed the Shield Bearers (*hypaspistai*).[22]

Arrian is the only surviving ancient writer to provide a detailed account of the Balkan campaign. His *Anabasis of Alexander*, written in the second century AD, is generally regarded as the most reliable source for the king's reign, despite a recent resurgence of faith in the works of Plutarch and the authors of the so-called vulgate tradition.[23] In the preface, he helpfully sets out his methodology. It was based on the accounts of two contemporaries of Alexander, who both wrote after his death: Aristoboulos, a court intellectual, and Ptolemy, his boyhood friend and Companion. Neither of their works has survived, making the *Anabasis* an invaluable source for the study of Alexander historiography.[24] But Arrian was a talent in his own right. His work was not a slavish reproduction of the original source material, but was written in his own style, employing a variety of literary models and incorporating personal opinions. He considered himself well-equipped for the task, having experience of military command and statecraft in addition to some philosophical interests. Alexander's deeds, he thought, had never been celebrated as they deserved, and so he sought to address this failure.[25]

It is a great relief to finally join up with the *Anabasis*. Up to this point, the reconstruction of Alexander's early life has relied heavily on Plutarch's patchwork of stories, and other anecdotes. With Arrian things are different; it feels like exchanging a barely identifiable footpath, overgrown and often non-existent, for a smooth stretch of asphalt. His narrative begins with Alexander's accession, and his election as *hegemon* of the League of Corinth, before moving swiftly on to the events of 335 BC. The Balkan campaign is believed to derive chiefly from Ptolemy's account; recalled from exile, he most likely took part as one of the Companion cavalrymen. Reading the *Anabasis* today is the closest we can get to experiencing something of what it was to ride with Alexander on that first campaign. Time, however, has worn away the clarity of Arrian/Ptolemy's words. Many of the topographic locators – the names of mountains, rivers and islands that signpost the army's route – have either long since disappeared, are confused or remain too general to be of use. Supplemental evidence, where possible, must be roped in to provide further insight. At present, there is still no 'definitive' route to follow, only possibilities. But despite the problems inherent in tracing Alexander's footsteps, the campaign remains of the utmost importance. It was a seminal moment in his reign, and provides valuable information about his character and the emergence of his military brilliance.

Alexander began by crossing the Philippoi or Drama plain, to the east of Amphipolis, a place that would later witness a series of world-altering events. In 42 BC, this flat marshy expanse saw the Roman armies of Octavian and Mark Antony collide with those of Brutus and Cassius. It was here that the hopes and dreams of a resurgent Republic sank into the quagmire of history, trampled underfoot by those ultimately in pursuit of individual rule. A hundred years later, the apostle Paul made a visit, spending time in Philippoi where he converted the first European, a woman named Lydia, to Christianity, seeding a faith that would soon consume Western civilisation. Alexander must also have felt the press of history as he led his army eastwards, the memory of his father stamped onto the horizon.

Philippoi had been the first of his self-named foundations, acquired in 356 BC, shortly after Alexander's birth; the lucrative gold mines concealed among its mountainous backdrop provided the funds for Macedon's further expansion. Philip had reorganised the region's power structure and environment, forming alliances with the neighbouring Thracians, draining the Philippoi plain, and

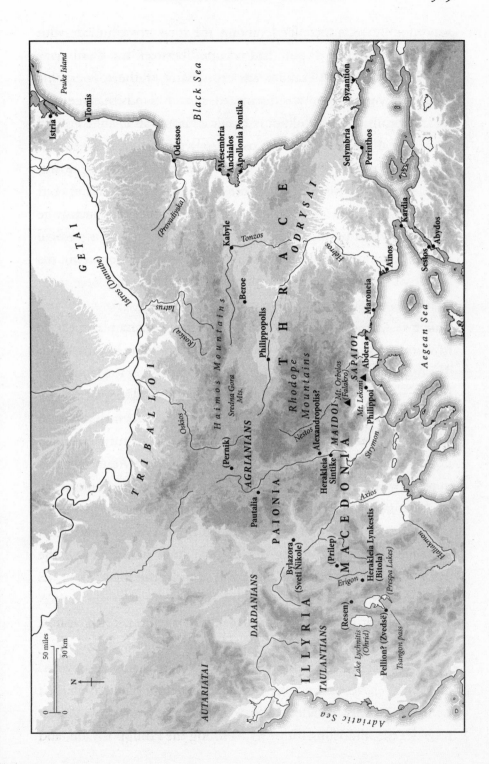

apportioning reclaimed land among the local communities. But recently a boundary dispute had occurred between the Philippians and Thracians, and Alexander was expected to arbitrate. In 1936, a fragmentary inscription was discovered, broken into nine pieces and reused within one of Philippoi's basilicas. It is possibly the earliest known of Alexander's decrees, commonly dated to 335–4 BC, and can be seen on display in the on-site museum. The writing, where legible, relates to his ruling concerning the dispute.[26] He followed his father's example, stipulating that the newly created lands were to be cultivated by the Philippians and subjected to the necessary royal levies. The implementation of his orders, along with the setting of boundaries between them and the Thracians, were to be overseen at a later date by two of his Companions, Leonnatos and Philotas.[27] An addendum to the royal orders concerns a stockpile of wood at Mount Dysoron that had also come to his attention. The mountain is probably to be identified with Mount Menoikion, to the north of Amphipolis, and suggests that Alexander spent some time before the expedition acquainting himself with the area's resources. He designated that it was to be left alone until he could decide on its future use. He may well have had the Asian invasion in mind when weighing up possible options, for such a commodity could be used to strengthen the fleet or provide extra siege equipment. Alexander was unsure; he needed to wait to see how events unfolded. In the meantime, by keeping hold of the timber, he made sure it didn't fall into the hands of unforeseen enemies. The inscription provides a fascinating insight into some of the peripheral issues that occupied Alexander's mind during his first year as king.

The Thracians' dissatisfaction with their land-grabbing neighbours may have boiled over into revolt on the news of Philip's death. Alexander decided to march into their territory. Arrian provides the directions: 'Starting from Amphipolis, he invaded the part of Thrace that belongs to the autonomous Thracians, with the city of Philip and Mount Orbelos on his left.'[28] This passage seems to indicate Mount Lekani as the intended destination, situated between Philippoi and the Nestos river, to the south of ancient Orbelos (probably Mount Falakro), a region occupied by the Thracian Sapaioi who may have remained autonomous during Philip's reign. Following Alexander's trail, the local roads draw the traveller up into the heart of the mountain, with its thick bushes, isolated villages and stony ground. Roving herds of goats, sometimes hundreds strong, sweep across the landscape, leaving cars stranded among a moving current of bleats and rattling bells. In such circumstances, there is little choice but to wait and count goats. Archaeological surveys of the area have revealed evidence of the region's intense mining activity, along with numerous fortified settlements that await further investigation.[29] Arrian uses the word 'invade' to describe Alexander's move into Sapaioi territory, but no military action is mentioned. His presence, along with that of the army, probably brought them swiftly back into line.[30]

The towering Rhodopes that divide the Aegean coast from the Thracian interior had now to be crossed or circumnavigated. Unfortunately, Arrian provides scant detail: 'then he crossed the river Nestos and is said in ten days to have reached Mount Haimos,' is all he says.[31] It is possible that Alexander decided to split his forces, each taking a different road north in order to maximise the Macedonian presence among the more remote and troublesome tribes, some traversing the mountains, others continuing along the coastal road towards the river Hebros (Evros). This route provided easy access to the Thracian interior, avoiding the Rhodopes, and must have been well known to the Macedonians from Philip's lengthy campaigns.[32]

The next barrier in their path was the Haimos mountains (today's Stara Planina or Balkan range). They rise in the distance across the Thracian plain, dark and ominous, the western reaches given additional protection by the adjoining Sredna Gora range, its tight valleys and inaccessible crags home to many a Thracian refuge. The Haimos took their name from the blood (*haima*) of the snake-monster Typhon, who was wounded here during his battle with Zeus over the supremacy of the heavens.[33] The thick forests and narrow rocky paths have witnessed many a battle across the millennia. In AD 811, the Byzantine emperor Nikephoros I and his army entered never to re-emerge; they were wiped out by the Bulgars, the assailants swamping the Byzantines like water over a drowning man. The victor Khan Krum was said to have later used the skull of Nikephoros as a drinking cup. The blood mountains have earned their name.

There are widely divergent views as to where Alexander intended to cross, and again details are lacking. Almost every pass has been championed by archaeologists and historians; a medley of Bulgarian villages and towns proudly proclaim that Aleksandâr Makedonski (Alexander the Macedonian, as he is called in these parts) came this way. There is one recent discovery, however, that sheds some light on the matter. In 2018, the Vatevi family collection from Plovdiv, one of the largest private collections of ancient military artefacts in Bulgaria, was published. Among its inventory were twelve sling bullets inscribed with Alexander's name on one side and Philip's on the other.[34] The names both appear in their genitive form and translate as '(belonging to the troops) of Alexander, son of Philip'. They appear to have been found together in the same area, and are likely related to the 335 BC campaign. The exact find-spot was not recorded, but, on current information, they were discovered beyond the Haimos mountains, in Bulgaria's north-eastern territories, suggesting that Alexander was active in this region; he had perhaps opted for one of the eastern passes, which were shorter and more accessible.[35]

It was here that Alexander confronted the first real challenge of the campaign. Another tribe of autonomous Thracians, along with some merchants from nearby Greek emporia, had taken up arms against him. They constructed a makeshift stockade across a stretch of high land, hoping to stop the Macedonian advance, and gathered their women, children and possessions inside. The approaching passage was steep enough for them to deploy their main offensive weapon – rock-loaded wagons. Alexander consulted with his Companions about what could be done to combat the threat. It was believed there was no easy way around the defenders; the gauntlet had to be run. This was perhaps not the whole truth. The Haimos boasts many passes and anyone familiar with the area would have been able to provide an alternative route. Either Alexander was given false information or, more likely, he was not willing to concede to the rebels. For Arrian, it is the first opportunity to establish Alexander's military excellence, and he makes the most of the event, providing a detailed account.

Alexander, he writes, employed a cunning stratagem to counter the dreaded wagons. He gave the following instructions for the advance: those on level ground, with adequate space, were to break formation on their approach, parting left or right in order to leave an avenue down which the wagons could pass. Any caught in the narrows, unable to move, were to crouch close together and link shields; the wagons, it was hoped, would then bound harmlessly over them. Trust between a general and his troops was fundamental to any success of an army. Without it, doubt would set in and unity would be liable to fracture and break. Alexander was taking a risk, but he had confidence in the well-drilled abilities of his men.

The front ranks of infantrymen likely swapped their small shields and long *sarissas* for the traditional armaments of hoplite warriors – shorter spears and larger shields – to provide extra safety and mobility. Alexander followed on the left wing with his royal guard,

the rest of the Shield Bearers and lightly armed Agrianian skirmishers, while archers took up position on the right. The vanguard
began their advance, edging forward, eyes scanning the way ahead.
The Thracians waited until they were in range before unleashing
their wagons, which crashed down the rocky hillsides with the
inevitability of Sisyphos' boulder. The men, remembering the words
of their commander, acted in unison, their discipline and coordination keeping them safe. The plan proceeded without a hitch; none
were lost in its execution. With the deadly wagons successfully
neutralised the Macedonians took heart. They let loose their war
cry and charged uphill towards the stockade. As they did so,
Alexander ordered the archers ahead to gain a better line of sight
on the attackers. The Thracians ran downhill to meet the enemy,
but the archers and advancing phalanx had no problem pushing
them back, and they fled before Alexander could launch his main
offensive from the left. Fifteen hundred of the enemy were killed,
while the others melted into the woodland. In the confusion, the
women and children were abandoned, becoming Alexander's first
spoils of war. He sent them to the coastal cities under the charge
of two of his Companions to be sold as slaves. The army, with
growing confidence in their king, then continued across the Haimos
and into Triballoi country.[36]

The Triballoi had quite the reputation in antiquity. They were
a byword for savagery – the archetypal barbarian – said to sacrifice
their own fathers and to possess evil eyes of such venom that some
could kill a man with a single stare.[37] Their heartlands were located
away to the west, between the Lom and Iskar rivers. Towards the
end of the fifth century BC, however, they had begun to expand
their political and military influence eastwards, at one point coming
to blows with Ateas' band of Scythians.[38] In 376/5 BC, hunger
drove them on a plundering raid as far south as Abdera, with an
army 30,000 strong.[39] The orator Isocrates attributed their rise in

power to a strong sense of unity: 'according to what all men say, [the Triballoi] are of one mind as are no other people on earth, but are bent on destroying not only those who border upon their territory and those who live in their neighbourhood but also all others whom they are able to reach.'[40] This was most likely a product of a succession of ambitious leaders. Arrian names Alexander's adversary as King Syrmos, probably the same man who had defeated Philip in 339 BC.[41] He had received advance warning of the Macedonian march and decided to evacuate his people to an island in the Danube, where some other Thracians had already sought refuge.[42] He then sent a large part of the army back to challenge the Macedonians. The two forces, one headed north and the other south, missed each other in their opposing movements, but as soon as Alexander heard about the Triballoi's location he turned around to force a confrontation. He came upon them late in the day, while they were busy making camp. They had occupied a strong defensive position – a wooded glen with hills protecting their flanks and the river Lyginos behind. The battle site has not been located, but it is conceivable that the batch of sling stones from the Vatevi collection come from this very encounter. Alexander immediately pressed for battle. He gathered his commanders around and set the strategy. With the memories of their previous defeat still raw in their minds, they would have needed little extra motivation to take on the old enemy.

The Triballoi formed up their line, plugging the glen's mouth like a stopper in the neck of an amphora. Alexander also made his preparations, opting for a deep formation in his phalanx with his cavalry in an advanced position. His intention may have been to disguise his numerical superiority in order to draw the enemy out of their defensive enclave, after which he could bring his cavalry into play. First, he aimed to raise the Triballoi's fabled bloodlust, to test the unity that Isocrates had praised so highly. Archers and slingers sallied out from the Macedonian line and began peppering the enemy with missiles. The plan worked. Unable to resist retaliation, the Triballoi broke cover and went on the attack. Alexander now sprang his trap. He ordered Philotas to take the Upper Macedonian cavalry and charge their right wing, where the enemy line had been over-extended. Herakleides and Sopolis did the same on the opposite wing with their cavalry divisions from Bottiaia and Amphipolis. The infantry phalanx and remaining cavalry took on the centre, with Alexander perhaps leading the way on foot. The fighting was fierce. The Triballoi managed to hold their own when the battle was at long range, while they were also talented with projectiles, but when the bulk of the infantry phalanx engaged, the cavalrymen picking off the outliers, they were quickly overwhelmed, and retreated through the densely wooded glen to the river. Three thousand perished in the flight, nightfall and the thick vegetation preventing further casualties. There had also been losses on the Macedonian side. Eleven cavalrymen and forty foot soldiers were killed. Alexander, always attentive in his obligations to the war dead, would have ordered them to be cremated and buried beneath an earthen mound before turning his mind to tracking down the remaining Triballian forces, who had returned to the Danubian island where Syrmos was waiting. Alexander had foreseen this occurrence – he may have become aware of the tactic during his time with Philip in the north. He now sought to link up with his flotilla of ships and launch an amphibious assault.

Arrian names the island as Peuke (Pine island).[43] It is here that the greatest division of opinion occurs among those who have studied Alexander's route. In antiquity, Peuke was firmly located in the Danubian Delta, a long way from Triballoi-controlled land and in the midst of Getai country.[44] Some modern scholars maintain the truthfulness of Arrian, while others suggest that he was either mistaken or that there was another island called Peuke further up-river.[45] Some further clues in the *Anabasis* suggest that the latter is more likely. Arrian states that the Lyginos river, where Alexander had defeated the Triballoi, was three days' travel from the Danube. The most credible candidates for the river concerned – the Rosica and Provadiyska – are more than three days' travel from the Danubian Delta. The account has undoubtedly been compressed in its retelling, and may be the cause of the confusion. One solution would be to separate out the events, the ships gathering at the mouth of the Danube, close to Peuke, before being escorted by a contingent of Macedonians up-river to where they were needed, weeks perhaps passing in between.[46] Unfortunately, the multitude of Danubian islands along the river's course and their ever-changing form make it almost impossible to ascertain the original location of the Triballian stronghold.

Once the ships had been assembled, Alexander loaded them with archers and infantry and set off for the island. The barbarians, however, descended to the water's edge and prevented them from landing. The steepness of the shore, combined with a swift-moving current, proved too much for the Macedonians. Alexander realised that he needed more ships to overcome the difficulties. Meanwhile, his army's presence on the banks of the river had drawn out other enemies.

The Getai occupied much of north-eastern Thrace. Following the expulsion of the Scythians, they now controlled both sides of the Danube. It's not known if these were the same Getai that had previously formed an alliance with Philip; they likely had more than one ruling dynast. If the cremated remains found in the antechamber of Tomb II belong to Meda, daughter of the Getic king Kothelas, then the alliance may quite literally have gone up in smoke. They had managed to gather a large force – 4,000 riders and 10,000 foot soldiers now arrayed themselves along the Danube's northern banks. To Alexander their presence invited attack, but there were also other factors that spurred him on. For the first time in Arrian's narrative he introduces the word *pothos* or longing as an added incentive for Alexander. It was a chance to encounter *terra incognita*, where his father had never set foot.[47] He decided to make the crossing at night. His small fleet were to carry the cavalry and weapons while the rest of the men were sent into the countryside to commandeer any watercraft they could get their hands on; some used mere fishing canoes carved from single tree trunks, others filled their leather tent covers with hay and floated across. Fifteen hundred cavalry and 4,000 infantry were safely landed on the opposite shore, amid a deep wheat field that further concealed their movements.

The army emerged from their cover at dawn. Alexander led the way with the infantry, who threshed the wheat with their *sarissas* to smooth the path for those following behind. On reaching open ground they changed formation. Alexander took the cavalry and occupied the right wing. Nikanor, another son of Parmenion, led

The Danube, Rousse region, Bulgaria

the infantry with the phalanx taking on a rectangular shape. They took the Getai completely by surprise, 'the solidity of the phalanx was terrifying, the onslaught of the cavalry violent,' writes Arrian.[48] The enemy withdrew to one of their settlements, around five kilometres inland, Alexander following. Their fortifications were not strong enough to repel the Macedonians and the Getai were put to flight, disappearing in the vast grasslands to the north, known as the Getic desert.[49] Alexander did not pursue. There was no need, and history did not favour those who penetrated into such territory.[50] He took the city, handing it over to his men to despoil, and then burnt it to the ground. On the banks of the Danube, Alexander sacrificed to Zeus the Preserver, Herakles, and the river itself for allowing them safe passage. On the same day, he returned with his men to base camp.

The Triballoi had been forced to watch on helplessly as the Macedonians decimated the Getic army. King Syrmos, along with the other Thracians on the island, made the sensible decision to surrender, and sent embassies to sue for peace. No details of the agreement have survived, but Alexander probably allowed Syrmos to keep his position in return for tribute and troop levies. Triballians were among the barbarian soldiers that later accompanied the main army to Asia.[51] Alexander appears to have spent much of the summer along the Danube making these arrangements. Among those who came to garner his friendship were some Celts who had recently settled on the Adriatic coast, men of great size and arrogance. Alexander drank with them and took the opportunity to ask what mortal thing they feared most in the world. He hoped that 'Alexander' would be their answer – an indication of his already sizeable ego – but, owing to the difficulty of their terrain and seeing that his aims for further conquest lay elsewhere, the Celts did not see him as a threat. They replied that the sky falling down on them was their principal concern, and that fear of the

Macedonians had not motivated their visit. Alexander later said to his friends, 'What braggarts Celts are!'[52]

His time in the Balkans would have witnessed many other feasts of friendship. The locals perhaps treated the Macedonians to the native dances that often accompanied such occasions, recreating acts of war, the dodging of missiles, the slaying of an enemy and deafening war cries.[53] Alliances were often cemented by toasts, the king and subject leaders downing horns of wine and then scattering the dregs over newly made comrades-in-arms. They also provided the opportunity for Alexander to personally acquaint himself with the power dynamics of the tribesmen. He would later select the most ambitious individuals to accompany him to Asia, leaving behind those that were less likely to cause trouble in his absence.[54] Alexander the Lynkestian was appointed General of Thrace, probably at some point during the campaign, and was left to administer the region and levy troops. Despite being the first to proclaim his support for his namesake following Philip's death, some suspicion may have remained – the appointment could be seen as a promotion, but equally as a shrewd political act, removing him from Macedonia and lessening his influence at court.[55]

Alexander then pushed westwards, towards the Oskios (Iskar) river, further into Triballian territory, lands which had probably been left untouched by Philip and were among Alexander's first real conquests as king.[56] Afterwards he headed south, to the headwaters of the Strymon river. The Agrianians, who occupied this region, were already well known to him. He had struck up a close relationship with their king, Langaros, who had visited Pella some time previously, perhaps during Alexander's regency in 340 BC. They had been part of the Thracian campaign from the start and had already proved their usefulness in battle, being crack light infantrymen of the highest repute and forming a special corps

1,000 strong.[57] Their capital is thought to have been at modern Pernik, south-west of Sofia, where a large medieval fortress overlies some Hellenistic remains. The site is positioned favourably between the Strymon valley and the Thracian plain, controlling access to both. During his time in this area, Alexander received a message from his western frontiers that the Illyrians were preparing for an imminent invasion. At the same time, he learned that the Autariatai, another Illyrian people to the north of Paionia, were threatening to ambush him during his march west. Alexander had not heard of these people before, but Langaros assured him that they were the least warlike of tribesmen. He offered to personally invade and lay waste their territory with a detachment of the Agrianian forces in order to keep them occupied. For the successful completion of this act, Alexander rewarded the king with great gifts including the promise of marriage to his half-sister Kynnane, newly widowed after the elimination of his cousin Amyntas. But after completing his mission, Langaros sickened and died and was unable to claim his prize.[58] The Agrianians, however, kept their loyalty, and remained among Alexander's most trusted troops.

ILLYRIAN STEEL

The Illyrians had been a constant menace throughout Philip's reign. Alexander may have had some experience in fighting them, and known some of the kings personally – it was to Illyria that he had gone during his self-imposed exile in 337/6 BC. Facing them in battle was another rite of passage that every Macedonian king had to endure. He marched westwards through Paionia to the river Erigon – the Crna Reka (Black River) – which loops across the large Pelagonian plain in Upper Macedonia.[59] The river is Arrian's only topographical signpost for the march, but he provides the end destination – the stronghold of Pellion.

Its location has not been positively identified, although there are various possibilities. Somewhere between Bitola and Lake Ohrid is one option, perhaps around Resen in North Macedonia where there was a direct route of invasion between Illyria and Upper Macedonia, via the Pelagonian straits, or even among the mountainous margins of the Pelagonian plain. But perhaps further to the south, in what is now Albania, is to be preferred.[60] In 2002, the British historian T.J. Winnifrith put forward the idea that Pellion was to be identified with the mountainous heights above the village of Zvezdë, where there are the remains of a fortified hilltop settlement.[61] It is yet to be excavated, but the acropolis can still be traced atop a protruding triangular pinnacle of rock, with terraces descending down the western side, the ground covered with ceramics and roof tiles. It occupies a key strategic location, controlling the road across the Korçë plain towards the crucial Tsangon pass, as well as another north–south route running between Lake Ohrid and Prespa, which was guarded by an earlier prehistoric wall. The topography fits the description of the battleground well and provides an evocative setting to consider what followed.

Alexander moved into these borderlands in August, the fields already shorn of their harvest but with fruit still ripening on the trees. According to Arrian, he made camp next to the river Eordaikos (most likely the modern Devoll that runs through south-eastern Albania), close to Pellion.[62] Kleitos, a son of the former Illyrian king Bardylis, was leading the enemy forces. They occupied the city and its surrounding wooded heights. Here he remained, poised on Macedon's borders, awaiting reinforcements from Glaukias, king of the Taulantians (another Illyrian people to the north-west), before they invaded. Alexander could not allow the two forces to combine and issued orders to assault the city's wall the next day.

At first light, the Illyrians arrayed themselves around Pellion. As part of their preparations they had procured three boys, three girls and three black rams from the local community. These were sacrificed in front of the Macedonian army – a morbid offering to their war god. Alexander and the Macedonians were well accustomed to their tactics of intimidation and had a few of their own. They advanced uphill, letting loose their war cry and brandishing their arms. Battle was joined and their superior discipline, training and weapons quickly made the difference. The Illyrians retreated, taking refuge behind the strong walls of Pellion. The Macedonians pursued and found the victims of the enemy's macabre war ritual lying lifeless on the ground. The battle now turned into a siege. Alexander encamped by the walls and began to make preparations to surround the city with a ditch and palisade. The plan would probably have worked had it not been for the timely arrival of Glaukias and his army. The odds suddenly turned against the Macedonians.

Alexander was now facing a dangerous situation. His thoughts turned to supplies that were running low. Philotas and a select band of cavalry were sent out into the surrounding lands, along with all the pack animals, to search for food. The move did not go unnoticed. Glaukias' men set off in pursuit and managed to occupy the high ground surrounding the Macedonians. Alexander became concerned that if nightfall isolated them they could fall prey to the raiding party. He promptly set off from camp with the Shield Bearers, the archers, the Agrianians and four hundred horsemen, the rest of the army remaining stationed at Pellion to ensure that the two Illyrian armies could not unite. His foresight proved invaluable and the rescue mission was successful, but his situation had not improved. The enemy still occupied the heights around the city, hundreds if not thousands of javelin-men, slingers, infantrymen and cavalry ready to rush down and attack the Macedonians. Alexander, in one of the only such occurrences in his life, decided to withdraw, but some of Glaukias' men had taken up position behind him, on the hills that overlooked the Eordaikos river and the narrow pass that led towards Macedonia and safety. Alexander had made a mistake in not holding the pass with a unit of men; it was a rare oversight. Taking all the factors into consideration, he decided to deploy a risky stratagem: psychological warfare.

Alexander was a lover of theatre and decided to put on a performance for those watching from the grandstand of the surrounding mountains. The men knew the script well, having practised it innumerable times in the build-up to the campaign. They assembled into battle formation, the phalanx consisting of files 120 men deep. On either wing, two hundred cavalrymen took up their positions. With the audience hooked, Alexander began to issue the commands. The infantry, in complete silence, raised their *sarissas* upright; another order had them lowered, as if ready to charge. Next they swung their weapons to the right, then to the left, waving like a field of wheat in a gentle summer breeze. The Illyrians watched in disbelief as the men moved forward, keeping their formation perfectly, wheeling one way then the other. The discipline, the practice and coordination were exceptional, the men were acting as if they were one body, one mind. The final part of the show was the most impressive. Suddenly, the infantry on the left sharpened into a wedge, the tips of their *sarissas* levelled at those Illyrians on the foothills closest to them. Alexander, leading the way, ordered the attack. The bewildered enemy abandoned their posts. The Macedonians now broke their silence. Banging spears against shields, they raised their shrieking war cry, *Alalai!* The rest of the Illyrians reacted in the predicted fashion, hastily retreating towards to the city's walls. Alexander's bluff had worked. He then turned his attention to the pass behind him. Some of the Taulantians still occupied a hill on the line of march. He rallied his bodyguards and Companion cavalrymen and charged them. They scattered on the Macedonians' approach, withdrawing to the mountains on either side. Alexander manned this advanced covering position with his Companions, also sending for the Agrianians and archers, and set about orchestrating the retreat.

The pass was narrow and forested, bounded on one side by a river and on the other by a lofty mountain with cliffs descending to the water's edge. There was not even space for men to march four abreast. The Tsangon pass, through which the Devoll flows, may be the one Arrian describes, although sedimentation, flood control and deforestation have greatly altered its appearance. The Shield Bearers crossed the river first, tramping across the shallows, and the battalions of heavy infantry followed. As soon as they had reached the other side they were under orders to form up and

The Tsangon pass

stretch their line to the left, so that the phalanx would appear solid the moment it had cleared the water. The Illyrians, with the rear of the Macedonian army left exposed, decided that now was the time to attack. Alexander waited until they were close enough to make a counter-charge from his hilltop, whereupon the phalanx below, raising their war cry once more, began advancing through the water. Under this combined assault the Illyrians were forced to withdraw. Alexander now gave orders for the Agrianians and archers to take up another defensive position at the river to help cover the retreat of the remaining forces. Alexander crossed the river safely, but noticed that some of the stragglers were once again falling prey to the Illyrians who were harrying the last of the men like wolves around a flock. He ordered the archers to shoot from mid-river to provide cover, with additional firepower provided by the artillery. The barrage worked and the Illyrians scattered once more. The army exited the pass having not lost a man. It was a masterclass of defensive manoeuvring.

No sooner had Alexander safely extracted the army than he began to plot his return. It was to be a surprise attack, a tactic that was especially effective against an ill-organised and undisciplined force. Three days passed before his spies reported that the Illyrians' defences had duly slackened. They were camped outside the city without palisade or ditch to protect them, no sentry posts were in operation and their line was spread out over the foothills and plain. Alexander, accompanied by the trusty Agrianians, Shield Bearers, archers and two battalions of heavy infantry, crept across the river by night, leaving orders for the rest of the army to follow when they had secured the crossing. On reaching the enemy camp, however, he decided not to wait for them, but to continue the assault with the forces that he had with him. His light troops stole in among the smouldering fires, tents and sleeping men sprawled out on the ground. Many were slaughtered where they lay, others were captured alive to be held as hostages. Some managed to rally; bleary eyed, they were suddenly confronted with the pressing phalanx, arranged in deep formation with the elite Shield Bearers packed into the wings. It was a rout. Kleitos abandoned Pellion, burning the city to the ground as he did so. The Macedonians pursued Glaukias and his forces to the surrounding mountains where they escaped and made their way back to their own territory. Alexander did not hunt them down; the objective had been achieved and no further risks were necessary. The Illyrians were silent for the rest of his reign.

This was not a great cavalry victory, like Alexander's later battles in Persia, nor was it the result of a successful siege, slowly crushing the enemy under the grindstone of Macedonian force. It was a clandestine attack, a night-time raid, carefully executed with skilled and experienced soldiers all silently obeying the commands of their leader. It is an early example of Alexander's deft understanding of strategy and adaptability, his desire to emerge victorious whatever the circumstances. For the army, it was the first taste of things to come. Under his leadership they never lost a battle.

In the conclusion to the *Anabasis*, Arrian takes a moment to consider the key ingredients that made Alexander a general without rival:

He had the most wonderful power to discern the right course, when it was still unclear, and was most successful in inferring from observed facts what was likely to follow. His skill in marshalling, arming and equipping a force, in raising the morale of his troops, filling them with confidence and banishing their fear in dangers by his own fearlessness was altogether most admirable. In fact, when what was to be done was clear, he displayed the utmost daring, and whenever he had to snatch a success from the enemy by anticipation, before any one could even apprehend what was to happen, he had a most wonderful ability to strike first.[63]

The hallmark of Alexander's generalship, evident from the beginning of his reign, was to lead by example. He did not ask his men to do anything that he would not undertake himself. According to Plutarch, he believed that boldness could triumph over fortune, courage over superior force.[64] Rivalry and competition were rife in Macedonian society and Alexander, as king, endeavoured to prove himself the best; had it not been for his early death, suggests Arrian, he would have gone on conquering, in competition with himself in default of any rival.[65] This Homeric spirit pervaded the army, spreading throughout the ranks, and Alexander rewarded individuals and battalions for their bravery, forever fostering the ethos of excellence among the men.

Occasionally, however, his ambition and willingness to lead from the front tipped over into recklessness, earning rebukes from his friends. Arrian believed that 'his rage in battle and passion for glory made him like others overcome by any other form of pleasure, and that he was not head-strong enough to keep himself out of dangers.'[66] In Illyria, he received the first of his recorded wounds, his head being struck by a stone, his neck by a cudgel.[67] As with Philip, his body became a biography of war, every scar a memory, every bump and callus a defeated foe. But his bravery in battle, as well as his willingness to share the hardships of the march, were of vital importance in keeping morale high, and the men loved him for it.

Accounts of his reign are littered with anecdotes that were held up to later generations as exemplars of strong leadership. In the aftermath of battle, he visited the wounded, examining their injuries and sharing war stories. According to Curtius, he took his exercises with the soldiers, and was in dress and bearing little different from any other; with such actions, despite his youth, he made himself beloved and worthy of respect.[68] On long marches, he would often go by foot, Leonidas' tough conditioning having prepared him for such feats from childhood. In the mountains of the Hindu Kush, he went about the exhausted men, the tiredness and cold already starting to close their eyes, lifting up those that were lying down and encouraging others with words of support. One moment he was with the centre of the column, then at the rear – anywhere his presence could motivate those who were struggling.[69] In the desert, with the army almost dying from thirst, a group of men managed to find some water in the hollow of a rock and brought it to Alexander in a helmet. He thanked the men for their great gift, he was as thirsty as the rest of them, but as he looked around the army, their faces sun-cracked and abraded by sand-heavy wind, he saw the longing in their eyes and knew he could not drink until the army had done the same. In front of everyone he poured away the precious water. Arrian reports that this act heartened the men so much that it was as if everyone had drunk what Alexander had discarded.[70] It was these feats of endurance, coupled with the army's astonishing pace and the occasional helping hand of fortune, that time and time again caught the enemy off guard.

Alexander's indefatigable energy drove his men on; he was something of a human dynamo, a freak, bottled lightning. But the scale of his conquests, the endless string of sieges and battles against those who resisted, confront the modern observer with the uncomfortable facts of reality. Tens of thousands died in his quest for empire. Arrian's account, especially of the later stages of his reign when Alexander pursued a policy of terror to secure his gains, makes for grim reading – villages were wiped out, entire populations butchered or enslaved. Even in the context of the times it was a chilling period of unremitting warfare. It is no wonder that he continues to divide opinion; killing, as the eminent historian Brian Bosworth once wrote, is arguably what Alexander did best.[71] Everyone who comes to his story must try to balance the narratives of glory with the human cost of conquest.

The Balkan campaign had provided the ideal opportunity for Alexander to prove his military credentials, and it helped further legitimise his kingship. There are failures and mistakes – the inability to take the Danubian island and neglecting to man the pass during the fight against the Illyrians – but, regardless, Alexander emerges as a commander of exceptional talent; when reading Arrian's account it is often hard to believe that he was only just into his twenties. The intensive military training that he received as a youth, along with the campaign experience accrued under Philip, had proved formative and his new position in overall command was one in which he thrived. But Alexander did not act alone; his achievements were also those of his men. He had inherited from his father a highly experienced and diverse army capable of bringing his plans to fruition, with subordinate officers of similar skill, expertise and ambition. It was the particular combination of Alexander's leadership and the abilities of his men that accounted for their remarkable string of successes. Yet the sternest test for the new king and his army was still to come. During Alexander's absence in the north, revolution had begun to stir in Greece once more.

II.

ACHILLES RESURRECTED

Alexander was dead, killed by the Triballoi. Or, at least, that is what the Athenian orators Demosthenes and Lycurgus claimed. According to one contemporary, they were so confident in their assertions that they all but displayed his body before the Assembly.[1] Among those they sought to convince was a group of Theban exiles also in attendance. With this news, they urged their Boiotian friends to conceive fresh hopes of freedom, to return to their homes and throw out the oppressive Macedonian garrison.

The orators were pulling on a particularly potent thread of persuasion. In 379 BC, Thebes had been in a similar situation, with the Spartans controlling the city. Every Theban knew the story: twelve brave countrymen had set out from Athens and wrestled back control in a stunning covert coup, killing the pro-Spartan leaders and forcing the resident garrison to surrender. The event had ushered in a golden age of Theban hegemony under such fine leaders as Pelopidas and Epameinondas. This appeal to the civic pride of the exiles worked – with ideas of fame and honour firing in their hearts, a new generation of would-be heroes set out in the footsteps of their illustrious fore-bears, hoping to replicate their achievements. But history can both inspire and mislead. The Macedonians were a wholly different prospect from the Spartans of old.[2]

The revolutionaries entered Thebes at night, aided by insiders who shared in their designs. Timolaos, a pro-Macedonian leader, was seized and killed, along with Amyntas, one of the garrison's soldiers.[3] An Assembly of leading citizens was quickly convened whereby the leaders of the coup put their case to the masses. They spoke glorious words of freedom and liberty: now was the time for rebellion, they said, but it was the rumours of Alexander's death that proved the decisive factor. Arrian says that they conjectured what they most desired; the Thebans readied themselves for another war with Macedon.[4]

The Kadmeian garrison was promptly put under siege, and surrounded with ditches and stockades. The Thebans tried to bribe the mercenaries among them, but they could not agree on a price. Aeschines later stated that it was for the sake of five talents that they remained loyal to their original paymasters.[5] Meanwhile, they sent out pleas for support to other city-states – to the Arkadians, Elians and Argives in the Peloponnese.[6] Demosthenes had promised Athenian aid and provided a cache of weapons to arm the liberators; he also urged the Assembly to vote for war. The news spread quickly across Greece, travelling north and into Illyria, to the ears of Alexander. He immediately realised the gravity of the situation and feared that, if he did not act quickly, the garrison would be lost and the revolt gain further momentum. Later, when he was asked how he had kept control of Greece, he replied, 'By never putting anything off.'[7]

The speed of Alexander's march defied belief, such was its blistering pace. His route south lay through Upper Macedonia, via Pelinna in Thessaly, passing Thermopylai and entering Boiotia. Within thirteen days, his army had covered some 440 kilometres to reach Onchestos, a mere fourteen kilometres from Thebes.[8] His

march had managed to outpace news of his movements, as was
surely his aim, and it was only when the army arrived at Onchestos
that word reached Thebes. The leaders of the revolt reacted predict-
ably: the distance, the speed, they just didn't think it possible.
They searched for alternative answers, suggesting that it was
Antipatros and a reserve Macedonian force from Pella; they were
annoyed with those who insisted that Alexander was leading the
army. He was dead, they maintained. It must be another Alexander,
perhaps the Lynkestian. They were wrong. It was Alexander, *the*
Alexander, very much alive and now within striking distance of
their city.[9]

Onchestos, positioned on the southern shores of Lake Kopais,
was famous for its bright-groved sanctuary of Poseidon and its
celebrated horse races. Philip had relocated the headquarters of
the Boiotian League here after his victory at Chaironeia, and the
site's infrastructure made it an ideal stopover for the army and a
convenient mustering point for local allies.[10] Diodorus claims that
Alexander now had more than 30,000 infantry, along with some
3,000 cavalry, under his command. The smaller force he had taken
through Thrace and Illyria had likely been supplemented with
fresh troops from Antipatros as well as the arrival of allies –
Phokians, perhaps the Thessalians as well, and Boiotians hostile
to Thebes – men from Plataia, Orchomenos and Thespiai. The
army was at full strength, roughly equal to that which had fought
at Chaironeia. Alexander was taking the threat seriously.[11]

The Thebans were now forced to confront the reality of the
situation. They held another Assembly, and it was decided to see
things through. Their allies, however, were not so sure. The
Athenians agreed to send troops but they held back, waiting to
see how things developed. The Arkadians advanced to the Isthmus
but ventured no further; Thebes was to fight on alone.[12] Around
this time a number of troubling omens were observed, as the

ancient authors loved to relate. The marshes at Onchestos started to make a frightening noise, like the bellowing of an enraged bull; a stream in Thebes was suddenly filled with blood; a spider's web in the temple of Demeter grew to the size of a *himation*, its iridescent rainbow of colours predicting a storm of mixed troubles; the city's statues started to perspire.[13] The gods feared for the Thebans.

The E03 national road follows Alexander's route south. It crosses the ridge of Onchestos and descends into the Teneric plain, entering a rich agricultural land. Thebes rises in the distance, a city where myths and legends gathered like maidens around a fountain. It was considered to be among Greece's most ancient settlements, founded by the travelling Phoenician hero Kadmos, who built his palace on the site's acropolis, which became known as the Kadmeia. Both Dionysos and Herakles were born here, as was the famous lyric poet Pindar, whose work Alexander admired. Athenian trage-dians plundered its heritage for good stories. Such well-known plays as the *Bacchae*, *Oedipus the King* and *Antigone* were set there, but, above all, Thebes was famed as a siege city. Before the Trojan War it had been the setting for the much-loved epic, the *Thebaid*, which retold the struggle between Oedipus' sons for the throne. Each of the seven gates had witnessed the clash of respective champions; the climax was a duel between the two leaders, Polyneikes and Eteokles. Both were slain, brother killing brother.[14] A generation later came the sequel, the *Epigoni*, which dealt with the sons of the attackers and their successful capture of the city. The cultural and mythical reputation of Thebes filled the imagin-ation of the traveller long before they saw its fabled walls. Such stories must have appealed to Alexander's sense of heroic emulation.

Thebes (modern Thiva) spreads across a series of low hills, perched Sphinx-like above the surrounding plains, streaked with the green of cultivated parsley and framed by the distant black outline of Mount Kithairon to the south. Today it is a small but busy provincial town; the Kadmeia, with its steep sides, resembles the bowl of an upturned lyre, blanketed with houses, shops and a tight gridwork of streets, many of which have been named after former Thebans of renown: Herakles' road, Pindar's street. Excavations have been opportunistic, carried out when modern development has allowed. Only a few islands of archaeology can be glimpsed among the high-rises, the rest has either been destroyed or still lies buried. Of horse-rich Thebes, Thebes of the seven gates, city of beautiful dances, not much remains.[15]

Alexander arrived towards the end of September, as the landscape was breathing its last heavy sighs of summer. It had been almost a year since he had last laid eyes on the city, when a show of force had successfully banished any ideas of revolt. He no doubt hoped that his return would produce the same outcome. The army encamped near the sanctuary of Iolaos, a companion of Herakles, which lies undiscovered somewhere to the north-east of the city. Here he awaited an embassy of reconciliation, but the Thebans,

Thiva (ancient Thebes)

far from considering surrender, launched a pre-emptive strike. A
small combined force of horse and foot sallied out from the city,
a volley of spears killing a few Macedonians before the attack was
quashed by Alexander's archers and light infantry.[16] If he had hoped
for a quick capitulation he was disappointed.

The defences of Thebes were considerable. The Kadmeia had
been walled since the Bronze Age. Amphion and Zethos, sons of
Zeus, were said to have built them, one using strength to assemble
the colossal stones, the other the sound of his lyre. In the fifth
century BC, the city had received an extra layer of protection – a
second ring of walls enclosing the area of Greater Thebes, three
metres thick with towers positioned along its length.[17] But there
was one weakness, and Alexander knew it. To the south, the walls
of the Kadmeia either converged with those of Greater Thebes or
ran very close to them. It was the closest he could get to the
garrison and the best place to attack, while it also enabled him to
control the road to Athens and cut off any prospect of outside
aid. On the second day, he moved his army around the city's
flanks, and took up the offensive position.

The Thebans had foreseen this stratagem and fortified the area
with two ranks of palisades, perhaps also with ditches, that stretched
between the two outermost projections of the southern walls. In
between, they stationed their main force of cavalry and infantrymen. Slaves, refugees and resident aliens (*metics*) were left to man
the walls. Meanwhile, they maintained pressure on the Macedonian
garrison on the Kadmeia. It was crucial that they should not be
able to link up with Alexander's troops, trapping the Thebans
between anvil and hammer.

Alexander assembled his siege engines and took three days to
prepare his assault. He let it be known, however, that there was
still one last chance for peace. A herald was sent towards the city
walls with an ultimatum, the usual precursor to battle. Plutarch

records that he asked for the surrender of the ringleaders of the rebellion – Phoenix and Prothytes – and offered amnesty to the rest, urging them to come over to his side and enjoy the peace common to all Greeks. Some inside the walls were tempted to accept the offer, but the returned exiles strengthened their resolve for continued resistance. With a flourish of bravado, they countered Alexander's demands, requesting the heads of the Macedonian garrison commanders instead.[18] As a final insult, they exposed the Common Peace for what they saw it as, a sham that was nothing more than an instrument of Macedonian control. As far as they were concerned, they were now on the side of the Persians and called upon the opposing Greeks to join them in liberating Greece from an oppressive tyrant. Diodorus says that this carefully aimed barb wounded Alexander deeply, and that he flew into a rage, stating that he would visit upon the Thebans the most extreme punishment.[19]

The two main sources for the battle – Arrian and Diodorus – differ in their accounts of what followed.[20] Diodorus relates that Alexander divided his forces into three units: the first was to attack the palisades, the second to confront the Theban battle line, the third being held back in reserve. It was to be a coordinated attack, initiated with the customary blast of the trumpet and war cries; a discharge of javelins would follow before hand-to-hand combat was joined. Arrian, drawing on Ptolemy, however, says that it was an unsanctioned act of bravery that began the assault, and his version appears to have the edge of realism. Perdikkas, who was in charge of the camp guard as well as a battalion of heavy infantry, charged the palisade with his men before Alexander had given the signal for battle, the breath of Ares driving them on. They managed to tear open a hole in the defences, breaking into the ranks of Thebans. Amyntas, son of Andromenes, quickly joined them with his own battalion.

Alexander, alerted to this development, brought the rest of the army up in support, sending in his archers and Agrianians to help. The rampant Perdikkas managed to fight his way through to the second palisade but was gravely wounded in the process and carried back to safety by his men. Once the two sides were fully engaged, the fighting was bloody and brutal.

Arrian is the only one to provide some key topographical clues to where the fighting took place. He says that the Macedonians managed to push the defenders into a sunken road that led past the sanctuary of Herakles. Part of the sanctuary was excavated in 2004–5, lying some forty metres south of the Kadmeian wall and the Elektrai gates, on Polyneikes street.[21] The land rises steeply at this point, up towards the Kadmeia. It was likely here, with their backs to the inner palisade, that the Thebans rallied; their city, their families, everything they knew and held dear was at stake. Urging each other on at the top of their voices, they went on the counter-attack. At first it was a success. Eurybotas, commander of Alexander's Cretan archers, was killed, along with seventy of his men; the Thebans' ferocity stunned the Macedonians and the rest fled back to the king who was waiting in reserve with his Shield Bearers. In their pursuit, the Thebans broke formation. Their blood was up, but now they encountered Alexander and the tightly packed phalanx of his best troops, and their resolve was broken on a rolling tide of spears. Badly outnumbered and tiring from the struggle, many began to fall on the road and among the grave-stones of the dead. The rest were pushed back to one of the side gates in the walls of Greater Thebes, perhaps somewhere close to the modern bus station. In the confusion, some of the Macedonians forced their way inside before the gates could be closed. It was probably around the same time that the Kadmeian garrison managed to free themselves from their confinement and joined the battle.[22]

The defenders were now doomed. Diodorus gives an alternative version of this key moment, suggesting that, during the fighting, Alexander had spotted an undefended postern gate and sent Perdikkas – the first time he is mentioned – with a band of men to capture it, which they did successfully, penetrating the city's walls.[23] Despite the discrepancies in the accounts, some broader points are clear: that it was the reserve forces that managed to wear down the Theban resistance, that one of the gates was eventually breached and that the Kadmeian garrison was able to break free, after which carnage ensued.

There was panic in the streets. Those who had been manning the walls fled to the agora, while the scattered advance guard attempted to rally at the Amphion Hill, situated beyond the northern tip of the Kadmeia. It was a symbolic spot; the raised earthen mound was said to have covered the tomb of Amphion, and perhaps of his brother Zethos as well, second founders of the city and builders of the Kadmeian walls. It is still there today, free of buildings, pine-clad and overlooked by the Archaeological Museum. In 379 BC, it was here that the revolutionaries had gathered their recently imprisoned comrades before issuing proclamations of liberty. It was now the location of the Thebans' last stand – history is not without its cruel synchronicities.[24] The Macedonians pressed hard, Alexander appearing here and there amid the blur of battle frenzy. Boukephalas was wounded in the melee, but fought on with his master rather being replaced, a feat that was long remembered.[25] Those who were not cut down made a dash for freedom. The Theban cavalry tore through the streets, trampling some of their own men in the process, the defenders streaming out of the city and onto the plain. Those unable or unwilling to escape were slaughtered, the scenes recalling those imagined by the local women in Aeschylus' *Seven Against Thebes*: 'foreign soldiers swarming in our streets, tearing, burning, destroying.'[26] Now it was a grim reality. The city that had inspired the most

celebrated playwrights of Classical Greece had become the setting
for one of history's greatest tragedies. Bodies began to pile up on
the streets, family homes were broken into, suppliants ripped from
their protective shrines. Alexander's Boiotian allies, along with the
Phokians, used the opportunity to exercise their hatred of their old
enemies. Arrian finishes his account of the battle with the sober
words, 'they spared neither woman nor child.'[27]

When the dust had finally settled, it was reported that over
6,000 Thebans had perished and more than 30,000 had been
captured. In the quest for loot, the Macedonian soldiers and their
allies set off in all directions to fill their personal coffers. It had
been a long campaign, a year's worth of marching, fighting and
killing; this was no lonely outpost in Thrace or Illyria, but one of
the richest cities in Greece, and it was time for the victors to gather
their spoils. One story became famous from this episode of the
city's demise, that of Timokleia.[28] She was of aristocratic birth and
was sister to Theagenes, the leader of the Thebans at Chaironeia
who had died during the fighting. A Thracian cavalry commander,
along with his men, occupied her property and enjoyed a feast
after the battle. He then summoned Timokleia to the bedchamber
and raped her. Afterwards she was forced to reveal whether there
was any silver or gold smuggled away. She admitted that, before
the fall of the city, she had ordered her maids to hide the family's
valuables at the bottom of a dry well in the garden. The Thracian
couldn't wait for dawn to investigate; he insisted on being shown
the site immediately. In the dark, semi-naked, he lowered himself
into the confined space. Timokleia then took revenge. With the
help of her servants, she rained rocks down on the thief, burying
him in a shower of stone. The crime was soon uncovered and the
Thracians took Timokleia to Alexander. She confessed to the
murder, but her noble appearance, family name and eloquent
words moved the king. He let her go without punishment, freed

her relatives from captivity, and declared that no other was to touch her household. It was a moment of magnanimity amid the mayhem.

More than five hundred Macedonians had been killed in the battle and Alexander's first duty was to bury them with honour. They were cremated, their remains interred under an earthen mound erected close to where the fighting had been the thickest. The ancient travel writer Pausanias saw it in the second century AD close to the Elektrai gates.[29] Despite the best efforts of archaeologists, however, it remains undiscovered.

The fate of the city and its people had now to be addressed. According to ancient custom all things conquered in war were the property of the conquerors, the city could be destroyed, the population sold into slavery.[30] But Alexander was aware that the eyes of Greece were upon him, and decided to put the matter to representatives of the Greek allies that were present. The Thebans had broken the Common Peace and this scaled-down meeting of the League of Corinth was to decide the punishment, the Macedonian king presiding in his role as *hegemon*. The Assembly was packed with those hostile to Thebes and vigorous arguments were promptly set forward for its destruction. Attention was drawn to Thebes' controversial past, including the Thebans' brutal treatment of other Boiotian communities and their 'Medising' during the Persian Wars. This last charge was not without irony; Macedonia too had then also fought for the Great King. Justin reports that one captive Theban, named Kleadas, was allowed to speak on his city's behalf.[31] He said that the Thebans had only revolted because they had heard that Alexander was dead, and that whatever wrong they had committed must be blamed on gullibility not disloyalty. Moreover, they had already paid a heavy price with the loss of their young warriors. His final entreaties were for the innocent soil of his homeland, which had been Philip's home during his teenage years, and had not only given birth to men but gods as well. This was a more pervasive line of argument. Herakles and Dionysos were immensely important to Alexander and were entwined with the city's history. The bedchamber of Semele, mother of Dionysos, could still be seen among the ruins of Kadmos' palace, vines growing around the ancient walls. Herakles' birthplace was preserved too, the house of his parents, Alkmene and Amphitryon, forming part of his sanctuary outside the Elektrai gates. How would history remember him if he destroyed one of the great centres of Greek culture?

Thebes was razed to the ground, its land apportioned among the allies and the population sold into slavery. The proceeds from the sales raised 440 talents of silver, a welcome injection of funds for the wars to come.[32] The Council had passed the resolution. There can be little doubt that Alexander was behind the decision, in which idealism was set against pragmatism, the latter eventually winning out. The strict measures taken by Philip after Chaironeia had proved inadequate to stop a return of Theban aggression. Rebellion had flared on the mere suggestion of Alexander's demise, underlining the fragility of the Common Peace. As with Olynthos, which his father had wiped from the map in 348 BC, the safest option was to destroy the city. This act of terrorism was to stand as a stark lesson for the rest of Greece.[33] All remaining Thebans were made outlaws, and it was made an offence to give any refuge, although some managed to find sanctuary in Athens and other places.[34] Finally, a garrison of Macedonians was to remain on the Kadmeia to control the surrounding lands. Alexander, however, did find some room to show clemency. Priests and priestesses were spared, as were Philip's former guest-friends and those who had voiced their opposition to war in the Theban Assembly. He forbade the burning of Pindar's house, placing a sign next to the building: 'Set not on fire the roof of Pindar, maker of song.'[35] The poet's descendants were also allowed to go free, and the city's holy places and sanctuaries similarly left alone.[36] But, regardless, that autumn in 335 BC Thebes ceased to exist. The orator Demades later said that it was as if one of Greece's eyes had been knocked out.[37]

Among the seized plunder, which was considerable, Alexander kept back a few pieces for himself. They included an aptly named painting, *On the Capture of a Town* by Aristides, later displayed in Pella's palace, and a magnificent chandelier that would travel with him to Asia Minor and was dedicated to Apollo at Kyme.[38] The ancient authors suggest that, later in life, he felt some remorse about the city's harsh punishment, but he never reversed his decisions, which remained in place right up to his death.[39] Instead, he continued his father's policy of favouring those Boiotian communities that had long suffered from Theban domination. The rebuilding of their settlements was accelerated and he tasked the mining engineer Krates with fixing the Bronze Age drainage system at Lake Kopais, which had long ago fallen into disuse; new cultivatable land was provided for the settlers, as his father had done at Philippoi. Alexander's actions changed both the social and physical environment of Boiotia.[40]

The sudden disappearance of Thebes, such a mighty and formidable city, had the appropriate repercussions. The other Greeks who had been looking to join the rebellion quickly reconsidered their positions, the Arkadians condemned to death those who had championed helping Thebes, the Elians recalled their exiled men who were favourable to Alexander, and the Aitolians sent embassies begging for forgiveness.[41] Athens, on hearing the news, had been plunged into turmoil. The celebrations of the Greater Eleusinian Mysteries were cancelled, the countryside evacuated, the citizens fearing that the Macedonian army would soon appear before their own walls.[42] As they had done the year before, they sent a belated embassy to Alexander, congratulating him on his campaigns in the north and for crushing the Theban rebellion. Alexander was well aware of their role in the affair, according to Plutarch. When presented with the letter from the Assembly he tossed it away in anger and stormed out on the envoys.[43] After further consideration, he sent a demand to Athens to surrender the anti-Macedonian ringleaders, the list including several of the city's leading men, Demosthenes among them.[44] Alexander had reportedly heard about some of the orator's derogatory comments regarding his person. During his march on Thebes he had resolved to prove his old enemy wrong. 'Demosthenes' he said, 'called me a boy while I was in Illyria and among the Triballi, and a youth when I was marching through Thessaly; I will show him I am a man by the time I reach the walls of Athens.'[45] When Alexander's demands were read out in a tense meeting of the Assembly, many began to look towards the elderly Phokion, who had always preached caution. He believed that such a sacrifice was necessary to preserve the city. Demosthenes, understandably, countered the proposal, and retold the fable of the sheep who surrendered their watchdogs to the wolves. Without them, he claimed, they would be at the mercy of Alexander, although this time he did not slander the king as a young Margites but called him the arch-wolf instead; that wolf was now at his door.[46] Demades, who had apparently been bribed by Demosthenes' supporters, took centre stage and persuaded the Assembly to try and save the men's lives. He read aloud a carefully worded decree that he wished to present to Alexander, imploring mercy for the accused and stating that their crimes would be dealt with internally, by the city's law courts. It was passed by the Assembly and a second embassy set out for Thebes, headed by Demades and Phokion, men more favourable to the king. The year was now getting on; Alexander's anger had abated and he was already thinking about the future.

The silver-tongued Demades found him much more agreeable, and persuaded him to acquiesce. There was to be peace between Athens and Macedon once again. The general Charidemos, who had informed Demosthenes of Philip's murder, was exempt from forgiveness and was sent into exile, promptly going over to Asia where he served as an advisor to the Great King Darius III.[47] The fate of Thebes was enough to ensure that the Athenians kept their word.

From now on Demosthenes was forced to accept the reality of Macedonian supremacy. He had hopes that the Persians would deal with Alexander, allowing a resurgence of Athenian power, but such an eventuality never came to pass. In 330 BC, he appeared in the law courts again, this time to defend the proposal to award him a crown shortly before Philip's murder. Aeschines had blocked the provisional decree, citing an unconstitutional action, and now decided the time was ripe to take down his old rival. Demosthenes, however, gave a brilliant performance. In his speech *On the Crown*, he defended his actions that led to the battle of Chaironeia and put the defeat down to the good fortune of the Macedonian king rather than anything else.[48] By reminding his fellow citizens of the treasured ideals that they had fought for, freedom and autonomy among them, he won over the crowd and secured an overwhelming victory. Aeschines left Athens, while Demosthenes finally got his crown.

After Alexander's death, in 323 BC, Demosthenes would re-emerge to champion the cause of freedom once more. Antipatros managed to crush the revolt and sent his agents to track down Demosthenes, who had fled to the island of Kalaureia (modern Poros). Before he could be apprehended, he took poison concealed in his pen and committed suicide – he who had lived by the pen died by the pen.[49] His statue was later set up in the Athenian Agora. On its base was carved the inscription:

If only your strength had been equal, Demosthenes, to your
wisdom,
Never would Greece have been ruled by a Macedonian Ares.[50]

The words fail to convey the complexity of the time in which
Demosthenes lived. He was no general, nor was he a man who
had the capacity to match the Macedonians on the battlefield; his
words were his sword and shield. Philip reportedly said that his
speeches were like soldiers because of their warlike power.[51] He can
be seen as the architect of the disaster at Chaironeia, someone
who failed to grasp the reality of the day, fighting against a Common
Peace that may have avoided bloodshed; or as the hero of Greek
liberty, refusing to bend to the demands of foreign invaders. Either
way, he is a tragic figure who had the singular misfortune to come
up against one of the ancient world's great military forces, and
two exceptional leaders in Philip and Alexander. Despite his failures, and through whichever filter we choose to view his life, he
remains one of the great characters of antiquity.

BRAND ALEXANDER

Alexander returned home after a long and tiring campaign, six
months and a thousand experiences older. With affairs seemingly settled, both within and outside the kingdom, he was finally
able to turn his thoughts to Persia. He summoned a War Council,
consulting with his Companions about when to launch the offensive and how best to conduct the operation. Parmenion had by
now returned from the east to help organise the army and report
on the current situation in Asia.[52] The expeditionary force under
his command had at first been very successful. They had crossed
the Hellespont early in 336 BC and had won over many coastal

cities and island communities in western Asia Minor, thereby depriving the Persians of crucial depots for their formidable fleet. A statue of Philip was set up in the sanctuary of Artemis in Ephesos, while altars in Eresos on Lesbos were dedicated to Zeus Philippios (Zeus Protector of Philip).[53] Initially, the Persians had not resisted their advance. Darius had been crowned king shortly before Philip's death and domestic issues, along with a possible revolt in Egypt, had dominated his immediate agenda. By early 335 BC, however, he was able to send 5,000 mercenaries to help counter-attack. Under the leadership of the Rhodian Memnon, who had previously stayed at Pella, they succeeded in pushing back the Macedonians, eventually eradicating all their previous gains.[54] Their foothold in Asia was now reduced to a small area around Abydos on the Hellespont, but crucially the bridgehead had been maintained. Parmenion, who had seen first-hand the riches of the East, strongly urged Alexander to undertake the expedition.[55] Plutarch also records an emissary from Ephesos, sent by the Greeks of Asia, who implored him to invade and liberate their cities.[56] Alexander was anxious to get started, but Parmenion and Antipatros advised him to take a wife and sire a child before embarking on the ambitious campaign. They both had numerous daughters who would provide a good match; he could probably have even taken one of each if he so desired. But Alexander did not take their advice. He replied that it would be a disgrace to sit at home celebrating a marriage and awaiting the birth of children when he had been elected commander-in-chief for the campaign by the Greeks, and had his father's invincible army ready to go.[57] It was a shrewd political decision. Philip's marriage on the eve of his own Persian expedition had thrown the royal family into turmoil, and Alexander did not wish to make the same mistake. Olympias was now back in a position of primacy and there could be no more trustworthy ally during his absence. Despite the year's heavy fighting, during which the army had travelled over two thousand kilometres, Alexander remained resolved upon conquest.[58] Europe was Philip's legacy, Alexander desired his own. He raised the men's ambitions for the campaign, pointing out the riches and glorious challenges that awaited them. The decision was made. In the spring they were to head east.

The end of the Macedonian year, in early October, was celebrated with appropriate pomp at Dion. Lavish sacrifices were offered at the altar of Olympian Zeus, in the shadow of broad Olympos, the meat distributed to all those present. A massive tent that could accommodate a hundred couches was set up to host the royal party, perhaps in the open ground between the city, the theatre, the Baphyras river and the sanctuary of Olympian Zeus, a patch of green edged with the browns and oranges of trees acquiring their autumnal tint. Here Alexander entertained Companions, ambassadors and other guests with magnificent banquets, just as he had seen his father do so many times in the past. Surplus booty from Thebes was likely handed out in another generous round of gift-giving, while each of the nine days of the festival programme was dedicated to an individual Muse with various athletic, dramatic and artistic contests thrilling the crowds. Celebrations continued at Aigai, the bad memories of Philip's murder expunged in a sea of merriment. Alexander had proved himself a capable successor.

It was the beginning of a new stage in his life, and in that year he may have found time to say goodbye to his old master Aristotle, who returned to Athens to found a philosophical school at the Lyceum. Alexander perhaps provided funds for the project. Aristotle's whereabouts and activities up this point are uncertain; he may have remained teaching at Mieza or helped out with the resettlement of his beloved Stageira. There is some indication that he had retained a degree of influence at the royal court and enjoyed

Philip's hospitality at Pella. The Athenians, according to one late source, later set up an inscription honouring his role in promoting the city's interests, perhaps referring to the settlement after Chaironeia which may have secured their lenient treatment.[59] Aristotle and Alexander would continue to communicate through letters. Among Aristotle's list of lost works are an advisory pamphlet *In Defence of Colonies*, addressed to Alexander, and another entitled *On Kingship*.[60] Alexander received similar works from Xenokrates and Theopompus, perhaps on request. They were designed to credit the writer and honour the recipient, adding an intellectual sheen to his reputation.[61] Apparently Aristotle's *On Kingship* had such an effect on Alexander that he would say to himself, 'Today, I have not been king; I have done good to no one,' if he had failed to perform a beneficial act.[62]

A later story reports that he was guarded when it came to others benefiting from Aristotle's teachings. Plutarch mentions a letter between the two where Alexander reprimanded his old teacher for divulging the secret doctrines that he had learned at his side.[63] It is of debatable authenticity and scholars have questioned the existence of any such secret works, but it may reflect some insecurity or jealousy on Alexander's part about others profiting from Aristotle's wisdom.

Although it is impossible to say to what extent master influenced pupil, Alexander did retain an interest in philosophy throughout his life, with a number of learned individuals joining his royal retinue.[64] He also copied Aristotle in the value he put on collecting information to better understand the world around him. During his time in Asia he commissioned works on Indian ethnography; his corps of surveyors and pacers (*bematistai*) recorded distances from place to place, and returning soldiers were able to provide Theophrastus with descriptions of previously unknown species of flora, which were included in his *Enquiry into*

Plants. Pliny the Elder preserves a tradition that Alexander aided Aristotle's research into zoology, ordering hunters, fishermen and fowlers from across Greece and Asia to provide his master with new information on birds and beasts, and that golden collars were placed around the necks of stags in order to keep track of their ages.[65] Such stories are likely embellishments, part of the package of romantic legends that surrounded Alexander and Aristotle's relationship, but there is no doubt that Alexander's campaigns were responsible for a revolution in Greek knowledge of the East. Arguably, it is this that remains the most tangible legacy of their time together.[66]

Over the winter, with preparations under way, Alexander had a chance to consider how best to record and present his future exploits. Around the same time, at Leibethra, to the south of Dion, a wooden statue of the mythical musician Orpheus, who was connected with the region, had begun to sweat, a troubling omen. There were concerns that it boded ill for the Persian expedition, but the seer Aristandros of Telmessos put Alexander at ease, providing a customarily favourable interpretation. He said that it merely represented the hard work awaiting those who wished to celebrate the king's actions in poetry and song.[67]

Alexander had no Homer to recount his deeds, as he was later to lament, nor a Pindar to sing his praises, but he needed to find somebody to tell his story.[68] He sent invitations to Ephorus, Xenokrates and Menedemos, all accomplished writers, but they unanimously rejected his offer, and so the task fell to Kallisthenes of Olynthos, who accepted.[69] He was a relative of Aristotle, and Alexander's old master probably helped secure his patronage. He had already established his credentials as a historian and had produced numerous works including a fourth-century Hellenic history, a monograph on the First Sacred War, perhaps at Philip's request, and a commentary on the *Iliad*'s catalogue of ships.[70]

He is said to have claimed that 'it was not he who had come to win fame from Alexander, but it would be his work to make Alexander renowned among men.'[71] Only a few meagre fragments from his *Deeds of Alexander* have survived, quoted by later authors; they reveal Kallisthenes' knowledge of Homer and Asiatic history, which were weaved into the narrative, playing into ideals of a heroic quest. No doubt each passage was scrutinised by Alexander, while some sections may even have been sent back from Asia to Greece, dispatches from the front that were designed to retain the hearts and minds of those left behind. Kallisthenes had to walk a fine line, keeping his patron happy while not sullying his own reputation. His official history of Alexander's campaigns was never finished, for Kallisthenes was executed (or died in custody) after being implicated in a plot to assassinate the king in 327 BC. His reputation as a historian was mixed among succeeding generations. Polybius included him among a list of learned men, along with Xenophon and Plato, while others wrote him off as a flatterer; Cicero called him a hack.[72] The loss of his work, regardless of its qualities, is of unparalleled significance as it closes a rare window onto Alexander's mind and how he wished to present himself.

Alexander may not have had the greatest literary talents at his disposal but he was far luckier when it came to the realm of art. He lived during a time of great artistic innovation, with access to a pool of immensely talented individuals. Philip's wealth and patronage had long drawn them to the royal court in Macedonia. A walk around Pella in the 330s BC would have revealed workshops of every kind – it was a powerhouse of creativity. The Pella Archaeological Museum now displays fragments of the city's rich artistic heritage. The first piece of artwork to be encountered, occupying pride of place in the entrance hall, is a bust of Alexander, a copy of a lost original found in nearby Giannitsa, the face that, as one art historian has eloquently stated, became the most influential in history.[73]

The dishevelled lion-like mane of hair, the tilt of the head and upward cast of the eyes, mark this out as an Alexander. As with Kallisthenes' history, this is how Alexander himself wished to be portrayed: the youthful king, his gaze fixed on some distant point between heaven and earth – Achilles resurrected. Interest in his own image had started early; he had already appeared in statue form alongside his father Philip in Olympia and Athens. He had been sculpted by men of reputation, the Athenian Leochares and probably also Euphranor and Chaireas.[74] But it was a rising star from the Peloponnesian city of Sikyon whom he came to favour, and who created the prototype for his royal portraiture.

The Giannitsa Alexander,
Pella Archaeological Museum

Lysippos had originally been a coppersmith before turning his daring hand to casting bronze. He combined technical proficiency with artistic flair to pioneer a new style of portraiture; he paid greater attention to the subject's hair and had a more nuanced appreciation of proportions than his predecessors. By reducing the size of the head and slimming down the body, he succeeded in making his statues appear somehow taller, more imposing. Their sinewy strength was displayed through dynamic poses that added vigour and movement, while there was a theatricality in the design that interacted with the viewer, pulling them around the works in order to consider them from all angles. Lysippos used to say that 'whereas his predecessors had made men as they really were, he made them as they appeared to be.'[75] By this he means that his statues retained something of the subject's personality, not just their idealised likeness. This concept was of great importance when it came to securing Alexander's admiration and patronage. Despite the feminine aspects of his appearance – the clean-shaven face, the melting eyes – Lysippos was able to preserve his leonine and virile nature. While the upwards gaze suggested both piety and *pothos*, his youthful appearance recalled victorious athletes and favoured heroes; he was able to give form to Alexander's inner excellence. It was this balance of youth and power that proved a winning combination. 'Eager to speak seems the statue of bronze, up to Zeus as it gazes,' an ancient observer felt compelled to engrave onto one particular Lysippian statue of Alexander. It seemed to say, 'Earth I have set under foot: Zeus, keep Olympus yourself!'[76]

This was the birth of a new type of ruler portraiture, but to what extent Alexander and Lysippos were influenced by existing fashions at the Macedonian court remains an open question. The miniature ivory heads recovered from Tomb II have much in common with Alexander's later portraiture. The twisting of their

necks, the sullen eyes, the clean-shaven faces, all suggest an established tradition. The school of royal pages may be the point of
origin. The boys, their heads filled with Homer, modelled their
appearance on existing portraits of their favourite gods and heroes
– Apollo, Dionysos, Herakles and Achilles – as well as victorious
athletes, who went unbearded in contemporary portraiture.[77]
Alexander did not change his style when he became king; although
he grew his sideburns long, he was never shown fully bearded, as
might have been expected. His image was already known and
widely disseminated, so there may have been no reason to change;
either that or he couldn't grow a very convincing beard. Nevertheless,
the differences between father and son's portraiture helped
Alexander forge his own identity. Old age had had its time, it was
now the youngster's turn.

Other artists also joined Lysippos in the elite circle of Alexander's
court favourites. They included Pyrgoteles the gem-cutter and the
famed painter Apelles, to whom he would give his mistress
Pankaste, the old man having fallen in love with her while painting
her portrait.[78] Roman sources record an edict whereby a monopoly
on Alexander's image was granted to these privileged few, likely a
fabrication that developed out of the king's unique preferences,
but they reveal a preoccupation with self-presentation that
Alexander sought to carefully control.[79] He was a master of propaganda, a man who, it was said, loved his own good name more
than his life or kingship.[80] During his reign his image and name
almost became separate entities, helping to create an almost mythical reputation that went before him like a battle standard.
Apparently he took to calling his men 'Alexanders', extensions of
his being; when fighting alongside another Alexander, he
commented, 'You at least will have to prove yourself a brave man
to live up to your name.'[81] The youngster, fired up with his king's
word, fought on only to be killed. But nowhere is brand Alexander

more alluring, and controversial, than when considering his claim that, not only was he divinely favoured, he was actually the son of a god.

According to the Alexandrian scholar Eratosthenes, writing in the third century BC, Olympias told Alexander the secret of his conception on the eve of his Persia campaign, and bade him be worthy of his divine parentage.[82] These may have been among the last words that mother and son shared in person.[83] The god credited with his siring was Ammon, an Egyptian deity (Amun) that the Greeks identified with Zeus.[84] His cult had already spread to the northern Aegean, the god being depicted wearing the skin and horns of a ram. At Aphytis, on the Pallene finger of the Chalkidike peninsula, he had a famous sanctuary.[85] It was rediscovered in the late 1960s at the pretty coastal town of Kallithea. Subsequent excavations have phased and dated the site. A Doric peristyle temple was built in the second half of the fourth century BC. A little to the east, an open-air corridor, an Egyptian feature, ran parallel to it, and was lined with monumental statues. It can be visited today. The site is sandwiched between hotels, sun-seekers and the enticing turquoise of the Aegean, a slice of Africa in northern Greece.[86] It was in the vicinity of this sanctuary, during the siege of Poteidaia in 356 BC, that Philip had first heard about the birth of Alexander. But Ammon also had links with Olympias' homeland. Herodotus, in his *Histories*, told the story of two black doves that had once flown north from Upper Egypt. One had settled in an oak tree at Dodona and began to speak in a human voice, the other made its home in the oasis of Siwah, in the Libyan desert, where Ammon's famous Oracle was established.[87] It was to this site in 331 BC that Alexander trekked. According to Arrian he already traced part of his lineage to the god, and by following in the footsteps of his ancestors, Herakles and Perseus, he hoped to confirm the rumours of his divine filiation.[88]

He was not disappointed. On the steps of the temple, set among a sea of evergreen palms and mirror-like pools of water, he was greeted by the priest as 'Son of Zeus'.[89] Later, inside the temple's innermost chamber, he put his questions to the priest, the god's mouthpiece on earth. Although ancient authors loved to speculate on what he asked, he probably never revealed the content of the conversation. Arrian says that he simply heard what his heart desired.[90]

A number of legends soon grew up around the subject of Alexander's mysterious genesis, some of which may have circulated during his lifetime. The first was that on the night before her wedding, Olympias' womb had been struck by a lightning bolt which produced a great sheet of flame that spread far and wide before fizzling out. Later it was said that Philip dreamed that he was sealing up Olympias' womb as one seals an amphora, the sign upon the seal, through the hazy recollection of his subconscious, appearing to be the figure of a lion. Aristandros the seer stated that Olympias was pregnant and that her son would be bold and lion-like. Finally, the most enduring of stories was that Philip had secretly observed his wife lying asleep next to a giant serpent, a god in disguise. Unsettled by the scene, he sent a friend to Delphi in order to consult the Pythia on the matter. Apollo commanded him to sacrifice to Ammon and to revere him above all other deities; the offending eye with which he had spied the secret union was fated to be blinded by an arrow. Alexander, apparently, neither confirmed nor denied the snake story, which rapidly became the most popular, adding to the mystic aura that surrounded him.[91]

These beliefs were not so uncommon for the time. The athlete Theagenes of Thasos was called the son of Herakles, the boxer Diagoras of Rhodes the son of Hermes; it was even said that Plato was fathered by Apollo. Aristandros had actually written on the matter, relating that a phantom in the guise of Apollo had made a night-time visit to Plato's mother.[92] Lecherous gods, it seems, were still interfering with the lives of mortals. What Alexander actually believed is impossible to recover, but Plutarch, perhaps, comes the closest to how he saw things. While conversing with an Egyptian philosopher about the nature of the gods, Alexander is said to have added his personal opinion, 'that while God [Zeus] is the father of all mankind, it is the noblest and best whom he makes especially his own'.[93]

Some of the Macedonian old guard, however, saw Alexander's publicised connection with Ammon as a slight against Philip. Kleitos the Black had aired this particular grievance at the fatal feast in Marakanda, suggesting that he was trying to disown his father.[94] There may be some truth in this: the wounds from their former rift, the dishonouring of Alexander and Olympias, had never properly healed, the shadow of Philip's achievements remaining ever-present throughout his life. But Philip was never completely set aside by Alexander. Instead, like Herakles before him, he had two fathers, one mortal, the other immortal. And in many ways, when it came to establishing links to the divine, Philip had set the standard.

Shortly before his assassination, in 336 BC, his statue had been shown enthroned among the gods, stressing their special relationship; surviving inscriptions show his name coupled with that of Zeus. In Macedonia's 'New Lands', Philip had also received godlike honours from grateful communities who no doubt wanted to retain his favour; it was the beginnings of a ruler cult.[95] Alexander, it could be argued, was merely following the path that his father had created, but in his own distinctive way. Alexander was awarded similar honours in Asia, and, although a slightly separate topic to his divine filiation, it further elevated his status and led to debates about whether he came to believe himself a living god. The template was set for future generations. His successors mimicked his portraiture, some creating their own mythical backstories, and the cult of kings became the norm. It was the dawn of a new age, though none was ever able to replicate the phenomenon of brand Alexander.

THE HELLESPONT, MAY 334 BC

They had come from Macedonia's mountain-ringed highlands, from its coastal plains and green river valleys; from Thrace, as far north as the banks of the Danube and the wilds of forested Illyria. From Greece they had come, from Thessaly, Boiotia, Attika and the Peloponnese, from the many islands that sparkle like stars in the Aegean's twilight-blue waters. There were fresh-faced youngsters and battle-scarred veterans, fathers, brothers, sons and strangers; men from villages, towns and beloved country farms; foot soldiers and cavalrymen mingled with skirmishers, scouts and strong-armed archers. Some wished for glory and plunder or just a steady wage, others had been rallied under the banner of revenge for Persian atrocities; 5,000 mercenaries had been bought with royal funds. Among them were men of many other trades: engineers and surveyors, physicians, priests and seers, smiths and merchants, while a band of intellectuals provided a gloss of high culture to the roving royal court. The enterprise was underpinned by a silent workforce of servants and slaves, performing those endless menial tasks that ensured the smooth running of the campaign. Finally, there were the animals, the pack-mules, cavalry mounts, sacrificial victims and mobile food sources that bleated, lowed and neighed among the many different dialects of their human masters. All were now under the ultimate command of their leader, Alexander. Many would never see their homelands again, including the king himself. It was an army unlike any other.

Around 35,000 men had come to Sestos on the Hellespont (modern Dardanelles); another 10,000 awaited them at Abydos, on the other side of the straits.[96] Antipatros was left behind to administer Macedonia with an army of 12,000 infantry and 1,500 horse. One hundred and sixty warships, along with a number of cargo vessels, had been provided by the Greeks and were now used to help transport the men across to Asia, their decks thudding under the rush of bare feet, the smell of pitch, brine and sweat clinging to every surface, the sailors hollering at each other like the seagulls riding the breeze above.[97]

Alexander had spent a considerable amount of money in his preparations. He was to cross over to Asia with only thirty days' worth of provisions and seventy talents left in the royal coffers. His debts were said by the naval officer Onesikritos to be two hundred talents.[98] Plutarch reports that, before leaving Macedonia, Alexander divided up his revenues from the royal lands, distributing them among his Companions. He 'assigned an estate to one, a village to another or the revenues of some port or community to a third,' he writes.[99] These gifts may have been granted in order to offset loans provided by the Companions or to strengthen loyalty. A recently discovered inscription from Kalindoia, in Bottike, among the 'New Lands' won by Philip during his annexation of Chalkidike, records that Alexander gave the city and its territory, which included three villages, to the Macedonians over the winter of 335–334 BC. It was a strategically important area, close to the main east–west road, with fine pastures for horse breeding; evidently Alexander was continuing his father's policy of population resettlement to provide extra security within the kingdom.[100]

Some of his closest friends, continues Plutarch, apparently became concerned that the king was giving away most of his land. Perdikkas, fully recovered after his wounding at Thebes and ready for the battles to come, asked him what he was leaving for himself. Alexander replied, 'My hopes!' Perdikkas, along with some others, thereby declined the property allotted to them, stating, 'Very well, then . . . those who serve with you will share those too.'¹⁰¹

Sestos was the mistress of the Hellespont. From the curving arch of sandy beach you can gaze across at Asia, a little over a kilometre away. These were the waters that Leander had swum each night to reach his lover Hero, where, during the Persian Wars, the Great King Xerxes had yoked the two continents together, bridging the gap with cables of papyrus, flax and 674 boats.¹⁰² His innumerable hordes had then marched west, in three separate columns, following three differing routes, across Aegean Thrace and into Macedonia. Alexander's march was the symbolic opposite. Setting out from his kingdom's heartlands, he had moved through a landscape that still remembered the Persian presence – the giant canal that had been driven through the neck of the Athos penin-sula, Doriskos, where Xerxes had counted his troops by the ten thousand, and across the many rivers that the army had reportedly drunk dry. At Sestos, he erected altars to those gods that were of particular relevance to the success of the campaign: Zeus, this time in the guise of protector of safe landings, the Argead ancestor Herakles, and Athena, patroness of the Pan-Hellenic crusade.¹⁰³ After the sacrifices had been made and the omens observed, Alexander left Parmenion in charge of organising the army's loading and transport while he and his entourage headed a little further down the peninsula. This land also had connections to another war story, one that was much dearer to the king.

The shrine and tomb of Protesilaos was near the Athenian colony of Elaious, set within a grove of tall elms and natural springs, green and cool under the springtime sun. 'Great-souled Protesilaos', as Homer called him, had been the first Greek victim of the Trojan War, but because he was the first to die, leaving behind a young wife and a half-built house, his name was immortalised, and in Elaious he was honoured as a god.[104] Alexander offered him sacrifices, hoping that his own landing on Asian soil might be more fortunate.[105] The smaller Macedonian fleet, composed of sixty ships of various sizes, was on hand to ferry the men across the Hellespont. Alexander boarded the fleet's flagship and made for the harbour of the Achaians on the opposite shore. In order to further secure a safe crossing, he sacrificed a bull to Poseidon and the Nereids at the midway point, tipping the beast into the strong-flowing waters along with libations poured from a golden cup.[106] He took control of the ship's rudder, guiding his ship towards the destination he had imagined since childhood – Asia, and the ruins of windy Troy. He was now twenty-one years old but underlying his youth was tough-edged experience. He had already fought in major battles, earning the respect of his fellow Macedonians. His quick and decisive actions had managed to secure the allegiances of the Balkan peoples and the League of Corinth. All threats within the kingdom had been eliminated. He had become known for his generosity to his allies and his severe treatment of his enemies. From his father, he had inherited the best fighting force in the ancient world, along with a tough constitution and a keen military mind. Olympias had helped foster his sense of destiny and his belief that he was touched by the divine. During his time in Thrace – it is not known exactly when – he had consulted an oracle of Dionysos and received a scorching endorsement of his future success. The priests, as was their custom, had poured wine upon the altar fire; the god's response was to be read in the flames. The answer shocked all those present, the fire leaping up towards the sky, even reaching above the temple's roof.[107] His mother had sought further assurances in Asia Minor, and an enquiry was sent to Apollo's Oracle at Kyzikos (or Zeleia) regarding her son's prospects of success. She received a set of mysterious instructions that, if followed, would ensure victory over the Persians.[108] The gods were with Alexander.

His numerous tutors and trainers, among them the stern Leonidas and whimsical Lysimachos, had helped mould his body and mind. Aristotle had imparted his wisdom. Trusty Boukephalas was there to carry him towards glory. Driving him on was his legendary *pothos*, that inner ambition to rival the feats of heroes, to do and see new and extraordinary things. His role models were there with him: Achilles in his personal copy of the *Iliad*, and a statuette of Herakles – Herakles of the table – a work by Lysippos.[109] His fellow Companions, the trusted clique of friends that had accompanied him from boyhood, who had shared in the many rites of passage that marked their transition into men of Macedon, had similar ambitions. The future was spread out before them like a giant canvas on which they could paint their own glorious deeds. Together they would see more of the world than any before them: the cultured cities of Asia Minor, the strange and mystic lands of Egypt with its pyramids, sphinxes and inaccessible oracles, the unimaginable wealth of Persia that made them the richest men in existence. Their journey would take them into far-flung Baktria and Sogdiana in modern Afghanistan, home to ferocious warrior tribesmen; in India they would battle against ranks of elephants and mighty foreign kings. They took with them their language, traditions, beliefs, and ideas on art and architecture, a distinctive Greco-Macedonian mix that would prove to be one of history's most enduring cultural exports, ready to be unpacked in a new land and disseminated through the king's many self-named city foundations. Their eleven years abroad would change the world in a profound way, although at that moment, cresting the rise and fall of the Hellespont's waves, they could never have known it.

Macedonia would become a shrine for their victories, the riches of Persia flowing back into town and country, enriching inhabitants and land alike. Following Alexander's first victory over a Persian force at the Granikos river, in 334 BC, Lysippos created a unique equestrian monument to be displayed at Dion, depicting twenty-five fallen Companions in bronze along with Alexander.[110] They were later hauled away to Rome, where they adorned the portico of Metellus, but before they vanished from history, copies were made, and one depicting the king has been retrieved from the Roman site of Herculaneum, which was buried by the eruption of Mount Vesuvius in AD 79. He is portrayed astride a rearing Boukephalas, the remains of a sword raised over an invisible enemy. This is the Alexander who now led his men into Asia.

Alexander at the battle of the Granikos

As the ship ran onto shore, the hull grating against the sand of a new continent, Alexander stood on the prow fully armed, ready for battle. He launched a spear into Asian land, then, leaping from the ship and into the surf, waded forward to claim his prize: his spear-won territory.[III] He was no longer a boy with a dream but a man on a mission. His invasion of the Persian Empire had begun.

AUTHOR'S NOTE

The story of the young Alexander is over, but for those wishing to know more about his career and conquests in Asia – the events that seared his name into history – please read on. A summary of this time is provided in the following pages, along with a brief discussion of his afterlife in Greece and the Balkans.

EPILOGUE

ALEXANDER IN THE EAST

After Alexander had paid his respects to his heroes at Troy, he linked up with the rest of the army and proceeded east. At the Granikos river he confronted a composite satrapal force. The invasion was almost over before it had begun. Having struggled through the waters, up the river's steep banks, and through a mass of defenders, Alexander and his Companions were charged by some Persian officers. He managed to kill the first, but two others were upon him before he could react. One of them sheared off a side plume of his helmet with an axe or sword. Alexander unhorsed him and drove a spear down into his chest. The other Persian now came up from behind, ready to deliver the death blow. In the nick of time, Kleitos the Black came to the king's rescue. There was a spray of blood as the offending arm was severed at the shoulder. It fell harmlessly onto the dusty ground and was quickly lost among the stamping hooves and rushing feet of the Macedonian advance. To the speed and shock of the tactics, to the savage bravery of the men, the Persians had no answer. Alexander had his first victory. The Gates of Asia had been smashed open.

The army continued south through present-day Turkey. Sardis, capital of Lydia and a key seat of Persian control, surrendered and Alexander then set about capturing the Greek cities along the coast.

Miletos was taken after a short siege, and Halikarnassos (with the exception of its citadels) followed shortly afterwards. It was around this time that Alexander temporarily disbanded his Pan-Hellenic fleet. Its maintenance was costly and it could not rival the Persian navy, so he adopted a land-based strategy to nullify the Persian threat, hoping to capture the remaining coastal strongholds, thereby depriving them of their base of operations and sources of manpower. He campaigned through Lykia and Pamphylia before cutting inland, heading north towards central Phrygia. At Gordion, he confronted the eponymous knot which connected an ox cart to its yoke. It was said to have been set up in the city's citadel by Midas, son of Gordios, with whom Alexander must have been familiar after living and studying in the heart of the 'Gardens of Midas' around Mieza. Whoever succeeded in untying the knot, local legend had it, could claim the rulership of Asia.

Accounts differ as to Alexander's actions. Some say that after a time spent examining the fist of cornel bark, the ends tucked inside leaving no sign of weakness, he took out his sword and severed the tie, declaring, 'Now it's undone.'[1] Others claimed that he simply removed the peg that connected the ox cart to its yoke. Regardless, it was an ingenious piece of propaganda and a timely boost in morale.

The first set-piece battle against Darius III and his vast impe-rial army came at Issos (Kilikia) in November 333 BC. The two sides formed up on either side of the Pinaros river, on a narrow plain that reduced the superiority of the Persian numbers. As at the Granikos, the Macedonians successfully crossed the water-course. Alexander, leading his right wing of Companion cavalry, exploited a gap in the enemy line and then charged diagonally at the centre where Darius was positioned – the Great King's flight was soon followed by the rest of his army. It was an emphatic victory.

Afterwards the Persian camp was plundered while the royal tent was set aside for Alexander. On gazing upon its opulent bathroom, aglitter with gold and pungent with the scent of exotic perfumes, the luxurious dining area replete with couches, tables and a banquet ready to be consumed, he was said to have remarked, 'So this, it seems, is what it is to be king.'[2] Later on, a begemmed casket, regarded as the most valuable item from Darius' treasures, was brought to Alexander. He used it to house his beloved copy of the *Iliad*.

Most of the Phoenician cities of the Levant surrendered without resistance as Alexander continued southwards. Darius had escaped to fight another day but it was essential that the Levantine coastline was secured, so protecting the Macedonian rear when it came to heading inland for the final showdown. Tyre, however, the main city located on a small islet offshore, denied Alexander access. It was promptly besieged, an action which turned into the lengthiest of Alexander's reign, lasting seven months. The Macedonian engineering corps once again proved its worth, eventually managing to build a causeway to the island city so that siege machines could be set against the walls. The arrival of ships from new allies allowed Alexander to surround the defenders, seaborne artillery and rams probed the defences, and the breakthrough came from the southern side, scenes of indiscriminate slaughter following. As at Thebes, the message was clear: resist and be destroyed. Nowhere is Alexander's single-mindedness and relentless pursuit of victory more evident. The taking of Tyre, along with Gaza a little later, essentially ended the threat of the Persian navy.

Egypt surrendered to Alexander on his approach, the locals welcoming him as a liberator, and he was bestowed with Pharaonic titles. On the edge of the Nile Delta he found an excellent site for a new settlement, the city that would eventually house his tomb – Egyptian Alexandria – and he also found time to consult the remote desert Oracle of Zeus Ammon at Siwah, where his divine filiation was confirmed. He then returned north.

Near Gaugamela in autumn 331 BC, in present-day northern Iraq, the Pan-Hellenic army faced Darius' forces once again. This time the Great King had chosen the perfect setting for battle, the wide plain, and prepared ground allowing him room to manoeuvre his overwhelming cavalry force and unleash two hundred scythed chariots. Alexander refused the entreaties of some of his Companions to attack by night, giving the celebrated rebuff, 'I will not steal my victory.'³ He was aware that his smaller army could easily be enveloped, and so, for the first time, formed a secondary or rear phalanx, which had the ability to turn around and combat any attack from behind. The overall formation resembling a rough trapezoid with reinforced flanks. His aim was essentially to get Darius to over-commit his cavalry, enabling a counter-offensive to be launched at their weakened line, but the strategy was a risky one, and would rely on the discipline, courage, and abilities of his men, but in this Alexander had every confidence.

Alexander began by advancing to the right, at an oblique angle, moving away from the prepared ground. Darius, concerned to keep his positional advantage and not to be outflanked, sent his cavalry to ride around the Macedonians and stop them from extending the line any further. A torrid battle soon developed on the flank as Alexander sent in his own troops to counter the threat, the tornadic movements of huge numbers of riders throwing up great clouds of dust. Darius now deployed his deadly scythed chariots but they proved largely ineffective. Their drivers were picked off by the light infantry. The men within the Macedonian phalanx parting their ranks to let other chariots pass through without damage, and they were then seized by the Shield Bearers and grooms. Meanwhile, the shifting Persian line, along with their large-scale commitment of cavalry against Alexander's right, had led to a thinning of their front, perhaps even a gap appearing somewhere on their centre left. This was what Alexander had been waiting for. He formed up his Companion cavalry into a flying wedge and, supported by some heavy and light infantry, charged at the point of weakness, spearing diagonally towards Darius. The fighting was brutal, *kopis* blades slashing, spears rammed into faces. The main Macedonian phalanx was now also upon the Persians, their tight array and bristle of *sarissas* causing havoc among the line. Darius witnessed their bloody advance from his chariot; before they got too close he fled once more, his centre and left wing collapsing behind him. Alexander pursued, but on the other side of the battlefield there was trouble. Parmenion's wing had been isolated and surrounded. Some Persian cavalry had ridden around the Macedonian left, and had attacked the baggage train. Alexander's movements had also caused a tear in his own line allowing other enemy riders to penetrate their ranks. Parmenion and his troops were now hard pressed on all sides, he sent a message to Alexander for aid. When word reached the king, he broke off his pursuit of Darius and returned towards the action, but in doing so, he ran into the fleeing enemy cavalry. Here the fighting was at its most desperate, some sixty Companions falling in the clash, many more being injured, yet Alexander managed to prevail. He then moved across to attack the enemy's right wing. By now, however, Parmenion and his Thessalian horsemen had turned the tide, the flight of Darius had become common knowledge and what was left of the Persian army disintegrated. Alexander set off once more in pursuit of the Great King. As at Issos, he managed to elude capture, although trust in his leadership had been dealt a fatal blow.

Alexander was later welcomed into Babylon where he was accorded the title 'king of the world'. He was only twenty-five.[4] He went on to capture the other royal centres, Sousa, Persepolis and Pasargadai, their treasuries making him the richest man on earth. With the Pan-Hellenic mission fulfilled, the opulent palace of Persepolis, a symbol of Achaimenid rule, was plundered, vandalised and burnt to the ground. Some ancient authors suggest that the blaze was the result of a drunken mistake, instigated by an Athenian courtesan called Thais, but it was more likely to have been a carefully considered act. The riches were first removed and the men were then allowed to take or destroy whatever was left. Excavations at the site suggest that the fire was set in many places simultaneously, targeting those buildings associated with Xerxes, who had sacked Athens; specially constructed stands perhaps allowed the army to watch the spectacle. The great war was over, revenge quenched by flames.[5]

Alexander then turned his attention to tracking down Darius. He was regrouping at Ekbatana, another royal centre to the north, but did not have the numbers for another battle and retreated towards the Caspian Sea. Alexander pursued and caught up with him beyond the Caspian Gates, where he had been stabbed by his followers and left to die. Alexander saw to Darius' burial arrangements and set his sights on tracking down the usurper and regicide, Bessos. It was a turning point in the campaign, where the motives of the League of Corinth began to fall away, leaving only those of the new king of Asia. Many of the allied troops were sent back home, but the Macedonians, and those tempted to prolong their service as mercenaries, went on with Alexander towards Baktria and Sogdiana (modern Afghanistan and Uzbekistan), the northern lands of the Persian Empire. Bessos, who had assumed the throne name Artaxerxes V, was later given up by his own men, but Alexander's efforts to fortify the frontier led to an uprising among the local chiefs and semi-nomadic peoples of the region. He would spend over a year dealing with this new war, dividing his forces to counter the enemy's guerrilla tactics, and bolstering the network of military outposts and settlements that had been established a little earlier, a strategy that mimics Philip's in Thrace all those years before. Like his father, he also took a new wife, the Baktrian noblewoman Rhoxane, to help consolidate his relationships with the local aristocracy.

This last development was just one of many ways in which Alexander attempted to reconcile Asiatic and Macedonian customs. He adopted certain elements of Persian dress and protocol, admitted foreign members into his court, retained the principles of Achaimenid administration, and began training Persian youths in the Macedonian manner. Plutarch believed he used this approach to establish authority through good will rather than force.[6] His father had done something similar while expanding Macedon's frontiers, but this progressive policy caused much resentment among some of the conservative Greeks and Macedonians who considered the Persians an inferior race. It was also the view of Aristotle, who may have communicated with his pupil on this very matter: 'Alexander did not follow Aristotle's advice,' recounts Plutarch, 'to treat the Greeks as if he were their leader, and other peoples as if he were their master; to have regard for the Greeks as for friends and kindred, but to conduct himself towards other peoples as though they were plants or animals.'[7]

This stage in the campaign is also marked by a number of internal issues. In 330 BC, Philotas, head of the Companion cavalry, was implicated in a plot to assassinate the king; he was tortured, found guilty and executed, along with the other conspirators. By association, Parmenion, Philotas' father, the man who had commanded the left wing in all Alexander's major battles, a veteran of Philip's reign and one of the most revered and powerful Macedonian noblemen, was also put to death. It's a matter of speculation whether there is any truth in the charges – Alexander may have fabricated them to eradicate the influence of a key faction within the army. When word reached Antipatros back home he was said to have remarked, 'If Parmenion plotted against Alexander, who is to be trusted? And if not, what is to be done?'[8]

The drunken argument and murder of Kleitos followed, and then, a little after Alexander's marriage to Rhoxane, the plot of the royal pages, which would have succeeded had not Alexander stayed drinking with his friends long into the night, depriving the youths who guarded his bedchamber of their window of opportunity. Kallisthenes, the campaign historian, who had objected to Alexander's adoption of Persian ways, especially an attempt to introduce a form of *proskynesis* (obeisance) at court, was also implicated, and later was either killed or died before trial.

In 327 BC, Alexander recrossed the Hindu Kush and headed east, into northern India, hoping to bring affiliate lands of the Persian Empire under his sway. At the Hydaspes (Jhelum) river the next year, he faced the army of the local king Poros. It was one of the most savage battles of his reign, at which the Macedonian cavalry eventually succeeded in enveloping the enemy and their terrifying ranks of war elephants. A special set of commemorative medallions was commissioned to celebrate the victory, but the occasion was also tinged with sadness. Boukephalas, Alexander's beloved horse, died around the same time, Alexandria Boukephala being built around his tomb.

The army pressed on. Alexander may have expected to encounter the eastern sea at any time, as Aristotle had suggested, but at the river Hyphasis (Beas) his demoralised and battle-fatigued soldiers refused to go any further. Alexander would never reach world's end.

For the return journey, a fleet had been constructed to ferry the men downriver towards the mouth of the Indus. It was not a peaceful procession: along the way they faced more resistance, Alexander's policy of terror often ended in massacres of the local inhabitants. At one Mallian settlement, modern Multan, Alexander, urging his lethargic troops on by personally leading the mission to scale the wall, was isolated inside the citadel where he suffered the most serious wound of his life. A massive arrow punctured his breastplate and lodged in his chest. Despite considerable blood loss his tough constitution saw him through and he recovered. The men, however, believed him dead – until he appeared once again in public a few days later, even managing to mount a horse to the deafening cheers of the army.

At the Indian Ocean the Cretan Nearchos, one of Alexander's boyhood comrades, was put in charge of the fleet that was to sail along the coast towards the Persian Gulf, while Alexander, together with a major portion of the army, returned to the centre of his empire via the Gedrosian desert, but lack of food and water, flash floods and the punishing heat took many lives. Although the ancient authors tend to exaggerate the scale of the disaster, it was a costly mistake. He regrouped at Karmania and spent the remaining years of his life in and around the Persian royal centres. At Sousa, he further pursued his policy of integration with Persian practices. A mass wedding was held with around ninety Companions marrying local brides, Alexander himself taking two women of Achaimenid lineage, Stateira and Parysatis. He now decided to discharge the veterans among the army, which caused another mutiny. The men, offended by the arrival of a 30,000-strong corps of Persian youths trained in the Macedonian manner, along with the assimilation of foreign cavalry forces into the army and Alexander's offensive Persian apparel, felt aggrieved that he was lessening their influence and future dependence on their countrymen. They were later reconciled, albeit after the ringleaders had been executed for sedition, and a grand feast was held to help heal the rift. Krateros, one of Alexander's most trustworthy generals and Companions, was appointed to lead them back to Macedonia, where he was to replace Antipatros as regent. The elderly steward had performed his duties well, putting down a revolt in Thrace and Greece, but his relationship with Alexander had become increasingly strained, in part owing to Olympias' hostile reports. No sooner had Krateros departed than Alexander was hit by the loss of another of his closest Companions, Hephaistion, who died after a short illness at Ekbatana in 324 BC. His funeral was greater than that of Philip. A section of Babylon's city wall was being dismantled to make room from the giant pyre. After Alexander had recovered from his manic grief he went back on the warpath, subduing the Kossaians, a mountain people based somewhere north of Sousa. Plans were now afoot for a new stage to the campaign. A large fleet was being constructed with the aim of taking Arabia, and there was even some talk that Alexander was toying with the idea of extending his empire westwards, but he would never embark on this new mission. He fell ill in Babylon in the summer of 323 BC and died eleven or twelve days later, on the night between 10 and 11 June. He was thirty-two. A Babylonian astronomical tablet soberly records the event, along with the local weather conditions: 'The king died; clouds . . .'[9]

Although rumours later circulated about a poisoning, Antipatros being accused in the sources, the length of Alexander's illness speaks against it. Eleven years of constant campaigning, illness and injury had undoubtedly taken its toll, weakening his natural defences and allowing a fever to conquer the man who had never lost a battle. He left no designated heir and when asked to whom he wished to leave his newly won empire, with his dying breath he is said to have declared, 'To the strongest.'[10]

Just who exactly that was to be quickly became a cause of contention. Perdikkas held the ring of power but there were disputes among the Companions and army about who should be king. Eventually an agreement was reached whereby Arrhidaios, Alexander's incapable half-brother, took on the mantle; he later shared the kingship with Alexander IV, born to Rhoxane a few months later, both kings being placed under the guardianship of Perdikkas. But it was not a lasting arrangement. Control of various parts of the empire were attributed to other powerful Macedonians, factions formed and a series of wars followed. Regions, cities, peoples and lands were carved up between them. Alexander's former Companions, Ptolemy and Seleukos, established the most long-lived kingdoms in Egypt and Asia respectively.

Aristotle died the year after Alexander, succumbing to disease aged sixty-two at Chalkis. Their relationship had reportedly soured towards the end of his reign, probably as a result of Kallisthenes' death. Alexander's 'kindly attentions', reports Plutarch, 'lacked their former ardour and affection towards him, and this was proof of estrangement'.[11] Aristotle never directly mentions Alexander in any of his works, although scholars debate whether a section on absolute kingship in the *Politics* acknowledges his new style of rulership, but according to Pliny the Elder, when the painter Protogenes was looking for new things to paint, Aristotle suggested the deeds of Alexander, because they were immortal.[12]

Alexander's surviving relatives, the last of the Argeads, were all eventually eliminated. His Illyrian half-sister, Kynnane, was killed as she travelled through Asia to propose a marriage between her daughter, Adea-Eurydike, and Arrhidaios-Philip III. The marriage did take place, but bride and groom were later murdered by Olympias back in Macedonia. In turn, she was put to death by Kassandros, Antipatros' son, at Pydna in 316 BC. Alexander IV vanishes from the record some years later, along with his mother, Rhoxane. Herakles, Alexander's illegitimate son by Barsine, who had grown up in Pergamon, also found himself at the centre of conflict between the Successors. He was brought back to Greece only to be secretly killed; the cremated body of an adolescent boy, accompanied by a gold oak wreath and contained in a bronze vessel, was discovered in 2008, near the sanctuary of Eukleia in Aigai. Archaeologists have suggested that the remains may be those of Herakles.[13] Alexander's sister Kleopatra, widowed after the death of Alexander the Molossian, was an enviable match for ambitious Companions but this also made her a threat, and she was killed at Sardis in 308 BC. Thessalonike, whom Kassandros had married, was murdered by her son. The Antipatrid dynasty which succeeded the Argead in Macedonia came to an end shortly afterwards. They were replaced by a line of Antigonid kings, descendants of Antigonos 'the One-eyed', a premier general of Philip's. Macedonia eventually fell to the Romans following their decisive victory at Pydna in 168 BC and the kingdom was absorbed into their growing empire. The glory days of Philip and Alexander had become but a distant memory.

During his lifetime, Alexander had never taken the Persian title 'King of Kings'. He had attempted to forge a new style of kingship, however there was another name associated with the Achaimenids that would become his own: there had been many 'Great Kings', but only one 'Great Alexander'.

ALEXANDER AND THE MACEDONIAN QUESTION

The following millennia witnessed many fluctuations in peoples and power dynamics in Macedonia – Romans, Byzantines, Bulgars and Ottomans all ruling for a time. By the beginning of the twentieth century, when it was still under Ottoman control, it was known as one of the most ethnically diverse regions in the Balkans, home to Turks, Greeks, Bulgarians, Serbs, Albanians, Jews, and Vlachs; the French even named a mixed salad, *la Macédoine*, after the area's bewildering array of peoples. But as the Ottoman Empire began to weaken – the sick man of Europe taking to his bed – surrounding powers began to eye up the possibility of expansion. Greece, Serbia and Bulgaria sought to impose their own nationalist agendas upon the region and its population in order to strengthen territorial claims. The past was weaponised, the Greeks claiming that the ancient Macedonians were of Hellenic descent, others that they were a distinct non-Greek people. The locals were caught in the middle of this propaganda war. The British journalist Henry Noel Brailsford, who spent time in the region during the early twentieth century, observed: 'The legend that Alexander the Great was a Greek goes out by one road, and the rival myth that Alexander was a Bulgarian comes in by the other.'[14] Following the expulsion of the Ottomans during the Balkan Wars (1912–13), Greece secured much of Macedonia's historical territory, with other peripheral areas being allocated to Bulgaria and Serbia, but the divisions of people and their assimilation into new nation-states led to conflicts over who had the right to call themselves Macedonians. It was the latest development of the so-called Macedonian Question.

The dispute escalated in 1991 when the Republic of Macedonia proclaimed its independence following the breakup of Yugoslavia. The new nation adopted the star or sun of Vergina for its national flag, while Skopje became thronged with monuments to Alexander and his father Philip. The Greeks, who saw these acts as cultural appropriation, held mass protests: the Alexander monument in Thessaloniki, a giant equestrian statue of the conqueror erected on the waterfront in 1974, was swamped with participants hosting banners proclaiming 'Macedonia is Greece'. It was a new phase in what has been called a 'global cultural war' waged between Greeks, Macedonians and their diaspora across the world, the politicised past in many ways masking long-held fears of conflicts and territorial change that have for centuries been a feature of life in this part of the Balkans.[15] In 2018 fresh steps were taken towards reconciliation

with the Prespa Agreement: Greece consented to withdraw its opposition to the Republic's accession to the EU, the Republic changed
its name to the Republic of North Macedonia – in order to differentiate it from the region of Macedonia in northern Greece – and
agreed to reconsider its monuments. The settlement continues to
divide popular opinion. Nationalism has become closely bound
up with differing historical ideas. For those who don't know the
difference between Greek Macedonia and the Republic of North
Macedonia, the situation can appear confusing. But what is clear
is that Alexander still matters – indeed that he remains central to
people's identity and perception of their place in the world. Few
historical figures have exerted such a persistent influence from
beyond the grave.

It was once a commonly held belief among sailors and fishermen
in Greece that Alexander's mermaid sister, *gorgona*, haunted the
waters of the Aegean, the creature occasionally emerging from the
salty depths during bad weather, asking the whereabouts of her
brother. Such pieces of folklore are now sadly dying out, but should
anyone have the misfortune to find themselves in the clutches of
a storm off the Greek coast, with wind-tossed waves threatening
a capsize, perhaps it is best to offer up the satisfactory answer that
is sure to placate the *gorgona*'s troubled mind and dissuade her
from the certain destruction of your vessel: that Alexander the
Great lives and reigns, as he surely still does, not only in legend,
but among the ruins of his homeland and the archaeological
discoveries that it has been this book's purpose to relate.

ENDNOTES

PROLOGUE

1. M. Andronikos, *The Chronicle of Vergina* (in Greek) (Athens, 1997), p. 118.
2. S. Drougou, 'Vergina. On the Tracks of the Macedonian Kings' in P. Valanavis (ed.) *Great Moments in Greek Archaeology* (Athens and Los Angeles, 2007) p. 265.
3. Andronikos, *The Chronicle of Vergina*, p. 119.
4. Drougou, 'Vergina. On the Tracks of the Macedonian Kings', p. 265.
5. M. Andronicos, *Vergina: The Royal Tombs and the Ancient City*, p. 70.
6. Andronikos, *The Chronicle of Vergina*, p. 151; Hamilakis, *The Nation and its Ruins: Antiquity, Archaeology and National Imagination in Greece* (Oxford, 2007), p. 151.
7. Plutarch, *Life of Pompey* 2.1 (Pompey and Alexander); Appian, *Mithridatic Wars* (24) 117 (577) (Pompey's cloak); Plutarch, *Life of Pompey* 13.4–5 (Pompeius Magnus); Plutarch, *Life of Julius Caesar* 11.3 (trans. B. Perrin, Loeb 99) (Caesar – a variation of the story is also related by Suetonius, *Julius Caesar* 7.1 where he felt remorse on encountering a statue of Alexander); Suetonius, *Augustus* 50.1 (Augustus' seal ring); Dio, *Roman History* 78.7.2 (Caracalla).
8. R. Stoneman, 'The Legacy of Alexander in Ancient Philosophy' in J. Roisman (ed.), *Brill's Companion to Alexander the Great* (Leiden, 2003), p. 325, and more generally on Alexander's legend, *Alexander the Great: A Life in Legend* (New Haven and London, 2008).
9. British Library Cotton MS Vitellius A XV folios 107r–131v (Alexander and Aristotle letter); *Perceforest* (Alexander and Arthur); Chaucer

Canterbury Tales 7.2631–70 (Alexander's fame). For general discussion on Alexander literature in Medieval Britain see D. Ashurst 'Alexander Literature in English and Scots' in Z.D. Zuwiyya (ed.) *A Companion to Alexander Literature in the Middle Ages* (Leiden and Boston, 2011) pp 255–290; G.Cary *The Medieval Alexander* (Cambridge, 1956).

10. E.N. Borza, *In the Shadow of Olympus: The Emergence of Macedon* (Princeton, 1990), p. 21.

11. *ID 1114: A handbook of Macedonia and surrounding territories. Compiled by the Geographical Section of the Naval Intelligence Division, Naval Staff, Admiralty* (London, 1921), p. 19. For the history of Macedonia's exploration see M.B. Hatzopoulos, 'A Century and a Lustrum of Macedonian Studies' in *Ancient World*, Vol. 4 (1981), pp. 91–108, 'Macedonian Studies', in R.J. Lane Fox (ed.), *Brill's Companion to Ancient Macedon. Studies in the Archaeology and History of Macedon, 650 BC–300 AD* (Leiden and Boston, 2011), pp. 35–42; Borza, 'The History and Archaeology of Macedonia: Retrospect and Prospect' in *Macedonia and Greece in Late Classical and Early Hellenistic Times. Studies in the History of Art*, Vol. 19 (Washington, 1982), pp. 17–30.

12. G.F. Abbott, *Macedonian Folklore* (Cambridge, 1903), p. 10.

I FIRE FROM HEAVEN

1. T. Desdevises-du-Dezert, *Géographie ancienne de la Macédoine* (Paris, 1863), p. 338.
2. The name Old Pella differentiates it from New Pella, another modern village a little to the west, close to the site of the Roman colony of Pella (est. 30 BC).
3. The early discoveries at Pella are summarised in P. Petsas, *Pella: Alexander the Great's Capital* (Thessaloniki, 1978); M. Siganidou and M. Lilimpaki-Akamati, *Pella: Capital of Macedonians* (Athens, 1996).
4. For ancient descriptions of Pella, on which these passages are based, see Strabo, *Geography* 7 frag. 20, Pseudo-Scylax, *Periplus* 66, Livy, *History of Rome* 44.46.4–9 (location, Phakos and surrounding lands); Solinus 13, Demosthenes, *On Halonnesus* (7) 16, Plutarch, *Life of Demetrius* 43.3 (Macedonian navy and ship sheds); Athenaeus, *Learned Banqueters* 7.328a (fish at Pella); Livy, *History of Rome* 42.51 (Athena 'Defender of the People'); Julius Pollux, *Onomasticon* ç15–16 (Pella wine); Pliny the Elder, *Natural History* 31.50 (cold streams).

5. I.M. Akamatis, 'Pella' in R.J. Lane Fox (ed.), *Brill's Companion to Ancient Macedon. Studies in the Archaeology and History of Macedon, 650 BC–300 AD* (Leiden and Boston, 2011), p. 394. The relocation of the capital from Aigai to Pella is not mentioned in the ancient sources and scholars are divided on whether it happened under Archelaos or Amyntas III. For discussion see M.B. Hatzopoulos and L.D. Loukopoulou, *Two Studies in Ancient Macedonian Topography. Meletemata* 3 (Athens, 1987) pp. 42–3; B. Raynor, *Kings, Cities, and Elites in Macedonia c.360–168 BC* (Oxford Diss., 2014), pp. 166–9; W. Greenwalt, 'Why Pella' in *Historia: Zeitschrift für Alte Geschichte* Bd. 48 H. 2 (1999), pp. 158–83.

6. On the etymology of Pella's name see M. Lilimbaki-Akamati, I. M. Akamatis, A. Chrysostomou and P. Chrysostomou, *The Archaeological Museum of Pella* (Athens, 2011), pp. 20–1.

7. Xenophon, *Hellenica* 5.2.13 (largest city in Macedonia); Strabo, *Geography* 7 frag. 20 (Philip's enlargement).

8. Thucydides, *Peloponnesian War* 2.100.2–3.

9. Aelian, *Historical Miscellany* 14.17, Pliny the Elder, *Natural History* 35.63.

10. Aeschines, *On the Embassy* 2.124, Plutarch, *Moralia* 603d.

11. Numerous construction dates for the palace's core have been suggested, spanning the entirety of the fourth century BC. See for example P. Chrysostomou, 'The Palace of Pella' in Lilimbaki-Akamati, Akamatis, Chrysostomou and Chrysostomou (eds.), *The Archaeological Museum of Pella*, pp. 58–66 (early fourth century BC, possibly connected to Archelaos' building programme); I. Nielsen, *Hellenistic Palaces* (Aarhus, 1999), pp. 84, 88; M.B. Hatzopoulos, 'Macedonian palaces: where king and city meet' in I. Nielsen (ed.), *The Royal Palace Institution in the First Millennium BC. Regional development and cultural interchange between East and West* (Athens, 2001), p. 191 (mid fourth century BC date, connected to Philip's reign); Raynor, *Kings, Cities, and Elites in Macedonia c.360–168 BC*, p. 183 (late fourth century BC date, during the kingship of Kassandros).

12. Mary Renault, *Fire from Heaven* (New York, 1969), p. 1.

13. D. Sweetman, *Mary Renault: A Biography* (San Diego, New York and London, 1993), pp 27 and 256.

14. C. Zilboorg, *The Masks of Mary Renault: A Literary Biography* (Columbia and London, 2001), p. 237.

15. These sources include: Book 17 of Diodorus Siculus, *Library of History*

(second half of the first century BC), Quintus Curtius Rufus, *The History of Alexander* – the first two books being lost (first century AD), Plutarch, *Life of Alexander* (early second century AD), Arrian, *Anabasis of Alexander* (first half of the second century AD*)*, Books 11–12 of Justin, *Epitome of the Philippic History of Pompeius Trogus* (*c.* 200 AD), and Pseudo-Callisthenes, *Greek Alexander Romance* (third century AD). Also of importance are Plutarch's essays 'On the Fortune or Virtue of Alexander I and II', and 'Sayings of Kings and Commanders', found in his *Moralia,* Books 15–17 of Strabo, *Geography* (early first century AD), Polyaenus, *Stratagems* (second century AD), the anonymous *Alexander Itinerary* (fourth century AD), and the *Epitome of the Deeds of Alexander the Great* and *On the Death and Testament of Alexander* from the so-called Metz Epitome (fourth-fifth century AD). For the collected fragments of lost Alexander historians, on which these later works were based, see C.A. Robinson, *The History of Alexander the Great: A Translation of the Extant Fragments, Vol. I* (Chicago, 1953).

16. Onesikritos, a naval officer in Alexander's fleet, and Marsyas of Pella, a boyhood companion of Alexander, both produced works dealing with the king's youth and upbringing: Diogenes Laertius, *Lives of Eminent Philosophers* 6.84 (Onesikritos' *The Education of Alexander*), Suda, s.v. 'Marsyas' (Marsyas' *On the Training of Alexander*). For further discussion of these works see T.S. Brown, *Onesicritus: A Study in Hellenistic Historiography* (Berkeley, 1947); W. Heckel, 'Marsyas of Pella, Historian of Macedon' in *Hermes*, Vol. 108 (1980), pp. 444–62.

17. Plutarch, *Life of Alexander* 1.2.

18. Sweetman, *Mary Renault*, p. 258.

19. Prior to the publication of *Fire from Heaven*, Renault had written *The Last of the Wine* (New York, 1956), *The King Must Die* (New York, 1958), *The Bull from the Sea* (New York, 1962) and *The Mask of Apollo* (New York, 1966).

20. For ancient references to Samothrace's fame see N. Lewis, *Samothrace, Vol. 1: The Ancient Literary Sources* (New York, 1958).

21. Lewis, *Samothrace, Vol. 1*, p. 70 (Mnaseas, frag. 27).

22. Diodorus Siculus, *Library of History* 5.49.6.

23. Justin's account, *Epitome to the Philippic History of Pompeius Trogus* 7.5.9–10, which suggests that Philip was first guardian of his nephew before being appointed king, is perhaps to be favoured over Diodorus' version of events, in *Library of History* 16.2.4–5, which states that he

succeeded directly as king after Perdikkas' death. See K. Buraselis, 'Royal *epitropeia*. Remarks on Kingship and Guardianship in Macedonia and the Hellenistic Kingdoms' in U. Yiftach and M. Faraguna (eds.), *Legal Documents in Ancient Societies VI. Ancient Guardianship: Legal incapacities in the Ancient World* (Trieste, 2017), pp. 59–74.

24. Diodorus Siculus, *Library of History* 16.4.1–7. For further discussion of this battle see N.G.L. Hammond, 'The Battle between Philip and Bardylis' in *Antichthon*, Vol. 23 (1989), pp. 1–9; K. Mortensen, 'The Career of Bardylis' in *Ancient World*, Vol 22.1 (1991), pp. 49–59; M.B. Hatzopoulos, 'Les limites de l'expansion Macédonienne en Illyrie sous Philippe II' in P. Cabanes, *L'Illyrie méridionale et l'Épire dans l'Antiquité* (1987), pp. 81–94.

25. Justin, *Epitome* 7.6.1–2.

26. Plutarch, *Moralia* 402b.

27. L. Durrell, *The Greek Islands* (London, 1978), p. 216.

28. Diogenes Laertius, *Lives of Eminent Philosophers* 6.59 (trans. R.D. Hicks, Loeb 185).

29. M. Belozerskaya, *To Wake the Dead* (New York and London, 2009), p. 42.

30. E.D. Bodnar and C. Foss, 'Diary II cont. 13' in *Cyriac of Ancona: Later Travels* (Harvard and London, 2003), p. 101. See also P.W. Lehmann, 'Cyriacus of Ancona's Visit to Samothrace' in K. Lehmann and P.W. Lehmann (eds.), *Samothracian Reflections: Aspects of the Revival of the Antique* (Princeton, 1973), pp. 3–56.

31. For archaeological reports of the Americans' work see the Samothrace series published by the New York Institute of Fine Arts. General archaeological guides include K. Lehmann, *Samothrace: A Guide to the Excavations and Museum* (New York, 1998); D. Matsas and A. Bakirtzis, *Samothrace: A Short Cultural Guide* (Athens, 2001); N. McGilchrist, *McGilchrist's Greek Islands 12. Lemnos with Aghios Efstratios and Samothrace* (London, 2010).

32. Livy, *History of Rome* 45.5.1–15. See B. Wescoat, 'The pilgrim's passage into the sanctuary of the Great Gods, Samothrace' in T.M. Kristensen and W. Friese (eds.), *Excavating Pilgrimage: Archaeological Approaches to Sacred Travel and Movements in the Ancient World* (London, 2017), p. 76.

33. Plutarch, *Moralia* 229d, 217c–d.

34. Plutarch, *Moralia* 217c–d (trans. F. Cole Babbitt, Loeb 245). Variations

of this anecdote are also attributed by Plutarch to the Spartan general Lysander (*Moralia* 229d) and an unknown Spartan (*Moralia* 236d).

35. B. Wescoat, *Samothrace, Vol. 9: The Monuments of the Eastern Hill* (Princeton, NJ and Athens, 2017), p. 75.

36. Strabo, *Geography* 10.3.7, Plato, *Euthydemus* 277d–e *(thronosis)*.

37. See Lewis, *Samothrace, Vol. 1*, pp. 35–6 (Ephorus, frag. 120).

38. P. Williams Lehmann and D. Spittle, *Samothrace, Vol. 5: The Temenos* (Princeton, 1982), pp. 267–9.

39. Plutarch, *Moralia* frag. 178 (*On the Soul*) (trans. F.H. Sandbach, Loeb 429).

40. G.E. Mylonas, *Eleusis and the Eleusinian Mysteries* (Princeton, 1961), pp. 261–74. See H. Bowden, *Mystery Cults in the Ancient World* (London, 2010), p. 38.

41. Lucretius, *Nature of Things* 6.1044–7 (trans. W.H.D. Rouse and M.F. Smith, Loeb 181).

42. Diodorus Siculus, *Library of History* 5.47.3–4.

43. Plutarch, *Life of Alexander* 2.1–2 (trans. B. Perrin, Loeb 99). A later variation of the same story is found in Himerius, *Orations* 9.12 (Lewis, *Samothrace, Vo.l 1*, p. 89). The marriage is also mentioned by Justin, *Epitome* 7.6.101–2. For discussion see J.R. Hamilton, *Plutarch: Alexander: A Commentary* (Oxford, 1969), pp. 2–3; W. Greenwalt, 'Philip and Olympias on Samothrace: A clue to Macedonian Politics during the 360s' in T. Howe and J. Reames (eds.), *Macedonian Legacies: Studies in Ancient Macedonian History and Culture in Honour of Eugene N. Borza* (Claremont (CA), 2009); pp. 79–106; E.D. Carney, *Olympias: Mother of Alexander the Great* (New York and London, 2006), pp. 12–15.

44. Plutarch's designation of Philip as a 'youth' – *meirakion* – a term which had an upper limit of twenty-one, and of Olympias as a 'child' – *pais* – suggests that the meeting took place earlier than 357 BC. However, considering Philip's movements and marriage policy 357 BC is more plausible.

45. Frontinus, *Stratagems* 2.5.19.

46. Justin, *Epitome of the Philippic History of Pompeius Trogus* 17.3.6 and Theopompus, frag. 355. See Carney, *Olympias: Mother of Alexander the Great*, pp. 5–6.

47. Quintus Curtius, *History of Alexander* 8.1.26.

48. The terms of this alliance were engraved on stelai and set up in Olynthos,

Macedonia and Delphi. A fragment of one stele was discovered near Olynthos and now resides in the Thessaloniki Archaeological Museum. See P.J. Rhodes and R. Osborne (eds.), *Greek Historical Inscriptions 404–323 BC* (Oxford, 2003), pp. 244–9, no. 50.

49. Plutarch, *Life of Alexander* 3.3–5 and *Moralia* 105b. For discussion see Hamilton, *Plutarch: Alexander: A Commentary*, pp. 7–8. The Illyrians had formed an alliance with Athens, Thrace and Paionia in late July 356 BC, but they were defeated by Parmenion while still collecting their forces and nothing came of the alliance. Parts of the stele bearing the terms of the alliance have been recovered from the Athenian Acropolis. See Rhodes and Osborne, *Greek Historical Inscriptions 404–323 BC*, pp. 254–9, no. 53.

50. Plutarch, *Life of Alexander* 3.4. See N.G.L. Hammond, 'The Regnal Years of Philip and Alexander' in *Greek, Roman and Byzantine Studies*, Vol. 33 (1992), pp. 355–73.

51. For folklore involving the three Fates in Macedonia see G.F. Abbott, *Macedonian Folklore* (Cambridge, 1903), pp. 126–8; L.A. Heuzey, *Le mont Olympe et l'Acarnanie: exploration de ces deux régions, avec l'étude de leurs antiquités, de leurs populations anciennes et modernes, de leur géographie et de leur histoire* (Paris, 1860), p. 139; H. Triantaphyllides, 'Macedonian Customs' in *Annual of the British School at Athens*, Vol. 3 (1896–7), pp. 207–14; A.J.B. Wace and M.S. Thompson, *The Nomads of the Balkans, an account of Life and Customs among the Vlachs of Northern Pindus* (London, 1914), p. 101.

52. I.M. Akamatis, 'The Cemetery in the Agora District' in Lilibaki-Akamati, Akamatis, Chrysostomou and Chrysostomou (eds.), *The Archaeological Museum of Pella*, pp. 40, 42.

53. Democritus, DK 68 B 275 (trans. K. Freeman, *Ancilla to the Pre-Socratic Philosophers* (Harvard, 1948), p. 116 (275)).

54. Soranus, *Gynecology* 2.6.10.

55. For rituals surrounding childbirth and infancy see V. Dasen, 'Childbirth and Infancy in Greek and Roman Antiquity' in B. Rawson (ed.), *A Companion to Families in the Greek and Roman World* (Malden (MA), Chichester and Oxford, 2011), pp. 291–314; R. R. Hamilton, 'Sources for the Athenian Amphidromia' in *Greek, Roman and Byzantine Studies*, Vol. 25 (1984), pp. 243–51; S. Hitch, 'From birth to death: life changing rituals' in E. Eidinow and J. Kindt (eds.), *The Oxford Handbook of Ancient Greek Religion* (Oxford, 2015), pp. 521–34.

56. S. Psoma, 'Naming the Argeads' in *KTÈMA*, Vol. 40 (2015), pp. 15–26.

57. Athenaeus, *Learned Banqueters* 4.129a, 10.434a–b, Aelian, *Historical Miscellany* 12.26 (Proteas).

58. Euripides, *Medea* 237–41 (trans. J. Morwood, Oxford World's Classics).

59. Strabo, *Geography* 7.7.8.

60. M.B. Hatzopoulos (ed.), *Macedonia: From Philip to the Roman Conquest* (Princeton, 1994), pp. 108–9, *Cultes et rites de passage en Macédoine. Meletemata* 19 (Athens, 1994), pp. 63–72.

61. F. Graf and S. Iles Johnston, *Ritual Texts for the Afterlife: Orpheus and the Bacchic Gold Tablets* (London and New York, 2007), pp. 40–45; M.W. Dickie, 'The Dionysiac Mysteries in Pella' in *Zeitschrift für Papyrologie und Epigraphik*, Bd. 109 (1995), pp. 81–6.

62. E.R. Dodds, *Euripides: Bacchae* (Oxford, 1944), p. xliv.

63. Poseidippus, AB 44. See J.N. Bremmer, 'A Macedonian Maenad in Posidippus (AB 44)', in *Zeitschrift für Papyrologie und Epigraphik*, Bd. 155 (2006), pp. 37–40.

64. Athenaeus, *Learned Banqueters* 5.198e, Polyaenus, *Stratagems* 4.1.1.

65. Athenaeus, *Learned Banqueters* 13.560f. Pseudo-Callisthenes, *Greek Alexander Romance* (3.22) compares Olympias to Kandake, queen of the African kingdom of Meroe, 'a woman above normal human size and of an almost godlike in appearance.' A third-century AD votive stele, currently in the Florina Archaeological Museum, is thought to depict Olympias, Alexander and Philip, with Olympias towering over the other two. See A. Rizakis and J. Touratsoglou, *Inscriptions of Upper Macedonia* (1985), p. 137, no. 148.

66. Plutarch, *Life of Alexander* 2.5. For Olympias and her association with the cult of Dionysos see Carney, *Olympias: Mother of Alexander the Great*, pp. 88–103.

67. Euripides, *Bacchae* 102–4, 698, 768.

68. Demosthenes, *On the Crown* 18.259–60.

69. Cicero, *On Divination* 2.135, alludes to one of Olympias' pet snakes. For surviving snake customs in Greece and the Balkan, see E.J. Håland, 'Saints and Snakes: Death, Fertility and Healing in Modern and Ancient Greece and Italy' in *Performance and Spirituality*, Vol. 2 No. 1 (2011), pp. 123–4; M. MacDermott, *Bulgarian Folk Customs* (London and Philadelphia, 1998), p. 66.

70. Lucian, *Alexander the False Prophet* 6–8.

71. Athenaeus, *Learned Banqueters* 13.557b.

72. Whether Satyrus' list is in chronological order is still debated. For discussion on the order of wives see A.M. Prestianni Giallombardo, "Diritto' matrimoniale, ereditario e dinastico nella Macedonia di Filippo II' in *Rivista storica dell'antichità*, Vol. 6–7 (1976–7), pp. 81–110; A. Tronson, 'Satyrus the Peripatetic and the Marriages of Philip' in *The Journal of Hellenistic Studies*, Vol. 104 (1984), pp. 116–26; E.D. Carney, *Women and Monarchy in Macedonia* (Oklahoma, 2000); M.B. Hatzopoulos, *Ancient Macedonia. Trends in Classics – Key Perspectives on Classical Research* (Berlin/Boston, 2020), pp. 138–42.

73. Polyaenus, *Stratagems* 8.60 (Illyrian queens), 8.44 (Thessalian aristocratic women – female founder in Thessaly), 6.1.2–5 (Jason of Pherai's exceptionally rich mother and her slaves; for discussion see M. Mili, *Religion and Society in Ancient Thessaly* (Oxford, 2015), pp. 79–85); Carney, *Olympias: Mother of Alexander the Great*, pp. 7–8, P. Cabanes, 'La place de la femme dans l'Épire antique, in *Iliria*, Vol. 13 No. 2 (1983), pp. 193–269 (Epeirote women).

74. For a general account of royal women in Macedonia see Carney, *Women and Monarchy in Macedonia* and 'Macedonian Women' in J. Roisman and I. Worthington (eds.), *A Companion to Ancient Macedonia* (Malden (MA), Chichester and Oxford, 2010), pp. 409–27; A. Kottaridi, 'Queens, princesses and high-priestesses: the role of women at the Macedonian court' in *Heracles to Alexander the Great. Treasures from the Royal Capital of Macedon, a Hellenic Kingdom in the Age of Democracy* (Oxford, 2011), pp. 93–126 and 'Women in Macedonia' in *Alexander the Great: Treasures from an Epic Era of Hellenism* (New York, 2004), pp. 89–114; S. Le Bohec-Bouhet, 'Réflexions sur la place de la femme dans la Macédoine antique' in A.-M. Guimier-Sorbets, M.B. Hatzopoulos and Y. Morizot (eds.), *Rois, cités, necropoles: institutions, rites et monuments en Macédoine. Actes des colloques de Nanterre (décembre 2002) et d'Athènes (janvier 2004). Meletemata* 45 (Athens, 2006), pp. 187–98.

75. Eurydike is often called Illyrian in the ancient sources but this is a likely slander as her father's name, Sirras, is a Lynkestian name and not attested in Illyria.

76. Justin, *Epitome* 7.4.5–7, 7.5.4–5 (the bad Eurydike); Aeschines, *On the Embassy* 2.26–9, Cornelius Nepos, *Iphicrates* 3.2 (the good).

77. See E.D. Carney, *Eurydice and the Birth of Macedonian Power* (Oxford, 2019); K. Mortensen, 'Eurydice: Demonic or Devoted Mother?' in *Ancient History Bulletin*, Vol. 6 (1992), pp. 156–71.

78. R.J. Lane Fox 'The 360's' in R.J. Lane Fox (ed.), *Brill's Companion to Ancient Macedon* pp. 261–2.

79. Plutarch, *Moralia* 401b, Justin, *Epitome* 9.7.13 (Myrtale). For discussion of the name changes see Carney, *Olympias: Mother of Alexander the Great*, pp. 93–6; G.H. Macurdy, *Hellenistic Queens: A study of woman-power in Macedonia, Seleucid Syria, and Ptolemaic Egypt* (Baltimore and London, 1932), p. 24; K. Mortensen, *Olympias: Royal Wife and Mother at the Macedonian Court* (University of Queensland Diss, 1997), p. 34. An alternative source for Olympias' new name was her devotion to the Olympian gods.

80. Diodorus Siculus, *Library of History* 18.2.2 (trans. R.M. Greer, Loeb 377). The Heidelberg Epitome says that Arrhidaios had epilepsy as well as a learning disability; see P. Wheatley, 'The Heidelberg Epitome: a Neglected Diadoch Source' in V. Alonso Troncoso and E.M. Anson (eds.), *After Alexander: The Time of the Diadochi (323–281 BC)* (Oxford, 2013), pp. 17–29. For further discussion of Arrhidaios' condition, see W.S. Greenwalt, 'The Search for Arrhidaeus' in *Ancient World*, Vol. 10 (1984), pp. 69–77; E.D. Carney, 'The Trouble with Philip Arrhidaeus' in *Ancient History Bulletin*, Vol. 15.2 (2001), pp. 63–89; G. Squillace, 'Olympias' Pharmaka? Nature, Causes, Therapies and Physicians of Arrhidaeus' Disease' in M. D'Agostini, E.M. Anson and F. Pownall (eds.), *Affective Relations and Personal Bonds in Hellenistic Antiquity: Studies in Honour of Elizabeth D. Carney* (Oxford and Philadelphia, 2020), pp. 51–61.

81. Plutarch, *Life of Alexander* 77.5 (trans. B. Perrin, Loeb 99).

82. E. Voutiras, *Marital Life and Magic in Fourth Century Pella* (Amsterdam, 1998).

83. Pliny the Elder, *Natural History* 7.124 and Athenaeus, *Learned Banqueters* 6.248f (Philip's eye injury). Also discussed in A.S. Riginos, 'The Wounding of Philip II of Macedon: Fact and Fabrication' in *The Journal of Hellenistic Studies*, Vol. 114 (1994), pp. 103–19.

84. Plutarch, *Life of Alexander* 9.3.

85. Arrian, *Anabasis of Alexander* 7.12.6.

86. See previous note.

87. Plutarch, *Life of Alexander* 39.7.

2 MEET THE MACEDONIANS

1. Herodotus, *Histories* 7.129. According to another tradition Herakles was responsible for opening up the pass; see Diodorus Siculus, *Library of History* 4.18.6–7, Lucan, *Civil War* 6.343–9.
2. Aelian, *Historical Miscellany* 3.1, Plutarch, *Moralia* 293c, Ovid, *Metamorphoses* 1.450–569.
3. Ovid, *Metamorphoses* 1.555–60 (trans. D. Raeburn, Penguin).
4. For the geography of ancient Macedonia and its natural resources, see N.G.L. Hammond, *A History of Macedonia, Vol. I: Historical Geography and Prehistory* (Oxford, 1972); C.G. Thomas, 'The Physical Kingdom' in J. Roisman and I. Worthington (eds.), *A Companion to Ancient Macedonia* (Malden (MA), Chichester and Oxford, 2010), pp. 65–80; E.N. Borza, *In the Shadow of Olympus: The Emergence of Macedon* (Princeton, 1990), pp. 23–57 and 'The Natural Resources of Early Macedonia' in W. Lindsay Adams and E.N. Borza (eds.), *Philip II, Alexander the Great and the Macedonian Heritage* (Washington, 1982), pp. 1–20; M. Girtzy, *Historical Topography of Ancient Macedonia: Cities and other Settlement-sites in the Late Classical and Hellenistic Period* (Thessaloniki, 2001).
5. Plutarch, *Moralia* 178b (trans. F. Cole Babbitt, Loeb 245).
6. For the Macedonian accent and pronunciation, see Pausanias, *Description of Greece* 4.29.3 and Plutarch, *Moralia* 292d–f ('b' and 'ph'). For discussion of language see M.B. Hatzopoulos, *La Macédoine. Géographie historique, langue, cultes et croyances, institutions* (Paris, 2006), pp. 47–8, 'Macedonia and Macedonians' in R.J. Lane Fox (ed.), *Brill's Companion to Ancient Macedon. Studies in the Archaeology and History of Macedon, 650 BC–300 AD* (Leiden and Boston, 2011), p. 44, 'Recent Research in the Ancient Macedonian Dialect. Consolidation and New Perspectives' in G.K. Giannakis, E. Crespo and P. Filos (eds.), *Studies in Ancient Greek Dialects: From Central Greece to the Black Sea. Trends in classics – Supplementary volumes*, 49 (Berlin and Boston, 2018), pp. 299–328.
7. *The Greek Anthology* 6.335 (*kausia*); Demosthenes, *Third Philippic* (9) 31 (slaves).
8. Polyaenus, *Stratagems* 4.2.1 (bathing); Athenaeus, *Learned Banqueters* 1.17f (hunting); Aristotle, *Politics* 7.2 (1324b) (killing a man).
9. N.G.L. Hammond, *The Macedonian State: Origins, Institutions and*

History (Oxford, 1989); E.M. Anson, 'The Meaning of the Term Macedones' in *Ancient World*, Vol. 10 (1985), p. 12.

10. Hesiod, *Catalogue of Women* frag. 7 (Loeb 503), Hellanicus, frag. 74.

11. For recent discussions on ancient Macedonian ethnicity, see J. Engels, 'Macedonians and Greeks' in Roisman and Worthington (eds.), *A Companion to Ancient Macedonia*, pp. 81–98; M.B. Hatzopoulos, 'Macedonians and other Greeks' in Lane Fox (ed.), *Brill's Companion to Ancient Macedon*, pp. 51–78, and 'Perception of Self and the Other: The Case of Macedon' in I.D. Stefanidis, V. Vlasidis and E. Kofos (eds.), *Macedonian Identities through Time: Interdisciplinary Approaches* (Thessaloniki, 2008), pp. 39–52; J. Hall, 'Contested Ethnicities: Perceptions of Macedonia within Evolving Definitions of Greek Identity' in I. Malkin (ed.), *Ancient Perceptions of Greek Ethnicity. Center for Hellenic Studies Colloquia* 5 (Harvard, 2001), pp. 159–86.

12. Herodotus, *Histories* 8.137–8.

13. See C.J. King, *Ancient Macedonia* (London and New York, 2018), pp. 14–17; S. Sprawski, 'The Early Temenid Kings to Alexander I' in Roisman and Worthington (eds.), *A Companion to Ancient Macedonia*, pp. 127–43, and 'Argead terminology' in W. Heckel, J. Heinrichs, S. Müller and F. Pownall (eds.), *Lexicon of Argead Makedonia* (2020), pp. 100–1.

14. For possible explanations of the addition and dating of the Karanos insertion, see W. Greenwalt, 'The Introduction of Caranus into the Argead King List' in *Greek, Roman and Byzantine Studies*, Vol. 26 (1985), pp. 43–9; G. Mallios, *Myth and History: The Case of Ancient Macedonia* (Aristotle University of Thessaloniki Diss., 2011), p. 192; J.C. Yardley and W. Heckel, *Justin: Epitome of the Philippic History of Pompeius Trogus* (Oxford, 1997), pp. 83, 98; S. Müller, 'The Symbolic Capital of the Argeads' in S. Müller, T. Howe, H. Bowden and R. Rollinger (eds.), *The History of the Argeads: New Perspectives* (Wiesbaden, 2017), pp. 183–98.

15. Justin, *Epitome* 7.1.7–12, Clement of Alexandria, *Protrepticus* 2.11 (Scholia).

16. Diodorus Siculus, *Library of History* 7.16.

17. Herodotus, *Histories* 1.56; M.B. Hatzopoulos, 'Herodotus (8.137–8), The Manumissions from Leukopetra, and the Topography of the Middle Haliakmon Valley' in P. Derow and R. Parker (eds.), *Herodotus and his World: Essays from a Conference in Memory of George Forrest* (Oxford, 2003), pp. 201–18.

18. The prehistoric tumuli cemetery of Aigai was excavated between 1949 and 1960 by Manolis Andronikos, a further season of excavation following in 1960–1 under the direction of Photias Petsas. See M. Andronikos, *An early Iron Age cemetery at Vergina, near Beroea* (in Greek) (Thessaloniki, 1961). An English summary of the finds can be found in M. Andronicos, *Vergina: The Royal Tombs and the Ancient City* (Athens, 1992), pp. 25–30. For Petsas' excavations see A. Bräuning and I. Kilian-Dirlmeier, *Die eisenzeitlichen Grabhügel von Vergina. Die Ausgrabungen von Photis Petsas 1960–1961* (Mainz, 2013).

19. Thucydides, *Peloponnesian War* 2.99–100.

20. There is a debate on whether the burials from around the Thermaic Gulf represent the local aristocracy or Macedonians. The former is more likely. For an overview and bibliography, see M.B. Hatzopoulos, *Ancient Macedonia. Trends in Classics – Key Perspectives on Classical Research* (Berlin/Boston, 2020), pp. 11–33. The finds from Archontikon are currently on display in the Pella Archaeological Museum.

21. I. Graekos, 'Trade and Exchange in the Macedonian Court' in *Heracles to Alexander the Great: Treasures from the Royal Capital of Macedon, a Hellenic Kingdom in the Age of Democracy* (Oxford, 2011), p. 68.

22. Justin, *Epitome* 7.2.6–12 (Aeropos); Herodotus, *Histories* 5.18–21, 9.45, Speusippus, *Letter to Philip* 3, Justin, *Epitome* 7.3.1–7 (Alexander I killing Persian envoys and helping Greeks at Plataia).

23. Quintus Curtius, *History of Alexander* 3.6.17.

24. Plutarch, *Life of Alexander* 5.4.

25. Polyaenus, *Stratagems* 8.60, Athenaeus, *Learned Banqueters* 13.560f (Kynnane). Olympias also supervised the education of her grandson Alexander IV, who was born after Alexander the Great's death: Diodorus Siculus, *Library of History* 18.49.4, 57.2.

26. Jerome, *Letters* 107.4.

27. Diodorus Siculus, *Library of History* 19.52.4.

28. Suda s.v. 'Leonnatos' (Leonnatos), Suda s.v. 'Marsyas' (Marsyas); Aelian, *Historical Miscellany* 12.26 (Proteas); Quintus Curtius, *History of Alexander* 3.12.16 (Hephaistion). Scholars often add other individuals such as Ptolemy, Lysimachos, Seleukos, Nikanor and Perdikkas to the group, but it is not known if they were Alexander's *syntrophoi* or later childhood friends. See W. Heckel, *The Marshals of Alexander's Empire* (London and New York, 1992); V. Alonso Troncoso, 'La *Paideia* del príncipe en el tiempo de los diádocos' in *Ancient History Bulletin*, Vol. 14.1

(2000), pp. 22–34; C.G. Thomas, *Alexander the Great in his World* (Malden (MA), Oxford and Victoria (Aus), 2007), p. 146.

29. Quintus Curtius, *History of Alexander* 5.2.20 (sisters' gift of clothes to Alexander).

30. Plutarch, *Life of Alexander* 22.5, *Moralia* 127b, 180a, 1099c.

31. Plutarch, *Life of Alexander* 25.4–5 (trans. author); J.R. Hamilton, *Plutarch: Alexander: A Commentary* (Oxford, 1969), p. 66. The incident is also mentioned in Plutarch, *Moralia* 179e–f, Pliny the Elder, *Natural History* 12.62.

32. A version of the *Alexander Romance* alludes to a weapons master in a list of young Alexander's tutors. See A.E. Samuel, 'The Earliest Elements in the Alexander Romance' in *Historia: Zeitschrift für Alte Geschichte*, Bd. 35 H. 4 (1986), pp. 427–37.

33. For education in ancient Greece, see H.I. Marrou, *A History of Education in Antiquity* (Wisconsin and London, 1956); F.G.A. Beck, *Greek Education 450–350 BC* (Oxford and New York, 1964); W.M. Bloomer (ed.), *A Companion to Ancient Education* (Malden (MA), Chichester and Oxford, 2015); M. Joyal, I. McDougall and J. C.Yardley (eds.), *Greek and Roman Education: A Sourcebook* (London and New York, 2009).

34. Aelian, *Historical Miscellany* 14.11 (trans. N.G. Wilson, Loeb 486), also Suda s.v. 'Philiskos'. Pseudo-Callisthenes, *Greek Alexander Romance* 1,13, mentions another grammarian, Polyneikes of Pella.

35. Aelian, *Historical Miscellany* 3.32 (trans. N.G. Wilson, Loeb 486), Pseudo-Callisthenes, *Greek Alexander Romance* 1.13.

36. Stobaeus, *Anthology* 4.205 Nr. 115, (Menaichmos, variations of this name are found in the *Greek Alexander Romance* 1.13); Suda, s.v. 'Anaximenes', *Greek Alexander Romance* 1.13 (Anaximenes).

37. W.A. Johnson, 'Learning to Read and Write' in Bloomer (ed.), *A Companion to Ancient Education*, pp. 137–48; R. Cribiore, *Gymnastics of the Mind: Greek Education in Hellenistic and Roman Egypt* (Princeton, 2001).

38. For the rhapsode and his performance in antiquity see J.M. González, *The Epic Rhapsode and his Craft: Homeric Performance in a Diachronic Perspective* (Washington, 2013); J.L. Ready and C.C. Tsagalis, *Homer in Performance: Rhapsodes, Narrators, and Characters* (Texas, 2018); R. Scodel, 'The story-teller and his audience' in R.L. Fowler (ed.), *The Cambridge Companion to Homer* (Cambridge, 2004).

39. Homer, *Iliad* 1.1–9 (trans. R. Fagles, Penguin).

40. Dio Chrysostom, *Orations* 4.39, Plutarch, *Life of Alexander* 8.2.

41. Homer, *Iliad* 3.217 (trans. R. Fagles, Penguin), Plutarch, *Moralia* 331c (favourite line). For Alexander and Achilles see R. Lane Fox, *Alexander the Great* (London, 1973), pp. 59–67; W. Ameling, 'Alexander und Achilleus: Eine Bestandsaufnahme' in W. Will and J. Heinrichs (eds.), *Zu Alexander der Grosse. Festschrift G. Wirth zum 60. Geburtstag am 9.12.86* (Amsterdam, 1988), pp. 657–92; A. Cohen, 'Alexander and Achilles – Macedonians and "Mycenaeans"' in J.B. Carter and S.P. Morris (eds.), *Ages of Homer* (Texas, 1995), pp. 483–505; W. Heckel, 'Alexander, Achilles, and Heracles: Between Myth and History' in P. Wheatley and E. Baynham (eds.), *East and West in the World Empire of Alexander: Essays in Honour of Brian Bosworth* (Oxford, 2015), pp. 21–33.

42. Homer, *Iliad* 11.783–4 (trans. A.T. Murray and W. F. Wyatt, Loeb 170) (Peleus to his son Achilles).

43. Arrian, *Anabasis of Alexander* 7.14.4–5, Dio Chrysostom, *Discourses* 2.33.

44. Plutarch, *Life of Alexander* 5.4.

45. Plutarch, *Life of Alexander* 24.6–8.

46. Pelagonia was another canton, to the north of Lynkestis; Derriopos was likely part of Pelagonia. Tymphaia was coupled with Parauaia. Atintania and Dassaretis are sometimes also included in the list of cantons by scholars. See M. Girtzy, *Historical Topography of Ancient Macedonia: Cities and other Settlement-Sites in the late Classical and Hellenistic Period* (Thessaloniki, 2001); N.G.L. Hammond, *A History of Macedonia, Vol. I*; Hatzopoulos, *Ancient Macedonia*, pp. 43–8.

47. Livy, *History of Rome* 45.30.6–7 (trans. A.C. Schlesinger, Loeb 396).

48. A.J.B. Wace and A.M. Woodward, 'Inscriptions from Upper Macedonia' in *Annual of the British School at Athens*, Vol. 18 (1911–12), p. 167.

49. For more information on the region's archaeology and ancient sites, see A.G. Vlachopoulos and D. Tsiafaki (eds.), *Archaeology: Macedonia and Thrace* (in Greek) (Athens, 2017).

50. M.W. Leake, *Travels in Northern Greece, Vol. III* (London, 1835), pp. 304–5; L.A. Heuzey, *Mission archéologique de Macédoine* (Paris, 1976), pp. 285–98.

51. For the history of the excavations and site guide in English, see G. Karamitrou-Mentessidi, 'Aiani – Historical and Geographical Context' in Lane Fox (ed.), *Brill's Companion to Ancient Macedon*, pp. 93–112,

and the Greek Ministry of Culture's archaeological guide, G. Karamitrou-Mentessidi, *Aiani* (Athens, 1996).

52. Many of these finds are currently on display in the Aiani Archaeological Museum.

53. Elimeia had a Trojan foundation myth (Stephanus of Byzantium, s.v. 'Elimeia'). The Orestians claimed descent from the Greek hero Orestes (Strabo, *Geography* 7.7.8), the Lynkestians from the Corinthian Bakchiads (Strabo, *Geography* 7.7.8). For further discussion see I.K. Xydopoulos, 'Upper Macedonia' in M. Tiverios, P. Nigdelis and P. Adam-Veleni (eds.), *Threpteria: Studies on Ancient Macedonia* (Thessaloniki, 2012), pp. 520–39.

54. J.R. Ellis, *Philip II and Macedonian Imperialism* (Princeton, 1976), p. 38.

55. G. Karamitrou-Mentessidi, *Voion – Southern Orestis: Archaeological and Historical Topography* (in Greek with English summary) (Thessaloniki, 1999).

56. Thucydides, *Peloponnesian War* 2.100 (Perdikkas II's cavalry raids and Archelaos' reforms), 4.124–8 (retreat against Lynkestians and Illyrians); Diodorus Siculus, *Library of History* 16.2.5 (defeat of Perdikkas III). See also Xenophon, *Hellenica* 5.2.40–42.

57. Diodorus Siculus, *Library of History* 16.3.1–2.

58. This development is mentioned among a number of reforms attributed to Alexander by a fragment of Anaximenes of Lampsakos, frag. 4 Which Alexander he is referring to has long been a subject of debate among scholars, but Alexander the Great is the most likely, being the only Alexander who needed no qualification. But Anaximenes is probably guilty of combining a number of earlier developments, attributing them to the most famous Macedonian king. That the original subdivision of the army took place under Philip is probable. See N.G.L. Hammond and G.T. Griffith, *A History of Macedonia, Vol. II 550–336 BC* (Oxford, 1979), pp. 406–49, 705–13, esp. pp. 419–20.

59. Frontinus, *Stratagems* 4.1.6.

60. Polyaenus, *Stratagems* 4.2.10.

61. Demosthenes, *Third Philippic* (9) 50–1.

62. The *sarissa*'s length varied over time, Theophrastus, *Enquiry into Plants* 3.12.2 says 12 cubits (18ft), while Asclepiodotus, *Tactics* 5.1 says 10 cubits (15ft). See N. Sekunda, 'The *Sarissa*' in *Acta Universitatis Lodziensis: Folia archaeologica*, Vol. 23 (2001), pp. 13–41.

63. The only reference to the size of the Macedonian shield is Asclepiodotus, *Tactics* 5.1 which says 8 palms (24 inches) in diameter.

64. Diodorus Siculus, *Library of History* 16.3, Arrian, *Anabasis of Alexander* 1.6.1. On the use of the *sarissa*, see N.G.L. Hammond, 'Training in the Use of the Sarissa and its Effect in Battle, 359–333 BC' in *Antichthon*, Vol. 14 (1980), pp. 53–63.

65. Plutarch, *Life of Aemilius Paulus*, 19.3–4.

66. Polybius, *Histories* 18.31.2–6, Plutarch, *Life of Aemilius Paulus* 16, Livy, *History of Rome* 44.37.11.

67. The term bodyguard is used to describe various units in the Macedonian army/court. See W. Heckel, *The Marshals of Alexander's Empire* (London and New York, 1993) and 'Somatophylakia: A Macedonian cursus honorum' in *Phoenix*, Vol. 40 (1986), pp. 279–94. Two of the seven, attested during Alexander's reign, slept in the royal chamber at night (Quintus Curtius, *History of Alexander* 8.6.22).

68. King, *Ancient Macedonia*, pp. 15, 32.

69. W. Heckel, J. Heinrichs, S. Müller and F. Pownall, *Lexicon of Argead Makedonia* (Berlin, 2020), pp. 109–14.

70. Aelian, *Tactics* 18.51.

71. R.E. Gaebel, *Cavalry Operations in the Ancient World* (Oklahoma, 2002), p. 31.

72. Diodorus Siculus, *Library of History* 16.4.4 (Bardylis, 359 BC), 16.85.5 (Chaironeia, 338 BC).

73. For more information on the Macedonian army see W. Heckel and R. Jones, *Macedonian Warrior: Alexander's Elite Infantrymen* (Oxford and New York, 2006); N. Sekunda, *The Army of Alexander the Great* (Oxford and New York, 1984) and 'The Macedonian Army' in Roisman and Worthington (eds.), *A Companion to Ancient Macedonia*, pp. 446–71; D. Karunanithy, *The Macedonian War Machine: Neglected aspects of the armies of Philip, Alexander and the Successors (359–281 BC)* (Barnsley, 2013); C.A. Matthew, *An Invincible Beast: Understanding the Hellenistic Pike-Phalanx at War* (Barnsley, 2015).

74. A number of large country houses, from Pieria to the Strymon, were discovered during the construction of the Egnatia highway. See P. Adam-Veleni, E. Poulaki and K. Tzanavari (eds.), *Ancient Country Houses on Modern Roads* (Athens, 2003).

75. Justin, *Epitome* 8.6.2 (trans. J.C. Yardley, American Philological Association).

76. M.B. Hatzopoulos, *Macedonian Institutions under the Kings. A Historical and Epigraphic Study (Vol. I) and Epigraphic Appendix (Vol. II). Meletemata* 22 (Athens, 1996), p. 482.

77. Athenaeus, *Learned Banqueters* 13.572d–e.

78. Theopompus, frags. 225b and 225a. Some believe that the figure is a scribal error for either 80 or 1,800, and that it may refer either to Philip's Companions or numbers of the Companion cavalry. See Hammond and Griffith, *A History of Macedonia, Vol. II*, pp. 395–7; J. Rzepka, 'How many Companions did Philip II have?' in *Electrum*, Vol. 19 (2012), pp. 131–5; Lane Fox, *Alexander the Great*, pp. 107–8 and 'Philip's and Alexander's Macedon' in Lane Fox (ed.), *Brill's Companion to Ancient Macedon*, p. 373.

79. Arrian, *Anabasis of Alexander* 4.12.14, Quintus Curtius, *History of Alexander* 5.1.42, 8.6.6.

80. The most thorough publication on the find is M. Tsimbidou-Avlonitou *The Macedonian Tombs of Phoinikas and Aghios Athanasios Thessaloniki* (in Greek but with English and Italian summaries (Athens, 2005).

81. Herodotus, *Histories* 5.17.

82. A.G. Zannis, *Le pays entre le Strymon et le Nestos: géographie et histoire (VIIe–IVe siècle avant J.-C.). Meletemata* 71 (Athens, 2014), pp. 194–202.

83. Seneca, *Natural Questions* 5.15.

84. Hatzopoulos, *Macedonian Institutions under the Kings Vol. I*, pp. 188–9, fn. 1, and 'Philippes' in J. Fournier (ed.), *Philippes, de la préhistoire à Byzance. Etudes d'archéologie et d'histoire. Bulletin de correspondance hellénique. Supplément* 55 (Athens, 2016), p. 104, and Ch. Koukouli-Chrysanthaki 'Philippi' in Lane Fox (ed.) *Brill's Companion to Ancient Macedon*, pp. 437–52.

85. Theophrastus, *On the Causes of Plants* 5.14.5–6.

86. Zannis, *Le pays entre le Strymon et le Nestos*, pp. 213–14.

87. Diodorus Siculus, *Library of History* 16.8.6.

88. For the dating of Philip's gold coinage, see Lane Fox, 'Philip's and Alexander's Macedon' in Lane Fox (ed.), *Brill's Companion to Ancient Macedon*, p. 368. For general discussion on Philip's coinage see K. Dahmen, 'The Numismatic Evidence' in Roisman and Worthington (eds.), *A Companion to Ancient Macedonia*, pp. 41–62; S. Kremydi, 'Coinage and Finance' in Lane Fox (ed.), *Brill's Companion to Ancient Macedon*, pp. 159–7; G. Le Rider, Le *monnayage d'argent et d'or de Philippe II frappé en Macédoine de 359 à 294* (Paris, 1977) and *Monnayage*

et finances de Philippe II, un état de la question. Meletemata 23 (Athens, 1996).

89. Hammond and Griffith, *A History of Macedonia, Vol. II*, pp. 438–44.
90. Diodorus Siculus, *Library of History* 16.53.3.
91. Diodorus Siculus, *Library of History* 16.54.3–4, Cicero, *Letters to Atticus* 1.16.12.
92. Athenaeus, *Learned Banqueters* 4.155b–f, 6.231b–c.
93. I.D. Loukopoulou, 'Macedonia in Thrace' in Lane Fox (ed.), *Brill's Companion to Ancient Macedon*, p. 470; D. Triantaphyllos, 'Excavations at the fort of Kalyva' (in Greek) in *Archaeological Work in Macedonia and Thrace, Vol. 2* (1988), pp. 443–58.
94. Arrian, *Anabasis of Alexander* 7.9.2–3. (trans. P.A. Brunt, Loeb 269).

3 GODS, WAR AND WINE

1. For excavations at the Pnyx and reconstructions of its various incarnations, see K. Kourouniotes and H.A. Thompson, 'The Pnyx in Athens: A study based on Excavations conducted by the Greek Archaeological Service' in *Hesperia: The Journal of the American School of Classical Studies at Athens*, Vol. 1 (1932), pp. 90–217; B. Forsén and G. Stanton (eds.), *The Pnyx in the History of Athens: Proceedings of an International Colloquium Organized by the Finnish Institute at Athens 7–9 October, 1994* (Athens, 1996); M.H. Hansen, *The Athenian Ecclesia, Vols. I and II* (Copenhagen, 1983 and 1989); S.I. Rotroff and J.K. Camp 'The Date of the Third Period of the Pnyx' in *Hesperia: The Journal of the American School of Classical Studies at Athens*, Vol. 65 No. 3 (1996), pp. 263–94.
2. On Demosthenes' upbringing and background, see I. Worthington, *Demosthenes of Athens and the Fall of Classical Greece* (Oxford, 2013), pp. 9–41; E. Badian, 'Demosthenes' rise to prominence' in I. Worthington (ed.), *Demosthenes: Statesman and Orator* (London, 2000), pp. 9–44; G. Martin (ed.), *The Oxford Handbook of Demosthenes* (Oxford, 2018).
3. Plutarch, *Life of Demosthenes* 7.1–2 (acting advice), 11.12 (exercises); *Moralia* 845a–b, Cicero, *Brutus* 142, Quintilian, *Institutes of Oratory* 11.3.6 ('Delivery, delivery, delivery').
4. For a detailed analysis of the speech see C. Wooten, *A Commentary on Demosthenes' Philippic I* (Oxford, 2008).

5. Demosthenes, *First Philippic* (4) 2–3 (trans. J.H. Vince, Loeb 238).

6. Aeschines, *Against Ctesiphon* (3) 167.

7. Demosthenes, *First Philippic* (4) 4 (trans. J.H. Vince, Loeb 238).

8. Demosthenes, *First Philippic* (4) 34, Harpocration, s.v. 'Sacred Trireme'.

9. On Philip's actions in Thessaly see D. Graninger, 'Macedonia and Thessaly' in J. Roisman and I. Worthington (eds.), *A Companion to Ancient Macedonia* (Malden (MA), Chichester and Oxford, 2010), p. 314; R.M. Errington, *A History of Macedonia* (Berkeley and Oxford, 1990), pp. 59–70.

10. Diodorus Siculus, *Library of History* 16.35.2, Polyaenus, *Stratagems* 4.2.38. Onomarchos had used an ingenious stratagem to counter the Macedonian phalanx. He positioned his mercenaries in front of a crescent-shaped mountain while concealing catapults on the nearby slopes. As the Macedonians advanced, the Phokians feigned retreat. Philip pursued, he was drawn into range and then hit by the artillery; in the confusion, Onomarchos' troops attacked, and the Macedonians fled in distress.

11. Diodorus Siculus, *Library of History* 16.35.2–3 (trans. C.L. Sherman, Loeb 389).

12. Polyaenus, *Stratagems* 4.2.38 (Philip retreating like a ram).

13. Justin, *Epitome of the Philippic History of Pompeius Trogus* 8.2.3.

14. J. Buckler, *Philip and the Sacred War* (Leiden, 1989), p. 75.

15. Diodorus Siculus, *Library of History* 16.35, 16.61.2, Eusebius, *Preparation for the Gospel* 8.14.33. Pausanias, *Guide to Greece* 10.2.5 preserves an alternative tradition whereby Onomarchos was killed by his own men.

16. Justin, *Epitome* 8.2.6 (trans. J.C. Yardley, American Philological Association).

17. Stephanus of Byzantium, s.v. 'Thessalonike', Diodorus Siculus, *Library of History* 19.35.5.

18. Demosthenes, *First Philippic* (4) 10–11 (trans. J.H. Vince, Loeb 238).

19. Demosthenes, *First Philippic* (4) 19 (trans. J.H. Vince, Loeb 238).

20. Demosthenes, *First Philippic* (4) 50.

21. Theopompus, frag. 127, Aesop, *Fables* 319.

22. Demosthenes, *Third Philippic* (9) 56, *On the False Embassy* 19.265.

23. Justin, *Epitome* 8.3.10.

24. Demosthenes, *Third Philippic* (9) 11.

25. Demosthenes, *First Olynthiac* (1) 5 (trans. J.H. Vince, Loeb 238).

26. Philochorus, frags. 49–51 relates that the first contingent consisted of 2,000 lightly armed troops (peltast mercenaries) and 38 triremes under

the command of Chares. The second was of 4,000 light infantry mercenaries, 18 triremes and 150 cavalry under Charidemos, which joined the
Olynthians to raid Poteidaia and Bottike. The last, comprising 2,000
Athenian hoplites, 17 triremes and 300 Athenian cavalry, were under
the ultimate control of Chares.

27. D.M. Robinson, *Excavations at Olynthus Part X: Metal and minor miscel-
laneous finds* (Baltimore, 1941), p. 421; J.W.I. Lee, 'Urban Combat at
Olynthus, in 348 BC' in P.W.M. Freeman and A. Pollard (eds.), *Fields
of Conflict: Progress and Prospect in Battlefield Archaeology. BAR* 958
(2001), p. 13.

28. Demosthenes *On the False Embassy* (19) 267. See also Diodorus Siculus,
Library of History 16.53.2.

29. Democritus, B230 D-K (trans K. Freeman, *Ancilla to the Pre-Socratic
Philosophers* (Harvard, 1948), p.112 (230)).

30. The months of the Macedonian calendar were as follows: Dios (October),
Apellaios (November), Audonaios (December), Peritios (January),
Dystros (February), Xandikos (March), Artemisios (April), Daisios
(May), Panemos or Panamos (June), Loos (July), Gorpiaios (August)
and Hyperberetaios (September). See M.B. Hatzopoulos, *Ancient
Macedonia. Trends in Classics – Key Perspectives on Classical Research*
(Berlin/Boston, 2020), p. 78. For Macedonian religion see M. Mari,
'Traditional Cults and Beliefs' in R.J. Lane Fox (ed.), *Brill's Companion
to Ancient Macedon. Studies in the Archaeology and History of Macedon,
650 BC–300 AD* (Leiden and Boston, 2011), pp. 453–66; P. Christesen and
S.C. Murray, 'Macedonian Religion' in Roisman and Worthington (eds.),
A Companion to Ancient Macedonia, pp. 428–45.

31. Livy, *History of Rome* 40.6.1–2 (Xandika purification rite). See also
Quintus Curtius, *History of Alexander* 10.9.11–3

32. Diodorus Siculus, *Library of History* 17.16.3–4. See M.B. Hatzopoulos
'Was Dion Macedonia's Religious Centre?' in P. Funke and M. Haake
(eds.) *Greek Federal States and their Sanctuaries: Identity and Integration.
Proceedings of an International Conference of the Cluster of Excellence
'Religion and Politics' held in Münster, 17.06. – 19.06.2010* (Stuttgart, 2013),
pp. 163–71; M. Mari, 'Le Olimpie macedoni di Dion tra Archelao e
l'età Romana' in *Rivista di filologia e di istruzione classica* 126.2 (1998),
pp. 137–69.

33. On the mountain sanctuary of Aghios Antonios see E. Voutiras, 'La
culte de Zeus en Macédoine avant la conquête romaine' in A.-M.

Guimier-Sorbets, M.B. Hatzopoulos, Y. Morizot (eds.) *Rois, cites, nécropoles: institutions, rites et monuments en Macédoine. Actes de Nanterre (décembre 2002). et d'Athènes (janvier 2004). Meletemata* 45 (Athens, 2006), pp. 333–46. Also Plutarch, *Moralia* frag. 191.

34. W.M. Leake, *Travels in Northern Greece, Vol. III* (London, 1835), p. 410.
35. For more information on Dion and its archaeology, see D. Pandermalis, *Dion: The Archaeological Site and the Museum* (Attika, 1997), *Discovering Dion* (Athens, 2000) and *Gods and Immortals at Olympus: Ancient Dion, City of Zeus* (New York, 2016).
36. Pandermalis, *Dion: The Archaeological Site and the Museum*, p. 17.
37. For Alexander and religion see L. Edmunds, 'The Religiosity of Alexander' in *Greek, Roman and Byzantine Studies*, Vol. 12 (1971), pp. 363–91; F.S. Niaden, 'Alexander the Great as a Religious Leader' in *The Ancient World*, Vol 42 No. 2 (2011), pp. 166–79, and *Soldier, Priest and God: A Life of Alexander the Great* (Oxford, 2018).
38. Marsyas of Pella, frag. 21.
39. On Aristandros of Telmessos see A. Nice, 'The Reputation of the "Mantis" Aristander' in *Acta Classica*, Vol. 48 (2005), pp. 87–102; C.A. Robinson, 'The Seer Aristander' in *American Journal of Philology*, Vol. 50 No. 2 (1929), pp. 195–7; M. Flower, *The Seer in Ancient Greece* (Berkeley, Los Angeles and London, 2008).
40. D. Pandermalis, 'New Discoveries at Dion' in M. Stamatopoulou and M. Yeroulanou (eds.), *Excavating Classical Culture. Recent Archaeological Discoveries in Greece. BAR* 1031 (Oxford, 2002), p. 99.
41. On the importance of feasts in Macedonian society see M. Mari, 'The Macedonian Background of Hellenistic Panegyreis and Public Feasting' in F. Van den Eijnde, J.H. Blok and R. Strootman (eds.), *Feasting and Polis Institutions. Mnemosyne Supplements* 414 (Leiden and Boston, 2018), pp. 297–314.
42. Diodorus Siculus, *Library of History* 16.55.1–2; Demosthenes, *On the False Embassy* 19.139 (slaves and cups).
43. Diodorus Siculus, *Library of History* 17.16.3–4.
44. Diodorus Siculus, *Library of History* 16.55.3–4, Aeschines, *On the Embassy* 2.156 (Satyros).
45. Athenaeus, *Learned Banqueters* 4.130b–c.
46. B. Barr-Sharrar, *The Derveni Krater: Masterpiece of Classical Greek Metalwork* (Princeton, 2008); P. Themelis and J. Touratsoglou, *The Tombs of Derveni* (in Greek with English summaries) (Athens, 1997).

47. On the importance of symposia in Macedonia see E.D. Carney, *King and Court in Ancient Macedonia: Rivalry, Treason and Conspiracy* (Swansea, 2015), pp. 225–64; A. Kottaridi, 'The Symposium' in D. Pandermalis (ed.), *Alexander the Great. Treasures from an Epic Era of Hellenism* (New York, 2004), pp. 65–88, and 'The Royal Banquet: a Capital Institution' in *Heracles to Alexander the Great: Treasures from the Royal Capital of Macedon, a Hellenic Kingdom in the Age of Democracy* (Oxford, 2011), pp. 167–80; N. Sawada, 'Social Customs and Institutions: Aspects of Macedonian Elite Society' in Roisman and Worthington (eds.), *A Companion to Ancient Macedonia*, pp. 392–9.

48. On drinking undiluted wine, see Diodorus Siculus, *Library of History* 16.87.1 (Philip); Athenaeus, *Learned Banqueters* 12.537 (Alexander).

49. Plutarch, *Life of Alexander* 70.1 says forty-one men died during one drinking competition in Asia.

50. Polybius, *Histories* 5.27.5–7, see W. Lindsay Adams, 'Macedonian Kingship and the right of petition' in *Ancient Macedonia*, Vol. 4 (1986), pp. 43–52.

51. Marsyas of Pella, frag. 11, Xenophon, *Anabasis* 6.1.1–16, Hesychius, *Lexicon* s.v. 'Karpaia'.

52. Diodorus Siculus, *Library of History* 16.87.1, Plutarch, *Life of Demosthenes* 20.3.

53. M.B. Hatzopoulos, *Macedonian Institutions under the Kings, Vol. 1. A Historical and Epigraphic Study. Meletemata* 22. (Athens, 1996), p. 129; S. le Bohec-Bouhet, 'The Kings of Macedon and the Cult of Zeus in the Hellenistic Period' in D. Ogden (ed.), *The Hellenistic World: New Perspectives* (Swansea, 2002), p. 45.

54. G. Karadedos, 'The Hellenistic Theatre at Dion' in *Ancient Macedonia*, Vol. 4 (1986), pp. 325–40; P. Adam-Veleni, *Theatre and Spectacle in Ancient Macedonia* (in Greek and French) (Thessaloniki, 2010), pp. 89–92; E. Moloney, 'Philippus in acie tutior quam in theatro fuit . . . (Curtius 9.6.25): The Macedonian Kings and Greek Theatre' in E. Csapo, H.R. Goette, J.R. Green and P. Wilson (eds.), *Greek Theatre in the Fourth Century BC* (Berlin and Boston, 2014), p. 240; L. Polacco, 'In Macedonia, sulle tracce di Euripe' in *Dioniso*, Vol. 56 (1986), pp. 17–30. The visible structure dates to Philip V's reign (*c.*200 BC), but it replaced an earlier structure going back to the late fifth century BC.

55. Plutarch, *Life of Alexander* 8.2–3.

56. Ammianus Marcellinus, *History* 16.5.4.

57. For Alexander's athletic competitions in Asia, see W. Lindsay Adams, 'The Games of Alexander the Great' in W. Heckel, L.A. Tritle and P. Wheatley (eds.), *Alexander's Empire: Formulation to Decay* (Claremont (CA), 2007), pp. 125–38. For theatrical performances and musical contests see B. Le Guen, 'Theatre, Religion, and Politics at Alexander's Travelling Royal Court' in Csapo et al. (eds.), *Greek Theatre in the Fourth Century BC*, pp. 249–74. See also L.A. Tritle, 'Alexander and the Greeks: Artists and Soldiers, Friends and Enemies' in W. Heckel and L.A. Tritle (eds.), *Alexander the Great: A New History* (Malden (MA), Chichester and Oxford, 2009), pp. 99–120.

58. Demosthenes, *Second Olynthiac* (2) 18–19 (trans. J.H. Vince, Loeb 238).

59. Aeschines, *On the Embassy* (2) 15–17.

60. Aeschines, *On the Embassy* (2) 97. Among the eleven envoys there were ten Athenians and one man representing the city's allies, Aglaocreon of Tenedos (Aeschines, *On the Embassy* (2) 20). For Aeschines' political career see E.M. Harris, *Aeschines and Athenian Politics* (Oxford, 1995).

61. Aeschines' *On the Embassy* (2) and Demosthenes' *On the False Embassy* (19) were delivered in 343 BC. Demosthenes had accused Aeschines of misconduct as an ambassador but failed to secure a conviction. Aeschines won the case by thirty votes. The embassies are also mentioned as part of a later court case in 330 BC: Aeschines, *Against Ctesiphon* (3) and Demosthenes, *On the Crown* (18).

62. Aeschines, *On the Embassy* (2) 34.

63. Aeschines, *On the Embassy* (2) 35 (trans. C.D. Adams, Loeb 106).

64. Plutarch, *Life of Demosthenes* 8.3.

65. Hermippus, frag. 63.8. For Amphipolis see Chapter 1.

66. Demosthenes, *On the False Embassy* (19) 235 (trans. C.A. Vince and J.H. Vince, Loeb 155).

67. Plutarch, *Life of Demosthenes* 16.4 (trans. B. Perrin, Loeb 99). See Aeschines, *On the Embassy* (2) 40–53.

68. Justin, *Epitome* 8.4.6.

69. Aeschines, *Against Timarchus* (1) 166–69 (the speech was delivered in spring 345 BC). See N. Fisher, *Aeschines: Against Timarchus* (Oxford, 2001), pp. 312–14.

70. Aeschines, *On the Embassy* (2) 112 (trans. C.D. Adams, Loeb 106).

71. Demosthenes, *On the Crown* (18) 32 (oath); *On the False Embassy* (19) 168 (prisoners).

72. Diodorus Siculus, *Library of History* 16.60.1–2.

73. Aeschines, *On the Embassy* (2) 142.

74. Diodorus Siculus, *Library of History* 16.60.1, Pausanias, *Guide to Greece* 10.3.1–3, Speusippus, *Letter to Philip* 8, Demosthenes, *Third Philippic* (9) 32.

75. Diodorus Siculus, *Library of History* 16.60.2, Demosthenes, *On the False Embassy* (19) 128.

76. Diodorus Siculus, *Library of History* 16.60.3.

77. Diodorus Siculus, *Library of History* 16.56.6–8; Pausanias, *Guide to Greece* 10.13.4. M. Scott, *Delphi: A History of the Center of the Ancient World* (Princeton and Oxford, 2014), p. 121 and 151; R. Meiggs and D. Lewis, *A Selection of Greek Historical Inscriptions to the End of the Fifth Century* BC (Oxford, 1988), no. 27.

78. Plutarch, *Life of Pericles* 1.5 (trans. I. Scott-Kilvert, Penguin).

4 FRIENDS

1. The story is recorded in Plutarch's *Life of Alexander* 6.1–5 (trans. I. Scott-Kilvert and T.E. Duff, Penguin – for following quotes). Pseudo-Callisthenes, *Greek Alexander Romance* 1.17, gives Alexander's age as fifteen when the event occurred, but an earlier age, around eleven, is more likely considering Philip's movements, as well as those of Demaratos of Corinth, who is associated with the story. See R. Lane Fox, *Alexander the Great* (London, 1973), p. 47.

2. The price of thirteen talents is given by Plutarch, and corroborated by Aulus Gellius, *Attic Nights* 5.2, citing Chares, Alexander's later court chamberlain. Pliny, *Natural History* 8.154, suggests the higher figure of sixteen talents. Both are likely historical exaggerations.

3. J.K. Anderson, *Ancient Greek Horsemanship* (Berkeley, Los Angeles and Cambridge, 1961), p. 15.

4. The Alexander Mosaic at Pompeii and Tomb II's hunting frieze at Vergina (see Chapter 9) both depict Alexander's horse, probably Boukephalas, as bay or chestnut.

5. See for example Xenophon, *On Horsemanship* 9.1–12 (dealing with a spirited horse).

6. Diodorus Siculus, *Library of History* 17.76.6, Aulus Gellius, *Attic Nights* 5.2.

7. For names related to branding marks, see Arrian, *Anabasis of Alexander* 5.19.5, Pseudo-Callisthenes, *Greek Alexander Romance* 1.15, Tzetzes, *Book of Histories* 1.28 (story 28) and Suda, s.v. 'Koppa Branded'. Other traditions attribute the name Boukephalas to a white blaze on his muzzle that resembled an ox-head or to the fact that the width of his head was like that of an ox (Arrian, *Anabasis of Alexander* 5.19.5, Strabo, *Geography* 15.1.29). For Thessalian branding see A. Aston and J. Kerr, 'Battlefield and Racetrack: The Role of Horses in Thessalian Society' in *Historia: Zeitschrift für Alte Geschichte*, Bd. 67 (2018), p. 14. The Pharsalian brand of an ox-head corroborates Pliny's statement (*Natural History* 8.154) that Philoneikos was from Pharsalos in Thessaly.

8. Arrian, *Anabasis of Alexander* 5.19.4–5, Plutarch, *Life of Alexander* 61, Pliny, *Natural History* 8.154, Strabo, *Geography* 15.1.29, Aelian, *On Animals* 16.3, Suda, s.v. 'Koppa Branded'. See also A.R. Anderson 'Bucephalas and his Legend' in *The American Journal of Philology*, Vol. 51 No. 1 (1930), pp. 1–21.

9. Plutarch, *Life of Alexander* 7.1 (trans. B. Perrin, Loeb 99).

10. Thucydides, *Peloponnesian War* 4.88, 5.6.1. Also see K. Sismanidis, *Ancient Stageira: Birthplace of Aristotle* (Athens, 2003), p. 13.

11. Aristotle, *Metaphysics* Book Alpha 1 980a.

12. For recent biographies of Aristotle, see J.A. Barnes, *Aristotle: A Very Short Introduction* (Oxford, 2000), E. Hall, *Aristotle's Way: How Ancient Wisdom Can Change Your Life* (London, 2018), C. Natali, *Aristotle: His Life and School* (Princeton and Oxford, 2013).

13. Vita Marciana 6. He was also known as the 'Nous' (the mind or brain).

14. K. Sismanidis, *Ancient Stageira: Birthplace of Aristotle* (Athens, 2003), p. 88.

15. For Aristotle's stay on Lesbos, see A.M. Leroi, *The Lagoon: How Aristotle Invented Science* (London and New York, 2014).

16. Diodorus Siculus, *Library of History* 16.2.3, Dio Chrysostom, *Orations* 49.5.

17. Athenaeus, *Learned Banqueters* 506e, 508e. A story corroborated by Speusippus, *Letter to Philip* II 12, and Pseudo-Diogenes' *5th letter of Plato*.

18. Diogenes Laertius *Lives of Eminent Philosophers* 3.40, Aelian *Historical Miscellany* 4.19.

19. Plutarch, *Life of Alexander* 7.2. Also *Vita Marciana* 5.18.

20. Diogenes Laertius, *Lives of Eminent Philosophers* 5.4, Tzetzes, *Book of Histories* 7.41 (story 140).

21. Strabo, *Geography* 7 frag. 35; Sismanidis, *Ancient Stageira*, pp. 39–45, 73–5; 'Stageira' in W. Heckel, J. Heinrichs, S. Müller and F. Pownall (eds.), *Lexicon of Argead Makedonia* (Berlin, 2020), pp. 477–8.

22. The French scholar A.H. Chroust, for example, argues for the fallacy of the tradition. See *Aristotle: New Light on his Ideas and on some of his Lost Works, Vol. 1* (Paris, 1973). The legends are examined in M. Brocker, *Aristoteles als Alexanders Lehrer in der Legende* (Bonn Diss., 1966).

23. Homer, *Iliad* 14.226.

24. Plutarch, *Life of Alexander* 7.3.

25. Aelian, *On Animals* 15.1. See N.G.L. Hammond, 'The Location of the Trout-River Astraeus' in *Greek, Roman and Byzantine Studies*, Vol. 36 (1995), pp. 173–6.

26. Also attested by Pseudo-Callisthenes, *Greek Alexander Romance*, 1.16.

27. See A. Koukouvou and E. Psarra, 'The Agora of Ancient Mieza. The Public Face of an Important Macedonian City' in *The Agora in the Mediterranean from Homeric to Roman Times. International conference, Kos, 14-17 April 2011* (in Greek with English summary) (Athens, 2011), pp. 223–37.

28. Conversation with Angeliki Kottaridi.

29. Aelian, *Historical Miscellany* 4.19.

30. J.Barnes, *Aristotle* (Oxford and New York, 1982), p. 5.

31. For full discussion see N.G.L. Hammond, 'Royal Pages, and Boys Trained in the Macedonian Manner during the Period of the Temenid Monarchy' in *Historia: Zeitschrift für Alte Geschichte*, Bd. 39 H. 3 (1990), pp. 261–90, and *The Macedonian State: The Origins, Institutions and History* (Oxford, 1989), pp. 53–8; S. Psoma, 'Entre l'armee et l'Oikos: dans le royaume de Macedoine' in A.-M. Guimier-Sorbets, M.B. Hatzopoulos and Y. Morizot (eds.), *Rois, cités, nécropoles: institutions, rites et monuments en Macédoine. Actes des colloques de Nanterre, (décembre 2002) et d'Athènes, (janvier 2004). Meletemata 45* (Athens, 2004), pp. 285–99; R. Strootman, *Court and Elites in the Hellenistic Empires: The Near East after the Achaemenids c.330–30 BC* (Edinburgh, 2014), pp. 136–44; E.D. Carney, 'Elite Education and High Culture in Macedon' in E.D. Carney, *King and Court in Ancient Macedonia: Rivalry, Treason, and Conspiracy* (Swansea, 2015) pp. 191–205.

32. Hammond, 'Royal Pages, and Boys Trained in the Macedonian Manner during the Period of the Temenid Monarchy,' p. 266.

33. Justin, *Epitome of the Philippic History of Pompeius Trogus* 13.1.12.

34. Diodorus Siculus, *Library of History* 17.65.1, Quintus Curtius, *History of Alexander* 5.1.42. Other scholars estimate 80–200 pages in the overall system; see, for example, N.G.L. Hammond and G.T. Griffith, *A History of Macedonia Vol. II, 550–336 BC* (1979, Oxford), p. 401 (85 royal pages) and Hammond, 'Royal Pages, and Boys Trained in the Macedonian Manner during the Period of the Temenid Monarchy,' p. 266 (200 royal pages).
35. See Strootman, *Court and Elites in the Hellenistic Empires*, p. 137.
36. For an overview of gymnasia in Macedonia, see P. Gauthier and M.B. Hatzopoulos, *La loi gymnasiarchique de Béroia. Meletemata* 16 (Athens, 1993), pp. 155–72.
37. The Beroia gymnasiarchical law stele currently resides in the Veroia Archaeological Museum (SEG 27.261). For discussion see Gauthier and Hatzopoulos, *La loi gymnasiarchique de Béroia*. English translations of the stele's text can be found in M.M. Austin, *The Hellenistic World from Alexander to the Roman Conquest: A selection of Ancient Sources* (Cambridge, 2006), pp. 203–7 and S.G. Miller, *Arete: Greek Sports from Ancient Sources* (Berkeley, Los Angeles and London, 2004), pp. 137–42. The Amphipolis ephebarchical law stele can be seen in the Amphipolis Archaeological Museum. For an English translation see M.B. Hatzopoulos, *Macedonian Lawgiver Kings and the Young* (Athens, 2016), pp. 25–31, and for dating see pp. 31–3.
38. Hatzopoulos, *Macedonian Lawgiver Kings and the Young*, pp. 42–5.
39. Hatzopoulos, *Macedonian Lawgiver Kings and the Young*, p. 44 (Theopompus T31).
40. Polybius, *Histories* 12.22.5–6 (trans. W.R. Paton, F.W. Walbank and C. Habicht, Loeb 159), Plutarch, *Moralia* 334d (trans. F. Cole Babbitt, Loeb 305).
41. See A. Chaniotis, *War in the Hellenistic World. A Social and Cultural History* (Malden (MA), Oxford and Victoria (Aus), 2005), p. 98; B. Meißner, 'Early Greek Strategic and tactical teaching and literature' in P. Rance and N.V. Sekunda (eds.), *Greek Taktika: Ancient Military Writing and its Heritage. Proceedings of the International Conference on Greek Taktika held at the University of Toruń, 7–11 April 2005* (Gdańsk, 2017), pp. 65–78.
42. Pseudo-Callisthenes, *Greek Alexander Romance* 1.13 (Alexander and mock fights); Athenaeus, *Learned Banqueters* 1.19a, Plutarch, *Life of Alexander* 39.3, 73.7 (ball playing). See L. O'Sullivan, 'Playing Ball in Antiquity' in *Greece and Rome*, Vol. 59 No. 1 (2012), pp. 17–33.

43. M.B. Hatzopoulos, *Cultes et rites de passage en Macédoine. Meletemata* 19 (Athens, 1994), pp. 55–61.

44. Herodotus, *Histories* 5.22 (foot race). Justin, *Epitome to the Philippic History of Pompeius Trogus* 7.2.14 records that Alexander I participated in various events.

45. Plutarch, *Moralia* 331b (trans. F. Cole Babbitt, Loeb 305). This anecdote also appears in *Moralia* 179d and *Life of Alexander* 4.5–6. The suggestion for Alexander to take part in the Olympics is attributed both to Philip and Alexander's friends.

46. For Philip's fondness for wrestling see Polyaenus, *Stratagems* 4.2.6, Plutarch, *Moralia* 602d, *Life of Eumenes* 1.1.

47. Plutarch, *Life of Alexander* 4.6.

48. For Alexander and athletics see W.L. Adams, 'The Games of Alexander' in W. Heckel, L.A. Tritle and P. Wheatley (eds.), *Alexander's Empire: Formulation to Decay* (Claremont (CA), 2007), pp. 125–38; T.S. Brown, 'Alexander and Greek Athletics, in Fact and in Fiction' in K.H. Kinzl (ed.), *Greece and the Eastern Mediterranean in ancient history and prehistory. Studies presented to Fritz Schachermeyr on the occasion of his 80th birthday* (Berlin and New York, 1977), pp. 76–88; D. Lunt, 'The Thrill and the Avoidance of Defeat: Alexander as a Sponsor of Athletic Contests' in *Ancient History Bulletin*, Vol. 28 (2014), pp. 119–34.

49. Plutarch, *Life of Alexander* 4.4–5.

50. Diogenes Laertius, *Lives of Eminent Philosophers* 5.1, Aelian, *Historical Miscellany* 3.19.

51. Diogenes Laertius, *Lives of Eminent Philosophers* 5.19 (trans. R.D. Hicks, Loeb 184).

52. Aristotle, *The Art of Rhetoric* 7.2.12 (1389a) (trans. H.C. Lawson–Tancred, Penguin); Isocrates, *Discourses: Antidosis* (15) 265 (wits and wool-gathering).

53. Diogenes Laertius, *Lives of Eminent Philosophers* 5.18.

54. Diogenes Laertius, *Lives of Eminent Philosophers* 5.20 (trans. R.D. Hicks, Loeb 184).

55. Pseudo-Callisthenes, *Greek Alexander Romance*, 1.16 (trans. R. Stoneman, Penguin).

56. Aristocles, *On Philosophy* frag. 2. C. Natali, *Aristotle: His Life and School* (Princeton, 2013), p. 43 fn. 85; G. Anagnostopoulos (ed.), *A Companion to Aristotle* (Malden (MA), Chichester and Oxford, 2009), pp. 8–9 (differences in views).

57. Plutarch, *Life of Alexander* 8.3.

58. J.A. Barnes, *Cambridge Companion to Aristotle* (Cambridge, 1995), p. 12.

59. Diogenes Laertius, *Lives of Eminent Philosophers* 5.2.

60. *Vita Marciana* 23.

61. Aristotle, *Nicomachean Ethics* 1.3 (1095a) (trans. J.A.K. Thomson, Penguin).

62. Isocrates, *Letters: To Alexander (5)*. See P. Merlan, 'Isocrates, Aristotle and Alexander the Great' in *Historia: Zeitschrift für Alte Geschichte*, Bd. 3 H.1 (1954), pp. 60–81.

63. Cicero, *Tusculan Disputations* 1.4.7.

64. Plutarch, Life of Alexander 54.3 (trans. B. Perrin, Loeb 99), Euripides, *Bacchae* 260.

65. Plutarch, *Life of Alexander* 54.1–2 (trans. B. Perrin, Loeb 99).

66. Plutarch, *Life of Alexander* 53.4 (trans. B. Perrin, Loeb 99).

67. Plutarch, *Life of Alexander* 8.1.

68. See W. Greenwalt, 'Macedonia's Kings and the Political Usefulness of the Medical Arts' in *Ancient Macedonia*, Vol. 4 (1987), pp. 213–22; B. Antela-Bernárdez and C. Sierra Martín, 'Alexander and the Medicine' in *Karanos*, Vol. 1 (2018), pp. 35–54.

69. Herodotus, *Histories* 8.135.

70. For Aristotle's zoological research, see D'A.W. Thompson, *Historia Animalium* (Oxford, 1910); H.D.P. Lee, 'Place-Names and the Date of Aristotle's Biological Works' in *The Classical Quarterly* Vol. 42 No. 3/4 (1948), pp. 61–7; A.M. Leroi, *The Lagoon: How Aristotle Invented Science* (London and New York, 2014). A useful guide to Vermion's flora is N. Babos, *Native Plants and Herbs of Mount Vermion* (Thessaloniki, 2015).

71. Galen, 12.967; L.C. Watson, *Magic in Ancient Grece and Rome* (London and New York, 2019), p. 105.

72. The 17th Ephorate of Prehistoric and Classical Antiquities, *Ancient Theatre of Mieza* (Veria, 2014), pp. 24–5; P. Adam-Veleni, *Theatre and Spectacle in Ancient Macedonia* (in Greek and French) (Thessaloniki, 2010), pp. 92–5.

73. Dio Chrysostom, *Orations* 53.1. For Aristotle on Homer, see R. Mayhew, *Aristotle's Lost Homeric Problems* (Oxford, 2019); N.J. Richardson, 'Aristotle's Reading of Homer and its Background' in R. Lamberton and J.J. Keaney (eds.), *Homer's Ancient Readers: The Hermeneutics of Greek Epic's Earliest Exegetes* (Princeton, 1992).

74. Plutarch, *Life of Alexander* 8.2, 26.1–2, Pliny the Elder, *Natural History*

7.107–9. Strabo, *Geography* 13.1.27 suggests Alexander annotated his copy of the *Iliad* along with Anaxarchos and Kallisthenes. Chares of Mytilene, Alexander's chamberlain, states that the king's pillow was actually the treasury that lay close to the king's bed, a Persian custom adopted after Issos (Athenaeus, *Learned Banqueters* 12.514e–f). See C. Brunelle, 'Alexander's Persian Pillow and Plutarch's Cultured Commander' in *The Classical Journal*, Vol. 112 No. 3 (2017), pp. 257–78.

75. Isocrates, *Discourses: To Philip (5)* 68. (trans. G. Norlin, Loeb 209).

76. Aeschines, *Against Ctesiphon* (3) 132.

77. P. Briant, 'History and Ideology: The Greeks and Persian Decadence' in T. Harrison (ed.), *Greeks and Barbarians* (New York, 2002), pp. 193–210.

78. See K. Vlassopoulos, *Greeks and Barbarians* (Cambridge, 2013); E.S. Gruen, *Rethinking the Other in Antiquity* (Princeton and Oxford, 2011); E. Jensen, *Barbarians in the Greek and Roman World* (Indianapolis and Cambridge, 2018); J. Morgan, *Greek Perspectives on the Achaemenid Empire. Persia Through the Looking Glass* (Edinburgh, 2016).

79. P. Cartledge, *Alexander the Great: The Hunt for a New Past* (London, 2004), pp. 93–5.

80. M.J. Olbrycht, 'Macedonia and Persia' in J. Roisman and I. Worthington (eds.), *A Companion to Ancient Macedonia* (Malden (MA), Chichester and Oxford, 2010), pp. 343–4. In support of Persian influence on the Macedonian court, see D. Kienast, *Philipp II von Makedonien und das Reich der Achamieniden* (Munich, 1973); against see R. Lane Fox, 'Alexander the Great: "Last of the *Achaemenids*"' in C. Tupin (ed.), *Persian Responses: Political and Cultural Interaction with(in) the Achaemenid Empire* (2007, Swansea), pp. 267–311.

81. Isocrates, *Letters: To Philip 2* (3) 3.

82. Polybius, *Histories* 3.6.10–14 (trans. W.R. Paton, F.W. Walbank, C. Habicht, Loeb 137).

83. Didymus, *On Demosthenes* cols. 12–13.

84. Diodorus Siculus, *Library of History* 16.69.7–8.

85. Diodorus Siculus, *Library of History* 16.71.1, Justin, *Epitome* 8.6.3–8, Demosthenes, *On Halonnesus* (7) 32. For alternative dating of Arybbas' removal see R.M. Errington, 'Arybbas the Molossian' in *Greek, Byzantine and Roman Studies*, Vol. 16 (1975), pp. 41–50.

86. Plutarch, *Life of Alexander* 5.1–2 (trans. B. Perrin, Loeb 99). Also in Plutarch, *Moralia* 342b–c.

87. Diodorus Siculus, *Library of History* 16.52.3–4. Quintus Curtius, *History*

of Alexander 5.9.1, 6.5.2, (Artabazos and his family fled to Philip's court in 352 BC and stayed until the mid 340s BC). Other Asian visitors included the Persian Sisines (Quintus Curtius, *History of Alexander* 3.7.11) and the Parthian Amminapes (Quintus Curtius, *History of Alexander* 6.4.25).

88. See previous note.

89. Diodorus Siculus, *Library of History* 16.52.5–8. According to Strabo, *Geography* 13.1.57, Aristotle's move to Lesbos may have been because of Persian pressure on Atarneus.

90. Demosthenes, *Fourth Philippic* (10) 32 (341 BC).

91. Greek Lyric Poetry, Vol. 5, Aristotle, p. 214–17 (trans. D.A. Campbell, Loeb 144). The song is found in Didymus, *On Demosthenes* col. 6, Athenaeus, *Learned Banqueters* 15.696a–697b and Diogenes Laertius, *Lives of Eminent Philosophers* 5.7–8. For discussion see A.L. Ford, *Aristotle as Poet: The Song for Hermias and its Contexts* (Oxford, 2011).

92. Arrian, *Anabasis of Alexander* 2.3.1, 3.1.5 and 7.16.1–2.

93. For the beginnings of what we today know as geography see J. Brotton, *A History of the World in Twelve Maps* (London, 2012).

94. See Brotton, *A History of the World in Twelve Maps*, pp. 28–9.

95. Aristotle, *On Meteorology* 1.13 (350a).

96. Arrian, *Anabasis of Alexander* 5.26.1–2 (trans. P.A. Brunt, Loeb 269).

97. Arrian, *Anabasis of Alexander* 5.26.4–5 (trans. P.A. Brunt, Loeb 269).

98. Philostratus, *Life of Apollonius of Tyana* 2.43, Pliny, *Natural History* 6.62–3.

99. Valerius Maximus, *Memorable Doings and Sayings* 8.13 ext 2, Plutarch, *Moralia* 466d, Aelian, *Historical Miscellany* 4.29.

100. Arrian, *Anabasis of Alexander* 1.8.1–3 (Perdikkas at Thebes); Quintus Curtius, *History of Alexander* 8.1.15–16 (Lysimachos and the lion); Appian, *Syrian Wars* (11) 57 (294–5) (Seleukos and the bull); Quintus Curtius, *History of Alexander* 7.4.32–8, Arrian, *Anabasis of Alexander* 3.28.3 (Erigyios and the enemy).

101. Diogenes Laertius, *Lives of Eminent Philosophers* 5.20.

102. For Hephaistion's career see W. Heckel *Who's Who in the Age of Alexander and his Successors. From Chaironeia to Ipsos (338–301 BC)* (Havertown (PA) and Barnsley, 2021), pp. 214–19.

103. Quintus Curtius, *History of Alexander* 3.12.17 (trans. J.C. Rolfe, Loeb 368). Also Diodorus Siculus, *Library of History* 17.37.6, 17.114.2.

104. Plutarch, *Moralia* 180d, 333a, 340a.

105. Diodorus Siculus, *Library of History* 17.114.3 (trans. C. Bradford Welles, Loeb 422).

106. Epictetus, *Discourses* 2.22.17–18 and Aelian, *Historical Miscellany* 12.7 describe Hephaistion as Alexander's *eromenos* – a younger lover of the *erastes*. Diogenes, *Epistles* 24 says that Alexander was ruled by Hephaistion's thighs. However, none of these accounts are contemporary and they are of dubious trustworthiness.

107. Aeschines, *Against Timarchus* (1) 133, 141–154.

108. K. Mortensen, 'Homosexuality in the Macedonian Court and Philip's Murder' in *Ancient Macedonia*, Vol. 7 (2007), pp. 371–87.

109. Theopompus, frag. 225b.

110. D. Ogden, 'Alexander's Sex Life' in W. Heckel and L.A Tritle (eds.), *Alexander the Great: A New History* (Malden (MA), Chichester and Oxford, 2009), pp. 203–4.

111. Quintus Curtius, *History of Alexander* 10.5.32, Plutarch, *Life of Alexander* 4.4–5, Arrian, *Anabasis of Alexander* 7.28.2.

112. Athenaeus, *Learned Banqueters* 10. 435a.

113. Athenaeus, *Learned Banqueters* 10.435a (Kallixeina); Aelian, *Historical Miscellany* 12.34 (Pankaste); Plutarch, *Life of Alexander* 21.4 (Barsine).

114. On Alexander's relationships see Ogden, 'Alexander's Sex Life' in Heckel and Tritle (eds.), *Alexander the Great*, pp. 203–17.

115. Plutarch, *Life of Alexander* 22.3 (trans I. Scott-Kilvert and T. E. Duff, Penguin).

116. For the importance of hunting in Macedonia see W.S. Greenwalt, 'The Iconographical Significance of Amyntas III's Mounted Hunter Stater' in *Ancient Macedonia*, Vol. 5 (1989), pp. 509–19; E.D. Carney, 'Hunting and the Macedonian Elite: Sharing the Rivalry of the Chase (Arrian 4.13.1)' in E.D. Carney, *King and Court in Ancient Macedonia: Rivalry, Treason and Conspiracy* (Swansea, 2015), pp. 235–81; N. Sawada, 'Social Customs and Institutions: Aspects of Macedonian Society' in Roisman and Worthington (eds.), *A Companion to Ancient Macedonia*, pp. 392–408; I. Graekos, 'War and Hunting: the world of the Macedonian king and his companions' in *Heracles to Alexander the Great: Treasures from the Royal Capital of Macedon, a Hellenic Kingdom in the Age of Democracy* (Oxford, 2011), pp. 49–58.

117. Athenaeus, *Learned Banqueters* 1.17f–18a.

118. Xenophon, *On Hunting* (boar hunting 10.1–23).

119. Polyaenus, *Stratagems* 4.2.16.

120. Theopompus, frag. 340; see also Pliny the Elder, *Natural History* 8.149; E. Baynham, 'Alexander's Pets: Animals and the Macedonian Court' in D'Agostini, Anson and Pownall (eds.), *Affective Relations and Personal Bonds in Hellenistic Antiquity : Studies in Honour of Elizabeth D. Carney* (Oxford and Philadelphia, 2020), pp. 127–42.

121. Plutarch, *Life of Alexander* 61.1.

122. Xenophon, *On Hunting* 10.3.

123. Xenophon, *On Hunting* 10.11–12.

5 CAMPAIGN

1. Plutarch, *Life of Alexander* 9.1.

2. Plutarch, *Moralia* 178b.

3. Plutarch, *Life of Demetrius* 42.3.

4. Plutarch, *Moralia* 179c–d.

5. Diodorus Siculus, *Library of History* 17.117.3–4, 18.2.4 (ring as symbol of power).

6. Isocrates, *Discourses: To Nicocles* (2) 18.

7. Suda, s.v. 'Antipatros', Athenaeus, *Learned Banqueters* 10.435d, Plutarch, *Moralia* 179b. On Antipatros and his career, see J.D. Grainger, *Antipater's Dynasty* (Barnsley, 2019); E.J. Baynham, 'Antipater: manager of kings' in I. Worthington and N.G.L. Hammond (eds.), *Ventures into Greek History* (Oxford, 1994), pp. 331–56.

8. Frontinus, *Stratagems* 1.4.13, Isocrates, *Letters: To Antipater* (4) (Antipatros at Pella); Theopompus frag. 217 (Thrace). See J.R. Hamilton, *Plutarch: Alexander: A Commentary* (Oxford, 1969), p. 22.

9. Valerius Maximus, *Memorable Doings and Sayings* 7.2 ext 10 (trans. D.R. Shackleton Bailey, Loeb 493).

10. Plutarch, *Life of Alexander* 39.3, 39.4–5 (Phokion and Olympias); *Life of Phocion* 18.1–3 (refusing gifts).

11. Valerius Maximus, *Memorable Doings and Sayings* 7.2 ext 10.

12. Patrick Leigh Fermor, *The Broken Road* (London, 2014), p. 42.

13. Homer, *Iliad* 13.298–301, *Odyssey* 8.361 (Ares); Hesiod, *Works and Days* 504–35, Tyrtaeus frag. 12, Orphic Hymns 80 (North Wind). For more information on the Thracians and Bulgarian archaeology see R.F. Hoddinott, *Bulgaria in Antiquity: An Archaeological Introduction* (London

and Tonbridge, 1975), *The Thracians* (London, 1981); J.–L. Martinez, A. Baralis, N. Mathieux, T. Stoyanov and M. Tonkova (eds.), *L'épopée des rois thraces: des guerres médiques aux invasions celtes (479–278 av. J.–C.). Découvertes archéologiques en Bulgarie* (Paris, 2016); J. Valeva, E. Nankov and D. Graninger (eds.), *A Companion to Ancient Thrace* (Malden (MA), Chichester and Oxford, 2015).

14. Herodotus, *Histories* 5.3.
15. Xenophanes, frag. 21 B16, Herodotus, *Histories* 5.6.
16. Thucydides, *Peloponnesian War* 2.97.4, Xenophon, *Anabasis* 7.3.25–34. See Z.H. Archibald, 'Macedonia and Thrace' in J. Roisman and I. Worthington (eds.), *A Companion to Ancient Macedonia* (Malden (MA), and Chichester, 2010), pp. 326–41.
17. Herodotus, *Histories* 5.3.
18. The principal study of the Odrysian kingdom remains Z.H. Archibald, *The Odrysian Kingdom of Thrace: Orpheus Unmasked* (Oxford, 1998).
19. Diodorus Siculus, *Library of History* 16.71.1–2.
20. D. Agre, *The Tumulus of Golyamata Mogila near the villages of Malomirovo and Zlatinitsa* (Sofia, 2011).
21. Homer, *Iliad* 10.434–41.
22. Strabo, *Geography* 7 frag. 40 (war cry); Livy, *History of Rome* 42.60.2 (headhunters). For further information on the Thracian army see *The Thracians 700 BC–AD 46* (Oxford and New York, 2001); J.G.P. Best, *Thracian Peltasts and their Influence on Greek Warfare* (Groningen, 1969); T. Stoyanov 'Warfare' in Valeva, Nankov and Graninger (eds.), *A Companion to Ancient Thrace*, pp. 426–42; C. Webber, *The Gods of Battle: The Thracians at War*, 1500 BC–AD 150 (Barnsley, 2011).
23. Demosthenes, *Third Philippic* (9) 49–50.
24. Polyaenus, *Stratagems* 4.2.13 and 4.2.4.
25. I. Hristov, 'Kozi Gramadi' in R. Ivanov (ed.), *Thracian, Greek, Roman and Medieval Cities, Residences and Fortresses in Bulgaria* (Sofia, 2015), pp. 1–80.
26. I. Hristov, *A Sanctuary of Zeus and Hera on Kozi Gramadi Peak in Sredna Gora* (Sofia, 2014).
27. I. Christov and M. Manov, 'Ancient Macedonian Sling Bullets from the Area of a Thracian Rulers' Residence near the Peak of Kozi Gramadi' in *Archaeologia Bulgarica*, Vol. 15 No. 1 (2011), pp. 21–33; E. Nankov, 'The Mobility of Macedonian Army in Thrace during the Reign of Philip II and the Inscribed Lead Sling Bullets from Kozi Gramadi' in

Bulgarian E-Journal of Archaeology, Vol. 5 No. 1 (2015), pp. 1–13; I. Hristov, 'Military Operations before the Walls of the Residence in 341 BC in Accordance with the Evidence of the Lead Sling-Balls from the Site' in *Kozi Gramadi. Studies of an Odrysian Ruler's Residence and Sanctuaries in Sredna Gora Mt. 8th–1st Centuries BC, Vol. II* (Sofia, 2012), pp. 79–89.

28. See E. Nankov, 'Inscribed Lead Sling Bullets from the Regional Museum of History in Shumen. New Data on the Campaigns in the Lands of the Getae in the Time of Philip II and Alexander III' in *Thracia and the surroundings. Proceedings of the National Scientific Conference, October 27–29, 2016* (title in Bulgarian) (2016), pp. 282–293 and *Markers of Mobility: Toward an Archaeology of the Sling in Ancient Thrace* (forthcoming); E. Paunov and D.Y. Dimitrov, 'New Data on the use of the War Sling in Thrace (4th–1st century BC)' in *Archaeologia Bulgarica*, Vol. 4 No. 3 (2000), pp. 44–57.

29. Demosthenes, *On the Chersonese* (8) 44, *Fourth Philippic* (10) 15.

30. Demosthenes, *On the Chersonese* (8) 14, Polyaenus, *Stratagems* 4.2.13.

31. Thucydides, *Peloponnesian War* 2.98.1–2. See P. Delev, *A History of the Tribes of South-Western Thrace in the First Millennium BC* (Sofia, 2014), p. 19; G. Mitrev, 'The Valley of the Strouma River in Antiquity' in *Advances in Bulgarian Science 2014* (Sofia, 2015), pp. 5–17.

32. Aristotle, *History of Animals* 8.65 (630a), Pausanias, *Guide to Greece* 10.13.1–2.

33. Plutarch, *Life of Alexander* 9.1. Also called Alexandreia by Stephanus of Byzantium, s.v. 'Alexandreia'. Not to be confused with modern Alexandroupolis, gateway to Samothrace in north-eastern Greece. See Z. Archibald, 'Alexandropolis' in M.H. Hansen and T.H. Nielsen, *An Inventory of Archaic and Classical Poleis: An Investigation Conducted by the Copenhagen Polis Centre for the Danish National Research Foundation* (Copenhagen, 2004), pp. 892–3; P.M. Fraser, *Cities of Alexander the Great* (Oxford, 1996), pp. 26, 29–30.

34. Conversation with Emil Nankov.

35. J.R. Hamilton, *Plutarch: Alexander: A Commentary* (Oxford, 1969), p. 22–3. For argument in favour of Alexander's rebellion see W.W. Tarn, *Alexander the Great, Vol. II* (Chicago, 1948), pp. 248–9, and against, N.G.L. Hammond and G.T. Griffith, *A History of Macedonia, Vol. II 550–336 BC* (Oxford, 1979), p. 558.

36. Arrian, *Anabasis of Alexander* 1.1.5–6 (autonomous Thracians in 335 BC).

37. In Asia, the army completed an entire city wall in twenty days. Arrian, *Anabasis of Alexander* 4.4.1.

38. See Z. Archibald, 'Cabyle' in Hansen and Nielsen, *An Inventory of Archaic and Classical Poleis*, pp. 893–4; Z. Archibald, 'Thracians and Sycthians' in D.M. Lewis, J. Boardman, S. Hornblower and M. Ostwald (eds.), *The Cambridge Ancient History. Vol. VI: The Fourth Century* (2nd edn, Cambridge, 1994), p. 470.

39. Theopompus, frag. 110 (trans. G.S. Shrimpton, *Theopompus the Historian* (Montreal and Kingston, London and Buffalo, 1991). On Philip's settlements in Thrace, see W. Lindsay Adams, '"Symmiktous Katoikisas" and the City Foundations of the Thracian Frontier' in *Thrace in the Graeco-Roman World: Proceedings of the 10th International Congress of Thracology, Komotini – Alexandroupolis, 18–23 October 2005* (2008), pp. 4–12, 'Philip II and the Thracian Frontier' in *Thrace Ancienne. Actes 2e Symposium international des études thraciennes, Vol. I., Komotini* (1997), pp. 81–8, and 'The Frontier Policy of Philip II' in *Ancient Macedonia*, Vol. 7 (2002), pp. 283–91; J.R. Ellis, 'Population Transplants by Philip II' in *Makedonika*, Vol. 9 (1969), pp. 9–16; E. Badian, 'Philip II and Thrace' in *Pulpudeva*, Vol. 4 (1983), pp. 51–71; R.A. Billows, *Kings and Colonists: Aspects of Macedonian Imperialism. Columbia Studies in the Classical Tradition* (Leiden, New York and Köln, 1995).

40. Justin, *Epitome* 8.5.12–13. (trans. J. C. Yardley, American Philological Association)

41. L.D. Loukopoulou, 'Macedonia in Thrace' in R.J. Lane Fox (ed.), *Brill's Companion to Ancient Macedon. Studies in the Archaeology and History of Macedon, 650 BC–300 AD* (Leiden and Boston, 2011), pp. 467–76; L.J. Bliquez, 'Philip II and Abdera' in *Eranos*, Vol. 79 (1981), pp. 65–79.

42. Diodorus Siculus, *Library of History* 16.71.2.

43. Arrian, *Anabasis of Alexander* 1.25.2, Diodorus Siculus, *Library of History* 17.62.5, Quintus Curtius, *History of Alexander* 10.1.44.

44. Demosthenes, *On the Chersonese* (8) and Hypothesis, *Third Philippic* (9) 35, *Philip's Letter* (12) 3, 11, 16. On the Macedonian fleet, see N.G.L. Hammond, 'The Macedonian Navies of Philip and Alexander until 330 BC' in *Antichthon*, Vol. 26 (1992), pp. 30–41; H. Hauben, 'Philippe II, fondateur de la marine macédonienne' in *Ancient Society*, Vol. 6 (1975), pp. 51–9; W.M. Murray, 'The Development of a Naval Siege Unit under Philip II and Alexander III' in T. Howe and J. Reames (eds.), *Macedonian Legacies* (Claremont (CA), 2008), pp. 31–55.

45. Demosthenes, *Philip's Letter* (12). For discussion see R.J. Lane Fox, 'Philip: Accession, Ambitions and Self-Presentation' in Lane Fox (ed.), *Brill's Companion to Ancient Macedon*, pp. 335–66; N.G.L. Hammond, 'Philip's Letter to Athens 1 – 340 BC' in *Antichthon*, Vol. 27 (1993), pp. 13–20.

46. Demosthenes, *Philip's Letter* (12) 1 (trans. J.H. Vince, Loeb 238).

47. Demosthenes, *Philip's Letter* (12) 23 (trans. J.H. Vince, Loeb 238).

48. Demosthenes' *Second Philippic* (6) is believed to be related to the embassy of Python of 344/3. See J. Trevett, *Demosthenes, Speeches 1–17* (Texas, 2011), pp. 100–12.

49. Plutarch, *Life of Demosthenes* 15.5, *Moralia* 840c (Aeschines). See also J. Buckler, 'Demosthenes and Aeschines' in I. Worthington (ed.), *Demosthenes: Statesman and Orator* (Oxford and New York, 2000), pp. 134–40.

50. Aristophanes, *Peace* 680 (cock of the walk on the Pnyx).

51. Demosthenes, *On the Peace* (5) 24.

52. Demosthenes, *Fourth Philippic* (10) 5–6.

53. Demosthenes, *On the False Embassy* (19) 294–5, 334 (Megara), 260 (Elis), 261 (Arkadia and Argos); *Third Philippic* (9) 29–30 (Philip the virus). For Euboia, see Demosthenes, *First Philippic* (4) 37, *Third Philippic* (9) 33, 57–8, 66, Aeschines, *Against Ctesiphon* (3) 87. Also P.A. Brunt, 'Euboea in the time of Philip II' in *The Classical Quarterly*, Vol. 19 No. 2 (1969), pp. 245–65.

54. Demosthenes, *Third Philippic* (9) 31 (trans. J.H. Vince, Loeb 238).

55. Demosthenes, *Third Philippic* (9) 65 (trans. J.H. Vince, Loeb 238).

56. Demosthenes, *On the Crown* (18) 244, Aeschines, *Against Ctesiphon* (3) 256 (Byzantion embassy).

57. Plutarch, *Life of Phocion* 14.1, *Moralia* 188b–c.

58. Arrian, *Anabasis of Alexander* 2.14.5 says that Perinthos had wronged Philip in some way but there are no details.

59. For more information on Perinthos, see B. Isaac, *The Greek Settlements in Thrace until the Macedonian Conquest. Studies of the Dutch Archaeological and Historical Society*, 10 (Leiden, 1986); M.H. Sayar, *Perinthos-Herakleia (Marmara Ereğlisi) und Umgebung. Geschichte, Testimonien, griechische und lateinische Inschriften* (Vienna, 1998).

60. Diodorus Siculus, *Library of History* 16.74–6; E.I. McQueen, *Diodorus Siculus: The Reign of Philip II: The Greek and Macedonian Narrative from Book XVI* (London, 1995), pp. 150–5.

61. Hammond and Griffith, *A History of Macedonia, Vol. II*, p. 572.

62. R.K. Sinclair, 'Diodorus Siculus and Fighting in Relays' in *The Classical Quarterly*, Vol. 16 No. 2 (1966), pp. 249–55.

63. Diodorus Siculus, *Library of History* 16.75.1–2, Demosthenes, *Answer to Philip's Letter* (11) 5, Arrian, *Anabasis of Alexander* 2.14.5.

64. Diodorus Siculus, *Library of History* 16.75.4 (trans. C. Bradford Welles, Loeb 422).

65. The siege of Selymbria is not directly attested in the ancient sources but is highly likely to have taken place. See Hammond and Griffith, *A History of Macedonia, Vol. II*, p. 574.

66. A. Moreno, 'Hieron: The Ancient Sanctuary at the Mouth of the Black Sea' in *Hesperia: The Journal of the American School of Classical Studies at Athens*, Vol. 77 No. 4 (2008). pp. 655–709.

67. Pindar, *Pythian Odes* 4.203–210, Apollonius of Rhodes, *Argonautica* 2.525–33, Polybius, *Histories* 4.39–6, Diodorus Siculus, *Library of History* 4.49.1–2.

68. Didymus, *On Demosthenes* cols. 10–11, Demosthenes, *On the Crown* (18) 73.

69. Demosthenes, *Answer to Philip's Letter* (11) 1 (Scholia). See Hammond and Griffith, *A History of Macedonia, Vol. II*, p. 574.

70. Athenaeus, *Learned Banqueters* 8.351c.

71. For Leon see Suda s.v. 'Leon', Plutarch, *Life of Phocion* 14, Philostratus, *Lives of Sophists* 1.2.

72. Demosthenes, *On the Crown* (18) 87, Didymus, *On Demosthenes* col. 11, Dionysius of Byzantium, *Through the Bosphorus* 14. Philip dismantling the temples of his enemies seems to be a literary topos: see Justin, *Epitome* 8.3.4, 5.5–6.

73. Vitruvius, *On Buildings* 2.345, Athenaeus, *On Machines* 10. For Polyeidos' *Helepolis* at Byzantion, see W.M. Murray, 'The Development of a Naval Siege Unit under Philip II and Alexander III' in T. Howe and J. Reames (eds.), *Macedonian Legacies* (Claremont (CA), 2008), p. 34 fn. 18. For torsion catapult see Hammond and Griffith, *A History of Macedonia, Vol. II*, p. 448; E.W. Marsden, *Greek and Roman Artillery: Historical Development* (Oxford, 1969), pp. 67–8.

74. Justin, *Epitome* 9.8.4–5.

75. Dionysius of Byzantium, *Through the Bosphorus* 65.

76. They were also aided by their Island allies (Chians, Koans, Rhodians, Tenedians). Diodorus Siculus, *Library of History* 16.77.1–3.

77. Hesychius of Miletus, frags. 26–7. See also Stephanus of Byzantium, s.v. 'Bosporos'.

78. Demosthenes, *Answer to Philip's Letter* (11) 5.

79. Hammond and Griffith, *A History of Macedonia, Vol. II*, pp. 579–81.

80. Justin, *Epitome* 9.1.8 (trans. J.C. Yardley, American Philological Association), Paul Orosius, *Seven Books of History against the Pagans* 3.13.4.

81. D. Campbell, *Ancient Siege Warfare: Romans, Greeks, Carthaginians and Romans 546–146 BC* (Oxford and New York, 2005), p. 31; E.W. Marsden, 'Macedonian Military Machinery and its Designers under Philip and Alexander' in *Ancient Macedonia*, Vol. 2 (1977), pp. 211–23, and *Greek and Roman Artillery: Historical development* (Oxford, 1969). For Alexander's engineers see D. Whitehead, 'Alexander the Great and the Mechanici' in P. Wheatley and E. Baynham (eds.), *East and West in the World Empire of Alexander the Great: Studies in Honour of Brian Bosworth* (Oxford, 2015), pp. 75–91; for his sieges see S. English, *The Sieges of Alexander the Great* (Barnsley, 2010).

82. *Alexander Itinerary* 6. For English translations see I. Davies, 'Alexander's Itinerary: An English Translation' in *Ancient History Bulletin*, Vol. 12 (1998), pp. 29–54; W. Heckel and J.C. Yardley, *Alexander the Great: Historical Texts in Translation* (Malden (MA), 2004). For authorship see R.J. Lane Fox, 'The Itinerary of Alexander: Constantius to Julian' in *The Classical Quarterly*, Vol 47 No 1 (1997), pp. 239–52.

83. Plutarch, *Life of Alexander* 4.1–4, *Moralia* 53d (Alexander's appearance). The tradition that he had different coloured eyes comes from the Romances and, as it was associated with magic and sorcery, is not to be trusted, although his eyes may well have been asymmetrical (Pseudo-Callisthenes, *Greek Alexander Romance* 1.13, Julius Valerius 1.7, Tzetzes 11.368.8). As regards his height, Pseudo-Callisthenes, *Greek Alexander Romance* 3.4, says that he was three cubits (4ft 6in/137cm) – surely an exaggeration, but other sources attest to his small stature compared with others (Quintus Curtius, *History of Alexander* 5.2.13, 7.8.9, 6.5.29, Arrian, *Anabasis of Alexander* 2.12.6). The idea that the tilt of his neck could be associated with ocular torticollis is not proven; the tilt was likely a stylistic trait emphasised in portraiture. The ancient descriptions of Alexander are collected in A. Stewart, *Faces of Power: Alexander's Image and Hellenistic Politics* (Berkeley, Los Angeles and Oxford, 1993), pp. 341–58.

84. Aelian, *Historical Miscellany* 12.14.

85. Dio Chrysostom, *Discourses* 2.1–2.
86. Dio Chrysostom wrote a lost *On the Virtues of Alexander* in no less than eight books, suggesting he was well acquainted with Alexander's life (Suda, s.v. 'Dion').
87. Frontinus, *Stratagems* 1.4.13, 13a. For discussion of this piece of evidence see Hammond and Griffith, *A History of Macedonia, Vol. II*, pp. 580–1.
88. Strabo, *Geography* 7.3.6, Ovid, *Tristia* 4.4.55.
89. R.F. Hoddinott, *Bulgaria in Antiquity: An Archaeological Introduction* (London and Tonbridge, 1975), p. 39, E. Nankov, *Markers of Mobility: Towards an Archaeology of the Sling in Ancient Thrace* (forthcoming).
90. Polyaenus, *Stratagems* 4.2.20. See J. Gardiner-Garden, 'Ateas and Theopompus' in *The Journal of Hellenic Studies*, Vol 109 (1989), pp. 29–40 (p. 30).
91. Jordanes, *Getica* 10.65. See Gardiner-Garden, 'Ateas and Theopompus'.
92. A. Minchev, 'Odessos' in D.V. Grammenos and E.K. Petropoulos (eds.), *Ancient Greek Colonies in the Black Sea ,Vol. I* (Thessaloniki, 2003), p. 222.
93. Ovid, *Tristia* 3.10.75 (trans. A.L. Wheeler, G.P. Goold, Loeb 151).
94. Ovid, *Tristia* 5.7.17 (trans. A.L. Wheeler, G.P. Goold, Loeb 151).
95. The king of the Histrianoi was either a local king who had taken control of the Greek polis of Histria or, more probably, a rival Scythian leader who controlled lands north of the Danube. See Pomponius Mela, *Geography* 2.1.7–8; I. Lazarenko, *The Scythians in Thrace (7th century BC–1st Century AD) Part I: Written Sources for Scythians in Thrace* (Sofia, 2015), p. 387.
96. Herodotus, *Histories* 4.118–144.
97. Lucian, *Long Lives* 10. For the Scythian army see E.V. Cernenko, *The Scythians 700–300 BC* (Oxford and New York, 1983). On Scythians in general see B. Cunliffe, *The Scythians: Nomad Warriors of the Steppe* (Oxford, 2019); R. Rolle, *The World of the Scythians* (London, 1989); St. J. Simpson and S. Pankova (eds.), *Scythians: Warriors of Ancient Siberia* (London, 2017).
98. D. Draganov, *The Coins of the Scythian Kings* (Sofia, 2016); Gardiner-Garden, 'Ateas and Theopompus,' p. 36. The five coins, dated between 353 and 347 BC, attest to Scythian presence in north-eastern Thrace from an early date.
99. Justin, *Epitome* 9.2.14, Lucian, *Long Lives* 10.
100. Frontinus, *Stratagems* 2.8.14. For a possible reconstruction of the battle, see R.E. Gaebel, *Cavalry Operations in the Ancient Greek World* (Oklahoma, 2002), pp. 153–4.

101. Justin, *Epitome* 9.2.15–16.

102. Athenaeus, *Learned Banqueters* 13.557b, Stephanus of Byzantium, s.v. 'Getia'.

103. Justin, *Epitome* 9.3.1–3, Didymus, *On Demosthenes* col. 13, Demosthenes, *On the Crown* (18) 67 and Scholia, Plutarch, *Moralia* 331b–c. See A.S. Riginos, 'The Wounding of Philip II of Macedon: Fact and Fabrication' in *The Journal of Hellenic Studies*, Vol. 114 (1994), pp. 103–19.

104. Justin, *Epitome* 9.3.3.

105. Plutarch, *Moralia* 331b–c (trans. F. Cole Babbitt, Loeb 305).

6 THE ROAD TO CHAIRONEIA

1. Aeschines, *Against Ctesiphon* (3) and Demosthenes, *On the Crown* (18) provide the main sources of information on the background and outbreak of the Fourth Sacred War. On dates, see discussion and notes in P. Londey, 'The Outbreak of the 4th Sacred War' in *Chiron*, Vol. 20 (1990), pp. 239–60.

2. Aeschines, *Against Ctesiphon* (3) 116 (trans. C.D. Adams, Loeb 106). The temple had been burnt down in 373 BC. For the outbreak of the Fourth Sacred War and following events, see Aeschines, *Against Ctesiphon* (3) 115–129, Demosthenes, *On the Crown* (18) 143–59.

3. Aeschines, *Against Ctesiphon* (3) 117 (trans. C.D. Adams, Loeb 106).

4. Didymus, *On Demosthenes* col. 11.

5. Diodorus Siculus, *Library of History* 16.84.2, Demosthenes, *On the Crown* (18) 169, Didymus, *On Demosthenes* col. 11.

6. On the special meeting and what took place see Demosthenes, *On the Crown* (18) 169–79, Diodorus Siculus, *Library of History* 16.84.1–5, Plutarch, *Life of Demosthenes* 18.1–2. Diodorus says that the meeting took place in the theatre, but is contradicted by Demosthenes' account, which suggests the Pnyx.

7. Pausanias, *Guide to Greece* 9.1.3. For Boiotian pigs insult see Pindar, *Olympian Odes* 6.89–90, *Dithyrambs* frag. 83.

8. For details on the embassies, see Demosthenes, *On the Crown* (18) 211–12, Didymus, *On Demosthenes* col. 11, Philochorus, frags. 56a and b, Plutarch, *Life of Demosthenes* 18–19, Diodorus Siculus, *Library of History* 16.85.3–4.

9. Hyperides, *Against Diondas* 1 (137r–136v), Demosthenes, *On the Crown* (18) 213.

10. Plutarch, *Life of Demosthenes* 18.2–4.

11. D. Guth, 'Rhetoric and Historical Narrative: The Theban-Athenian Alliance of 339 BC' in *Historia: Zeitschrift für Alte Geschichte*, Bd. 63 H. 2 (2014), pp. 151–65. For more on Hyperides' *Against Diondas* see N. Tchernetska, 'New Fragments of Hyperides from the Archimedes Palimpsest' in *Zeitschrift für Papyrologie und Epigraphik*, Bd. 154 (2005), pp. 1–6; C. Carey et al., 'Fragments of Hyperides' against Diondas from the Archimedes Palimpsest' in *Zeitschrift für Papyrologie und Epigraphik*, Bd. 165 (2008), pp. 1–19; R. Janko, 'Some notes on the New Hyperides (against Diondas)' in *Zeitschrift für Papyrologie und Epigraphik*, Bd. 170 (2009), p. 16.

12. Aeschines, *Against Ctesiphon* (3) 150–1.

13. See Guth, 'Rhetoric and Historical Narrative: The Theban-Athenian Alliance of 339 BC', pp. 151–65.

14. Polyaenus, *Stratagems* 4.2.8, Dinarchus, *Against Demosthenes* (1) 74, Aeschines, *Against Ctesiphon* (3) 146 (Gravia pass, Proxenos, Chares and 10, 000 mercenaries); Pausanias, *Guide to Greece* 10.36.2 (fortification at Ambrossos).

15. Polyaenus, *Stratagems* 4.2.3.

16. Aelian, *Historical Miscellany* 14.48.

17. Plutarch, *Life of Alexander* 57.2.

18. Polyaenus, *Stratagems* 4.2.8, Dinarchus, *Against Demosthenes* (1) 74, Aeschines, *Against Ctesiphon* (3) 146.

19. The fate of Amphissa is not directly referenced in the ancient sources. Strabo, *Geography* 9.4.8 implies that it was destroyed, but this is contradicted by Diodorus Siculus, *Library of History* 18.38.2. Philip probably took a lenient approach so as not to further antagonise the Thebans, with whom he thought peace was still a possibility.

20. Demosthenes, *On the Crown* (18) 216. An inscription (IG II² 1155) recording honours for a certain Athenian Boularchos, son of Aristoboulos, may relate to one or both of these battles. See S. Lambert, 'Dedications and Decrees commemorating military action in 339/8 BC' in A.P. Matthaiou and N. Papazarkadas (eds.), *Axon: Studies in Honour of Ronald S. Stroud* (Athens, 2015), pp. 233–46. Also see Polyaenus, *Stratagems* 4.2.14.

21. *Sylloge Tacticorum* 94.3 in G. Chatzelis and J. Harris, *A Tenth Century Byzantine Military Manual: The Sylloge Tacticorum* (Oxford and New York, 2017), p. 146 n. 450. See J. Rzepka, 'The First Battles of the

Chaeronea Campaign, 339/8 BC' in *Greek, Roman and Byzantine Studies*, Vol. 58 (2018), pp. 516–22.

22. Theophrastus, *Enquiry into Plants* 4.11.3 (wet year).

23. Aeschines, *Against Ctesiphon* (3) 150–1.

24. Plutarch, *Life of Camillus* 19.5 (date for the battle of Chaironeia).

25. Plutarch, *Moralia* 193e.

26. Plutarch, *Life of Demosthenes* 2.2.

27. D. Blackman, 'Hammond, Nicholas Geoffrey Lemprière' in *Oxford Dictionary of National Biography*. Hammond later wrote up his adventures in wartime Greece in *Venture into Greece: with the Guerrillas, 1943–1944* (London, 1983).

28. G. Sotiriades, 'Das Schlachtfeld von Chäronea und der Grabhügel der Makedonen,' in *Mitteilungen des Deutschen Archäologischen Instituts, Athenische Abteilung*, Vol. 28 (1903), pp. 301–30, and 'Untersuchungen in Boiotien und Phokis.1. Topographisches über Chaironeia. Das Stadtflüsschen Haimon und das Herakleion,' in *Mitteilungen des Deutschen Archäologische, Instituts Athenische Abteilung*, Vol. 30 (1905), pp. 113–20. Also J. Kromayer, *Antike Schlachtfelder in Griechenland. Bausteine zu einer antiken Kriegsgeschichte, Vol. I* (Berlin, 1903), pp. 127–98, revised in *Schlachten-Atlas zur antiken Kriegsgeschichte, Vol. IV* (Leipzig, 1926), p. 36.

29. N.G.L. Hammond, 'The Two Battles of Chaeronea' in *Klio*, Vol. 31 (1938), pp. 186–218, later revised and republished as 'The Victory at Chaeronea' in N.G.L. Hammond, *Studies in Greek History: A Companion Volume to A History of Greece to 322 BC* (New York, 1973), pp. 534–57. See additions to Hammond's ideas by W.K. Pritchett, 'Observations on Chaironeia' in *American Journal of Archaeology*, Vol. 62 (1958), pp. 207–311.

30. Plutarch, *Life of Demosthenes* 19.1–3.

31. Dinarchus, *Against Demosthenes* (1) 74. See J. Ma, 'Chaironeia 338: Topographies of Commemoration' in *The Journal of Hellenic Studies*, Vol. 128 (2008), pp. 72–91, for an alternative configuration; Boiotians on the left, Athenians on the right.

32. Diodorus Siculus, *Library of History* 16.85.7 (Chares), 88.1 (Lysikles); Aeschines, *Against Ctesiphon* (3) 143, Polyaenus, *Stratagems* 4.2.2 (Stratokles).

33. Plutarch, *Life of Demosthenes* 20.2, *Moralia* 845f.

34. Demosthenes, *On the Crown* (18) 237; Pausanias, *Guide to Greece* 7.6.3 (Achaians), 7.15.3 (Arkadians); Strabo, *Geography* 9.2.37 (Corinthians). For the Phokians, who probably fought on both sides (Pausanias, *Guide to Greece* 10.3.3 and 10.33.8), see N.G.L. Hammond and G.T. Griffith, *A History of Macedonia, Vol. II. 550–336 BC* (Oxford, 1979), pp. 592–3. For Akarnanians see P.J. Rhodes and R. Osborne (eds.), *Greek Historical Inscriptions 404–323 BC* (Oxford, 2003), pp. 380–4, no. 77. More generally, Justin, *Epitome* 9.3.8.

35. Plutarch, *Life of Alexander* 9.2.

36. Diodorus Siculus, *Library of History* 16.85.1. It's still debated by scholars whether Alexander was on foot or mounted during the battle, a detail not mentioned in the sources. The latter seems more likely. Cavalry had already fought during the campaign, and their important role in Alexander's army proved decisive in all his major pitched battles. The skeletal remains of the Thebans (to be discussed later in the chapter) suggest injuries from mounted aggressors, and the grave stele of Panchares (currently in the Archaeological Museum of Piraeus), who may have died in the fighting, shows an Athenian Hoplite versus a cavalryman.

37. Plutarch, *Moralia* 177c.

38. Plutarch, *Moralia* 761a. On the history of the Sacred Band see J.G. DeVoto, 'The Theban Sacred Band' in *Ancient World*, Vol. 23 No. 2 (1992), pp. 3–1; J. Romm, *The Sacred Band: Three Hundred Theban Lovers Fighting to Save Greek Freedom* (New York, 2021).

39. Diodorus Siculus, *Library of History* 16.86.1.

40. Diodorus Siculus, *Library of History* 16.85.5–6.

41. Diodorus Siculus, *Library of History* 16.85.5–6, says that the Macedonians had greater numbers, whereas Justin, *Epitome* 9.3.9 believed that they were outnumbered.

42. Arrian, *Anabasis of Alexander* 3.9.7–8 (trans. P.A. Brunt, Loeb 236).

43. Alexander made the same offerings before the battle of Issos in 333 BC (Curtius, *History of Alexander* 3.8.22). On gods of Chaironeia see Plutarch, *Life of Sulla* 17.4 (Apollo); *Life of Demosthenes* 19.2 (Herakles); Pausanias, *Guide to Greece* 9.41.3 (Zeus). On Macedonians and battle sacrifices, see R. Parker, 'Sacrifice and Battle' in H. Van Wees (ed.), *War and Violence in Ancient Greece* (Swansea, 2000), pp. 299–314.

44. Poseidippus, AB 31.

45. Aeschines, *Against Ctesiphon* (3) 130. A scholiast explains that certain

celebrants were seized by a shark as they bathed in the sea before the Eleusinian Mysteries.

46. Plutarch, *Life of Demosthenes* 19.1 (Pythia prophecies); Plutarch, *Life of Demosthenes* 20.1, Aeschines, *Against Ctesiphon* (3) 130 (Pythia Philippising); Aeschines, *Against Ctesiphon* (3) 131 (bad sacrifices).

47. Xenophon, *Agesilaus* 2.12 (trans. E.C. Marchant and G.W. Bowerstock, Loeb 183).

48. Polyaenus, *Stratagems* 4.2.2.

49. Polyaenus, *Stratagems* 4.2.2, Plutarch *Moralia* 259D (also attributed to Thegenes the Theban).

50. Polyaenus, *Stratagems* 4.2.7, Frontinus, *Stratagems* 2.1.9. This stratagem is also alluded to in Demosthenes' later funeral oration for the battle dead, *Funeral Oration* (60) 21.

51. N.G.L. Hammond, 'The Victory at Chaeronea' in N.G.L. Hammond, *Studies in Greek History: A Companion Volume to A History of Greece to 322 BC* (New York, 1973), pp. 544–5.

52. Diodorus Siculus, *Library of History* 16.86.3. On the cavalry and its probable role in the battle of Chaironeia, see M.A. Sears and C. Willekes, 'Alexander's Cavalry Charge at Chaeronea, 338 BCE' in *Journal of Military History*, Vol. 80 (2016), pp. 1,017–35.

53. See C. Willekes, 'Equine Aspects of Alexander the Great's Macedonian Cavalry' in T. Howe, E. Garvin and G. Wrightson (eds.), *Greece, Macedon and Persia: Studies in Social, Political and Military History in Honour of Waldemar Heckel* (Oxford and Philadelphia, 2015), pp. 47–58.

54. Diodorus Siculus, *Library of History* 16.86.3–4.

55. Frontinus, *Stratagems* 2.1.9.

56. Polyaenus, *Stratagems* 4.3.8 (charging nobly) (trans. P. Krentz and E.L. Wheeler, Ares), Plutarch, *Life of Alexander* 9.2.

57. Xenophon, *Agesilaus* 2.14 (trans. E.C. Marchant and G.W. Bowerstock, Loeb 183).

58. Plutarch, *Life of Pelopidas* 18.5 (trans. I. Scott-Kilvert and T.E. Duff, Penguin).

59. P. Cartledge, *Thebes: The Forgotten City of Ancient Greece* (London, 2020), pp. 229–30.

60. Plutarch, *Moralia* 845f. Also *Life of Demosthenes* 20.2.

61. Plutarch, *Life of Demosthenes* 20.3 (trans. B. Perrin, Loeb 99).

62. See G. Sotiriades, 'Excavation of Two Tombs next to Chaironeia' (in Greek) in *Praktika, Vol. 53-9* (1902), pp. 53–9, 'Das Schlachtfeld von

Chäronea und der Grabhügel der Makedonen,' in *Mitteilungen des Deutschen Archäologische Instituts. Athenische Abteilung*, pp. 301–30, 'Excavations at Chaironeia, Orchomenos, and Elatea' (in Greek) in *Praktika*, Vol. 35–57 (1904), pp. 35–57, and 'Chaironeia and Phokis excavations' (in Greek) in *Praktika*, Vol. 122–30 (1910), pp. 122–30.

63. Sotiriades, 'Das Schlachtfeld von Chäronea und der Grabhügel der Makedonen,' p. 308; C.W. Clairmont, *Patrios Nomos: Public Burial in Athens during the Fifth and Fourth Centuries BC. The Archaeological, Epigraphic-Literary and Historical Evidence* (Oxford, 1983), p. 242; A.S. Coolley, 'The Macedonian tomb and the battle of Chaironeia', *Records of the Past*, Vol. 3.5 (May 1904), pp. 131–43.

64. Ma, 'Chaironeia 338: Topographies of Commemoration', pp. 72–91; Coolley, 'The Macedonian Tomb and the battlefield of Chaironeia.'

65. Quintus Curtius, *History of Alexander* 5.4.3, Livy, *History of Rome* 36.8.3–6.

66. Diodorus Siculus, *Library of History* 17.21.4. The pick of the enemy booty may have been given to the division that most distinguished itself during the battle. The Thessalian cavalry was given this honour after the battle of Issos in 333 BC, when it was allowed to plunder Damaskos where the Persian army's treasures and baggage had been deposited (Plutarch, *Life of Alexander* 24.2).

67. Diodoros Siculus, *Library of History* 16.86.6.

68. Arrian, *Anabasis of Alexander* 7.3.1–66; such a sequence of events is related to have taken place during the cremation of the Indian wise man Kalanos, who was honoured by the army in Asia.

69. Pausanias, *Guide to Greece* 9.40.4.

70. Ma, 'Chaironeia 338: Topographies of Commemoration', p. 84. See also L. Phytalis, 'Investigations into the Chaironeia Polyandrion' (in Greek), in *Athenaion*, Vol. 9 (1880), pp. 347–52. The statue was erected sometime after the original burial.

71. See Romm, *The Sacred Band: Three Hundred Theban Lovers Fighting to Save Greek Freedom*.

72. For studies on the Chaironeia lion monument bones see Ma, 'Chaironeia 338: Topographies of Commemoration'; M.A. Liston, 'Skeletal Evidence for the Impact of Battle on Soldiers and Non-Combatants' in L.L. Brice (ed.), *New Approaches to Greek and Roman Warfare* (Hoboken (NJ), 2020), pp. 81–94.

73. Diodorus Siculus, *Library of History* 16.87.1–2 (trans. C. Bradford Welles, Loeb 422), Theopompus, frag. 236.
74. Homer, *Iliad* 2.215–20.
75. Justin, *Epitome* 9.4.1 (trans. J.C. Yardley, American Philological Association).
76. Lycurgus, *Against Leocrates* 41–2.
77. Pausanias, *Guide to Greece* 9.15.2, Justin, *Epitome* 9.4.6.
78. Diodorus Siculus, *Library of History* 18.56.7, Pausanias, *Guide to Greece* 1.34.1, Rhodes and Osborne, *Greek Historical Inscriptions 404–323 BC*, pp. 370–3, no. 75; Pausanias, *Guide to Greece* 9.1.8, 4.27.10 (Plataians, destroyed in 373), 9.37.3 (Orchomenians, destroyed in 371). D. Knoepfler, *Eretria: Fouilles et recherches, Vol. XI. Décrets érétriens de proxénie et de citoyenneté* (Lausanne, 2001), pp. 367–89, argues convincingly that Oropos was made independent after Chaironeia until 335, which goes against the sources. The Thespians dedicated a statue to Philip and scholars have suggested that this was a result of Philip also refounding the city (Dio Chrysostom, *Orations* 57.42).
79. Plutarch, *Moralia* 177e (trans. F. Cole Babbit, Loeb 245).
80. Plutarch, *Moralia* 177c–d (trans. F. Cole Babbit, Loeb 245).
81. Plutarch, *Moralia* 177e–f (trans. F. Cole Babbit, Loeb 245).
82. Justin, *Epitome* 9.4.4., Polybius, *Histories* 5.10 and Hyperides frag. B 19.2.
83. Aristotle, *Rhetoric* 3.1.7 (1365a).
84. Plutarch, *Moralia* 471e–f. Also P. Green, *Alexander of Macedon, 356–323 B.C. A Historical Biography* (Berkeley (LA), and London, 1991), p. 85 fn. 26.
85. Arrian, *Anabasis of Alexander* 1.16.7 (trans. P.A. Brunt, Loeb 236), Plutarch, *Life of Alexander* 16.8. See J.M. Hurwit, *The Acropolis in the Age of Pericles* (Cambridge and New York, 2004), p. 245.
86. Thucydides, *Peloponnesian War* 2.34.5.
87. P1136 – Translation reproduced with the kind permission of the Office of Management, Archaeological Museum of Kerameikos.
88. P695 – Translation reproduced with the kind permission of the Office of Management, Archaeological Museum of Kerameikos.
89. Pausanias, *Guide to Greece* 1.29.3. For the *Demosion Sema* see N.T. Arrington, 'Topographic Semantics: The Location of the Athenian Public Cemetery and Its Significance for the Nascent Democracy' in *Hesperia: The Journal of the American School of Classical Studies at Athens*, Vol. 79 No. 4 (2010), pp. 499–539. For the Kerameikos archaeological site in general, see U. Knigge, *The German Archaeological Institute in Athens:*

The Athenian Kerameikos: History, Monuments, Excavations (Athens, 1991);
E. Spathari, *Kerameikos: A Guide to the Monuments and the Museum*
(Athens, 2009).

90. Demosthenes, *On the Crown* (18) 290 (trans. H. Yunis, University of
Texas Press). See also IG II² 5226 – a fragmentary inscription found in
Athens that preserves a few lines of an epigram, also known from a
surviving literary source (the Palatine Anthology), which could also have
come from the epitaph of the Chaironeia dead or another unknown
monument – 'O Time, god who lookest upon all that befalls mortals,
announce our fate to all, how striving to save the holy land of Hellas,
we fell in the glorious Boeotian field' (*Greek Anthology*, 7.245). For
discussion see W.K. Pritchett *The Greek State at War, Vol. I* (Berkeley
and London, 1974), pp. 223–6.

91. Pausanias, *Guide to Greece* 1.29.11.

92. Demosthenes, *The Funeral Speech* (60) 23, Lycurgus, *Against Leocrates*
(1) 47.

93. Thucydides, *Peloponnesian War* 2.34.

94. Demosthenes, *On the Crown* (18) 285 (elected to speak at public funeral).
After the battle of Chaironeia he had left the city for a short time to
secure grain for the city. Aeschines, *Against Ctesiphon* (3) 159 accused
him of running away, but it was an important job and may have required
his diplomatic skills (Demosthenes, *On the Crown* (18) 248).

95. Diodorus Siculus, *Library of History* 16.88.2 (trans. C. Bradford Welles,
Loeb 422). Another Athenian general, Chares, likely fled to Asia in the
aftermath of the battle.

96. Demosthenes, *The Funeral Speech* (60) 36–7 (trans. N.W. De Witt and
N.J. De Witt, Loeb 374).

97. Demosthenes, *The Funeral Speech* (60) 37 (trans. N.W. De Witt and
N.J. De Witt, Loeb 374).

98. Demosthenes, *The Funeral Speech* (60) 24 (trans. N.W. De Witt and
N.J. De Witt, Loeb 374). Also Lycurgus, *Against Leocrates* 50.

99. Plutarch, *Life of Demosthenes* 21.3.

7 RECONCILIATION

1. Trans. from P.J. Rhodes and R. Osborne (eds.), *Greek Historical
Inscriptions 404–323 BC* (Oxford, 2003), pp. 372–9, no. 76 (IG II³ 1 318

frags A and B) © P.J. Rhodes and R. Osborne. Reproduced with the permission of the Licensor through PLSclear.

2. Aelian, *Historical Miscellany* 6.1, C. Roebuck, 'The Settlements of Philip II with the Greek States in 338 BC' in *Classical Philology*, Vol. 43 No. 2 (1948), pp. 73–92.

3. Diodorus Siculus, *Library of History* 17.3.3 (Ambrakia); Plutarch, *Life of Aratus* 23.4 (Corinth); Polybius, *Histories* 38.3.3 (Chalkis). These were the Macedonian 'Fetters of Greece'.

4. Polybius, *Histories* 18.14.1–5, 9.33.9–10; Demosthenes, *On the False Embassy* (19) 260–62 (for Philip's influence in the Peloponnese prior to Chaironeia).

5. Pausanias, *Guide to Greece* 8.7.4.

6. Pausanias, *Guide to Greece* 8.30.5.

7. Quintus Curtius, *History of Alexander* 6.3.1–3 mentions Sparta, Achaia and the Peloponnese in general as being subdued under Alexander's leadership or command.

8. Pausanias, *Guide to Greece* 8.28.1, Cicero, *On the Nature of the Gods* 3.22.57.

9. Pausanias, *Guide to Greece* 8.47.2, 4 (Kalydonian boar and Herakles), 8.11.7–8 (Epameinondas' grave).

10. Plutarch, *Moralia* 233e.

11. Polybius, *Histories* 9.28.7.

12. Justin, *Epitome* 9.5.3 (trans. J.C. Yardley, American Association of Philology).

13. This is where Alexander gathered the Council when he came to power (Plutarch, *Life of Alexander* 14.1), and likewise the Successor Demetrios the Besieger (Plutarch, *Life of Demetrius* 25.4) See H. Bowden, 'The Argeads and the Greek Sanctuaries' in S. Müller, T. Howe, H. Bowden and R. Rollinger (eds.), *The History of the Argeads: New Perspectives* (Wiesbaden, 2017), pp. 163–82; M. Flower, 'Alexander the Great and Panhellenism' in A.B. Bosworth and E.J. Baynham (eds.), *Alexander the Great in Fact and Fiction* (Oxford and New York, 2000), pp. 96–135.

14. Strabo, *Geography* 8.6.22.

15. T.T.B. Ryder, 'Demosthenes and Philip's Peace of 338/7 B.C', in *The Classical Quarterly*, Vol. 26 No. 1 (1976), pp. 85–7.

16. See S. Perlman, 'Greek Diplomatic Tradition and the Corinthian League of Philip of Macedon' in *Historia: Zeitschrift für Alte Geschichte*, Bd. 34 H.2 (1985), pp. 153–74.

17. See Bowden, 'The Argeads and the Greek Sanctuaries,' p. 173.

18. Rhodes and Osborne, *Greek Historical Inscriptions 404–323 BC*, pp. 372–9, no. 76.

19. Plutarch, *Life of Phocion* 16.4–5.

20. Herodotus, *Histories* 7.172.1, 175.1 (481/480 BC).

21. Hyperides mentions that a confederate force of 600 infantry and 60 cavalry were to be supplied by the Athenians, along with 20 ships mentioned elsewhere by Diodorus Siculus, *Library of History* 17.22.5. See Hyperides, *Against Diondas* 8 (175v–174r) 11–12 in C. Carey et al., 'Fragments of Hyperides' "Against Diondas" from the Archimedes Palimpsest' in *Zeitschrift für Papyrologie und Epigraphik*, Bd. 165 (2008), pp. 14 and 19.

22. M. Brosius, 'Why Persia became the enemy of Macedon' in W. Henkelman and A. Kuhrt (eds.), *A Persian Perspective: Essays in memory of Heleen Sancisi-Weerdenberg. Achaemenid History* 8 (Leiden, 2003), pp. 227–38.

23. Isocrates, *Discourses: To Philip* (5) 120–21; M.B. Hatzopoulos, *Ancient Macedonia. Trends in Classics – Key Perspectives on Classical Research* (Berlin/Boston, 2020), p. 162.

24. Isocrates, *Letters: To Philip* 2 (3) 5 (trans. L. Van Hook, Loeb 373).

25. Polybius, *Histories* 3.6.12–13 implies a similar motivation, arguing that religious obligations were a mere fabrication that concealed Philip's lust for glory and further riches.

26. Diodorus Siculus, *Library of History* 17.5–6, Aelian, *Historical Miscellany* 6.8, Plutarch, *Moralia* 337e. A Babylonian text suggests that Ochos died from natural causes rather than assassination; see C. Walker, 'Achaemenid chronology and the Babylonian sources' in J. Curtius (ed.), *Mesopotamia and Iran in the Persian period. Conquest and Imperialism, 539–331 BC* (London, 1997), pp. 17–25. On the timing of the campaign, see S. Ruzicka, 'A Note on Philip's Persian War' in *American Journal of Ancient History*, Vol. 10 No. 1 (1985), pp. 84–95.

27. Pausanias, *Guide to Greece* 5.4.9.

28. P. Schultz, 'Leochares' Argead Portraits in the Philippeion' in P. Schultz and R. von den Hoff (eds.), *Early Hellenistic Portraiture: Image, Style, Context* (Cambridge, 2007), pp. 205–33. See also R.F. Townsend, 'The Philippeion and fourth-century Athenian architecture' in O. Palagia and S. Tracy (eds.), *The Macedonians in Athens, 322–229 BC* (Oxford, 2003), pp. 93–101; E.D. Carney, 'The Philippeum, Women and the Formation

of a Dynastic Image' in W. Heckel, L.A. Tritle and P. Wheatley (eds.), *Alexander's Empire: Formulation to Decay* (Claremont (CA), 2007), pp. 27–60; S.G. Miller, 'The Philippeion and Macedonian Hellenistic Architecture' in *Mitteilungen des Deutschen Archäologischen Instituts, Athenische Abteilung*, Bd. 88 (1973), pp. 189–218.

29. Pausanias, *Guide to Greece* 5.20.9–10, 5.17.4 (the statue of Eurydike, which Pausanias mistakes for a daughter of Kynnane, Adea-Eurydike, who later became queen, and that of Olympias, had by his time been transferred to the temple of Hera). P. Schultz, 'Leochares' Argead Portraits in the Philippeion' in Schultz and von den Hoff (eds.), *Early Hellenistic Portraiture: Image, Style, Context*, p. 22, argues that the statues were of painted marble not chryselephantine, as stated by Pausanias. This idea is based on the cuttings for the statues; perhaps merely the head and arms were of gold and ivory. See also K.D.S. Lapatin, *Chryselephantine Statuary in the Ancient Mediterranean World* (Oxford, 2001), pp. 115–19.

30. Plutarch, *Life of Alexander* 9.3, Justin, *Epitome* 9.4.2.

31. Plutarch, *Life of Alexander* 9.3.

32. Plutarch, *Life of Alexander* 9.4 (trans. B. Perrin, Loeb 99), E.D. Carney, *Women and Monarchy in Macedonia* (Oklahoma, 2000), pp. 70–5.

33. Athenaeus, *Learned Banqueters* 13.557b (trans. S. Douglas Olsen, Loeb 327).

34. Diodorus Siculus, *Library of History* 17.16.2.

35. See A.B. Bosworth, 'Philip II and Upper Macedonia' in *The Classical Quarterly*, Vol. 21 No. 1 (1971), pp. 93–105.

36. Arrian, *Anabasis of Alexander* 3.5.6. See W. Heckel, 'Kleopatra or Eurydike?' in *Phoenix*, Vol. 32 (1978), pp. 155–8.

37. Plutarch, *Life of Alexander* 9.3–4 (trans. author).

38. Quintus Curtius, *History of Alexander* 8.4.27–30. On Macedonian marriages, see M. Renard and J. Servais, 'A propos du marriage d'Alexandre et de Roxane' in *L'Antiquité Classique*, Vol. 24 (1955), pp. 29–50; S.L. Ager, 'Symbol and Ceremony: Royal Weddings in the Hellenistic Age' in A. Erskine, L. Llewellyn-Jones and S. Wallace (eds.), *The Hellenistic Court: Monarchic Power and Elite Society from Alexander to Cleopatra* (Swansea, 2017), pp. 165–88. G.F. Abbott, who explored Macedonia in the early nineteenth century, mentions in *Macedonian Folklore* (Cambridge, 1903), pp. 158, 173 the local tradition of the bridal cakes, prepared by the family of the bride and consumed during the

wedding ceremony to signify the new union. Communal eating is still a common rite in many wedding ceremonies.

39. Plutarch *Life of Alexander* 9.4–5. See also Justin *Epitome,* 9,7.34 and Pseudo-Callisthenes, *Greek Alexander Romance* 1.21.

40. Plutarch, *Life of Alexander* 5.2 (trans. B. Perrin, Loeb 99). See E.A. Fredricksmeyer, 'Philip and Alexander: Emulation and Resentment' in *Classical Journal,* Vol. 85 No. 4 (1990), pp. 300–15.

41. Plutarch *Life of Alexander* 50.4–5.

42. Quintus Curtius, *History of Alexander* 8.1.20–1, 8.2.8–9.

43. Quintus Curtius, *History of Alexander* 8.1.24–5.

44. Arrian, *Anabasis of Alexander* 4.8.7 (trans. P.A. Brunt, Loeb 236).

45. Quintus Curtius, *History of Alexander* 8.1.49 (trans. J. C. Rolfe, Loeb 369).

46. Arrian, *Anabasis of Alexander* 4.8.9 (trans. author).

47. Plutarch, *Life of Alexander* 51.5. See Euripides *Andromache* 695 (trans. J. Morwood, Oxford World's Classics).

48. For further discussion on the death of Kleitos, see E.D. Carney, 'The Death of Clitus' in *Greek, Roman and Byzantine Studies,* Vol. 22 (1981) pp. 149–60; L.A.Tritle, 'Alexander and the Killing of Cleitus the Black' in W. Heckel and L.A. Tritle (eds.), *Crossroads of History: The Age of Alexander* (Claremont (CA), 2003), pp. 127–46; A.B. Bosworth, *A Historical Commentary on Arrian's History of Alexander, Vol. II. Commentary on Books IV-V* (Oxford, 1995), pp. 51–68.

49. Plutarch, *Life of Alexander* 9.3 (Olympias). Demosthenes, *Second Olynthiac* (2) 18, *Response to the Letter of Philip* (11) 9, Justin, *Epitome* 9.8.17 (jealous and selfish Philip).

50. Justin, *Epitome* 9.8.11.

51. For passes of the Pindos, see N.G.L. Hammond, 'Prehistoric Epirus and the Dorian Invasion' in *Annual of the British School in Athens,* Vol. 32 (1932), pp. 131–79, and *Epirus: the Geography, the Ancient Remains, the History and Topography of Epirus and Adjacent Areas* (Oxford, 1967); G.A. Pikoulas, 'The Crossings of the Pindus and Philip II' (in Greek) in *Ancient Macedonia,* Vol. 7 (2007), pp. 209–20; M.B. Hatzopoulos, L.D. Loukopoulou and M.B. Sakellariou, *Epirus: 4,000 years of Greek History and Civilisation. Greek Lands in History, Vol.II* (Athens, 2005).

52. C.C. King, *Lament from Epirus: An Odyssey into Europe's Oldest Surviving Folk Music* (New York and London, 2018), pp. 218–19.

53. Kitsos Harisiadis' recording is one of the best. It can be found on iTunes or YouTube.

54. G. Pliakou, 'The basin of Ioannina in central Epirus, northwestern Greece, from the Early Iron Age to the Roman period' in *Archaeological Reports for 2017–18*, No. 64 (2018), pp. 133–51.

55. G. Pliakou, 'Searching for the seat of the Aeacids' in G. De Sensi Sestito and M. Intrieri (eds.), *Sulla rotta per la Sicilia: L'Epiro, Corcira e l'occidente* (Pisa, 2011), pp. 89–108.

56. Hyperides, *In Defence of Euxenippus* (4) 24–6 (Olympias and the Athenians). For Macedonian links to the sanctuary see Euripides, *Archelaus* frag. 228a. For more information on Dodona, see S. Dakaris, *Archaeological Guide to Dodona* (Athens, 2010); D. Chapinal-Heras, *Experiencing Dodona: The Development of the Epirote Sanctuary from Archaic to Hellenistic Times* (Berlin, 2021).

57. For the published tablets see S. Dakaris, I. Vokotopoulou, A.F. Christides and S. Tselikas (eds.), *The Oracular Tablets of Dodona from the Excavations of D. Evangelides, Vols. I–II* (Athens, 2013). Some can be viewed online at www.dodonaonline.com. For more information on the Oracle, see H.K. Parke, *The Oracles of Zeus, Dodona, Olympia, Ammon* (Oxford, 1967).

58. Plutarch, *Life of Alexander* 9.6 (trans. I. Scott-Kilvert and T.E. Duff, Penguin). Also related in *Moralia* 70b–c, 179c.

59. Justin, *Epitome* 9.7.6.

60. Plutarch, *Moralia* 179c, suggests that both Olympias and Alexander were reconciled to Philip. Pseudo-Callisthenes, *Greek Alexander Romance* 1.22 suggests reconciliation with both.

61. Quintus Curtius, *History of Alexander* 8.1.25–6 (trans. J.C. Rolfe, Loeb 369).

62. Hammond believed that Alexander was given some mission by Philip and that Greek gossip turned it into exile. N.G.L. Hammond, 'Alexander's Campaign in Illyria' in *The Journal of Hellenic Studies*, Vol. 94 (1974), p. 87 fn. 35, and 'The Western Frontier in the Reign of Philip II' in *Ancient Macedonian Studies in Honour of Charles F. Edson* (Thessaloniki, 1981), p. 213 fn. 28.

63. Plutarch, *Life of Alexander* 10.1–3. For recent discussions of the so-called Pixodaros affair, see M.B. Hatzopoulos, 'A Reconsideration of the Pixodarus Affair' in B. Barr-Sharrar and E.N. Borza (eds.), *Macedonia and Greece in Late Classical and Early Hellenistic Times. Studies in the History of Art*, Vol 19 (Washington, 1982), pp. 59–66; S. Ruzicka, 'The "Pixodarus Affair" Reconsidered Again' in E.D. Carney and D. Ogden

(eds.), *Philip and Alexander the Great: Father and Son, Lives and Afterlives* (Oxford, 2010), pp. 3–11; V. French and P. Dixon, 'The Pixodarus Affair: Another View' in *Ancient World*, Vol. 13 (1986), pp. 73–82.

64. S. Drougou, 'Vergina – the Ancient City of Aegae' in R.J. Lane Fox (ed.), *Brill's Companion to Ancient Macedon. Studies in the Archaeology and History of Macedon, 650 BC–300 AD* (Leiden and Boston, 2011), pp. 254–5.

65. Plutarch, *Life of Alexander* 10.3. Arrian suggests this exile occurred earlier with the dishonouring of Olympias, presumably in relation to the argument at the wedding feast in 337 BC (*Anabasis of Alexander* 3.6.5). This dishonouring may relate to Kleopatra's name change to Eurydike. See W. Heckel, 'Kleopatra or Eurydike?' in *Phoenix*, Vol. 32 (1978), pp. 155–8.

66. On Kynnane see Arrian, *History of the Successors* frags. 1.22–24 and Polyaenus, *Stratagems* 8.60. Also W. Heckel, 'Kynnane the Illyrian' in *Rivista storica dell'antichita*, Vol. 13–14 (1986), pp. 193–200; W.S. Greenwalt, 'The Marriageability Age at the Argead court: 360–317 BC' in *Classical World*, Vol. 82 (1988), pp. 93–7.

8 THE FINAL ACT

1. L. Heuzey and H. Daumet, *Mission archéologique de Macédoine* (Paris, 1876), p. 178.

2. L. Heuzey, *Le mont Olympe et l'Acarnanie: exploration de ces deux régions, avec l'étude de leurs antiquités, de leurs populations anciennes et modernes, de leur géographie et de leur histoire* (Paris, 1860), p. 189.

3. Heuzey and Daumet, *Mission archéologique de Macédoine*, p. 177–9. An English translation of his first descriptions of the area can be found in S. Drougou and C. Saatsoglou-Paliadeli, *Vergina: The Land and its History* (1998), pp. 52–68.

4. L. Heuzey, *Le Mont Olympe et l'Acarnanie: exploration de ces deux régions*, p. 190. Palatitsia's sixteenth-century church of Aghios Demetrios, recently restored and home to some exquisite murals, gives an excellent example of what Heuzey was describing. Set into the exterior walls are elements from a bygone age – an ashlar block still preserving its finely cut edges, the great circular face of an upended column drum. Inside, the church's internal pillars rest on more reused drums, honeycombed

with holes, a natural feature of the local volcanic rock from which they
were carved.

5. Heuzey and Daumet, *Mission archéologique de Macédoine*, p. 177.
6. Heuzey and Daumet, *Mission archéologique de Macédoine*, pp. 181–3.
7. Justin, *Epitome to the Philippic History of Pompeius Trogus* 7.1.7–12 suggests
    that Karanos, a mythical founder of the Macedonian kingdom, had taken
    over a city called Edessa, which he renamed as Aigai; it was believed that
    at some later point in history the city had reverted to its original name.
    Some had already started to doubt the Aigai–Edessa identification,
    including Tafel and Papazoglou, but it was Hammond's arguments that
    proved crucial in the Aigai–Vergina identification, an idea that was also
    being considered by Robin Lane Fox. See N.G.L. Hammond, 'The
    Archaeological background to the Macedonian kingdom' in *Ancient
    Macedonia*, Vol. 1 (1970), pp. 53–67, *A History of Macedonia, Vol. I Historical
    Geography and Prehistory* (Oxford, 1972), pp. 156–9, 'The Location of
    Aegae' in *The Journal of Hellenic Studies*, Vol. 117 (1997), pp. 177–9; R.
    Lane Fox, *Alexander the Great* (London, 1973). For the history of the
    debate, see M.B. Hatzopoulos, *Ancient Macedonia. Trends in Classics – Key
    Perspectives on Classical Research* (Berlin/Boston, 2020), pp. 8–11.
8. A. Kottaridi, 'The Palace of Aegae' in R.J. Lane Fox (ed.), *Brill's
    Companion to Ancient Macedon. Studies in the Archaeology and History
    of Macedon, 650 BC–300 AD* (Leiden and Boston, 2011), pp. 297–333.
9. Diodorus Siculus, *Library of History* 16.92.1–3.
10. The 'tomb of Eurydike' has yet to be fully published but descriptions
    can be found in M. Andronikos, 'Vergina, Excavations of 1987' (in
    Greek) in *Archaeological work in Macedonia and Thrace*, Vol. 1 (1987),
    pp. 81–8, and R. Ginouvès and M.B. Hatzopoulos (eds.), *Macedonia:
    From Philip II to the Roman Conquest* (Princeton, 1994), pp. 154–61.
11. See Kottaridi, 'The Palace of Aegae', Lane Fox (ed.), *Brill's Companion
    to Ancient Macedon*, p. 332.
12. See C. Saatsoglou-Paliadeli, 'The Palace of Vergina-Aegae and its
    surroundings' in I. Nielsen (ed.), *The Royal Palace Institution in the First
    Millennium BC: Regional Development and Cultural Interchange between
    East and West* (Athens, 2001), pp. 201–13.
13. Theopompus, frag. 27. See Kottaridi, 'The Palace of Aegae' in Lane Fox
    (ed.), *Brill's Companion to Ancient Macedon*, p. 324.
14. Athenaeus, *Learned Banqueters* 13.557e, Diodorus Siculus, *Library of
    History* 17.2.3–4.

15. Diodorus Siculus, *Library of History* 16.91.2. Attalos may have been in co-command of the expedition force, along with Parmenion (Diodorus Siculus, *Library of History* 17.2.4). Justin, *Epitome* 9.5.8 also adds a third commander, Amyntas, though his patronymic is not given, making it difficult to be sure who he was. See E.I. McQueen, *Diodorus Siculus: The Reign of Philip II. The Greek and Macedonian Narrative from Book XVI* (London, 1995), p. 171.

16. Diodorus Siculus, *Library of History* 16.91.2 (trans, C. Bradford Welles, Loeb 422), Pausanias, *Guide to Greece* 8.7.6.

17. Justin, *Epitome* 10.1–3, Diodorus Siculus, *Library of History* 17.5.3–6.3. On the reign of Darius III see P. Briant *Darius in the Shadow of Alexander* (London, 2015).

18. Diodorus Siculus, *Library of History* 16.92.3–4, (trans. C. Bradford Welles, Loeb 422).

19. Diodorus Siculus, *Library of History* 16.93.4–5.

20. For discussion of this story see M.B. Hatzopoulos, 'The reliability of Diodorus' account of Philip's assassination' in C. Bearzot and F. Landucci (eds.), *Diodoro e l'altra Grecia: Macedonia, Occidente, Ellenismo nella Biblioteca storica. Atti del Convegno, Milano, 15–16 gennaio 2004* (Milan, 2005), pp. 43–65, and *La mort de Philippe II. Une étude des sources. Meletemata 76* (Athens, 2018).

21. Justin, *Epitome* 9.6.5–6 suggests that Pausanias was also raped by Attalos and his fellow diners.

22. Diodorus Siculus, *Library of History* 16.94.1 says that in this design Pausanias was encouraged by the words of his tutor, the sophist Hermokrates (also called Hermokles by Valerius Maximus in *Memorable Doings and Sayings* 8.14.4), who when asked how one might become most famous, replied that it would be by killing the one who had accomplished most; for just as long as he was remembered, so long would his slayer be remembered. McQueen, *Diodorus Siculus: The Reign of Philip II*, pp. 178–9 has rightly seen this story as of dubious worth, being similar to Kallisthenes' exhortation to the royal page Hermolaos who later conspired against Alexander (Plutarch, *Life of Alexander* 55.2, Arrian, *Anabasis of Alexander* 4.10.3).

23. Stobaeus, *Anthology* 4.34.70, Suetonius, *Twelve Caesars, Caligula* 57.4, Josephus, *Jewish Antiquities,* 19.94–6.

24. S. Drougou, *The Ancient Theatre of Vergina* (Thessaloniki, 2017), p. 26; P. Adam-Veleni, *Theatre and Spectacle in Ancient Macedonia* (in Greek

and French) (Thessaloniki, 2010), pp. 77–81, 153–5.

25. E.N. Borza, *In the Shadow of Olympus: The Emergence of Macedon* (Princeton, 1990), pp. 255–6; E. Moloney, '*Philippus in acie tutior quam in theatro fuit* . . . (Curtius 9.6.25): The Macedonian Kings and Greek Theatre' in E. Csapo, H.R. Goette, J.R. Green and P. Wilson (eds.), *Greek Theatre in the Fourth Century BC* (Berlin and Boston, 2014), p. 246.

26. Diodorus Siculus, *Library of History* 16.93–4, Justin, *Epitome* 9.6–7. On the different sources and traditions of Philip's murder, see Hatzopoulos, *La mort de Philippe II* and 'The reliability of Diodorus' account of Philip's assassination' in Bearzot and Landucci (eds.) *Diodoro e l'altra Grecia*, pp. 43–65.

27. It was later claimed that a depiction of a chariot adorned the hilt of Pausanias' dagger. Philip had apparently been told by an oracle to beware at all times of four-horse chariots, and he took appropriate actions to do so, giving orders for such vehicles within his kingdom to be unyoked and even avoiding the place in Boiotia that was called Chariot; but he could not escape the blade of Pausanias, and so the chariot finally took its victim. See Cicero, *Concerning Fate* 3.5, Aelian, *Historical Miscellany* 3.45, Valerius Maximus, *Memorable Doings and Sayings* 1.8 ext 9.

28. Stobaeus, *Anthology* 4.34.70.

29. Diodorus Siculus, *Library of History* 16.94.4.

30. Arrian, *Anabasis of Alexander* 1.25.2, Quintus Curtius, *History of Alexander* 7.1.6, *Alexander Romance* 1.24, Hatzopoulos, *La mort de Philippe II*.

31. For possible reconstructions of the events, see N.G.L. Hammond, '"Philip's Tomb" in Historical Context' in *Greek, Roman and Byzantine Studies*, Vol. 19 (1978), pp. 331–50; Hatzopoulos, *La mort de Philippe II*.

32. S.E. Psoma, 'Innovation or Tradition? Succession to the Kingship in Temenid Macedonia' in *Tekmeria*, Vol. 11 (2012), pp. 73–87.

33. Plutarch, *Moralia* 178f (trans. F. Cole Babbitt, Loeb 245).

34. Pseudo-Callisthenes, *Greek Alexander Romance*, 1.26. See Quintus Curtius, *History of Alexander* 10.7.14, for the symbolism of strapping on a cuirass.

35. Pseudo-Callisthenes, *Greek Alexander Romance*, 1.26 suggests the theatre as the setting, although the palace courtyard is another possibility (conversation with Angeliki Kottaridi).

36. Alexander's speech is related in Diodorus Siculus, *Library of History* 17.2.1–3 and Justin, *Epitome* 11.1.1–10, although when and where it happened is not clearly attested.

37. Quintus Curtius, *History of Alexander* 10.6.12, 10.7.14–15 (spears and shields); Quintus Curtius, *History of Alexander* 10.7.7, Plutarch, *Life of Demetrius* 17.5 (hailing as king).

38. On oaths see Quintus Curtius, *History of Alexander* 7.1.29–30, Polybius, *Histories* 15.25.11. It's unknown if the king reciprocated the oath, as was the custom in Epeiros (Plutarch, *Life of Pyrrhus* 5.2–3). See N.G.L. Hammond, 'The Continuity of Macedonian Institutions and the Macedonian Kingdoms of the Hellenistic Era' in *Historia: Zeitschrift für Alte Geschichte*, Bd. 49 H. 2 (2000), pp. 141–60; F.W. Walbank, 'Macedonia and Greece', in F.W. Walbank, A.E. Austin, M.W. Frederiksen and R.M. Ogilvie (eds.), *Cambridge Ancient History. Vol. VII part I: The Hellenistic World* (2nd edn, Cambridge, 1984), p. 226.

39. Papyrus Oxyrhynchus XV 1798.

40. Diodorus Siculus, *Library of History* 17.2.3. See Quintus Curtius, *History of Alexander* (10.9.11–15) on the army's purification after death of Alexander in 323 BC.

41. R. Strootman, *Courts and Elites in the Hellenistic Empires: The Near East After the Achaemenids, c.330 to 30 BCE* (Edinburgh, 2014), pp. 210–32.

42. On the death rituals of the Greeks, see R. Garland, *The Greek Way of Death* (New York, 1985).

43. Papyrus Oxyrhynchus XV 1798 (fir tree pyre).

44. Diodorus Siculus, *Library of History* 16.94.4.

45. See Papyrus Oxyrhynchus XV 1798, *Alexander Itinerary* 5, Pseudo-Callisthenes, *Greek Alexander Romance* 1.24, Justin, *Epitome* 9.7.10. For the papyrus' restoration see P.J. Parsons, 'The Burial of Philip?' in *American Journal of Ancient History*, Vol. 4 (1979), pp. 97–101.

46. Aristotle, *Politics* 5.10 (1311a36).

47. For a selection of writings exploring the possibility that others were involved in Philip's murder, see E. Badian, 'Once More the Death of Philip' in *Ancient Macedonia*, Vol. 7 (Thessaloniki, 2007), pp. 389–406; W. Heckel, T. Howe and S. Müller, '"The giver of the bride, the bridegroom, and the bride." A study in the murder of Philip and its aftermath' in T. Howe, S. Müller and R. Stoneman (eds.), *Ancient Historiography on War and Empire* (Oxford, 2017), pp. 145–67; E.D. Carney, 'The

Politics of Polygamy: Olympias, Alexander and the Murder of Philip' in *Historia: Zeitschrift für Alte Geschichte*, Bd. 41 H. 2 (1992), pp. 169–89; Hatzopoulos, *La morte de Philip II*.

48. Polyaenus, *Stratagems* 4.2.3; see Chapter 6.

49. Justin, *Epitome* 11.2.1–2.

50. Quintus Curtius, *History of Alexander* 7.1.6–8. 'Guilt', as seen from later trials under Alexander, could be as trivial as not reporting knowledge of hostile intentions, association with the assassin, etc. See A.B. Bosworth, 'Philip II and Upper Macedonia' in *The Classical Quarterly*, Vol. 21 No. 1 (1971), pp. 93–105; E.D. Carney, 'Alexander the Lyncestian: The Disloyal Opposition' in *Greek, Roman and Byzantine Studies*, Vol. 21 (1980), pp. 23–33. For sons of Aeropos and possible Argead descent, see N.G.L. Hammond, 'Some Passages in Arrian concerning Alexander' in *The Classical Quarterly*, Vol. 30 No. 2 (1980), pp. 455–76.

51. Quintus Curtius, *History of Alexander* 7.1.7. See previous note.

52. Quintus Curtius, *History of Alexander* 8.6.28 (killing of relatives of the condemned). Regarding the sons of Arrhabaios, Amyntas may be the same man mentioned in a position of command in the Asia expeditionary force. For Neoptolemos' flight see Arrian, *Anabasis of Alexander* 1.20.10.

53. Arrian, *Anabasis of Alexander* 2.14.5, Quintus Curtius, *History of Alexander* 4.1.12.

54. Plutarch, *Life of Alexander* 10.4 (trans. B. Perrin, Loeb 99). Euripides *Medea* 5.287–9.

55. Plutarch, *Life of Alexander* 10.4, Justin, *Epitome* 9.7.1.

56. Justin, *Epitome* 9.7.14 (trans. J.C. Yardley, American Philological Association).

57. Justin, *Epitome* 9.7.12.

58. Pausanias, *Guide to Greece* 8.7.7.

59. Diodorus Siculus, *Library of History* 17.2.4–6.

60. Justin, *Epitome* 11.2.3. See W. Heckel, 'Philip II, Kleopatra and Karanos' in *Rivista di Filologia e di Istruzione Classica*, Vol. 107 (1979), pp. 385–93; P. Emberger, 'The Problem of Karanos. Philip II and his Non-Existent Son' in *Diomedes*, Vol. 6 (2013), pp. 27–32; and R.J. Lane Fox, 'Philip's and Alexander's Macedon' in Lane Fox (ed.), *Brill's Companion to Ancient Macedon*, p. 385. Karanos' name, that of the mythical founder of the Macedonian line of kings, suggests that he was a concubine's son; Alexander's illegitimate son by his mistress Barsine was called Herakles,

which may indicate a naming tradition for such children. See S. Psoma, 'Naming the Argeads' in *KTÈMA*, Vol. 40 (2015), pp. 15–26.

61. Plutarch, *Moralia* 327c (trans. F. Cole Babbit, Loeb 305).

62. Quintus Curtius, *History of Alexander* 6.9.17–8. See also Justin, *Epitome* 12.2.3 (Delphic Oracle prediction of plot from within Macedonia).

63. IG VII 3055.

64. For reconstructions of Amyntas' possible conspiracy see J.R. Ellis, 'Amyntas Perdikka, Philip II and Alexander the Great' in *The Journal of Hellenic Studies*, Vol. 91 (1971), pp. 15–24; L. Prandi, 'A few Remarks on the Amyntas "Conspiracy"' in W. Will (ed.), *Alexander der Grosse: eine Welteroberung und ihr Hintergrund: Vorträge des Internationalen Bonner Alexanderkolloquiums, 19-21.12.1996* (Bonn, 1998), pp. 91–101; I. Pafford, 'Amyntas Son of Perdikkas, King of the Macedonians, at the Sanctuary of Trophonios at Lebadeia' in *The Ancient World*, Vol. 42.2 (2011), pp. 211–22. For the defection of Amyntas, son of Antiochos see Diodorus Siculus, *Library of History* 17.48.2, Arrian, *Anabasis of Alexander* 1.17.9 and 1.25.3, Quintus Curtius, *History of Alexander* 3.11.18. On *proxenos* awards see P.J. Rhodes and R. Osborne *Greek Historical Inscriptions 404–323 BC* (2003, Oxford) pp. 370–373 no. 75.

65. Arrian, *Anabasis of Alexander* 1.5.4.

66. J.R. Ellis, 'The first months of Alexander's reign' in E.N. Borza and B. Barr-Sharrar (eds.), *Macedonia and Greece in Late Classical and Early Hellenistic Times. Studies in the History of Art*, Vol. 19 (Washington, 1982), pp. 69–73.

67. Plutarch, *Life of Alexander* 11.1 (trans. B. Perrin, Loeb 99).

9 RETURN OF THE KING

1. L. Heuzey and H. Daumet, *Mission archéologique de Macédoine* (Paris, 1876), p. 233. Also recorded in Heuzey's earlier work, L. Heuzey, *Le Mont Olympe et l'Acarnanie: exploration de ces deux régions, avec l'étude de leurs antiquités, de leurs populations anciennes et modernes, de leur géographie et de leur histoire* (Paris, 1860), p. 200.

2. Heuzey and Daumet, *Mission archéologique de Macédoine*, pp. 233–4.

3. Y. Hamilakis, *The Nation and its Ruins: Antiquity, Archaeology, and National Imagination in Greece* (Oxford, 2007), pp. 125–6.

4. M. Andronicos, *Vergina: The Royal Tombs and the Ancient City* (Athens, 1984), p. 55–6.

5. M. Andronikos, *The Chronicle of Vergina* (in Greek) (Athens, 1997), p. 7. The following story of the Great Tumulus' excavation is also based on the following accounts: M. Andronikos, 'The Excavation of the Great Tumulus of Vergina' (in Greek with English summary) in *Athens Annals of Archaeology*, Vol. 9 (1976), pp. 123–30, 'Vergina: The Royal Graves in the Great Tumulus' in *Athens Annals of Archaeology*, Vol. 10 (1977), pp. 40–72, 'Plenary Papers: The Tombs at the Great Tumulus of Vergina' in J.N. Coldstream and M.A.R. Colledge (eds.), *Greece and Italy in the Classical World: Acta of the 11th International Congress of Classical Archaeology* (London, 1979), pp. 39–56, and *Vergina: The Royal Tombs and the Ancient City*; S. Drougou, 'Vergina: On the Tracks of the Macedonian kings' in P. Valavanis (ed.), *Great Moments in Greek Archaeology* (Athens and Los Angeles, 2007), pp. 256–71.

6. Andronikos, 'The Excavation of the Great Tumulus of Vergina', p. 130 (ten were found that year, bringing the total to at least nineteen by 1976).

7. S. Drougou and C. Saatsoglou-Paliadeli, *Vergina: The Land and its History* (Athens, 2005), p. 44.

8. Plutarch, *Life of Pyrrhus* 26.6–7 (trans. I. Scott-Kilvert and T.E. Duff, Penguin).

9. Andronikos, *The Chronicle of Vergina*, p. 65. Also recounted in Drougou and Saatsoglou-Paliadeli, *Vergina: The Land and its History*, p. 48.

10. M. Andronikos, 'Vergina and Aegae', in *To Vima Newspaper* (3 October 1976), 'The Excavation of the Great Tumulus of Vergina'. Also mentioned in Hamilakis, *The Nation and its Ruins*, p. 149.

11. M. Andronikos and M. Fotiadis, 'The Royal Tomb of Philip II: An Unlooted Macedonian Grave at Vergina' in *Archaeology*, Vol. 31 No. 5 (1978), p. 3.

12. Andronikos, *The Chronicle of Vergina*, p. 72.

13. Andronicos, *Vergina: The Royal Tombs and the Ancient City*, pp. 64, 100.

14. Andronicos, *Vergina: The Royal Tombs and the Ancient City*, p. 66.

15. M. Andronikos, *Vergina II: The 'Tomb of Persephone'* (in Greek) (Athens, 1994). Andronikos put forward the idea that it was created by a famous painter called Nikomachos (Pliny the Elder, *Natural History* 35.108). The 'Abduction of Persephone' was among his repertoire and he was noted for the rapidity of his compositions.

16. Andronicos, *Vergina: The Royal Tombs and the Ancient City*, p. 87; A. Kottaridi, *Macedonian Treasures: A Tour through the Museum of the Royal Tombs of Aegae* (Athens, 2011), p. 25.

17. See D. Grant, *Unearthing the Family of Alexander the Great. The Remarkable Discovery of the Royal Tombs of Macedon* (Yorkshire/ Philadelphia, 2019), pp. 139–41.

18. Dimensions from C. Saatsoglou-Paliadeli, *Vergina: The tomb of Philip, the mural with the hunt* (in Greek) (Athens, 2004), p. 49.

19. Andronicos, *Vergina: The Royal Tombs and the Ancient City*, p. 219. The unrobbed Macedonian tomb was near Karytsa, Pieria. The unlooted cist or box tombs at Derveni had been discovered in 1962, hinting at the riches that elite tombs normally possessed.

20. Andronikos, *The Chronicle of Vergina*, p. 107.

21. Andronicos, *Vergina: The Royal Tombs and the Ancient City*, p. 68.

22. M. Andronikos, 'Vergina: The Royal Graves in the Great Tumulus', p. 52 and *Vergina: The Royal Tombs and the Ancient City*, p. 70.

23. Andronicos, *Vergina: The Royal Tombs and the Ancient City*, p. 70.

24. Andronicos, *Vergina: The Royal Tombs and the Ancient City*, p. 73.

25. See previous note.

26. A.-M. Guimier-Sorbets, 'Mobilier et décor des tombes macédoniennes' in R. Frei-Stolba and K. Gex (eds.), *Recherches récentes sur le monde hellénistique. Actes du colloque en l'honneur de Pierre Ducrey (Lausanne, 20-21 novembre 1998)* (Bern and Oxford, 2001), pp. 217–29.

27. Andronicos, *Vergina: The Royal Tombs and the Ancient City*, p. 78.

28. B. Tsgarida, 'The golden wreath of Myrtale from Vergina' in *Amitos, An Honorary Volume for Professor M. Andronikos* (Thessaloniki, 1987), pp. 907–14.

29. Andronicos, *Vergina: The Royal Tombs and the Ancient City*, p. 228.

30. Andronicos, 'Vergina: The Royal Graves in the Great Tumulus', p. 72, *Vergina: The Royal Tombs and Ancient City*, p. 231.

31. Hamilakis, *The Nation and its Ruins*, p. 152.

32. Andronicos, *Vergina: The Royal Tombs and the Ancient City*, p. 226.

33. Diodorus Siculus, *Library of History* 19.11.1–9 (death of Arrhidaios-Philip and Adea-Eurydike), 19.52.5, and Diyllus frag. 1 (burial of the royal pair in Aigai, along with Kynnane).

34. *Greek Anthology* 7.238 (Philip II buried at Aigai); Diodorus Siculus, *Library of History* 19.52.5 (Arrhidaios-Philip buried at Aigai).

35. For an overview of the arguments, see M.B. Hatzopoulos, 'The Burial of the Dead (at Vergina) or the Unending Controversy on the Identity of the Occupants of Tomb II' in *Tekmeria*, Vol. 9 (2008), pp. 91–118; Grant, *Unearthing the Family of Alexander the Great*. For a flavour of

the academic disagreement see E.N. Borza and O. Palagia, 'The Chronology of the Macedonian Royal Tombs at Vergina' in *Jahrbuch des Deutschen Archäologischen Instituts*, Vol. 122 (2007), pp. 81–125; R.J. Lane Fox, 'Introduction: Dating the Royal Tombs at Vergina' in Lane Fox (ed.), *Brill's Companion to Ancient Macedon. Studies in the Archaeology and History of Macedon, 650 BC – 300 AD* (Leiden and Boston, 2011), pp. 1–34.

36. See for example on the pottery assemblage, S. Drougou, *Vergina: The Pottery from the Great Tumulus* (in Greek) (2005, Athens); on the painted frieze, C. Saatsoglou-Paliadeli, *Vergina: The tomb of Philip, the mural with the hunt* (in Greek) on papyri finds from within the tomb, R. Janko, 'Papyri from the Great Tumulus at Vergina, Macedonia' in *Zeitschrift für Papyrologie und Epigraphik*, Bd. 205 (2018), pp. 195–206. At the time of writing reports are still expected on the weapons, jewellery and other items.

37. Hatzopoulos, 'The Burial of the Dead (at Vergina) or the Unending Controversy on the Identity of the Occupants of Tomb II'. See also N.G.L. Hammond, '"Philip's Tomb" in Historical Context' in *Greek, Roman and Byzantine Studies*, Vol. 19 (1978), pp. 331–50.

38. J.E. Dimacopoulos, *A Shelter in the Style of a Tumulus. Vergina, An Underground Archaeological site and museum in the type of a crypt* (Athens, 1995). For a good general guide to the museum and finds, see Kottaridi, *Macedonian Treasures: A tour through the Museum of the Royal Tombs of Aigai.*

39. Andronicos, *Vergina: The Royal Tombs and the Ancient City*, p. 97; A. Kottaridi, 'Royal pyres from the necropolis of Aegae' (in Greek) in *Ancient Macedonia*, Vol. 6 (1999), pp. 631–41, 'Burial Customs and beliefs in the royal necropolis of Aegae' in *Heracles to Alexander the Great: Treasures from the Royal Capital of Macedon, a Hellenic Kingdom in the Age of Democracy* (Oxford, 2011), pp. 131–66, 'Macedonian Burial customs and the funeral of Alexander the Great' in *Alexander the Great: From Macedonia to the Oikoumene* (Veria, 1999), pp. 113–20, and *Macedonian Treasures: A Tour through the Museum of the Royal Tombs of Aigai*, pp. 60–3; T.G. Antikas, 'Horses and Heroes in the tomb of Philip II' in *Minerva*, Vol. 13 No. 1 (2002), pp. 46–9.

40. Pseudo-Callisthenes, *Greek Alexander Romance* 1.24.

41. Justin, *Epitome of the Philippic History of Pompeius Trogus* 11.1.4.

42. Plato, *Phaedo* 117c.

43. Andronicos, *Vergina: The Royal Tombs and the Ancient City*, pp. 165–6.

44. It's debatable whether this shield was purely ceremonial or was used in battle, but perhaps the latter is more likely. Plutarch reports that the mercenaries who had fought for the Phokians during the Third Sacred War had similar, richly adorned shields: 'gilded shields of purple with amber and ivory inlaid' (Plutarch, *Life of Timoleon* 31.1).

45. Pliny the Elder mentions that asbestos was used for the robes of royalty to keep their ashes separate from the pyre (*Natural History* 19.19)

46. T.G. Antikas and L.K. Wynn-Antikas, 'New finds from the Cremains in Tomb II at Aegae Point to Philip II and a Scythian Princess' in *International Journal of Osteoarchaeology*, Vol. 26 (2015), pp. 682–92, at p. 685.

47. Antikas and Wynn-Antikas, 'New finds from the Cremains in Tomb II at Aegae Point to Philip II and a Scythian Princess,' p. 684.

48. Grant, *Unearthing the Family of Alexander the Great*, pp. 143–60.

49. The most recent estimate, around 160cm (+/- 3.37cm), is based on the preserved left tibia. Antikas and Wynn-Antikas, 'New finds from the Cremains in Tomb II at Aegae Point to Philip II and a Scythian Princess', p. 685. But previous researchers have suggested a wider range between 160 and 170cm although they concede that some bone shrinkage may have occurred during cremation. N.I. Xirotiris and F. Langenscheidt, 'The Cremations from the Royal Macedonian Tombs of Vergina' in *Archaeological Ephemeris* (1981), pp. 142–60.

50. Antikas and Wynn-Antikas, 'New finds from the Cremains in Tomb II at Aegae Point to Philip II and a Scythian Princess', p. 686, Demosthenes, *On the Crown* (18) 67 and Scholia (67.124). See also A.S. Riginos, 'The Wounding of Philip II of Macedon: Fact and Fiction' in *The Journal of Hellenic Studies*, Vol. 114 (1994), pp. 103–19.

51. Nicholas Hammond was first to propose that Philip took a Scythian wife, a daughter of King Ateas, during his 339 BC campaign, and that she was to be identified with the woman in the antechamber. The authors of the most recent study have endorsed this view, putting forward new evidence to support her identity, but there is no written evidence to suggest that Philip had such a wife or concubine. Considering the similarities between Getic and Scythian culture and warfare, Meda, who is historically attested, is just as likely. See Hammond, '"Philip's Tomb" in Historical Context', and Antikas and Wynn-Antikas, 'New finds from the Cremains in Tomb II at Aegae Point to Philip II and a Scythian Princess.'

52. Andronicos, *Vergina: The Royal Tombs and the Ancient City*, p. 228 originally proposed an age range of 23–27; Xirotiris and Langenscheidt, 'The Cremations from the Royal Macedonian Tombs of Vergina' amended the range to 20–30; Antikas and Wynn-Antikas, 'New finds from the Cremains in Tomb II at Aegae Point to Philip II and a Scythian Princess' estimate 32, plus or minus 2 years.

53. Herodotus, *Histories* 4.93–4, 5.4 (Getai and belief in immortality); Thucydides, *Peloponnesian War* 2.96 (same mode of warfare as Scythians); Stephanus of Byzantium s.v. 'Getia' (sacrificing themselves on death of husband; Stephanus mentions Philip's wife while recounting the tradition). Excavations of Getic tombs in north-eastern Thrace may provide some evidence of this ritual; see for example the Sveshtari tomb where a female skeleton was discovered in the antechamber with a fatal wound to the occipital bone. See P. Delev, 'Lysimachus, the Getae and Archaeology' in *The Classical Quarterly*, Vol. 50 No. 2 (2000), p. 398.

54. On the frieze see Andronicos, *Vergina: The Royal Tombs and the Ancient City*, pp. 100–18; C. Saatsoglou-Paliadeli, *Vergina: The tomb of Philip, the mural with the hunt* (in Greek); H.M. Franks, *Hunters, Heroes, Kings: The Frieze of Tomb II at Vergina* (Princeton, 2012); Kottaridi, *Macedonian Treasures: A Tour through the Museum of the Royal Tombs of Aigai*, pp. 43–7; A. Cohen, *Art in the Era of Alexander the Great: Paradigms of Manhood and their Cultural Traditions* (Cambridge and New York, 2010). Andronikos, supporting a theory of Karl Schefold, thought that it may be a work of Philoxenos of Eretria, a pupil of Nikomachos; Aristides, a son of Nikomachos, has more recently been proposed by Saatsoglou-Paliadeli.

55. For the mountain lion (*Panthera leo*) in Macedonia see Herodotus, *Histories* 7.124–7, Aristotle, *History of Animals* 7 (8) 14–15 (606b), Pausanias, *Guide to Greece* 9.40.8–9. See also numismatic evidence in V. Alonso Troncoso, 'The Animal Types on the Argead Coinage, Wilderness and Macedonia' in T. Howe and F. Pownall (eds.), *Ancient Macedonians in the Greek and Roman Sources. From History to Historiography* (Swansea, 2018), pp. 137–62.

56. Kottaridi, *Macedonian Treasures: A Tour Through the Museum of the Royal Tombs of Aigai*, p. 46.

57. Justin, *Epitome* 11.2.1.

58. Andronikos originally believed that the antechamber had been constructed separately, at a later time, but this was challenged by one

of his engineering colleagues who oversaw the conservation of the tomb and concluded that both main and antechamber were built as one. See Andronicos, *Vergina: The Royal Tombs and the Ancient City*, p. 220; C. Zambas, 'Restoration of the retaining wall of the tomb of Philip B' (in Greek), in *Archaeological excavations in Macedonia and Thrace*, Vol. 13 (1999), pp. 553–65.

59. Other such graveside structures have also been discovered at Aiani and Pella, suggesting a more widespread custom than was previously believed. Pseudo-Callisthenes, *Greek Alexander Romance* 1.25 preserves a story that Alexander visited his father's memorial, but it is misplaced at Pella.

60. Plutarch, *Life of Alexander* 11.2.

61. Justin, *Epitome* 7.2.2–4.

62. Others have suggested that Alexander IV's burial was undertaken by Kassandros. See W.L. Adams, 'Cassander, Alexander IV and the Tombs at Vergina' in *Ancient World*, Vol. 22 (1991), pp. 27–33; V. Alonso Troncoso, 'Some Remarks on the Funerals of the Kings: From Philip II to the Diadochi' in P. Wheatley and R. Hannah (eds.), *Alexander and his Successors: Essays from the Antipodes* (Claremont (CA), 2009), pp. 276–98.

63. Diodorus Siculus, *Library of History* 18.4.1–6; Andronicos, *Vergina: The Royal Tombs and the Ancient City*, pp. 62, 229–30.

10 ALEXANDER IN CHARGE

1. Plutarch, *Life of Demosthenes* 22.1; Aeschines, *Against Ctesiphon* (3) 77, 219.

2. Plutarch, *Life of Demosthenes* 22.1, Aeschines, *Against Ctesiphon* (3) 160.

3. Plutarch, *Life of Phocion* 16.6.

4. Plutarch, *Life of Demosthenes* 22.1, Aeschines, *Against Ctesiphon* (3) 77, 160.

5. For some examples of Demosthenes' praise of Philip see *First Philippic* (4) 4, *Second Olynthiac* (2) 23, *On the Chersonnese* (8) 11–12.

6. Plutarch, *Life of Demosthenes* 23.2, Aeschines, *Against Ctesiphon* (3) 160.

7. Aeschines, *Against Ctesiphon* (3) 173, Dinarchus, *Against Demosthenes* (1) 10, 18, Diodorus Siculus, *Library of History* 17.4.7–9. Plutarch, *Life of Demosthenes* 23.1 mentions Demosthenes' entreaties to Macedonian generals suggesting that not only Attalos was approached. Alexander

later uncovered letters between Demosthenes and Darius' generals in Sardis (Plutarch, *Life of Demosthenes* 20.5, *Moralia* 847f).

8. Diodorus Siculus, *Library of History* 17.3.3–5, Pseudo-Demosthenes, *On the Treaty with Alexander* (17) 235.

9. Polyaenus, *Stratagems* 4.2.23 records an event not mentioned in any other source: that the Thessalians blocked the Tempe pass and forced Alexander to cut steps into nearby Mount Ossa, which later became known as 'Alexander's Ladder' and from which they circumnavigated the blockade. A recent study of the story suggests that it is either a fiction – it certainly has the flavour of folklore – or is related to Alexander's predecessor and uncle, Alexander II. See S.T. Sprawski, 'Alexander at Tempe (Polyaenus 4.3.21): Old Memories for "Tourists" during the Roman Era' in S.G. Gouloulis and S.T. Sdrolia (eds.), *Aghios Dimitrios: History, Art, and historical topography of the monastery and surroundings* (title in Greek) (Larissa, 2010), pp. 433–44.

10. Diodorus Siculus, *Library of History* 17.4.1, Justin, *Epitome of the Philippic History of Pompeius Trogus* 11.3.1–2. Aeschines, *Against Ctesiphon* (3) 160 records that the Thessalians had voted to march against Athens, Philostratus, *Heroicus* 53.16, that Alexander spared Phthia, for Achilles' sake, during his 'enslavement' of Thessaly. Phthia was Achilles' mythical home and may have been given special concessions by the new *archon* of the Thessalian league in honour of his boyhood hero.

11. Aeschines, *Against Ctesiphon* (3) 161 (trans. C.D. Adams, Loeb 106), Diodorus Siculus, *Library of History* 17.4.4–9, Aeschines, *Against Ctesiphon* (3) 161, Plutarch, *Life of Demosthenes* 23.3. Plutarch puts this event in 335 BC, which is a mistake.

12. Arrian, *Anabasis of Alexander* 1.1.3.

13. Arrian, *Anabasis of Alexander* 1.1.2.

14. Diodorus Siculus, *Library of History* 17.4.9, Arrian, *Anabasis of Alexander* 1.1.1–3. Also Plutarch, *Life of Alexander* 14.1 (misdated to 335/4 BC).

15. Plutarch, *Life of Alexander* 14.1–3 (trans. B. Perrin, Loeb 99), also recounted in his *Moralia* 332a–b and 605d; Arrian, *Anabasis of Alexander* 7.2.1–2, Diogenes Laertius, *Lives of Eminent Philosophers*, 6. 32, 60, Cicero, *Tusculan Disputations* 5.32.92, Dio Chrysostom, *Discourse* 4. On the origins of this story, see P.R. Bosman, 'King meets Dog: The origin of the meeting between Alexander and Diogenes' in *Acta Classica*, Vol. 50 (2007), pp. 51–63. For its fame and various uses in historical tradition, see R. Stoneman, 'The Legacy of Alexander in Ancient Philosophy' in

J. Roisman, *Brill's Companion to Alexander the Great* (Leiden, 2003), pp. 325–45; M. Buora, 'L'incontro tra Alessandro e Diogene. Tradizione e significato' in *Atti dell' Istituto Veneto di Scienze, Lettere ed Arti*, Vol. 132 (1973–4), pp. 243–64.

16. Plutarch, *Life of Alexander* 14.4 (trans. I. Scott-Kilvert and T.E. Duff, Penguin), Diodorus Siculus, *Library of History* 17.93.4.

17. Diodorus Siculus, *Library of History* 16.25.3, 16.27.1. Pseudo-Callisthenes, *Greek Alexander Romance* 1.45 toys with this tradition. For some discussion on trying to unravel the source behind Plutarch's story, see L. O'Sullivan, 'Callisthenes and Alexander the Invincible God' in P. Wheatley and E. Baynham (eds.), *East and West in the World Empire of Alexander: Essays in Honour of Brian Bosworth* (Oxford, 2015), pp. 35–52; A.B. Bosworth, *Alexander and the East: The Tragedy of Triumph* (Oxford, 1996), p. 166 fn. 3, who suggests that the Delphi story was probably invented as an explanation of Alexander's later epithet 'invincible'.

18. Justin, *Epitome* 12.2.3. Another piece of Delphic advice is discussed by the ancient authors in relation to Alexander's time in Persia (Plutarch, *Life of Alexander* 37.1, Polyaenus, *Stratagems* 4.3.27, Quintus Curtius, *History of Alexander* 5.4.10). The Pythia had apparently told him to trust in a local wolf (*lykos*) during his march. The prophecy was fulfilled in 331/0 BC when Alexander advanced on Persepolis. The Persian gates (in the Zagros mountains), which protected the approach, were held by the enemy and Alexander sought a way around them. He trusted in a local citizen and shepherd from Lykia (perhaps called Lykios or dressed in a wolf skin, thereby tallying with the Oracle's cryptic words) who showed him the way. Plutarch records that Alexander received the instruction while still a boy, which seems unlikely, and the oracle is generally regarded as a fiction. See J.R. Hamilton, *Plutarch: Alexander: A Commentary* (Oxford, 1969), p. 97; W. Heckel, J. Hierichs, S. Müller and F. Pownall (eds.), *Lexicon of Argead Makedonia* (Berlin, 2020), p. 369.

19. Arrian, *Anabasis of Alexander* 1.1.4, Plutarch, *Moralia* 327c.

20. Ch. Koukouli-Chyrsanthaki, 'Amphipolis' in R.J. Lane Fox (ed.), *Brill's Companion to Ancient Macedon. Studies in the Archaeology and History of Macedon, 650 BC–300 AD* (Leiden and Boston, 2011), p. 420.

21. For discussion of the size of the Balkan army see N.G.L. Hammond, 'Alexander's Campaign in Illyria' in *The Journal of Hellenic Studies*, Vol. 94 (1974), pp. 79–80; N.G.L. Hammond and F.W. Walbank, *A History of Macedonia, Vol. III, 336–167 BC* (Oxford, 1988), p. 32.

22. N.G.L. Hammond and G.T. Griffith, *A History of Macedonia, Vol. II, 550–336 BC* (Oxford, 1979), pp. 705–13; M.B. Hatzopoulos, *Macedonian Institutions under the Kings Vol. I, A Historical and Epigraphic Study. Meletemata 22.* (Athens, 1996), pp. 269–70, and 'L'organisation de la guerre macédonienne. Philippe II et Alexandre' in P. Contamine, J. Jouanna and M. Zink (eds.), *La Grèce et la guerre . Actes du 25e colloque de la Villa Kerylos a Beaulieu-sur-Mer les 3 et 4 octobre 2014. Cahiers de la Villa «Kerylos»*, Vol. 26 (Paris, 2015), pp. 105–20.

23. The so-called vulgate authors, who are believed to have drawn upon a lost Hellenistic history of Alexander written by Cleitarchus, include Diodorus Siculus, *Library of History* (Book 17), Quintus Curtius Rufus, *History of Alexander*, Pompeius Trogus, via Justin, *Epitome*, and the anonymous author of the *Metz Epitome*. For Arrian's work see A.B. Bosworth, *A Historical Commentary on Arrian's History of Alexander, Vol. I and II* (Oxford, 1980 and 1995) and *From Alexander to Arrian: Studies on Historical Interpretation* (Oxford, 1998); P.A. Stadter, *Arrian of Nicomedia* (Carolina, 1980).

24. Arrian, *Anabasis of Alexander* 1.1.1 (Preface).

25. Arrian, *Anabasis of Alexander* 1.12.1–5.

26. For a full discussion of the text and possible dates, see C. Vatin, 'Lettre addressée a la cité de Philippes par les ambassadeurs auprès d'Alexandre' in *Praktika*, Vol. 259–70 (Athens, 1984), pp. 259–70; L. Missitzis, 'A Royal Decree of Alexander the Great on the Lands of Philippi' in *Ancient World*, Vol. 12 (1985), pp. 3–14; N.G.L. Hammond, 'The King and the Land in the Macedonian Kingdom' in *The Classical Quarterly*, Vol. 38 No. 2 (1988), pp. 382–91, and 'Inscriptions concerning Philippi and Calindoea in the reign of Alexander the Great' in *Zeitschrift für Papyrologie und Epigraphik*, Bd. 82 (1990), pp. 167–75. For a later date see M.B. Hatzopoulos, *Ancient Macedonia. Trends in Classics – Key Perspectives on Classical Research* (Berlin/Boston, 2020), pp. 164–9.

27. It is not known whether this was Parmenion's son or another individual of the same name.

28. Arrian, *Anabasis of Alexander* 1.1.5 (trans. author).

29. Zannis, *Le pays entre le Strymon et le Nestos: géographie et histoire (VIIe–IVe siècle avant J.-C.). Meletemata 71 (Athens, 2014)*, pp. 168–70.

30. Diodorus Siculus, *Library of History* 17.8.1.

31. Arrian, *Anabasis of Alexander* 1.1.5 (trans. author). The stock phrase 'and is said' is often used by Arrian to denote information not taken from

his primary sources, Ptolemy and Aristoboulos; he may have struggled to find any evidence pertaining to the direction of the march. Various ideas as to Alexander's route have been put forward by modern scholars. See T. Spiridonov, 'La marche d'Alexandre le Grand en Thrace antique et les tribus entre Stara Planina et le Danube' in *Thracia*, Vol. 4 (1977), pp. 225–33; D. Boteva, 'An Attempt at Identifying Alexander's route towards the Danube in 335 BC' in *Jubilaeus*, Vol. 5 (2002), pp. 27–31; A. Fol, 'La route d'Alexandre le Grand en Thrace au printemps de 335 av.n.è' in *Alexander the Great: 2300 Years after his death* (title in Greek) (Thessaloniki, 1980), pp. 131–3; N.G.L. Hammond, 'Some Passages in Arrian concerning Alexander' in *The Classical Quarterly*, Vol 30 No. 2 (1980), pp. 455–76; T. Stoyanov, 'Spatial Pattern and Economic Development of Northeastern Thrace – 7th–2nd centuries BC' in *Pistiros et Thasos. Structures économiques dans la péninsule balkanique aux VII–II siècles avant J.-C. Textes réunis par Mieczyslaw Domaradzki.* (Opole, 2000), pp. 55–67; K. Yordanov, 'The Politician and Statesman Philip II during his first years of government (359–357 BC)' (Bulgarian with English summary) in *Studia Thracica*, Vol. 7 (2000), pp. 105–30; M. Madzharov, *Roman Roads in Bulgaria: Contribution to the development of Roman road system in the provinces of Moesia and Thrace* (Veliko Tarnovo, 2017); Bosworth, *A Historical Commentary on Arrian's History of Alexander, Vol. 1*, pp. 51–71; J. Illiev, 'Rhodope Mountains and the Thracian Campaign of Alexander the Great in 335 BC' in *Bulletin of the Stara Zagora Historical Museum*, Vol. 4 (2011), pp. 276–84.

32. The respective distances to the Haimos, both through the Rhodopes and along the coastal/Evros road, were achievable in Arrian's given time frame – ten days from the Nestos. According to Thucydides, *Peloponnesian War* 2.97 a man travelling light only needed eleven days to journey from Abdera (at the mouth of the Nestos) to the Danube.

33. Apollodorus, *Library of Greek Mythology* 1.6.3.

34. N. Torbov, *Antique Weapons (11th century BC 5th century AD): From Stone to Gunpowder. Vatevi Collection, Vol. II* (Sofia, 2018); M. Manov and N. Torbov, 'Inscribed Lead Sling Bullets with the Name of Alexander the Great and with Other Names and Symbols Found in Thrace' in *Archaeologia Bulgarica*, Vol. 20 No. 2 (2016), pp. 29–43; E. Nankov, *Markers of Mobility: Toward an Archaeology of the Sling in Ancient Thrace* (forthcoming).

35. For the passes in this region and archaeological surveys, see T. Stoyanov,

'Spatial Pattern and Economic Development of Northeastern Thrace – 7th–2nd centuries BC' in *Pistiros et Thasos*, pp. 55–67. See also A. Jochmus, 'Notes on a Journey into the Balkan or Mount Haemus, in 1847' in *Journal of the Royal Geographical Society of London*, Vol. 24 (1854), pp. 36–85.

36. Arrian, *Anabasis of Alexander* 1.1.6–13, Polyaenus, *Stratagems* 4.3.11. For modern discussion of this event see Bosworth, *A Historical Commentary on Arrian's History of Alexander, Vol I*. pp. 54–6; W. Heckel, '"Synaspismos", Sarissas and Thracian Wagons' in *Acta Classica*, Vol. 48 (2005), pp. 189–94; T. Howe, 'Arrian and "Roman" Military tactics. Alexander's Campaign against the Autonomous Thracians' in T. Howe, E.E. Garvin and G. Wrightson (eds.), *Greece, Macedon and Persia: Studies in Social, Political, and Military History in honour of Waldemar Heckel* (Oxford and Philadelphia, 2015), pp. 87–93; E.F. Bloedow, 'On "Wagons" and "Shields": Alexander's crossing of Mount Haemus in 335 BC' in *Ancient History Bulletin*, Vol. 10 (1996), pp. 110–30.

37. Aristotle, *Topics* 2.11 (115b) (patricide); Pliny the Elder, *Natural History* 7.16 (death stare). On the Triballoi and their territory, see F. Papazoglou, *The Central Balkan Tribes in Pre-Roman Times* (Amsterdam, 1978) and N. Theodossiev, *North-western Thrace from the fifth to the first century BC. BAR 859* (Oxford, 2000).

38. Frontinus, *Stratagems* 2.3.20.

39. Diodorus Siculus, *Library of History* 15.36.1–4, Aeneas Tacticus, *How to Survive a Siege* 15.8–10.

40. Isocrates, *Discourses: Panathenaicus* (12) 227–8 (trans. G. Norlin, Loeb 229).

41. A small brass plaque from central Romania bearing the king's name in Greek has recently been published. It is a modern piece, but those who have studied it suggest that it may be a copy of an older original. Syrmos is depicted in heroic fashion, mounted on a horse with a spear in one hand. His head is encased in a massive helmet, similar to one spectacular example discovered in Romania. See N. Ursulescu and S. Tofan, 'A possible epigraphic attestation of King Syrmos' (in Romanian with French summary), in *Thraco-Dacica*, Vol. 22 (2001), pp. 99–106.

42. Arrian, *Anabasis of Alexander* 1.2.3, Plutarch, *Life of Alexander* 11.3.

43. Strabo, *Geography* 7.3.8 in a rare comparative account, perhaps also drawing on Ptolemy, confirms this topographical detail.

44. The Danubian Delta island of Peuke no longer exists but is believed to

have been either between the two southernmost branches of the river's outlets or a little further south, on the Dunavat peninsula which forms the right bank of the St George branch. See G. Romanescu, O. Bounegru, C.C. Stoleriu, A. Mihu-Pintilie, C. Ionut Nicu, A. Enea and C. Oana Stan, 'The ancient legendary island of Peuce: myth or reality' in *Journal of Archaeological Science*, Vol. 53 (2015), pp. 521–35. Also Plutarch, *Moralia* 342c, and *Alexander Itinerary* 7.16, which assume an identification with the Delta island.

45. For discussion see Bosworth, *A Historical Commentary on Arrian's History of Alexander, Vol. I*, p. 57.

46. P.A. Brunt, in the Loeb translation of Arrian's *Anabasis of Alexander*, suggests that Alexander found the ships at the mouth of the Danube, but 'up river' is closer to the original reading. See N.G.L. Hammond, 'The Macedonian Navies of Philip and Alexander until 330 BC' in *Antichthon*, Vol. 26 (1992), p. 36.

47. Arrian, *Anabasis of Alexander* 1.3.5.

48. Arrian, *Anabasis of Alexander* 1.4.3–4 (trans. P.A. Brunt, Loeb 236).

49. Strabo, *Geography* 7.3.14, 7.3.17. The grassland desert extended from the Danube to the Dniester.

50. For the disastrous Scythian campaign of the Great king Darius I, see Strabo, *Geography* 7.3.14, Herodotus, *Histories* 4.118–42.

51. Diodorus Siculus, *Library of History* 17.17.3–4.

52. Arrian, *Anabasis of Alexander* 1.4.8 (trans. P.A. Brunt, Loeb 236), Strabo, *Geography* 7.3.8.

53. Xenophon, *Anabasis* 6.1.1–16, 7.3.18–25.

54. Frontinus, *Stratagems* II.3, Justin, *Epitome* II.5.3.

55. Perdikkas, who had taken control of the Orestian and Lynkestian battalion, may have replaced Alexander the Lynkestian.

56. This detail comes from a fragmentary papyrus, part of an unknown work on Alexander now held by the British Library. See W. Clarysse and G. Schepens, 'A Ptolemaic Fragment of an Alexander History' in *Chronique d'Égypt*, Vol. 60 (1985), pp. 30–47; N.G.L. Hammond, 'A Papyrus Commentary on Alexander's Balkan Campaign' in *Greek, Roman and Byzantine Studies*, Vol. 28 (1987), pp. 331–47.

57. During the Balkan campaign the Agrianians were combined with the archers and numbered 2,000 (Arrian, *Anabasis of Alexander* 1.6.6). Five hundred made the crossing with Alexander into Asia in 334 BC (Diodorus Siculus, *Library of History* 17.17.4), later reinforcements bringing the

number up to 1,000 (Arrian, *Anabasis of Alexander* 4.25.6, Quintus Curtius, *History of Alexander* 5.3.6).

58. Arrian, *Anabasis of Alexander* 1.5.1–5.

59. In order to reach it, he either went via the Kyustendil Pass, on the border of Bulgaria and North Macedonia, or along the Strymon, through Maidoi territory – the Maidoi are mentioned by another fragment of the British Library papyrus – before heading west to the Erigon. In its lower reaches, the river is sheathed in precipitous mountainous gorges and is largely inaccessible. Alexander probably took a detour via present-day Prilep.

60. Of the various proposals for Pellion's location, for somewhere in the neighbourhood of Bitola, in North Macedonia, see A.B. Bosworth, 'The Location of Pellion (Arrian Anabasis 1.5.5)' in H.J Dell (ed.) *Ancient Macedonian Studies in Honor of Charles F. Edson* (Thessaloniki, 1981), pp. 87–97, and 'The Location of Alexander's Campaign against the Illyrians in 335 BC' in B. Barr-Sharrar and E.N. Borza (eds.) *Macedonia and Greece in Late Classical and Early Hellenistic Times: Studies in the History of Art*, Vol. 10 (1982), pp. 74–84. Alternatively, for somewhere in southern Albania see N.G.L. Hammond, 'Alexander's Campaign in Illyria' in *The Journal of Hellenic Studies*, Vol. 94 (1974), pp. 66–87, and 'The Campaign of Alexander against Cleitus and Glaucias' in *Ancient Macedonia*, Vol. 2 (1977), pp. 503–9; T.K.P. Sarantis, 'Alexander the Great's battle around Pellion' (in Greek) in *Ancient Macedonia*, Vol. 3 (1983), pp. 247–65; G. Karamitrou-Mentessidi, *Voion – South Orestis* (Thessaloniki, 1999), pp. 264–7; F. Papazoglou, *Les villes de Macédoine à l'époque romaine. Bulletin de correspondence hellénique. Supplément 16*, (Paris, 1988) pp. 242–4; M.W. Leake, *Travels in Northern Greece, Vol. III* (London, 1835), p. 323. For Selca e Poshtme, to the west of Ohrid, see N. Ceka, 'Le ville illyrienne de la Basse-Selce' in *Illiria*, Vol. 2 (1972), pp. 197–9, and *The Illyrians to the Albanians* (Tirana, 2013).

61. T.E. Winnifrith, *Badlands and Borderlands: A History of North Epirus/ Southern Albania* (London, 2002), pp. 143–52.

62. For the events that follow see Arrian, *Anabasis of Alexander* 1.5.5–12 – 1.6.1–11.

63. Arrian, *Anabasis of Alexander* 7.28.2–3 (trans. P.A. Brunt, Loeb 269).

64. Plutarch, *Life of Alexander* 58.1–2.

65. Arrian, *Anabasis of Alexander* 7.1.4–5.

66. Arrian, *Anabasis of Alexander* 6.13.4 (trans. P. Mensch, Landmark).

67. Plutarch, *Moralia* 327b.

68. Arrian, *Anabasis of Alexander* 1.16.5–6, 2.12.1 (visiting wounded); Quintus Curtius, *History of Alexander* 3.6.19–20 (training with the men).

69. Quintus Curtius, *History of Alexander* 7.3.17–18.

70. Arrian, *Anabasis of Alexander* 6.26.1–3. Other versions have slight variations: Quintus Curtius, *History of Alexander* 7.5.9–12, Plutarch, *Life of Alexander* 42.3–6, Polyaenus, *Stratagems* 4.3.25, Frontinus, *Stratagems* 1.7.7.

71. A.B. Bosworth, *Alexander and the East: The Tragedy of Triumph* (Oxford, 1996), p. iii.

11 ACHILLES RESURRECTED

1. For the rumours surrounding Alexander's death, see Demades, *On the Twelve Years* 1.17; he attended the speeches of Demosthenes and Lycurgus. Both Justin, *Epitome of the Philippic History of Pompeius Trogus* 11.2.8 and the Pseudo-Callisthenes, *Greek Alexander Romance* 1.27 suggest that an eyewitness to Alexander's death in battle was presented to the Assembly to substantiate their claims. Arrian, *Anabasis of Alexander* 1.7.2, relates a variation of the rumour, that Alexander's death had occurred in Illyria instead of Triballia. It was without doubt widely believed considering the subsequent actions of the Thebans. See also Aelian, *Historical Miscellany* 12.57.

2. The 379 BC Theban coup is related in vivid detail by Plutarch in his *Life of Pelopidas* 8–12. Also in Plutarch, *Moralia* 575b–598f, Xenophon, *Hellenica* 5.4.1–12, Nepos, *Pelopidas* 2–3.

3. Arrian, *Anabasis of Alexander* 1.7.1, names the two men as Timolaos and Amyntas, although he states that both were part of the garrison force. Perhaps Timolaos was a pro-Macedonian Theban as Demosthenes, *On the Crown* (18) 295 includes him among those who took bribes from Philip.

4. Arrian, *Anabasis of Alexander* 1.7.3.

5. Aeschines, *Against Ctesiphon* (3) 240.

6. Diodorus Siculus, *Library of History* 17.8.5 (Arkadians, Argives, Elians); Arrian, *Anabasis of Alexander* 1.10.1–2 (Arkadians, Elians).

7. Scholia A on Homer, *Iliad* 2.435, referenced in Onasander, *The General* (trans. Illinois Greek Club, Loeb 156), p. 435 fn. 1.

8. Arrian, *Anabasis of Alexander* 1.7.5. See N.G.L. Hammond, 'The March of Alexander the Great on Thebes in 335 BC' in *Alexander the Great: 2300 years after his death* (title in Greek) (Thessaloniki, 1980), pp. 171–81.

9. Arrian, *Anabasis of Alexander* 1.7.6.

10. The League had previously been based at Thebes. For reports on the latest archaeological work at Onchestos, see the Columbia University website, Onchestos Excavation Project: www.onchestos.mcah.columbia. edu.

11. Diodorus Siculus, *Library of History* 17.9.3,17.13.5.

12. Aeschines, *Against Ctesiphon* (3) 240 and Dinarchus, *Against Demosthenes* (1) 18–21 relate that the Arkadians met with envoys from both Antipatros and the Thebans at the Isthmus. They initially rebuffed the former but were still unwilling to commit themselves to the Theban cause. The Theban envoys approached Demosthenes for bribe money, nine or ten talents, which he was either unable or unwilling to provide, and so the Arkadians remained where they were.

13. For the troubling omens, see Diodorus Siculus, *Library of History* 17.10.2–5, Aelian, *Historical Miscellany* 12.57, Pausanias, *Guide to Greece* 9.6.2.

14. The original, which formed part of the Epic Cycle, is lost, but Statius' *Thebaid* preserves the story, and it was reworked by Aeschylus in his *Seven Against Thebes* and Euripides in his *Phoenician Women*.

15. Thiva has an excellent archaeological museum on-site. For more information on the city's history and archaeology, see D.W. Berman, *Myth, Literature, and the Creation of the Topography of Thebes* (Cambridge, 2015); P. Cartledge, *Thebes: The Forgotten City of Ancient Greece* (London, 2020); N. Rockwell, *Thebes: A History* (London and New York, 2017); S. Symeonoglou, *The Topography of Thebes from the Bronze Age to Modern Times* (Princeton, 1985).

16. Arrian, *Anabasis of Alexander* 1.7.7–9.

17. For Thebes' fortifications see Symeonoglou, *The Topography of Thebes from the Bronze Age to Modern Times*, pp. 117–22.

18. Plutarch, *Life of Alexander* 11.4. There has been much academic debate over the respective identities of Philotas and Antipatros and whether the Thebans meant Philotas, son of Parmenion, and Antipatros, steward of Macedonia. If so, the demand for their surrender was outrageous. However, these names are common and Philotas, not the son of Parmenion, is attested as one of the garrison commanders (Diodorus

Siculus, *Library of History* 17.8.7). It is therefore likely that Antipatros was simply the name of another of the garrison commanders.

19. Diodorus Siculus, *Library of History* 17.9.6.

20. Arrian, *Anabasis of Alexander* 1.8.1–8, Diodorus Siculus, *Library of History* 17.11–14. Also Plutarch, *Life of Alexander* 11.4–6.

21. See V.L. Aravantinos, 'The Inscriptions from the Sanctuary of Herakles at Thebes: An Overview' in N. Papazarkadas (ed.), *The Epigraphy and History of Boeotia: New Finds, New Prospects* (Leiden, 2014), pp. 149–209. A ditch running parallel to the southern edge of the hill was discovered during the investigation which may belong to the Theban defences erected for the showdown with Alexander.

22. Plutarch, *Life of Alexander* 11.5.

23. Diodorus Siculus, *Library of History* 17.12.3–4. Polyaenus, *Stratagems* 4.3.12 states that it was Antipatros who led a covert mission to secure the postern gate. He may have been confused with the garrison commander of the same name. Antipatros, Philip and Alexander's faithful Companion and steward, had probably been left behind in Macedonia during the campaign.

24. Xenophon, *Hellenica* 5.4.8–9.

25. Pliny the Elder, *Natural History* 8.154.

26. Aeschylus, *Seven Against Thebes* 220–1 (trans. P. Vellacott, Penguin).

27. Arrian, *Anabasis of Alexander* 1.8.8.

28. Plutarch, *Moralia* 259d, *Life of Alexander* 12.1–3, Polyaenus, *Stratagems* 8.40.

29. Pausanias, *Guide to Greece* 9.10.1.

30. Aristotle, *Politics* 1.6 (1255a3), Xenophon, *Cyropaedia* 7.5.73.

31. Kleadas and his speech is mentioned only by Justin, *Epitome* 11.4.1–6, which makes its authenticity suspect. However it likely deals with themes that must have been discussed at the meeting.

32. Cleitarchus, frag. 1, Diodorus Siculus, *Library of History* 17.14.1, 4 (440 talents).

33. Diodorus Siculus, *Library of History* 17.14.4, Polybius, *Histories* 4.23.8–9, 38.2.13–4, Plutarch, *Life of Alexander* 11.5–6.

34. On the punishment of the Thebans, see Arrian, *Anabasis of Alexander* 1.9.9–10, Diodorus Siculus, *Library of History* 17.14.1–4, Plutarch, *Life of Alexander* 11.5–6, Hyperides, *Funeral Speech* 17, Aelian, *Historical Miscellany* 13.7. For the Thebans' flight to Athens, see Pausanias, *Guide to Greece* 9.7.1, Justin, *Epitome* 11.4.9. For Akraiphiai see Pausanias, *Guide to Greece* 9.23.3.

35. Dio Chrysostom, *Discourses* 2.33 (trans. J.W. Cohoon, Loeb 257), Pliny the Elder, *Natural History* 7.109.

36. Polybius, *Histories* 5.10.6–8. Pausanias, in the second century AD, was still able to describe many of the sanctuaries that had not been destroyed (see *Guide to Greece* Book 9 (Boiotia), for descriptions of Thebes).

37. Demades, *On the Twelve Years* 65. Thebes was eventually refounded by the Successor Kassandros in 316 BC, with the consent of the other Boiotians. Money and services were provided by many individuals and cities across the ancient world (Diodorus Siculus, *Library of History* 19.54.1–3). An inscription relating to the donations for the city's refoundation has been recovered, put on display in Thiva's Archaeological Museum and published. See Y. Kalliontzis and N. Papazarkadas, 'The Contributions to the Refoundation of Thebes: A New Epigraphic and Historical Analysis' in *Annual of the British School at Athens*, Vol. 114 (2019), pp. 293–315.

38. Pliny the Elder, *Natural History* 35.98–9 (Aristides painting), 34.14 (chandelier).

39. Arrian, *Anabasis of Alexander* 2.15.2–5; Plutarch, *Life of Alexander* 13.1–3 (remorse).

40. See S.D. Garland, 'A New Boiotia? Exiles, Landscapes, and Kings' in S. Garland (ed.), *Boiotia in the Fourth Century BC* (Pennsylvania, 2016), pp. 147–64.

41. Arrian, *Anabasis of Alexander* 1.10.1–2. For a history of Aitolia's relations with Macedon see A.B. Bosworth, 'Early relations between Aetolia and Macedon' in *American Journal of Ancient History*, Vol. 1 (1976), pp. 164–81.

42. Arrian, *Anabasis of Alexander* 1.10.2–3, Plutarch, *Life of Alexander* 13.1.

43. Alexander's rejection of the letter is mentioned in Plutarch, *Life of Phocion* 17.4.

44. The names and numbers of the men requested by Alexander differ in the various ancient accounts. See Bosworth, *A Historical Commentary on Arrian's History of Alexander. Vol I* (Oxford, 1980), pp. 91–5.

45. Plutarch *Life of Alexander* 11.3 (trans. I. Scott-Kilvert and T.E. Duff, Penguin).

46. Plutarch, *Life of Demosthenes* 23.1–5.

47. Arrian, *Anabasis of Alexander* 1.10.6. Also Justin, *Epitome* 11.4.11.

48. Demosthenes, *On the Crown* (18) 300.

49. Plutarch, *Life of Demosthenes* 29–30, *Moralia* 847a–b.

50. Plutarch, *Life of Demosthenes* 30.5 (trans. I.Scott–Kilvert, T. E. Duff, Penguin).

51. Plutarch, *Moralia* 845d.

52. See M.M. Kholod, 'The Macedonian Expeditionary Corps in Asia Minor (336–225 BC)' in *Klio*, Vol. 100 No. 2 (2018), pp. 407–46.

53. Arrian, *Anabasis of Alexander* 1.17.11 (Philip's statue in Ephesos); A. Ellis-Evans, 'The Tyrants Dossier from Eresos' in *Chiron*, Vol. 42 (2012), pp. 183–210 (altars to Zeus Philippos).

54. Polyaenus, *Stratagems* 5.44.5, Diodorus Siculus, *Library of History* 17.7.1–10.

55. Plutarch, *Life of Alexander* 49.7.

56. Plutarch, *Moralia* 1126d.

57. Diodorus Siculus, *Library of History* 17.16.2. See E. Baynham, 'Why Didn't Alexander Marry Before Leaving Macedonia? Observations on Factional Politics at Alexander's Court in 336–334 BC' in *Rheinisches Museum für Philologie*, Neue Folge, Bd. 141 H. 2 (1998), pp. 141–52.

58. By author's estimates he covered 2,740 km (1,700 miles).

59. Plutarch, *Moralia* 603d (Pella); Ibn Abi Usaibia, *Life of Aristotle* 18 (inscription).

60. R. Lane Fox, *Alexander the Great* (London, 1973), p. 54 includes *Alexander's Assembly* and the *Glories of Riches*, mentioned among Aristotle's lost works, as possible other pamphlets sent to Alexander.

61. Cicero, *Letter to Atticus* 12.40.2 (Theopompus); Plutarch, *Moralia* 1126d (Xenokrates).

62. Sir D. Ross, *The Works of Aristotle, Vol. 12: Selected Fragments* (Oxford, 1952), p. 65. Also attributed to the Roman emperor Titus (Suetonius, *Titus* 8.1).

63. Plutarch, *Life of Alexander* 7.3–5. See G. Boas, 'Ancient Testimony to Secret Doctrines' in *The Philosophical Review*, Vol. 62 No. 1 (1953), pp. 79–92.

64. Plutarch, *Life of Alexander* 27.6 (Psammon). See W.Z. Rubinsohn, 'The Philosopher at Court: Intellectuals and Politics in the Time of Alexander the Great' in *Ancient Macedonia*, Vol. 5 (1993), pp. 1301–27.

65. Pliny the Elder, *Natural History* 8.44, 8.119. Alexander may however have provided some funds for Aristotle's zoological research (Athenaeus, *Learned Banqueters* 9.398e), although Aelian, *Historical Miscellany* 4.19, attributes this to Philip. See J. Romm, 'Aristotle's Elephant and the Myth of Alexander's Scientific Patronage' in *The American Journal of Philology*, Vol. 110 No. 4 (1989), pp. 566–75.

66. For Alexander's role in expanding geographic knowledge, see H.-J. Gehrke, 'The "Revolution" of Alexander the Great: Old and New in the World's View' in S. Bianchetti, M.R. Cataudella and H.-J. Gehrke (eds.), *Brill's Companion to Ancient Geography* (Leiden and Boston, 2015), pp. 78–97. All fragments mentioning the surveyors (*bematistai*) are collected in C.A. Robinson, *The History of Alexander the Great: A Translation of the Extant Fragments, Vol. I.* (Chicago, 1953), pp. 35–43. For trees and plants see Theophrastus, *Enquiry into Plants* 4.4.4 (banyan), 4.4.5 (jackfruit and banana), 4.4.8 (cotton).

67. Arrian, *Anabasis of Alexander* 1.11.1–2, Plutarch, *Life of Alexander* 14.5.

68. Arrian, *Anabasis of Alexander* 1.12.1–2.

69. Plutarch, *Moralia* 1043d. For Kallisthenes as official historian of the campaign, see Justin, *Epitome* 12.6.17. He is called *epistolographos* – probably the equivalent of secretary – in a fragment from a Hellenistic library catalogue from Tauromenion. See F. Battistoni, 'The Ancient Pinakes from Tauromenion. Some New Readings' in *Zeitschrift für Papyrologie und Epigraphik*, Bd. 157 (2006), pp. 169–80; F. Pownall, 'Was Kallisthenes the tutor of Alexander's Royal Pages?' in T. Howe and F. Pownall (eds.), *Ancient Macedonians in the Greek and Roman Sources. From History to Historiography* (Swansea, 2018), pp. 59–76.

70. The collected fragments of Kallisthenes can be found in C.A. Robinson, *The History of Alexander the Great*, pp. 45–77. See also L. Pearson, *The Lost Histories of Alexander the Great* (New York, 1960), pp. 22–49; W. Heckel, 'Creating Alexander: The Official History of Kallisthenes of Olynthos' in R.A. Faber (ed.), *Celebrity, Fame, and Infamy in the Hellenistic World* (Toronto, 2020), pp. 199–216.

71. Arrian, *Anabasis of Alexander* 4.10.1–2 (trans. P.A. Brunt, Loeb 236).

72. Polybius, *Histories* 12.4.12b (flatterer), 6.7.45.1 (list of learned men), Cicero, *Letters to Quintus* 16 (2.2.4).

73. A. Stewart, *Faces of Power: Alexander's Image and Hellenistic Politics* (Berkeley, Los Angeles and Oxford, 1993), p. 6.

74. Pliny the Elder, *Natural History* 34.78 (Euphranor), 34.75 (Chaireas).

75. Pliny the Elder, *Natural History* 34.65 (trans. H. Rackham, Loeb 394).

76. Plutarch, *Moralia* 335b (trans. F. Cole Babbitt, Loeb 305).

77. Stewart, *Faces of Power*, pp. 74–5.

78. Pliny the Elder, *Natural History* 35.86.

79. Pliny the Elder, *Natural History* 35.86, Valerius Maximus, *Memorable Doings and Sayings* 8.11 ext 2, Horace, *Epistles* 2.1.240, Plutarch, *Moralia* 335a–c.

80. Plutarch, *Life of Alexander* 42.2.

81. Polyaenus, *Stratagems* 4.3.1, Plutarch, *Life of Alexander* 58.3–4.

82. Plutarch, *Life of Alexander* 3.1–2. Plutarch also records an alternative tradition that Olympias was annoyed at Alexander's claim to divine sonship, and that she repudiated the idea, stating, 'Alexander must cease slandering me to Hera' (Hera being the immortal wife of Zeus renowned for punishing those who fooled around with her husband). This story however is probably based on a letter recorded by Aulus Gellius in his *Attic Nights* (3.4.1–2) and is most likely fictional.

83. Corroborated by Arrian, *Anabasis of Alexander* 4.10.2.

84. Ammon was the Greek name for the Egyptian god Amun-Re, the most important god in the Egyptian pantheon, syncretised with Zeus by the Greeks.

85. For Ammon's cult in Greece, see C.J. Classen, 'The Libyan God Ammon in Greece before 331 BC' in *Historia: Zeitschrift für Alte Geschichte*, Bd. 8 H. 3 (1959), pp. 349–55.

86. See E. Juri 'The Sanctuary of Zeus Ammon' (in Greek with English summary) in *Athens Annals of Archaeology*, Vol 3.3 (1971), pp. 356–67, B. Tsigarida, *The Sanctuary of Zeus Ammon at Kallithea (Chalcidice)*' in *Kernos*, Vol. 24 (2011), pp. 165–81.

87. Herodotus, *Histories* 2.55.

88. Arrian, *Anabasis of Alexander* 3.3.1–2.

89. Plutarch, *Life of Alexander* 27.5. For discussion see A.B. Bosworth, 'Alexander and Ammon' in K.H. Kinzl (ed.), *Greece and the Eastern Mediterranean in ancient history and prehistory: Studies presented to Fritz Schachermeyr on the occasion of his eightieth birthday* (Berlin and New York, 1977), pp. 51–75.

90. Arrian, *Anabasis of Alexander* 3.4.5.

91. These stories are related by Plutarch at the beginning of his *Life of Alexander* (2–3). Tertullian, *On the Soul* 46, also discusses the seal in the shape of a lion and gives Ephorus (the fourth-century BC historian) as his source. Also Livy, *History of Rome* 26.19.7–8 (snake sire). For discussion see A. Collins, 'Callisthenes on Olympias and Alexander' in *Ancient History Bulletin*, Vol. 26 (2012), pp. 1–14; D. Ogden, *Alexander the Great: Myth, Genesis and Sexuality* (Exeter, 2011); P. Goukowsky, *Essai*

sur les origines du mythe d'Alexandre (336–270 av. J.-C.) Vol. I (Nantes, 1978).

92. Pausanias, *Guide to Greece* 6.11.2 (Theagenes son of Herakles); Scholia to Pindar, *Olympian Odes* 7 (Diagoras son of Hermes); Origen, *Against Celsus* 6.8, Diogenes Laertius, *Lives of Eminent Philosophers* 3.2 (Plato son of Apollo).

93. Plutarch, *Life of Alexander* 27.6. (trans. I. Scott-Kilvert and T.E. Duff, Penguin) Also Plutarch, *Moralia* 180d.

94. Plutarch, *Life of Alexander* 50.6.

95. See M. Mari, 'The Ruler Cult in Macedonia' in B. Virgilio (ed.), *Studi ellenistici*, Vol. 20 (2008), pp. 219–68. See also R.J. Lane Fox, 'Philip: Accession, Ambitions, and Self-Presentation' in R.J. Lane Fox (ed.), *Brill's Companion to Ancient Macedon: Studies in the Archaeology and History, 650 BC–300 AD* (Leiden and Boston 2011), pp. 335–66.

96. The figures for the army are given by Diodorus Siculus, *Library of History* 17.17.3–5, Arrian, *Anabasis of Alexander* 1.11.3, Plutarch, *Life of Alexander* 15.1, *Moralia* 327d–e, Justin, *Epitome* 11.6.2. For discussion see M. Thompson, *Granicus 334 BC: Alexander's first Persian Victory* (Oxford and New York, 2007), pp. 40–44.

97. For ships see Arrian, *Anabasis of Alexander* 1.11.6. These 160 warships likely represented those mustered from the Greeks in accordance with their military obligations under the League of Corinth. A separate Macedonian fleet, some 60 warships, may also have been present at the Hellespont, its larger warships (but not smaller and more mobile craft) were probably included in Justin's overall figure of 182 ships for the Asiatic campaign (*Epitome*, 11.6.2, also Orosius *Seven Books of History against the Pagans* 3.16.1 - 180 ships). For discussion see N.G.L. Hammond, '*Macedonian Navies of Philip and Alexander until 330 BC*' in *Antichthon*, Vol. 26 (1992) pp. 30-41.

98. Plutarch, *Life of Alexander* 15.1–2. He was said to have inherited only around 60 talents from Philip, and debts of 500 talents on becoming king (Arrian, *Anabasis of Alexander* 7.9.6, Quintus Curtius, *History of Alexander* 10.2.24). Arrian says he borrowed 800 talents (*Anabasis of Alexander*, 7.9.6).

99. Plutarch, *Life of Alexander* 15.2 (trans. I. Scott-Kilvert and T.E. Duff, Penguin).

100. See I.P. Vokotopoulou, 'An Inscription of Kalindoia' (in Greek) in *Ancient Macedonia*, Vol. 4 (1986), pp. 87–114; P. Adam-Veleni, *Kalindoia:*

An Ancient City in Macedonia (Thessaloniki, 2008); N.G.L. Hammond, 'Inscriptions concerning Philippi and Calindoea in the Reign of Alexander the Great' in *Zeitschrift für Papyrologie und Epigraphik*, Bd. 82, (1990), pp. 167–75; Hatzopoulos, *Macedonian Institutions under the Kings. Vol. I. A Historical and Epigraphic Study. Meletemata 22* (Athens, 1996), pp. 121–2.

101. Plutarch, *Life of Alexander* 15.2–3 (trans. I. Scott-Kilvert and T.E. Duff, Penguin), *Moralia* 342e.

102. Herodotus, *Histories* 7.36.

103. Arrian, *Anabasis of Alexander* 1.11.7. Justin, *Epitome* 11.5.6, embellishes the tale, turning the three altars into twelve.

104. Homer, *Iliad* 16.286 (great souled Protesilaos), 2.700–2 (half built house and widow); Pausanias, *Guide to Greece* 1.34.2 (honoured as a god). The tomb of Protesilaos is often identified with the Karaağaçtepe mound at the end of the Gallipoli peninsula. See C.B. Rose, *The Archaeology of Greek and Roman Troy* (Cambridge, 2014), pp. 61–2.

105. Arrian, *Anabasis of Alexander* 1.11.5.

106. Arrian, *Anabasis of Alexander* 1.11.6–7.

107. Suetonius, *Life of Augustus* 94.5.

108. *Greek Anthology* 14.114. See M.R. Kaiser-Raiss 'Philip II und Kyzikos' in *Schweizerische Numisamatische Rundschau*, Vol. 63 (1984) p. 40. Olympias apparently accompanied her son to the river Strymon (*Alexander Itinerary* 7).

109. Statius, *Silvae* 4.6.59–70, Martial, *Epigrams* 9.43.

110. Arrian, *Anabasis of Alexander* 1.16.4.

111. Arrian, *Anabasis of Alexander* 1.11.7, Justin, *Epitome* 11.5.10.

EPILOGUE: ALEXANDER IN THE EAST

1.   Arrian, *Anabasis of Alexander* 2.3.7 (trans. P. Mensch, Landmark).

2.   Plutarch, *Life of Alexander* 20.8 (trans. I. Scott-Kilvert and T.E. Duff, Penguin).

3.   Plutarch, *Life of Alexander* 31.7 (trans. I. Scott-Kilvert and T.E. Duff, Penguin).

4.   A. Sachs and H. Hunger, *Astronomical Diaries and Related Texts from Babylonia, Vol. 1: Diaries from 652 BC to 262 BC* (Vienna, 1988), p. 179.

5. For a recent discussion of the event, see F.L. Holt, *The Treasures of Alexander the Great. How One Man's Wealth Shaped the World* (Oxford, 2016), pp. 77–85.

6. Plutarch, *Life of Alexander* 47.3.

7. Plutarch, *Moralia* 329b (trans. F. Cole Babbitt, Loeb 305).

8. Plutarch, *Moralia* 183f (trans. F. Cole Babbitt, Loeb 245).

9. Sachs and Hunger, *Astronomical Diaries and Related Texts from Babylonia, Vol. I*, pp. 206–7; R.J. Van Der Spek, 'Review of G.F. Del Monte (1997) Testi dalla Babilonia Ellenistica, Vol. I: Testi Cronografici' in *Orientalia*, Vol. 69 No. 4 (2000), p. 435.

10. Arrian, *Anabasis of Alexander* 7.26.3 (trans. P. Mensch, Landmark).

11. Plutarch, *Life of Alexander* 8.3–4 (trans. B. Perrin, Loeb 99).

12. Aristotle, *Politics* 3.13 1284a3–16, Pliny the Elder, *Natural History* 35.106.

13. A. Kyriakou, 'Exceptional Burials at the Sanctuary of Eukleia at Aegae (Vergina): The Gold Oak Wreath' in *Annual of the British School at Athens*, Vol. 109 (2014), pp. 251–85.

14. H.N. Brailsford, *Macedonia: Its Races and Their Future* (London, 1906), p. 103.

15. M. Featherstone, *Global Culture: Nationalism, Globalization, and Modernity* (London, 1990), p. 10. See L. Danforth, *The Macedonian Conflict: Ethnic Nationalism in a Transnational World* (Princeton, 1995).

GLOSSARY

Key Individuals, Peoples and Places

Abydos – Port city on the Asian side of the Hellespont (Dardanelles).

Achaia/ Achaians – Region/people in north Peloponnese, also one of Homer's names for the Greeks who fought at Troy.

Achaimenids – Persian royal dynasty.

Aeschines – Athenian statesman (*c.*397–*c.*322 BC). Political rival of Demosthenes, and advocate of peace with Macedon.

Agrianians – Thracian or Paionian tribe/people from the upper reaches of the river Strymon (Struma) in present-day western Bulgaria.

Aiani – City in the Elimeia, Upper Macedonia. Identified with the archaeological site at Megali Rachi, south of Kozani in present-day Western Macedonia (northern Greece).

Aigai – Ancestral capital of ancient Macedon, identified with the archaeological site next to the village of Vergina, Emathia, present-day Central Macedonia (northern Greece).

Aitolia/Aitolians – Region/people in present-day Western Greece.

Akarnania/Akarnanians – Region/people in present-day Western Greece.

Alexander I – Argead king (*c*.498–454 BC), son of Amyntas I, also known as the 'Philhellene'.

Alexander II – Argead king (370–368 BC), son of Amyntas III and Eurydike.

Alexander III – 356–323 BC. Son of Philip II and Olympias. Argead king (336–323 BC), also known as Alexander the Great.

Alexander IV – Argead king (323–309 BC), son of Alexander and Rhoxane.

Alexander Lynkestis – Companion of Philip II and Alexander, from Lynkestis, Upper Macedonia.

Alexander the Molossian – Molossian king (342–330/29 BC), brother to Olympias and uncle to Alexander the Great, married his niece Kleopatra in 336 BC.

Alexandria (Egypt) – City on the Nile Delta in Egypt, Alexander's most famous foundation, and location of his tomb (now lost).

Alexandropolis – City in Thrace, founded by Alexander in 340 BC during his time as regent, perhaps to be identified with a hill near Laskarevo, in present-day south-western Bulgaria.

Almopia – Region of Lower Macedonia, to the north of Emathia, in present-day Central Macedonia (northern Greece).

Amphiktyonic Council of Delphi/Amphiktyons – The Delphic Amphiktyony was composed of representatives from the surrounding regions of Greece. The Amphiktyons (Council members) helped administer the Delphic Oracle and sanctuary and had the ability to declare Sacred War on any transgressors.

Amphipolis – City close to the mouth of the Strymon river, on the eastern borders of Macedon, present-day Central Macedonia (northern Greece).

Amphissa/Amphissians – Lokrian people/city west of Delphi, their actions provoked the Fourth Sacred War, declared in 339 BC.

Amyntas III – Argead king (*c*.393–370 BC), father of Philip II, grandfather of Alexander the Great. Amyntas had two royal wives,

Gygaia, who bore him three sons – Archelaos, Arrhidaios, and Menelaos – and Eurydike of Lynkestis, with whom he had four children – Alexander, Perdikkas, Philip and a daughter Eurynoe.

Amyntas – Son of Perdikkas III, cousin of Alexander the Great, passed over as king whilst still young. Later married to Kynnane, they had a single daughter together, Adea (Adea-Eurydike).

Anaximenes – Rhetorician and historian from Lampsakos, on the northern coast of Asia Minor, present-day Turkey, reportedly one of Alexander's early tutors.

Antipatros – Prominent general, adviser and Companion of Philip II and Alexander, who often governed Macedonia during their absences.

Apelles – Famous painter, a court favourite of Alexander.

Aphytis – City on the Pallene finger of the Chalkidike peninsula in present-day Central Macedonia (northern Greece), famous for the sanctuary of Zeus Ammon in its territory.

Archelaos – Argead king (413–399 BC).

Argeads – Royal clan or family of Macedon.

Argos/Argives – City/people in north-eastern Peloponnese.

Aristandros – Seer from Telmessos in Lykia, Asia Minor (present-day Turkey), part of the Macedonian royal court under Philip II and Alexander.

Aristoboulos – Intellectual from Chalkidike, perhaps with some engineering expertise, who joined Alexander's Asiatic campaign and later wrote a history about it. Along with Ptolemy's lost work, it was a principal source for Arrian's *Anabasis of Alexander*.

Aristotle – Philosopher from Stageira, Chalkidike (384–322 BC). Tutor to Alexander, and founder of a philosophical school at the Lyceum in Athens.

Arkadia/Arkadians – Region/people in central Peloponnese.

Arrhidaios-Philip III – Argead king (323–317 BC) son of Philip II and Philinna, half-brother of Alexander.

Artabazos – Persian nobleman, father of Barsine.

Artaxerxes III (Ochos) – Achaimenid Great King (358–338 BC).

Artaxerxes IV (Arses) – Achaimenid Great King (338–336 BC).

Arybbas – Molossian king (c.373–342 BC), uncle of Olympias and Alexander the Molossian.

Atarneus – City in Asia Minor, present-day western Turkey.

Ateas – Scythian king in the Dobruja. Killed in battle by Philip II in 339 BC.

Athens/Athenians – City/people located in Attika, south-central Greece.

Attalos – Companion of Philip II. Uncle and guardian of Kleopatra-Eurydike (Philip's seventh wife).

Audata-Eurydike – Illyrian wife of Philip II, probably from the family of the Illyrian king Bardylis (defeated by Philip in 359 BC). Mother of Kynnane.

Babylon – Ancient city on the Euphrates river in present-day Iraq.

Baktria – Ancient region in Central Asia. Along with Sogdiana, Baktria was one of the upper satrapies of the Persian Empire.

Bardylis – Illyrian king, possibly Dardanian, defeated by Philip II in 359 BC.

Barsine – Daughter of the Persian nobleman Artabazos, married to the Rhodian commanders Mentor and then Memmon. Later Alexander's mistress who bore him an illegitimate son, Herakles.

Bessos/Artaxerxes V – Persian nobleman and satrap of Baktria, who proclaimed himself Great King after the defeat of Darius III.

Boiotia/Boiotians – Region/people in central Greece, home to the powerful city-state of Thebes.

Bottiaia or Bottia – Region of Lower Macedonia in present-day Central Macedonia (northern Greece), also known as Emathia.

Boukephalas – Thessalian stallion, Alexander's beloved horse.

Byzantion/Byzantines – City/people on the northern edge of the Bosphoros, located on the site of present-day Istanbul, Turkey.

Chaironeia – Village in Boiotia, site of the famous battle between Philip II and a coalition of Greek peoples in summer 338 BC.

Chalkidike – Peninsula in present-day northern Greece with three jutting fingers of land – Pallene, Sithonia, and Akte (or Athos). Home to the powerful Chalkidike League, led by the city of Olynthos, which was destroyed by Philip II in 348 BC.

Chares – Athenian general who opposed Philip II's operations in the Propontis, and central Greece.

Chersonese – Present-day Gallipoli peninsula.

Corinth – Ancient Greek city-state in north-eastern Peloponnese that controlled the Isthmus.

Darius III (Kodomannos) – Achaimenid Great King (336–330 BC).

Delphi – City in Phokis, central Greece, home to the famous Oracle of Apollo, one of the four great Pan-Hellenic sanctuaries of ancient Greece.

Demades – Athenian statesman who rose to prominence after the battle of Chaironeia.

Demaratos of Corinth – Prominent pro-Macedonian nobleman from Corinth, friend of Philip II and Alexander the Great.

Demosthenes – Athenian statesman (384–322 BC), famous opponent of Macedon.

Diogenes of Sinope – Cynic philosopher who lived in a storage jar, and divided his time between Athens and Corinth.

Dion – Sacred city in Macedonia, located at the foot of Mount Olympos and famed for its end of year festival of Olympian Zeus and the Muses held in autumn.

Dobruja – Region south of the Danube Delta controlled by the Scythians before Philip's victory in 339 BC, present-day north-eastern Bulgaria and south-eastern Romania.

Dodona – Home to the sanctuary and Oracle of Zeus Naios, located south of Ioannina, in Epeiros.

Edessa – Macedonian city in present-day Central Macedonia.

Ekbatana – Ancient city in Media, Asia, located in present-day Iran, one of the Achaimenid royal centres.

Elaious – City on the Chersonese (Gallipoli) peninsula, famous for its sanctuary of Protesilaos.

Elateia – City in Phokis, central Greece. Occupied by Philip in 339 BC, during the Fourth Sacred War.

Elimeia – Canton of Upper Macedonia, present-day Kozani regional unit in Western Macedonia, northern Greece. Also known as Elimiotis.

Elis/Elians – Region/people in eastern Peloponnese.

Emathia – Region of Lower Macedonia, present-day Central Macedonia (northern Greece), it was also known as Bottiaia or Bottia.

Eordaia – Canton of Upper Macedonia, but incorporated into the Argead kingdom early on in its history. Located in present-day Western Macedonia (northern Greece).

Epeiros – Region of north-western Greece, home to Molossians, Chaonians, and Thresprotians.

Ephesos – Greek city in Asia Minor, present-day western Turkey.

Erigyios – Boyhood friend and Companion of Alexander, originally from Lesbos but a naturalised Macedonian, brother of Laomedon.

Euboia/Euboians – Island/people off the east coast of central Greece, present-day Evia.

Eumenes – A Greek from Kardia, a city on the Chersonese, secretary and head of royal chancellery during Philip II and Alexander's reign.

Europa – Daughter of Philip II and Kleopatra-Eurydike.

Eurydike – Lynkestian wife of Amyntas III, with whom she had four children – Alexander, Perdikkas, Philip and Eurynoe. Grandmother of Alexander the Great.

Gaugamela – Site of Alexander's second battle against the Great King Darius III and his Persian forces in 331 BC, located in present-day northern Iraq.

Getai – One of the most numerous of Thracian peoples, active in northern Thrace, around the Danube and Dobruja (present-day Bulgaria and Romania).

Glaukias – King of the Illyrian Taulantians. Fought Alexander at Pellion during his Balkan campaign of 335 BC.

Gordion – Capital city of Phrygia in Asia Minor (present-day Turkey), home to the Gordian knot which Alexander severed in 333 BC.

Granikos – River in Phrygia, Asia Minor (present-day Turkey) site of Alexander the Great's first victory over Persian forces in spring 334 BC.

Halikarnassos – City of Karia in Asia Minor, present-day Bodrum in western Turkey.

Halos – City in Thessaly on the main road south to Thermopylai.

Harpalos – Boyhood friend and Companion of Alexander from Elimeia, Upper Macedonia.

Hellenike (Lanike) – Nurse of Alexander, and sister of Kleitos the Black.

Hellespont – Present-day Dardanelles, ancient crossing point between Europe and Asia.

Hephaistion – Boyhood friend and closest Companion of Alexander.

Herakles – Illegitimate son of Alexander and Barsine.

Hermeias – Tyrant of Atarneus and Assos, in Asia Minor, present-day western Turkey.

Hydaspes – River in northern India, present-day Jhelum (Pakistan), site of Alexander's battle with Indian the king Poros in 326 BC.

Illyria/Illyrians – Region/people to the north-west of Macedonia, comprising a number of peoples/tribes, the Dardanians, Taulantians, and Autariatai being the most prominent.

Isocrates – Athenian rhetorician. Supporter of a Pan-Hellenic campaign against Persia.

Issos – Town in south-western Kilikia, Asia Minor, present-day southern Turkey. The first major battle between Alexander the Great and Darius III was fought in its vicinity in November 333 BC.

Isthmia – Famous for its sanctuary of Poseidon outside Corinth, which was the location of one of the four Crown Games. After the battle of Chaironeia (338 BC), it became the setting for the formation of the League of Corinth.

Kadmeia – Acropolis of Thebes.

Kalindoia – City in northern Bottike, Macedonia. Located near present-day Kalamoto, Central Macedonia (northern Greece).

Kallisthenes – Greek from Olynthos (Chalkidike), relative of Aristotle, official historian of Alexander's Asian campaigns.

Karanos – Argive founder of Aigai and royal family of Macedon.

Karanos – Possible illegitimate son of Philip II.

Kardia – City in the Chersonese, present-day Gallipoli peninsula.

Karia – Region in Asia Minor (present-day western Turkey), ruled by the Hekatomnid dynasty.

Kassandros – Companion of Alexander, son of Antipatros.

Kersobleptes – Odrysian king, adversary of Philip II, finally defeated in the late 340s BC, whereby his territory came under Macedonian control.

Kilikia – Region of Asia Minor, present-day southern Turkey.

Kleitos (Illyrian) – Illyrian king, son of Bardylis, fought against Alexander in 335 BC at the fortress of Pellion.

Kleitos the Black – Companion of Philip II and Alexander, brother to Alexander's nurse, Lanike.

Kleopatra – Daughter of Philip II and Olympias, younger sister of Alexander the Great. Married her uncle Alexander the Molossian in 336 BC.

Kleopatra-Eurydike – Macedonian noblewoman, niece of Attalos, and Philip II's seventh wife, mother of Europa.

Kothelas – Getic king, father of Meda (Philip II's sixth wife).

Krateros – Companion of Alexander from Orestis, Upper Macedonia.

Kynnane – Daughter of Philip and his Illyrian wife Audata-Eurydike. Half-sister of Alexander. Married Prince Amyntas, perhaps in 336 BC, widowed shortly afterwards. Mother of Adea-Eurydike.

Kytinion – City in Doris, central Greece.

Lakedaimonia/Lakonia/Lakedaimonians – Region/people in south Peloponnese, also known as Spartans from the name of their lead city – Sparta.

Langaros – King of the Agrianians and friend of Alexander. Died sometime in the second half of 335 BC.

Laomedon – Boyhood friend and Companion of Alexander, originally from Lesbos, but a naturalised Macedonian, brother of Erigyios.

Larissa – City in northern Thessaly, northern Greece.

Lebadeia – City on the western frontier of Boiotia, present-day Livadia (central Greece).

Leonidas – Molossian, relative of Olympias, boyhood tutor or overseer of Alexander's early education.

Leonnatos – Boyhood friend and Companion of Alexander, from Lynkestis, Upper Macedonia..

Lokris/Lokrians – Regions/peoples in central Greece.

Lycurgus – Athenian statesman active during the reign of Alexander the Great.

Lynkestis – Canton of Upper Macedonia, present-day Florina regional unit, Western Macedonia (northern Greece).

Lysimachos – An Akarnanian, from western Greece, tutor of Alexander with whom he shared a love of Homer.

Lysimachos – Possible boyhood friend and Companion of Alexander.

Lysippos – Famous sculptor from Sikyon in northern Peloponnese. Court favourite of Alexander.

Macedonia/Macedon/Macedonians – Region/kingdom/people located in present-day northern Greece.

Maidoi – Thracian people located around the middle reaches of the river Strymon (Struma) in present-day south-western Bulgaria.

Marsyas – Boyhood friend and Companion of Alexander, later wrote about the prince's upbringing.

Meda – Getic wife of Philip II, daughter of Kothelas.

Memnon of Rhodes – Mercenary commander from Rhodes, brother of Mentor, and husband of Barsine.

Mentor of Rhodes – Mercenary commander from Rhodes, brother of Memnon, originally married to Barsine before Memnon.

Methone – Greek city on the coast of Pieria in present-day Central Macedonia, northern Greece.

Mieza – Macedonian city on the slopes of Mount Vermion in Emathia, present-day Central Macedonia (northern Greece). Location of 'Aristotle's School'.

Miletos – Greek city and port in Karia, Asia Minor, present-day western Turkey.

Molossia – Kingdom in Epeiros, north-western Greece.

Nearchos – Boyhood friend and Companion of Alexander, originally from Crete, but a naturalised Macedonian.

Nektanebo II – Last Egyptian pharaoh, and father of Alexander the Great according to the fictionalised *Alexander Romance*.

Neoptolemos – Actor from the island of Skyros, spent time at the court of Philip II and was present during the king's assassination in autumn 336 BC at Aigai.

Nikesipolis – Thessalian wife of Philip II from Pherai, mother of Thessalonike.

Ochomenos – Boiotian city, central Greece.

Odrysians – Thracian people, in the fourth century BC they were the most powerful of Thracian tribes/people, forming a supra-tribal state that controlled most of Thrace south of the Haimos mountains, present-day Bulgaria and European Turkey.

Oitia/Oitians – Region/people around Mount Oiti in central Greece.

Olympia – Sanctuary of Olympian Zeus located in Elis, in north-western Peloponnese, one of the four great Pan-Hellenic sanctuaries in Greece.

Olympias – Molossian wife of Philip II, mother of Alexander the Great and Kleopatra.

Olympos – Home of the gods, highest mountain in Greece, located between north-eastern Thessaly and south-eastern Macedonia.

Olynthos – City in Chalkidike, leader of the Chalkidikian League. Destroyed by Philip II in 348 BC.

Onchestos – Famous for its sanctuary of Poseidon, north of the Thebes, situated on the fringes of Lake Kopais in Boiotia.

Onesikritos – Greek naval officer of Alexander's from Astypalaia, credited with a work on Alexander's upbringing.

Onomarchos – Phokian general active during the Third Sacred War. Killed in battle against Philip II in 352 BC.

Orestis – Canton of Upper Macedonia, present-day Kastoria regional unit, Western Macedonia (northern Greece).

Oropos – Coastal city located between Boiotia and Attika, central Greece.

Paionia/Paionians – Region/people to the north of Macedonia, in present-day Republic of North Macedonia.

Pangaion – Mountain in eastern Macedonia, situated between Amphipolis and Philippoi (northern Greece).

Parmenion – Companion and premier general of Philip II and Alexander.

Parysatis – Persian wife of Alexander. Youngest daughter of former Great King Artaxerxes III (Ochos).

Passaron – Capital of Molossia, in Epeiros, now believed to be under the castle of Ioannina on the shores of Lake Pamvotis (northern Greece).

Pausanias – Companion of Philip II from Orestis, Upper Macedonia. Assassinated Philip II in the theatre at Aigai in autumn 336 BC, and was killed shortly after.

Pella – Macedonia's greatest city, co-capital with Aigai, located in present-day Central Macedonia, close to the Thermaic Gulf (northern Greece). Birthplace of Alexander the Great.

Pellion – Fortress on the border of Illyria and Macedonia, perhaps to be identified with Zvezdë in south-eastern Albania. Location of key battle during Alexander's Balkan campaign 335 BC.

Perdikkas – Boyhood friend and Companion of Alexander from Orestis, Upper Macedonia.

Perdikkas I – Argead king. Descendant of Temenos of Argos, founder of the Macedonian royal family.

Perdikkas II – Argead king (c.450–c.413 BC).

Perdikkas III – Argead king (365–360 BC), son of Amyntas III and Eurydike.

Perinthos – City on the Propontis (Sea of Mamara), besieged by Philip II in 340 BC.

Persepolis – City in Persia. One of the key royal centres of the Persian Empire, located in present-day Iran.

Persian Empire/Persians – Ancient empire/people in Asia, their heartlands were located in present-day southern Iran.

Peuke island – Island on the Danube, where Thracian and Triballoi peoples fled in 335 BC on Alexander's approach. Probably not to be identified with an island of the same name in the Danube Delta, and, at present, remains unlocated.

Peukestas – Companion of Alexander from Mieza.

Phalaikos – Phokian general active during the Third Sacred War.

Pherai – City in western Thessaly, northern Greece.

Phila – Elimeian wife of Philip II.

Philip II – 382–336 BC. Son of Amyntas III and Eurydike. Argead king 360–336 BC, father of Alexander the Great.

Philip the Akarnanian – Physician from Akarnania, western Greece, personal doctor of Alexander.

Philippoi – City in western Thrace, formerly Krenides, a colony of Thasos. Philip's first known self-named (re) foundation. Located in present-day Eastern Macedonia and Thrace, northern Greece.

Philokrates – Athenian statesman, influential in forming the peace of 346 BC, which bears his name.

Philotas – Companion of Alexander, son of Parmenion.

Phokion – Athenian statesman, nicknamed 'the Good', active during the reigns of Philip II and Alexander.

Phokis/Phokians – Region/people in central Greece.

Phrygia – Ancient region of Asia Minor, present-day Turkey.

Pieria – 'The Rich land', a region in Macedonia, between the Pierian and Olympos mountain range and the sea, stretching from the Haliakmon river in the north to the Peneios in the south, present-day Central Macedonia (northern Greece).

Pixodaros – Karian dynast and satrap. Involved with Philip II and Alexander regarding marriage to his daughter in 337/6 BC.

Plataia – Boiotian city, central Greece.

Plato – Philosopher, founder of the Academy school in Athens, died in 347 BC.

Poros – India king, defeated by Alexander in the battle of the Hydaspes river in 326 BC.

Poteidaia – City in the Chalkidike, located on the Pallene finger of the peninsula, present-day Kassandreia in Central Macedonia (northern Greece).

Propontis – Sea of Marmara.

Ptolemy – Boyhood friend and Companion of Alexander from Eordaia, Upper Macedonia. Later wrote a history of Alexander's campaign (now lost). Along with Aristoboulos' work, it was a principal source for Arrian's *Anabasis of Alexander*.

Pydna – Port city in Pieria (Macedonia) on the Thermaic Gulf located in present-day Central Macedonia (northern Greece).

Pyrrhos – King of Epeiros (319–272 BC).

Rhoxane – Baktrian noblewoman, daughter of Oxyartes, first wife of Alexander. Mother of Alexander IV.

Samothrace – Island in the northern Aegean, home to the sanctuary of the Great Gods.

Scythia/Scythians – Region/people occupying the steppe-lands between the Danube and Don, and across into Central Asia. Nomadic peoples, and famous horse-riders.

Seleukos – Possible boyhood friend and Companion of Alexander from Europos-by-the-Axios, in Lower Macedonia.

Sestos – Port city on the European side of the Hellespont (Dardanelles).

Siwah – Oasis in Egypt, home to the sanctuary and Oracle of Zeus Ammon.

Sogdiana – Region in Central Asia north of Baktria, present-day Tajikistan/Uzbekistan.

Sousa – Ancient city in Asia, one of the royal centres of the Persian Empire, located in present-day Iran.

Stageira – City on the Chalkidike peninsula, north of Athos, located in present-day Central Macedonia (northern Greece). Home to Aristotle. Destroyed by Philip II in 349/8 BC but refounded a little later.

Stateira – Persian wife of Alexander. Daughter of former Great King Darius III.

Tarsos - City in Kilikia, present-day southern Turkey.

Temenos – A king of Argos, descendant of Herakles, and ancestor of the royal family of Macedon, the dynasty is referred to as 'Temenid' by some ancient authors.

Tempe – A narrow 8-kilometre-long gorge between Mount Ossa and Olympos, on the border of Macedonia and Thessaly. One of the most famous gateways into the kingdom of Macedon.

Theagenes – Theban general, brother to Timokleia, commander of the coalition phalanx at Chaironeia in 338 BC where he was killed.

Thebes/Thebans – Boiotian city/people in central Greece. Among the most powerful of city-states in Greece, fought against Philip II during the battle of Chaironeia, destroyed by Alexander the Great in 335 BC.

Theophrastus – Peripatetic philosopher and colleague of Aristotle from Lesbos.

Theopompus – Greek historian from Chios, visitor to the Macedonian court, wrote a universal history of the fourth century BC focusing on the deeds of Philip II.

Thermopylai – The 'Hot Gates', a narrow passage between mountain and sea located next to the Malian Gulf, the principal gateway into central Greece.

Thespiai – Boiotian city, central Greece.

Thessalonike – Daughter of Nikesipolis of Pherai and Philip II.

Thessaly/Thessalians – Region/people in northern Greece, south of Macedonia.

Thrace/Thracians – Region/peoples located to the east of Macedonia, in present-day European Turkey, Bulgaria and parts of Romania.

Timokleia – Theban noblewoman, sister of Theagenes (general at Chaironeia), present in Thebes in 335 BC during Alexander's sacking of the city.

Triballia/Triballoi – Region/people, either Thracian or Illyrian, located north of the Haimos mountains in Thrace, present-day Bulgaria.

Tymphaia – Canton of Upper Macedonia, often paired with

Parauaia, present-day Grevena regional unit, Western Macedonia (northern Greece).

Tyre – Phoenician port-city, in present-day Lebanon. Besieged and captured by Alexander in 332 BC.

Upper Macedonia – Mountainous region to the west of Lower Macedonia. Today, Upper Macedonia encompasses much of Western Macedonia, northern Greece.

ACKNOWLEDGEMENTS

My sincere thanks go to my agent Donald Winchester, at Watson, Little Ltd, who first saw potential in the idea of a book on the young Alexander, and Arabella Pike at William Collins, who commissioned the work and provided invaluable feedback on the early drafts. Thanks also go to the rest of the HarperCollins team, who helped bring the final book to fruition.

In 2019, I was lucky enough to live for a year in northern Greece, and my stay was greatly enriched by the generosity and kindness of a number of individuals. My landlord Kostas and his family helped me settle in an apartment on Herakles Road in Veroia and invited my parents and me to a memorable Easter feast. Evanthia Kalaitzidou and her husband Panayiotis welcomed me into their home and lives, sharing numerous plates of delicious local food, blissful hours of conversation and introducing me to new friends. Anastasia Tanampasi, an exceptionally talented young historian, spent innumerable hours helping me with my Greek, offering translations and information on various aspects of regional history and tradition. Ioannis Graekos patiently answered my barrage of archaeological questions, Laura Wynn-Antikas treated me to some idyllic lunches in Pydna, and Charis Tsoungaris took me on a memorable tour of the wilds of Western Macedonia. I'm incredibly grateful for their friendship.

During my travels around Greece and the Balkans, I was fortunate to meet many archaeologists who kindly spoke to me about their work. I'm in awe of their passion, enthusiasm and willingness to share information on their latest finds. They include Angeliki Kottaridi, who also provided access to Aigai's palace reconstruction project, Athanasia Kyriakou at the site's sanctuary of Eukleia, Bonna Wescoat at Samothrace, Ioannis Akamatis at Pella, the British–American–Greek team working at Olynthos, Angelos Zannis at Philippoi, Lyudmil Vagalinski and his team at the excavations of Herakleia Sintike, Emil Nankov at Sofia, Igor Lazarenko and Aleksander Minchev at Varna, Zoran Rujak at Strumica, and, finally, Kliti Kallamata at Korçë, who showed me the intriguing tombs at Selca e Poshtme, which I would never have found without him, and the possible location of Pellion above present-day Zvesdë. I was deeply saddened to hear of his passing in 2020.

My research was greatly aided by the excellent staff at Veroia's Public Library, the British School at Athens and London's Institute of Classical Studies, whose collections have allowed me to track down even the most remote references. A number of experts in the field of Macedonian studies kindly took the time to read the manuscript and certain chapters, providing invaluable feedback and corrections: Miltiades Hatzopoulos, Charis Tsoungaris, Chrysoula Saatsoglou-Paliadeli, Laura Wynn-Antikas, Emil Nankov, Richard Stoneman and Paul Cartledge. Mary Ruskin also provided insightful comments on the proof copy. It goes without saying that any errors in the text are mine alone. A special thanks to all.

Lastly, to my family (Clan Rowson), to whom this book is dedicated: my parents Brian and Jill, brother Ed and sister-in-law Catherine and their kids – Elias, Max and Victoria – and my eldest brother Tom, who read innumerable chapter drafts and never failed to offer encouraging words – for their constant love and support, a most heartfelt thank you.

Text Permissions

ARRIAN, VOLUME I, translated by P.A. Brunt, Loeb Classical Library Volume 236, Cambridge, Mass.: Harvard University Press, Copyright © 1976 by the President and Fellows of Harvard College. Loeb Classical Library ® is a registered trademark of the President and Fellows of Harvard College. Used by permission. All rights reserved.

ARRIAN, VOLUME II, translated by E. Iliff Robson and P.A. Brunt, Loeb Classical Library Volume 269, Cambridge, Mass.: Harvard University Press, first published 1933. Loeb Classical Library ® is a registered trademark of the President and Fellows of Harvard College. Used by permission. All rights reserved.

DEMOSTHENES, VOLUME I, translated by J.H. Vince, Loeb Classical Library Volume 238, Cambridge, Mass.: Harvard University Press, first published 1930. Loeb Classical Library ® is a registered trademark of the President and Fellows of Harvard College. Used by permission. All rights reserved.

DIODORUS OF SICILY, VOLUME VIII, translated by C. Bradford Welles, Loeb Classical Library Volume 422, Cambridge, Mass.: Harvard University Press, Copyright © 1963 by the President and Fellows of Harvard College. Loeb Classical Library ® is a registered trademark of the President and Fellows of Harvard College. Used by permission. All rights reserved.

GREEK LYRIC, VOLUME V, edited and translated by David A. Campbell, Loeb Classical Library Volume 144, Cambridge, Mass.: Harvard University Press, Copyright © 1993 by the President and Fellows of Harvard College. Loeb Classical Library ® is a registered

INDEX

Abdera, 170, 314
Abydos (on Hellespont), 347, 359
Achilles, 31–2, 62–5, 150, 287, 290, 362
actors, 84, 102, 104, 105–6, 107, 238, 252–3, 257
Adea (daughter of Amyntas/ Kynnane), 239, 284, 377
Aeropos (Lynkestian nobleman), 261, 264
Aeropos (brother of Perdikkas), 51–2, 55
Aeschines, 107–8, 111–13, 171, 172, 186–8, 209, 301, 345
Aeschylus, 104, 140, 257, 339
Agamemnon, 62, 64
Agesilaos II, Spartan king, 143
Aggitis river cave (near Drama), 78
Agrianians, 305, 320–1, 323, 325–6
Aiakos (god), 31–2, 133, 300
Aiani, ancient Elimeia, 66–70, 68
Aigai, ancient: Andronikos' discoveries at, 1–3, 6, 267–83, 285–98; cemetery/necropolis, 1–3, 53–4, 267, 269, 270, 273, 275, 286, 297–8; rediscovered by archaeologists, 1–3, 6, 8, 41, 53–4, 239, 243–6, 249, 267–83, 285–98; and emergence of Pella, 15–16; etymology of name, 52, 53; as 'hearth' of Macedonian kingdom, 53, 96, 247–8; end-of-year festival of Olympian Zeus (336 BC), 96–105, 131, 239, 246–53, 254–9, 348; palace of, 239, 243–6, 247–52, 249; Heuzey's discoveries at Palatitsia, 243–6, 267; Hammond's Aigai–Vergina theory, 246, 269–70; sanctuary of Eukleia, 248, 378; theatre of, 248, 254–9, 255 see also Megali Toumba (Great Tumulus), Aigai
Aiolian tribe, 50
Aitolia, 31, 343
Albania, 66, 322
Aleuad family, Larissa, 87
Alexander (Oliver Stone film), 39, 151
Alexander I, Macedonian king, 36, 55, 73, 77–8, 131

Alexander II, Macedonian king, 36, 55
Alexander Itinerary (fourth century AD), 178
Alexander IV (son of Alexander), 284, 297, 377
Alexander Romance, 5, 135, 287–8
Alexander Sarcophagus, Sidon, 152
Alexander the Great: afterlife of, 3–5, 379–80; images of, 3, 6, 8, 18, 152, 225, 226, 279, 289, 294, 351–4, 352, 363; entombed in Egyptian Alexandria, 4–5, 297; death of in Babylon (323 BC), 4, 284, 376; and spread of Greek/Macedonian culture, 4, 169, 350, 362, 379–80; character, 5–6, 20, 57, 116–19, 146, 230–3, 237–8, 262, 296, 328, 340–2; fictionalised accounts of, 5, 17–19, 20–2, 135, 151; moral issues over warfare/rule of, 6, 94–5, 329–30, 340; birth of in Pella (356 BC), 13, 15, 34–5, 36–7, 40; as son of a god, 40, 354–8; status as Philip's most capable son, 43, 128–9, 227; formal education, 45–6, 56–61, 99, 104, 115; relationship with mother, 45, 228–9, 264; offerings to the gods, 59, 99, 306, 319, 360, 361; physical education programme, 59, 129, 131, 132–3, 329, 362; and Homeric epics, 63–5, 79, 141; speech at Opis (324 BC), 80; use of annihilation, 94–5, 319, 329–30, 342, 372; at Dion Olympia, 99–105; famed as heavy drinker, 103; as admirer of great Athenian playwrights, 104, 138, 140; first eyewitness account of, 111; military training, 115, 129, 130–1, 132–3; relationship with father, 116–19, 184–5, 226, 227–9, 230, 237–8, 251–2, 258, 357; self-named foundations, 118, 146, 167–8, 297, 369–70, 374; formal education at Mieza, 123–9, 132–3, 134, 135–8, 139, 141, 146, 148–9, 155, 156–7, 362; physical appearance, 134, 178, 352, 354; as fascinated by Persia, 144–5; *pothos* (ardent desire/longing) of, 146, 147–8, 318, 353, 362; sexuality of, 150, 151; and hunting, 151–5, 294; wives of, 151, 373, 374, 375; as regent of Macedon, 156–8, 166–8, 170;

corps, 74, 176, 177–9, 305, 369; guerrilla warfare, 74, 158; Alexander's speech to at Opis (324 BC), 80; Xandika festival, 96, 128, 305; and the gymnasia, 127, 128, 129–31; slingers, 164, 174, 198, 315–16, 324; Thracian mercenaries in, 164; Alexander's acumen/leadership, 193, 203–4, 260, 313–14, 315–16, 318–19, 324–30; 367–8, 370–1; formation at battle of Chaironeia, 197–8; burial mound at Chaironeia, 205–7, 206; Alexander expands Companions within, 306–7; infantry (Shield Bearers. formerly Foot Companions), 306–7, 313–14, 323, 325–7, 338, 370; Agrianian troops, 320–1, 323, 325–6; astonishing pace of, 329, 332–3; corps of Persian youths, 375

Arrhabaios (son of Aeropos), 261, 262, 264, 295

Arrhidaios (half-brother of Alexander), 42, 43, 45, 227, 238, 264; brief reign as king, 284, 376–7

Arrian (historian): *Anabasis of Alexander*, 80, 307–8, 327; and *pothos* concept, 146; and Philip's marriage to Kleopatra, 228; and murder of Kleitos, 233; and murder of Philip, 257; on the Balkan campaign, 307–8, 310–11, 313, 316–17, 318, 319, 321–2, 330; on military leadership, 327, 328; on Theban revolt, 332; on battle at Thebes, 337, 338, 340

art: decorative metalwork (toreutics), 159–60; in 'Eurydike's tomb,' 247–8; at palace of Aigai, 250; 'Abduction of Persephone' mural, 273–5, 275, 286; in Tomb I, 273–5, 275, 286; in Tomb II, 276–7, 279, 280, 281–2, 289, 290, 293–4, 353–4; hunting frieze in Tomb II, 276, 289, 293–4, 296; Vergina Star/Sun, 280, 379; in Pella, 351–2, 352; artists in Alexander's elite circle, 353–4; Lysippos' sculpture, 353–4, 362, 363

Artabazos (fugitive satrap), 144

Artashata (satrap of Armenia), 252

Artaxerxes III (Ochos), Achaimenid King, 143, 145, 174, 224

Artaxerxes IV (Arses), Achaimenid King, 224, 252

Arthurian legend, 5

Arybbas (Molossian king), 31, 32, 37, 143

Ashmolean Museum, Oxford, 17–18

Asklepios (healing god), 126, 219

Ateas (Scythian king), 181–3, 183, 292, 314

Athenaeus (writer), 227

Athenian League, Second, 87, 110, 173, 209–10

Athens: and growing power of Macedon, 24, 33–4, 44, 81, 83, 86–7, 89–91, 105–6; women's lives in, 41; Pnyx (site of democratic Assembly), 82–3, 84–7, 110, 172, 189–91; Social War (357–355 BC), 87, 90, 173; embassies to Pella, 106–13; Peace of Philokrates (346 BC), 112–14, 141–2, 170–2; Plato's Academy, 121–2, 127, 137, 211; Aristotle's Lyceum, 127, 137, 348; and the Byzantines, 172–3; war with Macedon starts (340 BC), 175–7; and Amphiktyonic Council, 186–8; embassy to Thebes, 189–92; coalition

against Philip, 189–95, 196–209, 215–16; Philip's peace terms after Chaironeia, 209–11, 349; Alexander's only visit to, 211–13; the Acropolis, 212–13; *Demosion Sema* (public cemetery), 213–15; funeral of Chaironeia war dead, 213, 215–16; Golden Age, 213; sacked by Xerxes (480 BC), 213, 223, 372; Epigraphical Museum, 217–18, 222; French School in, 243; awards gold crown to Philip (336 BC), 247; and Philip's death, 299–300; submits to Alexander, 301; revolt against Alexander, 331, 332, 333; and razing of Thebes, 343–5; suicide of Demosthenes, 345–6

athletes, 131–2, 221, 356

Attalos (Companion), 227, 229, 230, 252, 254, 262, 264, 300

Audata (wife of Philip), 40, 42, 45, 56, 239

Augustus, Roman emperor (Octavian), 4, 308

Autariatai (Illyrian people), 321

Babylon, 4, 146, 284, 371, 376

Bagoas (treacherous eunuch), 252

Baktria, 144, 230, 231, 362, 372

Balkan campaign, Alexander's, 309; entire campaign season reserved for, 303–4; Amphipolis as base for, 305, 308, 310–11; Arrian as source, 307–8, 310–11, 313, 316–17, 318, 319, 321–2, 330; as seminal moment in reign, 308; in Thrace, 310–18; and the Triballoi, 314–17, 319, 320; and the Getai, 317–19; feasts of friendship during, 319–20; and Agrianians, 320–1, 323, 325–6; and the Illyrians, 321–7, 328, 330, 332, 344; battle for Pellion, 322–7; failures and mistakes, 324, 330; end of, 346

Balkan Wars (1912–13), 379

Bardylis, King of Illyria, 23, 31, 40, 70

Barsine (mistress of Alexander), 144, 151, 377

Beroia (modern Veroia), 129–31

Bessos (Artaxerxes V), 372

Black Sea, 89, 166, 175, 176, 177, 179–81

Boiotia, 150, 188, 189, 191–3, 194–6, 265, 301, 331, 340, 341, 343

Boiotian League, 188, 210, 333

Bosphoros, 175, 177

Bosworth, Brian, 330

Boukephalas (horse), 3, 116–19, 237, 362, 363, 363; death of, 118, 374; at battle of Chaironeia, 203; wounded at Thebes, 339

boxing, 132, 356

Brailsford, Henry Noel, 379

Bulgaria, 159–60, 162–4, 165–7, 179–80, 312, 318–21, 379

Byzantion (modern-day Istanbul), 172–3, 174, 176–7, 179, 181, 182

Caracalla, Roman emperor, 4

Caspian Sea, 118, 146, 147–8, 372

Celts, 126, 270, 273, 275, 286, 297–8, 319–20

Chaireas (sculptor), 352